Most Holy Warrior

The Biblical Story of Jesus Christ Before Bethlehem

Michael K. Pasque

Foreword

Prayer

Heavenly Father. You know me well. You know that I have a dreadful tendency to make this all about me. It is not all about me. None of it is about me. It is all about you. Help me not to even look down that pathway, let alone take a first faltering step down it. That pathway is defined by darkness and forays there always end poorly.

Free my heart, Father, from that which I cannot free myself. Help me to focus on Jesus. When I look at Him, I see things as they really are. I see myself indebted beyond comprehension such that any worldly debt or hurt or threat or fear seems so trivial. His uncreated light illuminates everything. Only in the light of His Spirit with my eyes focused on Him can I write words that will have eternal consequences to the people who read or hear them.

Remind me of my truly wretched state so that my heart stays humble. And, at the same time, remind me of my extraordinary eternal value, my eternal status as a child of God, a prince of the kingdom—all bought and paid for by the shed blood of my Savior, Jesus—for only then can I show them the joy that is the heart of my relationship with you.

I have nothing—which you didn't give me.
I am nothing—which you didn't make me.
I know nothing—except by your Holy Spirit.
I do nothing—except in the Holy Name of Jesus.

The LORD is a warrior

—Exodus 15:3

"You are my war club, my weapon for battle—

> *with you I shatter nations,*

> *with you I destroy kingdoms,*

> *with you I shatter horse and rider,*

> *with you I shatter chariot and driver,*

> *with you I shatter man and woman,*

> *with you I shatter old man and youth,*

> *with you I shatter young man and maiden,*

> *with you I shatter shepherd and flock,*

> *with you I shatter farmer and oxen,*

> *with you I shatter governors and officials."*

—Jeremiah 51:20-23

Chapter 1

Introduction
This Book is About Jesus Christ

This book is about Jesus Christ. It cannot be about anything or anyone else. Like it or not, recognize it or not, live like it or not, *Jesus is the focal point of our existence.* This cry finds its origin in the deep chambers of our eternal heart. It echoes through the Word of God. From beneath the outstretched arms of the cherubim it tells us that it simply cannot be any other way. Jesus is the very focal point of our existence.

Most true believers have no trouble understanding and accepting the premise that Jesus Christ is not only the focal point of our lives, but of all history. Once again, whether we choose to acknowledge this fact in our daily lives or not, Holy Scripture is nonetheless unwavering in this revelation. Who else after all has been exalted *"to the highest place"*? Who else has a name that is *"above every name"*? Who else will command the undivided attention of *every* heart, *every* knee, and *every* tongue?

> *Therefore God exalted him to the highest place and gave him the name that is above every name, that at the name of Jesus every knee should bow, in heaven and on earth and under the earth, and every tongue confess that Jesus Christ is Lord, to the glory of God the Father.*
>
> —Philippians 2:9-11 (emphasis added)

Surely the statement that there is no name above the Name of Jesus makes Him the whole point of our existence, and therefore the whole point of every minute of our every day. This statement finds its logical substantiation in the realization of just a single fact: Jesus is *the* Son of God, the *only* Son of God. This statement ties Jesus personally to every man, and yet at the same time extends the discussion beyond our comprehension. After all, can we really even comprehend what it means for Jesus to be *"the radiance of God's glory and the exact representation of his being"*?

In the past God spoke to our forefathers through the prophets at many times and in various ways, but in these last days he has spoken to us by his Son, whom he appointed heir of all things, and through whom he made the universe. The Son is <u>the radiance of God's glory</u> and the <u>exact representation of his being</u>, sustaining all things by his powerful word. After he had provided purification for sins, he sat down at the right hand of the Majesty in heaven.

—Hebrews 1:1-3 (emphasis added)

This logical progression takes us to the bottom line. Jesus is not just a "part" of the solution to the problems of man. He is God. In His uniqueness Jesus is most holy, being entirely *set apart* from everyone and everything. In His divinity He is the whole answer to every question voiced by the lips of mankind. In fact, every thing, every moment, and every person reach the fullness of their meaning, their very reason for existence, only in relation to the Person of Jesus Christ. In this truth is excitement for the human heart, which is now only partially known—for it inexplicably anticipates the fullness of the ultimate unknowable fulfillment of God's promise.

But also spawned in the midst of this truth—in this realization of the knowledge of the Person of Jesus Christ—is a soft voice that arises to ever-beckon us to the eternal and infinite truth that "there is even more." No matter what stage of life we occupy when we first acknowledge the sovereign kingship of Jesus, from the moment of hearing that soft voice, our life's adventure becomes ever seeking this "even more."

This book, therefore, is about Jesus Christ precisely because we, deep in our hearts, want *even more*. This desire is woven into the very fabric of our human nature. Truth be told, most of us—in the depths of our very human, typically selfish hearts—want *special* knowledge about Jesus. We want knowledge about Jesus that nobody else possesses. We can't help it. Our natural tendency toward self-orientation, combined with our heart's inherent craving for Jesus, leaves us unrepentantly fettered to this seemingly selfish desire. There should however be no feelings of guilt—this unique and very personal knowledge is precisely what Jesus offers to each of us.

He who has an ear, let him hear what the Spirit says to the churches. To him who overcomes, I will give some of the hidden manna. I will also give him a white stone with a new name written on it, known <u>only</u> to him who receives it.

—Revelation 2:17 (emphasis added)

This book is about only a tiny facet of the special knowledge that we seek. In fact, on the pages of this book we seek the answer to only a single question. We seek the answer to a quirky little question regarding the Son of God that at first glance might not seem very important at all. But, in focusing on the answer to this question—on this special knowledge—a whole new perspective on the Biblical knowledge of our Lord and Savior may well be within our grasp. New perspectives on the written Word of God change everything. They have the potential to illuminate—to shed special light upon—every other verse in the Bible. In fact, the new perspective we seek may add an entirely new facet to our understanding of the Person of Jesus Christ because it is specifically about Him. One question forms the foundation of our quest:

What exactly was the Person of Jesus Christ up to before Bethlehem—during the events that are described by the books of the Old Testament?

With so many avenues of Biblical investigation, why would we concern ourselves with seeking an answer to this question? The answer is simple. The special knowledge that our hearts crave is found there. Knowledge of Jesus that can be found nowhere else is found in the Old Testament and becomes obvious only in seeking to answer this question. As simple as it seems, this question is the implement by which a vast wealth of undiscovered knowledge of the King of kings can be mined from the written words of the Old Testament prophets.

With this in mind and with the Bible as our authoritative source, what can be known regarding the whereabouts and actions of Jesus during the time encompassed by the words of Old Testament scripture? First of all, Jesus Christ, perfect God and perfect man, was not only involved in every aspect of the creation (John 1:1-3) but was indeed *"chosen"* for His specific role *"before"* the creation of the universe.

He was chosen before the creation of the world, but was revealed in these last times for your sake.

—1Peter 1:20

It doesn't make sense then that this same Person that is described as being both *"chosen before the creation"* and also the very focal point of all history would then be relegated to a minor role in the huge portion of world history that is encompassed by Old Testament scripture. In other words, it is simply inconceivable that Jesus was just sitting on the sidelines of the championship game waiting for the coach to put Him in after the half-time entertainment. Every chapter, every page, indeed every word of the Pentateuch, Prophets and Psalms must somehow be exclusively and expressly about Him. Holy Scripture itself in fact supports the validity of this assumption:

> *"You diligently study the Scriptures because you think that by them you possess eternal life. These are the Scriptures that testify <u>about me</u>, yet you refuse to come to me to have life."*
>
> —John 5:39-40 (emphasis added)

> *"If you believed Moses, you would believe me, for he wrote <u>about me</u>. But since you do not believe what he wrote, how are you going to believe what I say?"*
>
> —John 5:46-47 (emphasis added)

We must also acknowledge the perfection of Holy Scripture. The Living Word (Jesus) and the written Word (the Bible) are the very expression of God to mankind. The written Word is eternal. It is perfect.

> *The law of the LORD is perfect, reviving the soul. The statutes of the LORD are trustworthy, making wise the simple.*
>
> —Psalm 19:7

God's written Word must also be infinite, because in its unknowable depths it is the perfect expression of the infinite God. By its very nature it simply can't be anything less than infinitely perfect and perfectly infinite in the depth of this expression. Only in eternity will the infinite depth of the written Word—and its equally infinite expression of the Living Word, Jesus—be fully appreciated.

> *To all perfection I see a limit; but your commands are <u>boundless</u>.*
>
> —Psalm 119:96 (emphasis added)

One thing is abundantly clear from this discourse. There is simply no way that Jesus was just sitting off stage during the events of the Old Testament. There is no way that He was just waiting for His Bethlehem cue to walk upon the stage of history, to enter the course of a story that is already two thirds over and that is totally about Him. Indeed, when taken in context of what we know of the Living God, we know that the reverse must be true. Jesus in fact must have been involved in every single moment of the Old Testament.

Your <u>laws</u> endure to this day, for <u>all</u> things serve <u>you</u>.
—Psalm 119:91 (emphasis added)

The acceptance of this truth—that Jesus had to be involved in the every moment of the Old Testament—regrettably gives only fleeting satiety to hungry hearts. Indeed, following immediately on the tail of that answer is yet another more pressing question regarding the extent—and more importantly the nature—of His involvement. It would be the each choice to simply limit our vision of the Old Testament involvement of Jesus. We could picture Him standing watchfully by, only observing and directing the events of the history of Israel. And yet can we really believe that He who donned the very physical flesh of mankind to enter the creation and experience every detail of physical life in our world would really choose anything less than full engagement? Jesus has, after all, never done anything halfway. His life, death on the cross, and resurrection attest immeasurably to this fact. Indeed, this quick answer is not enough because it does not fit the known attributes of the fullness and perfection of our Savior. There has to be more.

This book is precisely focused upon that something more. Its premise is simple:

The Son of God—the very focal point of literally everything—must have had a completely physical, utterly emotional, and very literally palpable role in the events and adventures that are encompassed by Old Testament history.

The quest for information regarding the nature of the involvement of Jesus Christ in the adventures of the Old Testament begins and ends solely in the Bible. There are in fact many incidents described in Old Testament Scripture that are held by most scholars to be appearances of God or of the incarnate Jesus Christ. They are referred to as *theophanies* and *Christophanies*, respectively. Many of these events will be reviewed in the course of this book. Indeed, they form the foundation of this adventure. And yet there are also many other less recognized events that have much to offer in unveiling the true nature of the Old Testament role of Jesus. Every one of these events is described in scripture for a reason. No doubt that the New Testament is foundational in the revelation of Jesus. Even so, only an in-depth search into the mysterious revelation of the Old Testament can complete the fullness of the knowledge of Jesus.

The heart of the Old Testament revelation of Jesus is found in exploring the precise *nature* of His Old Testament involvement. Further still, the nature of his involvement is defined by examining the complete spectrum of roles that He plays in the various events of the Old Testament. This is where we walk a narrow mountain crest with steep slopes of deception on either side. And yet this is also where our hearts drive us hard in search of the truth about Jesus. Only here does the Son of God fully manifest His role as the link between the created and the Uncreated, the finite and the Infinite, the temporary and the Eternal. Only here is Jesus revealed as an incarnate, physical participant in a great struggle, *"a great war"* (Daniel 10:1).

Here also is where our hearts quicken as we see the full revelation of the role of Jesus as a *warrior*. Here is where we fully unearth attributes that at first might be considered contrary to all that is revealed of Jesus in the New Testament. And yet we will make the case that the Word of God has never hidden the fact that the very same Son of God who was the perfect manifestation of the compassionate mercy and love of God is also a ferocious warrior. In fact, in almost every key event of the Old Testament we will document evidence of the physical, hands-on participation of the Son of God in His extraordinary role as a warrior Commander—and this forms the foundational hypothesis of this book:

> *The Old Testament role of Jesus Christ was as the fully embodied warrior Commander of warriors in the army of the Lord. His mission during the 33 years described by the gospel accounts was the salvation of all who would accept the eternal life that is offered in His sacrifice on the cross. So also was His warrior mission during the Old Testament the preservation of God's remnant in the nation of Israel.*

From the very first step of our testing of this hypothesis, we can be assured that the Author of Holy Scripture, the Holy Spirit, must be—by the very nature of God—a perfectly efficient Writer. He can never be described as being verbose. He is God. God is perfectly efficient in everything that He does. There are no wasted motions by God and we can rest assured that there are no wasted words in His writing. By every known criterion, the written Word of God is perfectly complete. There is not a single word, letter, or punctuation mark that could have been left out. There is not a single thing that was left out that should have been included. God has told us in the Holy Scriptures precisely what He wants us to know. We need no more than that which is written there—and yet our hungry hearts crave every morsel of that which has been given.

We must therefore plunge headfirst into a study of the Old Testament adventures of Jesus Christ because there is information about Jesus to be found there that cannot be found anywhere else. The fullness of the attributes that describe Jesus cannot be known without going there. Most notably, there is knowledge of the Person of Jesus Christ that can only be developed in the setting of *war* supplied by the uniquely battle-tempered events of the Old Testament. This is no casual quest. In the only *eternal* quest of this life, we seek the fullness of the knowledge of Jesus that we are intended to take into eternity. In this quest, we face endless frustration without the knowledge of Jesus as the warrior Commander of the army of the Lord, which is found exclusively in the text of the Old Testament.

Before we start, there are two foundational ground rules by which this discourse must be judged. First, the theology established on these pages can never contradict or stand in opposition to a single word of the Bible. This is simply not negotiable.

Of even more importance, this book must also be judged by the most important of all of the rules regarding the exposition of real truth: this text must never do anything except exalt the Holy Name of Jesus Christ. In doing anything less than exalting Jesus, it is not just a waste of time—it is meaningless and it is wrong. As an academic pursuit, as an intellectual exercise, or as an avenue of worldly gain, these studies into the evidence for the role of Jesus during Old Testament times are meaningless. From an eternal perspective, our investigation has merit only as it elevates and deepens our understanding, knowledge, reverence, obedience, service, fearful awe—and love—of the only Person who matters, *Jesus*. May these criteria stand in judgment of every word that follows.

Chapter 2

The *"Commander of the Army of the Lord"* *"A Drawn Sword In His Hand"*

Jericho. The entire fighting force of the Israelite nation had just crossed the Jordan River after annihilating the armies of Og king of Bashon and Sihon king of the Amorites. The nation's heart had been circumcised. The Israelites were focused on God and their intentions were to do exactly as He had commanded them. They were wholeheartedly advancing forward in response to God's directive to occupy the Promised Land. It was in this setting that Joshua, the new leader of the Israelite nation, had a brief encounter with an unnamed warrior.

Now when Joshua was near Jericho, he looked up and saw a man standing in front of him with a drawn sword in his hand. Joshua went up to him and asked, "Are you for us or for our enemies?"

"Neither," he replied, "but as commander of the army of the LORD I have now come." Then Joshua fell facedown to the ground in reverence, and asked him, "What message does my Lord have for his servant?"

The commander of the LORD's army replied, "Take off your sandals, for the place where you are standing is holy." And Joshua did so.

Now Jericho was tightly shut up because of the Israelites. No one went out and no one came in. Then the LORD said to Joshua, "See, I have delivered Jericho into your hands, along with its king and its fighting men."

—Joshua 5:13-6:2

This brief account from the book of Joshua is as enigmatic as it is intense. Joshua is apparently alone outside of Jericho when he encounters *"a man."* This meeting is described by a total of six sentences, suggesting that this was a relatively short encounter. Even so, the conclusions that can be drawn regarding the individual who confronted Joshua are profound. From this brief text, six key attributes of Joshua's challenger can be discerned.

First, he is *a man*. He is not described as some sort of vague, free-floating apparition. Nor is he described as an angel—at least not in the classic scriptural sense. Joshua encounters a menacing, flesh-and-blood man whose very palpable presence immediately demands and receives Joshua's full and undivided attention.

Second, the man is a warrior. The presence of *"a drawn sword in his hand"* is not metaphorical. The man standing before Joshua is at war and he has a very real sword in his hand. Joshua was very familiar with swords. A sword was the most common weapon of his day. There is no chance that he misinterpreted what he saw.

This sword is not symbolic. It is not an allegorical symbol, for instance, of the Word of God. Nor is it an ivory-handled, never-meant-to-be-used, dress sword as seen on the belts of military commanders or chiefs-of-state. The picture that is conveyed is not that of a man casually standing before Joshua with his hand resting on the jewel-encrusted hilt of his sheathed ceremonial dress sword. This warrior's sword is drawn and it is meant for battle. This warrior means business.

Third, the man did not draw the sword *after* he met Joshua. His sword was already in his hand. The fact that the man has his sword drawn at the exact time that he encounters Joshua suggests that he is either already in a fight or at the least feels immediately threatened by another warrior or military force. Whoever or whatever that threat might be, it is close enough to prompt him to actually draw his sword. This is not a trivial point. A sword in a hip scabbard can be drawn in a split second. The realization of the perceived threat must be imminent. This warrior is prepared for a fight.

Fourth, this individual's demeanor suggests an ominous and somewhat obscure purpose. He pointedly assures Joshua that he is *"neither"* for Israel or for their enemies. More importantly he then identifies himself, *"as the commander of the army of the LORD."* This statement sends Joshua straight to the ground on his face in reverence. Although his purpose remains intentionally in doubt, and the full nature of his appearance is unknown, something about this claim leaves Joshua no room for contesting his statement. Joshua's response is immediate and unconditional. Joshua knew that he was in the presence of an individual who commands reverence.

Fifth, as surprisingly unconditional as Joshua's reaction is, it is nothing compared to this warrior's response to Joshua's unhesitating reverence. This man does not tell Joshua in a hushed and hurried manner to get up out of his reverent posture, as is seen in the Apostle John's angelic encounter in the book of Revelation:

> *I, John, am the one who heard and saw these things. And when I had heard and seen them, I fell down to worship at the feet of the angel who had been showing them to me.*
>
> *But he said to me, "Do not do it! I am a fellow servant with you and with your brothers the prophets and of all who keep the words of this book. Worship God!"*
>
> —Revelation 22:8-9 (emphasis added)

Not only does this warrior not admonish Joshua, he responds to Joshua's accommodating query with a demand for even further reverence.   This is no ordinary angel standing before Joshua.   His command for Joshua to remove his sandals confirms Joshua's reverent posture to the holiness before him.

Finally, this mysterious warrior voices his demand for reverence in nearly the exact same words as the demand made to Moses from the burning bush.   This warrior tells Joshua to take off his sandals for the place where he is standing is holy.

> *The commander of the LORD's army replied, "Take off your sandals, for the place where you are standing is holy." And Joshua did so.*
>
> —Joshua 5:15 (emphasis added)

> *"Do not come any closer," God said. "Take off your sandals, for the place where you are standing is holy ground."*
>
> —Exodus 3:5 (emphasis added)

The similarity between these two statements recorded by two different authors in two entirely different books of the Bible is no coincidence. No angel (or any other being for that matter) who serves in the army of God in any capacity would ever consider mimicking the holy words of God in this manner. Only one conclusion can be drawn from the information gleaned from this cryptic passage in the book of Joshua. As many commentators have written, the warrior speaking to Joshua is God.

There is only one God.   The three unique Persons of the Triune God are inseparable in their nature as God.   Nonetheless, the warrior who challenged Joshua can be more precisely identified.   After all, Jesus Himself tells us—with a little help from the Pharisees—that it was in fact *His* voice that emanated from the burning bush.

Jesus replied, "If I glorify myself, my glory means nothing. My Father, whom you claim as your God, is the one who glorifies me. Though you do not know him, I know him. If I said I did not, I would be a liar like you, but I do know him and keep his word. Your father Abraham rejoiced at the thought of seeing my day; he saw it and was glad."

"You are not yet fifty years old," the Jews said to him, "and you have seen Abraham!"

"I tell you the truth," Jesus answered, "before Abraham was born, I am!" At this, they picked up stones to stone him, but Jesus hid himself, slipping away from the temple grounds.

—John 8:54-59 (emphasis added)

The Pharisees' immediate response to His statement is to attempt to stone Him. The Pharisees knew exactly what Jesus was saying. Jesus was claiming to be the source of the voice emanating from the burning bush that revealed the eternal name *"I AM."*

God said to Moses, "I AM WHO I AM. This is what you are to say to the Israelites: 'I AM has sent me to you.'"

—Exodus 3:14

The author of the book of Hebrews further confirms that it was indeed Jesus who was the source of the voice in the burning bush.

By faith Moses, when he had grown up, refused to be known as the son of Pharaoh's daughter. He chose to be mistreated along with the people of God rather than to enjoy the pleasures of sin for a short time. He regarded disgrace for the sake of Christ as of greater value than the treasures of Egypt, because he was looking ahead to his reward. By faith he left Egypt, not fearing the king's anger; he persevered because he saw him who is invisible.

—Hebrews 11:24-27 (emphasis added)

The conclusions drawn from these facts are not trivial in their significance. The man who suddenly appeared before Joshua with sword in hand, ready for a fight, has very few words to say. The few words he says, nevertheless, are precise in their intention. He repeats the exact same command to Joshua outside of Jericho that he had given Moses from inside the burning bush. His intention is clear. He is identifying himself as the source of the voice in the burning bush. Jesus Himself told us that He was the source of that voice. There is only one conclusion that can be drawn from these facts. The man who confronted Joshua was Jesus Christ.

The establishment of the identity of Joshua's challenger makes this incident specifically relevant to our quest for knowledge regarding the nature of the role of Jesus Christ in the Old Testament. In this regard, the answers to several key questions pertaining to Joshua's encounter hold particular promise.

First of all, the timing of this appearance is critical. Why would Jesus make such a stunning appearance to Joshua immediately before the battle of Jericho? Why would Jesus be leading troops—for He told Joshua that He is the *"commander of the army of the LORD"*—into a fight just as Joshua and the Israelites are approaching their powerful enemies at Jericho?

This appearance was not a random, unplanned encounter. To the contrary, its timing is precise. The battlefield presence of this sword-wielding warrior must somehow have a direct bearing upon the outcome of this first great battle against the walled cities of the Promised Land.

Secondly, why would Jesus, the omnipotent Son of God, appear with a sword in His hand? The sword was a common weapon of that day intended for close-in combat. The all-powerful Son of God needs no weapon against any foe, let alone a hand-held sword. What is going on here?

Holy Scripture is precise. The presence of a drawn sword in the description of this scene cannot be disregarded as irrelevant. It is included for the express purpose of fully characterizing the nature and role of Jesus in the Old Testament. Jesus is physically present in this scene as a man and He holds a sword in His hand. He is a warrior. Something or someone is threatening Jesus in this scene and He apparently has a very real fight ahead of Him. Further still, the timing of His appearance strongly suggests that the outcome of this fight may well determine the outcome of the assault on Jericho.

In light of these facts, the presence of a drawn sword in His hand is of critical importance. Despite being the omnipotent Son of God, Jesus is going into battle with a weapon just like every other man on every other battlefield of that day. Despite being able to win the battle by merely speaking victory into existence, for some reason Jesus has chosen to fight as a common man would fight. This changes everything. Not only is Jesus palpably present, but the outcome of the Israelite assault on Jericho seems to be literally dependent upon the sword fighting skill of Jesus.

This fact is not lost on Joshua. The battle preparedness of the menacing warrior who challenged him was the very first thought on Joshua's mind. Joshua's initial response to this confrontation tells us that he was obviously very impressed by the appearance—sword and all—and apparent fighting capability of this man. For sure, the man who stood before him must have been a fearsome warrior. If he had the appearance of a slightly built weakling who could barely lift the sword he held, the first question out of Joshua's mouth would not have concerned whether he was for Israel or for her enemies.

If Jesus is headed into a fight, then who are His adversaries? His opponents have not been precisely defined by the text of this passage. Nevertheless, there are several reasonable deductions that can be made about them. These opponents must have—in one way or another—something to do with the defense of the walled city of Jericho. They are most likely either the actual occupants of Jericho or some sort of otherworldly army that is allied with them. Whoever they are, it is probable that their defeat will herald the fall of the city of Jericho. It is also very likely that His enemies are susceptible to the blows of a sword. Jesus would not have the weapon drawn if it was not effective against the enemies that stood before Him on the battlefield that day.

Finally, what can be known regarding the warrior's intriguing answer to Joshua's question of allegiance? In this quest to fully define the nature and role of Jesus in the events of the Old Testament, the complexities of His relationship to the nation of Israel are obviously paramount. The cryptic answer, *"Neither,"* supplies foundational evidence in the reconstruction of this complex Old Testament relationship. The Old Testament story of Israel is a war story. With the Warrior of warriors now standing before him, Joshua knew that the answer to his question would foretell the fate of Israel during every moment of Old Testament battle history. This critical topic will be dealt with in much greater detail later.

In summary, the man Joshua encounters is a warrior who anticipates mortal, close-in, hand-to-hand combat—and soon. This warrior is none other than Jesus Christ, the Son of the Living God. And yet, this warrior isn't going to "speak" the victory into existence and save the day by vanquishing his enemies with the Word of his mouth. This is the book of Joshua, not the book of Revelation. Instead, this warrior—Jesus—is going to do battle the old fashioned way. Hand-to-hand combat, swords flashing in the sun, and the clanging sound of metal striking metal all seem to be the expectation of this day. Amazingly enough, the timing of His appearance suggests that the outcome of the battle that Jesus will physically fight with drawn sword will directly influence the outcome of the Israelites assault on the walled city of Jericho.

This passage from the book of Joshua has engendered as many questions as it has answered. If the case has been made that Jesus assumed the role of a leader of warriors in the Old Testament, then what are the specifics of His military assignment? And most critically, the need for the omnipotent Son of God to carry a common steel sword into battle deserves even further Biblical investigation. Joshua has whetted our appetite. Our hearts tell us that we can know even more. A second critical passage from the book of Daniel will build further upon the foundation laid by this mysterious encounter described in the book of Joshua.

Chapter 3

Daniel's Special Messenger
"The Prince of the Persian Kingdom Resisted Me Twenty-one Days"

Babylon. The Jewish remnant was in exile. The conquest of Judah by the armies of Nebuchadnezzar was a distant, yet still fresh memory among the Israelite survivors. The horrific accounts of the destruction of Jerusalem and the burning of the Holy Temple were still fresh in the prophet Daniel's ears. And yet, Babylon—the predator—had itself now become prey. The conqueror had been conquered. The Babylonian empire had fallen to the Medes and Persians. It was the third year of the reign of Cyrus, king of Persia. Daniel, an exile, stood on the banks of the Tigris River.

The stage is set in the book of the prophet Daniel for one of the most unique and spectacular visions described in the Bible. It is so breathtaking that it literally sucks the strength right out of Daniel. Even though they do not see the vision itself, Daniel's companions are overcome with terror. From this radiant vision, a brilliantly arrayed messenger speaks to Daniel. There is something about this messenger that is different. He is no ordinary angel. Daniel is obviously overwhelmed by this unnamed messenger's appearance, as he renders a very vivid description of him.

> *I looked up and there before me was a man dressed in linen, with a belt of the finest gold around his waist. His body was like chrysolite, his face like lightning, his eyes like flaming torches, his arms and legs like the gleam of burnished bronze, and his voice like the sound of a multitude.*
>
> —Daniel 10:5-6 (emphasis added)

The description of the man whom Daniel encounters is unique in the Old Testament. It is significantly different than all other such physical descriptions of any of the many colorful messengers found there. And yet our interest is piqued because we have read this description before. In fact, it is nearly an exact duplicate of a description given by the apostle John in the New Testament book of Revelation.

> *I turned around to see the voice that was speaking to me. And when I turned I saw seven golden lampstands, and among the lampstands was someone "like a son of man," dressed in a robe reaching down to his feet and with a <u>golden sash around his chest</u>. His head and hair were white like wool, as white as snow, and <u>his eyes were like blazing fire</u>. <u>His feet were like bronze glowing in a furnace</u>, and <u>his voice was like the sound of rushing waters</u>.*
>
> —Revelation 1:12-15

Special note must be made of the similarity in Daniel's description of his messenger's eyes and those of the fully revealed Jesus described in the book of Revelation. This description of the messenger's eyes as being like *"flaming torches"* is duplicated nowhere else in scripture except in three passages from the book of Revelation. In addition to the above passage, two other passages from Revelation—both of which are clearly identified as describing Jesus—also speak of eyes *"like blazing fire."*

> *"To the angel of the church in Thyatira write: <u>These are the words of the Son of God</u>, whose <u>eyes are like blazing fire</u> and whose feet are like burnished bronze.*
>
> —Revelation 2:18 (emphasis added)

> *His <u>eyes are like blazing fire</u>, and on his head are many crowns. He has a name written on him that no one knows but he himself.*
>
> —Revelation 19:12 (emphasis added)

The two descriptions—Daniel's and John's—are incredibly similar. The one critical difference between the two is that in the book of Daniel the man's identity remains shrouded in mystery while in the book of Revelation that identity is clearly revealed. In the book of Daniel the man is most pointedly and purposefully not named, while in the book of Revelation that person is openly revealed as none other than Jesus Christ. In fact, the only person who is identified in the Bible who has *"eyes of blazing fire"* is Jesus—pointedly and specifically in the Revelation 2:18 verse above. A reasonable conclusion is supported by these facts. The person described in the tenth chapter of the book of Daniel—from His flaming eyes to His bronze legs and to the voice like the sound of a multitude—is also Jesus. The similarities can hardly be by random happenstance. The Holy Spirit obviously wanted us to make this connection.

The very deliberate nature of the anonymity of the messenger in Daniel will be discussed in depth later. A brief comment is appropriate now. In both of the two previous angelic messenger visitations described in the book of Daniel (chapters 8 and 9) the messenger is quite purposely named. In both instances it is the angel Gabriel who delivers the message. We cannot help but notice that not only is there no mention of Gabriel in chapters 10 and 11, but despite a dazzling and detailed description of this obviously unique messenger, no name is given. Despite delivering one of the lengthiest and most detailed prophetic discourses in the Bible, this messenger's identity remains quite intentionally shrouded in mystery. This very fact must arouse our suspicion.

As previously discussed, nothing written in the Word of God is there by random chance. One must ask, therefore, why the identity of the long-winded messenger to the prophet Daniel would be so conspicuously withheld. The Holy Spirit had to have a reason to not reveal his identity, or we can be assured that He would have revealed it. If, as we might quite reasonably expect, this were Gabriel yet again delivering this special message, surely we would know it. Despite the obvious fact that Chapter 10 follows Chapters 8 and 9 in the text of the Bible, this description of an angelic messenger is clearly not a continuation of the previously described visits. The text of Chapter 10 makes it quite clear that the encounter that is being described is entirely separate. Surely, if this were Gabriel again, he would have been named again. Instead, the messenger of Chapter 10 is treated differently, set apart, and special—even in comparison to the mighty angel Gabriel. Certainly this very special treatment of this mysterious messenger adds even more strength to the argument that this messenger is the incarnate Son of God.

Most would agree then that the interpretation of the evidence found in the first portion of this passage from the book of Daniel is relatively straightforward. Daniel appears to be describing yet another lightly shrouded appearance of Jesus in the Old Testament. It is in the interpretation of the rest of the passage that our problems begin.

In the second part of the description of Daniel's encounter, we are treated to several statements that can only be described as unsettling. We find ourselves reading comfortably along, believing that we are listening to the words of Jesus Christ, when out of the blue Daniel throws us a curve ball. His messenger tells Daniel that, *"… the prince of the Persian kingdom resisted me twenty-one days.*

Then Michael, one of the chief princes, came to help me, because I was detained there with the king of Persia" (Daniel 10:13; emphasis added).

What? Jesus, the only Son of God, was *"resisted"* by *"the prince of the Persian kingdom"* and *"detained"* with the *"king of Persia"*? How in any stretch of the imagination can that possibly be true? How can the immortal, omnipotent Son of God be detained by anyone—let alone one of the presumed heavenly powers that *He* in fact created? This suggestion seems to have carried this whole "warrior" thing just a bit too far. After all, it is one thing to state that Jesus appeared to Joshua with a sword in hand. It is another thing altogether to state that the wartime intentions of the Son of God were forcibly restrained—and by a created being!

The answer to this perplexing question is not as far-fetched as one might expect. It is found in the answer to another very similar question: How could that very same Son of the Living God—being in nature *fully* God—be crucified on a wooden cross like a common criminal?

The answer to this second question is obviously the answer to both questions. The Son of God *chose*, in humble submission to the will of His Father, to be humbled before man in the crucifixion—*and He likewise chose to participate in the adventures of the Old Testament in a similarly humbled, emptied fashion.* This is a bold statement. When viewed through the classic perspective of modern Christian teaching, most might well argue that it would be incorrect to make such a statement about Jesus Christ.

The assumption that this is Jesus speaking to Daniel is obviously the hinge point of the interpretation of this passage. Everything turns on this assumption. Either it is Jesus—and we have an incredible insight into the nature of His role in the Old Testament—or we have simply misinterpreted the first half of the passage in relation to the second.

Several possibilities may be available to explain away this seemingly insolvable conundrum and arrest our panic attack. The first is that the incredible similarity between the description of Daniel's messenger and the description of Jesus in the book of Revelation is just a coincidence. This possibility poses obvious problems to the faithful reader of Holy Scripture, for coincidences simply don't happen in the Bible. The physical descriptions in these two passages leave very little room for coincidence, as it is readily apparent that they are nearly identical. Biblical history is recorded as God has decreed and the words of the Bible, as we have discussed, are crafted with perfection. Calling the similarities of the two descriptions a "coincidence" is no solution to our problem. God means exactly what He says and says exactly what He means.

Another similar explanation might be that some angels happen to bear a striking resemblance to the Son of God in their otherworldly appearance. Certainly, there are plenty of other descriptions of angels that are clearly identified as someone other than Jesus. Their description, although almost always impressive, is never as dazzling as this one of a man with a *"face like lightning"* and *"eyes like flaming torches."*

A solution to this Daniel 10 dichotomy that appears commonly in Old Testament commentaries is that there are in fact *two* persons speaking to Daniel in this passage. In other words, our identity problem is solved by presuming that the person in the first half of the passage whose description resembles that of Jesus in the book of Revelation was then supervened by a second person who subsequently delivered the longwinded speech to Daniel. The only problem with this is that we are given no textual confirmation that there was ever more than one person involved in this scene. Quite to the contrary, the flow of the text seems to strongly support the contention that only one person is encountered in this vision.

> *So I was left alone, gazing at this great vision; I had no strength left, my face turned deathly pale and I was helpless. Then I heard him speaking, and as I listened to him, I fell into a deep sleep, my face to the ground. A hand touched me and set me trembling on my hands and knees.*
>
> *He said, "Daniel, you who are highly esteemed, consider carefully the words I am about to speak to you, and stand up, for I have now been sent to you." And when he said this to me, I stood up trembling.*
>
> *Then he continued, "Do not be afraid, Daniel. Since the first day that you set your mind to gain understanding and to humble yourself before your God, your words were heard, and I have come in response to them. But the prince of the Persian kingdom resisted me twenty-one days. Then Michael, one of the chief princes, came to help me, because I was detained there with the king of Persia. Now I have come to explain to you what will happen to your people in the future, for the vision concerns a time yet to come." While he was saying this to me, I bowed with my face toward the ground and was speechless.*
>
> —Daniel 10:8-15 (emphasis added)

Although arguable, further support of the conclusion that the entire passage is about Jesus is found in the whole tone of the passage in Daniel 10. It is a tone of staggering awe. Daniel finds himself immediately on his face before this messenger. Jesus tells Daniel to arise and stand, which Daniel does, only to once again immediately bow down with his face to the ground. This is no ordinary angel. Indeed, this messenger offers no exclamatory protest against Daniel's immediate prostration as previously noted in John's angelic encounter in the Book of Revelation. Quite to the contrary, this messenger's very presence obviously commands fear, respect, and immediate submission. Once again, no ordinary angel would allow Daniel to worship him. No ordinary angel would allow Daniel's prostrate reverence to continue for even a moment.

This particular argument, however, is not without its detractors. One can argue, for instance, that there is little difference between Daniel's response to this messenger and his response to the angelic visitation of Gabriel described in Daniel 8. In a description that is in many ways similar to that in Chapter 10, the mere presence of this angelic messenger—who is clearly named Gabriel—also sends Daniel flat on his face.

> *While I, Daniel, was watching the vision and trying to understand it, there before me stood one who looked like a man. And I heard a man's voice from the Ulai calling, "Gabriel, tell this man the meaning of the vision."*
>
> *As he came near the place where I was standing, I was terrified and fell prostrate. "Son of man," he said to me, "understand that the vision concerns the time of the end." While he was speaking to me, I was in a deep sleep, with my face to the ground. Then he touched me and raised me to my feet.*
>
> —Daniel 8:15-18 (emphasis added)

Most notably, Daniel also records no admonition from Gabriel against the reverence offered by Daniel. It must also be noted, however, that Daniel was presumably also in the presence of Jesus in this scene. The *"voice from the Ulai"* that commands Gabriel to *"tell this man the meaning of the vision"* (Daniel 8:16) is almost assuredly that of the Commander of the army of the Lord, Jesus. In other words, Jesus is also present in this encounter. The holiness that always surrounds Him most assuredly commands this scene and is most likely that which sent Daniel to the ground in front of Gabriel.

It is also not clear whether Daniel's posture before Gabriel is really one of worship. There is considerable evidence from the text suggesting that he has been physically blown onto his face or, as the wording suggests, fallen *"terrified"* rather than in reverence. No doubt Gabriel is clearly a powerful presence. One cannot help but notice, nonetheless, that the spectacular nature of the adjectives used in the description of our mysterious messenger in Daniel 10 is unrivaled by that of the rather plain description of Gabriel given in chapter 8.

As convincing as all of our arguments may be regarding the identification of Daniel's messenger as Jesus Christ, the Holy Spirit saves one of the most interesting until last. Even the most ardent of skeptics toward the case made thus far cannot help but be impressed by the fascinating nature of the next clue.

Some Biblical clues seem purposely hidden. As Solomon stated, *"It is the glory of God to conceal a matter; to search out a matter is the glory of kings"* (Proverbs 25:2). Such is the case with this clue. It is hidden right out in the open. Out of the blue, as this very same messenger continues to speak to Daniel, his carefully recorded words reveal another startling clue to his true identity. This same unidentified messenger begins a prophetic discourse in chapter 11 with a specific phrase that cannot help but pique our interest. His words are very precisely chosen. He uses a phrase that rings familiar to all students of the NIV translation of the Bible:

> *"Now then, I tell you the truth: Three more kings will appear in Persia, and then a fourth, who will be far richer than all the others. When he has gained power by his wealth, he will stir up everyone against the kingdom of Greece."*
>
> —Daniel 11:2 (emphasis added)

The phrase *"I tell you the truth"* is used 79 times in the NIV translation of the Bible. 79 times. It is only used once in the entirety of the Old Testament, and that is here at the beginning of the 11th chapter of the Book of Daniel—right in the middle of the discourse by this mysterious messenger. As you have probably already guessed, in every single one of the other 78 times that it is used—all of which occur in the New Testament—it is by none other than Jesus Christ.

Admittedly, this portion of the book of Daniel was originally written in Hebrew while the New Testament gospel accounts were in Greek. Thus the *actual* words that are spoken in these two passages are not the same. They are not even translated as the same in other translations of the Bible. Nonetheless, the meaning of the translations is nearly identical and the intention is clear. That intention is not found elsewhere in the text of the Bible except in these 78 passages. The NIV authors translated both phrases as *"I tell you the truth"* for a reason. Surely, this is no coincidence that they took two completely different passages and translated them into the exact same five-word statement. This can't be anything less than a carefully crafted clue left by God for all who might seek to know more regarding the true nature of His Son, Jesus. This clue leaves little doubt about the identity of the *"man"* who is delivering this cryptic message to Daniel.

When viewed in its entirety, this passage from the book of Daniel is remarkable in its revelation. In specific regard to the overarching premise of this book, the identity of the messenger combined with the content of the message makes this scriptural passage one of the most important in the Bible. It has the potential to significantly alter the perspective through which the whole of Old Testament scripture is viewed. In particular, if this is Jesus speaking to Daniel then this passage provides several clues that illuminate His Old Testament role:

1. Jesus had just been *sent* (like a soldier on a mission) to Daniel (Daniel 10:11).
2. Jesus had appeared *in response to Daniel's prayer* (Daniel 10:12).
3. *Jesus was delayed* twenty-one days *because* the *prince* of the Persian kingdom *resisted* him (Daniel 10:13).
4. Jesus *needed* help from *the archangel Michael*, one of the *"chief princes,"* *because* He was *detained* with the king of Persia (Daniel 10:13).
5. Soon Jesus will return *to fight against* the prince of Persia and He will presumably have another fight ahead of Him when the prince of Greece comes next (Daniel 10:20).
6. The only one who *supports Jesus* against them is Michael (Daniel 10:21).
7. Likewise, Jesus took His stand *to support and protect Michael* in a previous conflict during the first year of Darius the Mede (Daniel 11:1).

In summary, we can know for certain that the role of Jesus in the Old Testament was not that of a casual bystander. He was physically involved in the day-to-day events in the life of the nation of Israel. His role was that of a warrior. He took commands from a higher source, just like all warriors. The evidence seems to support the fact that Jesus had to actually fight the fight with drawn battle sword in hand. At least to some degree, He was emptied of His Godly power—most certainly at least regarding His fighting ability.

This emptiness extended to the point of needing the help of the mighty warrior angel, Michael. In a similar fashion, Michael in turn needed his battle support. Theirs seems to be the true camaraderie of warriors who have shared the throes of mortal combat. They apparently shared that very special bond that only warriors who stand back-to-back in battle can know. In many ways, this camaraderie was similar to that shared by Jesus and His disciples during His gospel ministry. Further still, the parallel to the New Testament role of Jesus in our salvation is readily apparent. For example, we also share the very special camaraderie of knowing Jesus in His suffering.

Further still, this passage assures us once again of the importance of our physical bodies and the way that we interact with the physical world around us. Indeed, this passage emphasizes the fact that Jesus specifically chose to not just speak the battle victories of the Old Testament into existence. He clearly could have done it the same way that we are told He will do it in the great end-times battles ahead. He is fully God. Nonetheless, for His own reasons—most assuredly having to do with the will of His Father—Jesus was instead embodied in the physical form of a man and fought alongside the angels. We cannot help but be reminded of the similarities between the nature of this Old Testament role and that of the Messiah Jesus who emptied and humbled Himself to the point of being crucified by and for the very human beings that He created and came to redeem.

Obviously, none of us were present to witness Jesus during the time described by the four gospel accounts. None of us witnessed Him speaking words of compassion and mercy as he cured the ill, raised the dead, and spoke with joy of the eternal life that He would share with those who would believe. Likewise, we are only left to imagine our Savior, the only Son of God, in His equally captivating Old Testament role as the warrior protector of the nation of Israel. Only in our imaginations can we see Him rising with sword drawn to stand in the gap between the righteous remnant of Israel and their enemies. What fierce battles must have raged around Him and against such awesome foes. What panoramic battle scenes must have swirled violently around him as He stood back-to-back with fellow warriors in the army of the Lord. No modern day warrior or movie idol—no matter how stunning—could even approach the battlefield glory of this Champion of champions, Hero of heroes, and Warrior of warriors.

The Old Testament descriptions of Joshua and Daniel's encounters with Jesus Christ change everything. The perspective on the most important Person in the entirety of the creation that they introduce is the foundation from which we move forward. These passages open an illuminating window into the many other episodes in the Old Testament where an embodied Son of God appears to be directly and palpably involved in the fight for the nation of Israel. With these introductory passages from Joshua and Daniel as our foundation, let's begin our search through the Old Testament for the physical presence of Jesus.

Chapter 4

The Setting of the Old Testament
"A Great War"

Daniel, an exile, stood on the banks of the Tigris River. He had been through three weeks of sheer misery. He had denied himself before his God. He had eaten no meat. He longed for the fruit of the vine. His skin was parched and cracked for lack of soothing lotion. The salt in the sweat that ran freely in the Babylonian sun seared his wounds. He had humbled himself before God in remembrance of the sin of his people. He had suffered. He had placed the plight of his people at the foot of the altar of God. *"In the third year of Cyrus king of Persia, a revelation was given to [him]. Its message was true and it concerned a great war."*

War. The most dominant single feature of the Old Testament is war. The Old Testament is the story of the nation of Israel and the story of the nation of Israel is a war story. Whether it is the individual struggle of a single heroic Israelite warrior or great battles involving the entire army of the nation of Israel, the setting of war is the dominant background feature of the history of Israel. The discipline, terror, and violence of hand-to-hand conflict—whether between individual warriors or between nations—is the furnace of affliction that God most commonly utilized to test the hearts of His chosen people. If Jesus is to have the primary role in the story of *"a great war,"* it should not be surprising that His role is that of a warrior.

Indeed, this description of Daniel's vision—that *"it concerned a great war"*—sets the tone for not only the prophetic content of the message that follows, but also for the entirety of the Old Testament. Daniel wants us to know that all of the events of the Old Testament are part of an epic struggle, a war, a fight. He wants us to know that everything that occurs in the history of Israel is somehow intertwined in a complex manner with the events of—and in the setting of—*"a great war."*

Old Testament scholars generally agree—especially in light of the rest of chapter 11—that this part of the book of Daniel is telling us of much more about a great war than just a detailed prophecy regarding a future progression of real world conquerors. To the contrary, his message emphasizes that the real world events that are described in the Old Testament scriptures—and in secular history—were not all that was going on during those tumultuous times. It seems, instead, to emphasize the importance of another great war that has been occurring since the beginning of time in an invisible world whose course runs parallel to ours. From the evidence that is tendered in this vision, there can be no doubt that this mysterious parallel otherworld is indeed also engulfed in a great war.

By every glimpse we get of it in this chapter and throughout the Bible, mysterious angels, demons, unknown princes, kings, authorities, and powers inhabit this otherworld, this parallel universe—and it seems to be nearly entirely consumed with a war between two opposing sides. This is indeed the great war that exists— and has existed since the dawn of mankind—between the forces of good and the forces of evil. This, in and of itself, is not surprising, for all of us are familiar with the many references in the Bible to war between the good angels and the bad. Certainly the repeated reference to the struggle between the archangel Michael and Satan is a hallmark of this war.

But the passages reviewed in the last two chapters even further amplify the significance of this great war. They reveal that Jesus Himself was palpably involved in this fight. Jesus was not just sitting in some heavenly throne room casting out strategic commands. To the contrary, these passages suggest that He was in fact steeped in the throes of the sword-swinging, metal-clanging-against-metal, hand-to-hand combat that took place between the heavenly warriors of God and Satan's rebellious legions of evil. The implications of such a revelation are profound when taken in the light of the rest of Holy Scripture.

The Bible reveals many things about this great war between the forces of good and evil. First and foremost, we know that the ultimate outcome of the war that has dominated our universe since the fall of Satan is already assured. God—the Creator of the whole show—will not be denied. His plan for ultimate victory is perfect. The death and resurrection of Jesus Christ are the exclusive guarantors of the victory of good over evil. Just as Jesus is the whole point of the creation, so also is His single most profound act of individual warfare that which exclusively decides the outcome of the conflict.

Despite the surety of the outcome of this great war, we can know with similar surety that still the fight must actually be fought. Just as we must fight the fight every day of our lives—despite the assurance of our salvation in the shed blood of Jesus Christ—so also did the Old Testament spiritual war that embroiled the nation of Israel have to be fought. There have always been—and will be for the foreseeable future—battles that must be fought in the actual implementation of

God's planned outcome. This need for close-in combat is precisely by God's design and is a product of His divine wisdom. It is our part of this great war. It was also Jesus' role in the Old Testament. This is where theology meets reality. The written Word of God has never strayed from this truth. From the first word to the last, the Bible makes it clear that it is God's good pleasure that we face those battles in our world now and that His mighty angels fight them in the spiritual world that parallels ours.

We know a fair bit about our battles — at least that part of them that we can see, hear, feel, and taste. We know all about the conflict between the true Commander of our heart and the usurper, our rebellious human nature. These are true battles. Our magnificently designed heart is the most holy battlefield of all battlefields. And by God's exacting design, this fight is unavoidable in our lives.

But we really know very little about the battle that rages behind the scenes, the battle in the dimension into which our eyes cannot peer and our ears cannot hear. Holy Scripture states, nonetheless, that the outcome of the warfare in the spiritual otherworld really matters. This otherworld warfare has a direct and profound impact upon what happens in our world — their battles influence ours. There is also considerable scriptural evidence that our battles — most specifically the prayers of our hearts, the thoughts of our minds, and the actions of our bodies — influence their battles, too. The information we do have suggests that the activities of the two universes are complexly and delicately interwoven in a masterful tapestry of struggle and war.

Accordingly, we can know that in the times of the Old Testament patriarchs, kings, and prophets, someone actually had to fight the battle in the spiritual otherworld of war that paralleled theirs. Enemies existed. Challenges were thrown down. Battle lines were formed. Metal sword clanged against metal sword as the conflicts swayed in the throes of brute force and battle strategy. And precisely here is the meat of this book. Precisely here is where we must know how the Son of God fit into this whole battle scenario. Precisely here, we want to know what exactly was the role of our embodied Savior in these battles.

The first question regarding the role of Jesus in this great epic conflict was posed by the visitor's message in the 10th chapter of the book of Daniel. This is a question that we will discuss at great length. We simply can't avoid it. This mandatory first question involves the specific power yielded by this special messenger, this Prince, this Commander of the army of the Lord. For if Jesus remains fully empowered as the Son of the Omnipotent God, then there really is no battle, is there? There can never be any real contest against God. Jesus is Creator and Sustainer of all. He is god. There is no power in the universe that can oppose Him.

And yet the 10th chapter of the book of Daniel tells us that this is not how this great war has played out. In the latter parts of this chapter, the messenger reveals that the Prince of Persia delayed him in coming to speak with Daniel. If our automatic assumption of the fullness of the deity of Jesus Christ is the perspective through which we interpret this passage, we immediately run headlong into stark contradictions. How can this *"Prince of Persia"* delay Jesus, the Son of the Living God? Even if this Persian prince is the mightiest of the dark powers of the otherworld, Satan himself, he cannot stand—even for an instant—in opposition to God. And most certainly, Jesus would not need the help or assistance of any angel—even the archangel Michael—for anything.

If, however, Jesus is fully emptied of His power as an equal Member of the Trinity, this delay by the Prince of Persia becomes a more plausible scenario. If Jesus is the fully, infinitely emptied, 100%-man, incarnation of the Living God described in the New Testament, then we have a battle on our hands. Indeed, if *"we see Jesus, who was made a little lower than the angels"* (Hebrews 2:9), as steeped in mortal combat against the darkest and most powerful angel ever created, then we have a very plausible explanation for this enigmatic scriptural text—with weighty implications.

Although some may easily dismiss this explanation, its exploration represents an extraordinary opportunity to know more fully the depths of submission and obedience to the Father's will demonstrated by the Son of the Living God. One might at first be tempted to respond, "So what?" Yet one might also realize what an extraordinary revelation it would be to know that Jesus was involved in a very real, palpable manner in every single event documented in the Old Testament.

As implausible as all of this may seem, even the skeptic must agree that it seems equally silly to believe that the Person of Jesus Christ sat idly by during the pivotal events of the Old Testament—the battles of this great war. Even the skeptic must find it hard to deny the hard reality that faces each of us squarely—that Jesus is above and before and beyond all things. How could even a single word of the Old Testament *not* be about Him? Truly, we are once again reminded that the whole of the Bible is about no one else.

*Then I said, "Here I am, I have come—it is written **about me** in the*
scroll."

—Psalm 40:7 (emphasis added)

The implications of Jesus emptied *to the point of needing help* sends shudders through modern day Christian theology. Yet, most amazingly, by scriptural standards this is not as outlandish as it might seem at first glance. The passage from the Book of Daniel after all is not the only place in Old Testament Scripture where we are told that *"the LORD"* needed assistance in battle. For example, in the revealing *"Song of Deborah"* found in the book of Judges, a similar statement is made.

Barak and Deborah have just won a great battle over the forces led by Sisera, the commander of a large Canaanite army that had been oppressing the nation of Israel. Deborah's song tells us of the battle. She exalts those who rose to stand beside them in battle and chides those who did not. Then, in the middle of the song Deborah refers to a battle fought not in the real world, but rather in this mysterious otherworld of war. In this passage we see further support for the premise that the mighty battles fought in this parallel world have a direct impact upon events in our world.

"From the heavens the stars fought, from their courses they fought
against Sisera. The river Kishon swept them away, the age-old river,
the river Kishon. March on, my soul; be strong! Then thundered the
horses' hoofs—galloping, galloping go his mighty steeds.

'Curse Meroz,' said the angel of the LORD. 'Curse its people bitterly,
because they did not come to help the LORD, to help the LORD against
the mighty.'"

—Judges 5:20-23 (emphasis added)

What a battle scene these verses describe. Surely this battle involves more than what we can see with our eyes. We are told of a battle in which angels (*"stars"*) *"from the heavens"* fight on *"mighty steeds."* These warriors are from the heavens. They are not of this world. And yet they ride into battle on great battle horses! As if this isn't unsettling enough, the next revelation regarding this great battle catches us completely off guard. We are also told to bitterly curse the people of Meroz, *"for they did not come to help the LORD"* in His battle against *"the mighty."*

Again, one cannot help being amazed at the concept that *"the LORD"* would need help in battle. Yet that is precisely what these verses state. Indeed, it is *"the angel of the Lord"* himself—the warrior Jesus we will soon argue—who is being quoted as having cried out *"Curse Meroz."* Visions of the Son of God caught up in the throes of fierce battle against mighty foes immediately come to mind. The battle sways too and fro with the Jesus right there in the thick of the fight. The pressure from the fearsome enemy becomes oppressive. Jesus cries out as the battle sways dangerously against them. Others must rally to His assistance when Meroz fails to answer the battle call. This scene could be right out of the movie *Braveheart!*

This passage also speaks much of the palpable ferocity of the otherworld warfare that surrounded the fledgling nation of Israel in its early days. How can we not be left craving to know more of this holy battle? We are nevertheless left standing with only the lingering sweet taste of this knowledge of Jesus—for Meroz is never again mentioned in the Bible.

A discussion of the emptiness of Jesus in His incarnation into the creation cannot be considered complete without also mentioning that these Old Testament examples are not the only time that angels assisted Jesus. Despite the fact that Jesus was fully empowered by the Holy Spirit to perform incredible miracles during the three-years of ministry described by the gospel accounts, He somehow still needed the assistance of angels. Once again, the question regarding why the Son of God would need help from anyone is answered by the degree of voluntary emptying that is described by the New Testament accounts. Two New Testament examples readily illustrate this point. The first is the fact that angels *"attended"* Jesus after His temptation in the desert.

> *At once the Spirit sent him out into the desert, and he was in the desert forty days, being tempted by Satan. He was with the wild animals, and <u>angels attended him</u>.*
>
> —Mark 1:12-13 (emphasis added)

The loyalty and faithfulness of fellow soldiers-in-arms who share the hard-earned camaraderie born in the fury and chaos of battle is hinted at by this description of Jesus at war in the desert. Even more exemplary is the description of the sorrows of Jesus in the Garden of Gethsemane, where we are told that angels not only *"appeared to him,"* but very specifically also *"strengthened him."*

He withdrew about a stone's throw beyond them, knelt down and prayed, "Father, if you are willing, take this cup from me; yet not my will, but yours be done."

An angel from heaven appeared to him and strengthened him. And being in anguish, he prayed more earnestly, and his sweat was like drops of blood falling to the ground.

—Luke 22:41-44 (emphasis added)

Our Old Testament examples—especially that described in Daniel 10 above—posed the question regarding the incarnate Son of God needing help from *any* created individual. These New Testament examples answer the question. The facts are clear. Jesus was fully emptied in His incarnation. The angels would not have been there to *"strengthen"* Him in the Garden of Gethsemane or *"help"* Him against *"the king of Persia"* if He did not in fact need to be strengthened and helped in these real world situations. The Bible is pure truth. As we have discussed, its words are precise. God says exactly what He means and means exactly what He says.

The possibility that Jesus appeared also in the Old Testament emptied of His divine power therefore really should not surprise us. After all, He emptied Himself into the literal skin of mankind at His birth in Bethlehem. Is it possible that Jesus did indeed bow to the will of the Father in accepting the humbled state that we acknowledge in His birth as a fragile human baby in Bethlehem—but instead actually accepted it from the very moment of His creation of the universe? Could His acceptance of this humbled state from the very beginning have mandated His need for the assistance of His warrior angel comrades? Despite our natural inclinations to the opposite, the Bible strongly reveals the fullness of the emptying of Jesus.

When I consider your heavens, the work of your fingers, the moon and the stars, which you have set in place, what is man that you are mindful of him, the son of man that you care for him? You made him a little lower than the heavenly beings and crowned him with glory and honor.

—Psalm 8:3-5 (emphasis added)

But we see Jesus, who was made a little lower than the angels, now crowned with glory and honor because he suffered death, so that by the grace of God he might taste death for everyone.

—Hebrews 2:9 (emphasis added)

The Holy Spirit would not tell us that Jesus was *"made"* into a state that placed Him *"a little lower than the angels"* if it was not critical to our understanding of the fullness of the Son of God's role in every event of the both the New and Old Testaments. The choice of the adjective *"little"* in this description is not random. The terminology utilized by the Holy Spirit is precise. It is exacting in its perfection. The Holy Spirit wanted us to be able to piece together the whole story and fully understand the significance of this critical passage from the book of Daniel. He wanted us to know that the fact that Jesus was made a *"little"* lower than the angels put Him palpably right in the middle of the fight.

Yet equally so are we reminded that Jesus is not some weakling noncombatant. He is in fact a force to be reckoned with in this battle in which He is so totally engaged. We are told, after all, in the passage from Daniel 10 that it is none other than Jesus alone who rallies to the assistance of Michael in his battle *"in the first year of Darius the Mede."* Furthermore, if not from the very beginning, at least by the time we see Jesus at Jericho, He is in fact the *"commander of the army of God."* He undoubtedly could have named Himself as such. He obviously could have gotten the command promotion just on the basis of who His Father was. Most likely, however, this is a command position that He attained the old fashioned way—He earned it.

So, what exactly was Jesus doing in the middle of the fray throughout the history chronicled by the books of the Old Testament? We must remember that the ministry of Jesus to us on earth was not just our salvation. He also came to show us things. He came to tell us of the Father, the salvation offered by God, the way we are to conduct ourselves in the lives that God has fashioned for us, and the good news of the kingdom of God. He came to show us a better way.

We can only guess that this may also have been Jesus' role in the parallel world of near continual war that coursed through the events of the Old Testament. The angels did not need redemption, but they did need leadership. After all, the original defection had occurred in the heart of Lucifer—at the highest leadership level. Suddenly the loyal angels found themselves in a fight. The lines were drawn between two clearly delineated and incompatible sides. The differences between the two sides were like black and white, like pure light and blackest darkness. They were not subtle. They could not help but square off against each other. The dark side already had its rebellious leader, Satan. So also did the other side need a leader. The loyal angels needed to be shown the way in the great struggle in which they found themselves embroiled from the moment evil was found in the heart of Lucifer. They needed a leader in this great war—a leader who would stand back-to-back with them in the fury of the fight.

More importantly, we must remember that there are warrior attributes of the Messiah that are repeatedly referred to throughout the Old Testament and then again in the New Testament book of Revelation. It may be hard for some of us to accept the fact that there is nearly as much said about the role of Jesus as our *avenger of blood* as there is said about His role as our *kinsman redeemer*. We can't—despite our natural inclination to do so—separate one from the other. Jesus became man to be the interface, the high priest, the bridge between created man and uncreated God. As much as we naturally gravitate toward the loving, compassionate Redeemer described in great detail on the pages of the New Testament, we cannot avoid the fact that the Word of God reveals a day of great wrath that will someday come like a flood upon this world. Jesus is—and always has been—a mighty, awesome and awful warrior—whether we like it or not. In light of the countless prophetic references to the very specific role Jesus will play on *"the great day of the Lord"* (Zephaniah 1:14), this exploration into the Old Testament role of Jesus as a mighty warrior is not so far fetched after all.

Before we can fully understand how the fullness of the nature of Jesus is revealed in the Old Testament scriptures and before we can discuss further scriptural references to the specific role of Jesus in the battles of the Old Testament times, we first need to explore the concept and importance of the fullness of the emptying of the Son of God in His incarnation.

Chapter 5

The Importance of This Discussion
The True Nature of Jesus: Fully God, Fully Man

If, as the preceding discussion suggests, Jesus was the warrior who both met Joshua outside of Jericho and delivered the message to Daniel in Daniel 10-11, then we have a problem. Classic Christian theology does not encompass the possibility that Jesus was reduced to the status of an embodied warrior who was actually engaged in the mechanics of physical battle during Old Testament history. Even if we were to grudgingly acquiesce to His participation in Old Testament battle, to state that He was actually dependent in battle upon the assistance of other angelic warriors would fall somewhere between heresy and insanity. Classic Christian teaching simply does not tolerate that which would be considered by most to be a somewhat blatant diminution of the one and only Son of God.

Still, this analysis of these critical scriptural passages cannot be so readily dismissed as heretical or even inconsequential. To the contrary, such complex and difficult scriptural passages as these offer much to the seeking heart. In the pursuit of the full knowledge of Jesus Christ, comprehending the complexities of His *fully God and yet simultaneously fully man* nature may be the most difficult task that we face. These are, nonetheless, the most important of discussions and the most critical of journeys into the written Word of God. Indeed, in the exploration of the immeasurable depth of the mystery of the true nature of Jesus Christ lies the fullness, the totality in fact, of our eternity as sons and daughters of the living God.

What then *can* we know about this complex interaction between the God-nature and the man-nature of Jesus? Further still, what can we know about *our* relationship to God as it pertains to this dual nature of our Redeemer? The foundation of this discussion is well established. God is entirely *set apart* from us. He is uncreated Creator and we are created. He is infinite and we are finite. He is eternal and we are transient. He is not just *a whole bunch* better and more holy and more powerful and more intelligent than we. Instead, He is entirely different than us in every metric that can be applied—and to a degree that is incomprehensible and even unimaginable to us.

We can also most emphatically know that we ourselves will never *be* God. Even so, that which the Bible so confidently tells us is that we will spend eternity in a very special relationship with God. We will enjoy a very special interaction with our Creator. Somehow, it is our eternal destiny to have the same—yet different—relationship to the Father that Jesus, His *only* Son, enjoys.

In fact, we are told that in the moment of the surrender of our hearts to Jesus, we have in fact already become sons and daughters of the Living God. And yet we are also told that Jesus is the one and only true Son of God. We are also told that we are being transformed into the likeness of Jesus—but of course know fully well that we will always fall immeasurably short of Him. We will not become Jesus. We will not become God. We will become *like* Jesus and we will become sons and daughters of the living God. And we know that precisely in the midst of this delicate, complex, mysterious interaction between the Divine and the not divine, the Uncreated and the created, the Infinite and the finite, the Eternal and the transient—between God and man—lies our eternity in the living God. The shed blood of Jesus Christ has exclusively and entirely purchased this eternal life for us.

We must not shy away from this discussion. We must repeatedly remind ourselves of its importance. This is not some esoteric discussion of little or no relevance to the daily lives of common Christians. Quite to the contrary, this discussion is of critical importance to all who call upon the most holy Name of Jesus Christ. Its critical nature is revealed in one fact. Jesus became man for all eternity. Our world is not 1st or 5th or 305th in a series of projects that God is keeping Himself busy with for the foreseeable future. No chance. *This is it.* This is the whole show. God says in His Word that this is it—that He has revealed *all* in His Holy Word.

> *Surely the Sovereign LORD does nothing without revealing his plan to his servants the prophets.*
>
> —Amos 3:7

Jesus became man *for eternity* because He is to be the focal point of our relationship to God *for eternity*. He is the interface, the bridge between the infinite, uncreated, eternal, Holy God and the finite, created, unholy man. He is our connection to that to which we cannot, by our very nature, be connected.

> *In the sight of God, who gives life to everything, and of Christ Jesus, who while testifying before Pontius Pilate made the good confession, I charge you to keep this command without spot or blame until the*

appearing of our Lord Jesus Christ, which God will bring about in his
own time—God, the blessed and only Ruler, the King of kings and
Lord of lords, who <u>*alone is immortal*</u> *and* <u>*who lives in*</u>
<u>*unapproachable light,*</u> *whom* <u>*no one has seen or can see.*</u> *To him be*
honor and might forever. Amen.

—1Timothy 6:13-16 (emphasis added)

As our connection, Jesus must *remain* in this position in order to maintain our relationship with the Mighty God. As such, He is—very literally—our *everything*.

And he is the head of the body, the church; he is the beginning and the
firstborn from among the dead, so that in <u>*everything*</u> *he might have*
the <u>*supremacy*</u>.

—Colossians 1:18 (emphasis added)

Jesus is our eternity. He is not just our ticket to life, to God's eternal dance of love. He is the blinding pure light, focal point of the entirety of God. He is the focus of all of God's attention and *He* will be focused precisely and exclusively *on us* in His role as our connection to the Father, as our high priest—for eternity.

The LORD *has sworn and will not change his mind: "You are* <u>*a priest*</u>
<u>*forever,*</u> *in the order of Melchizedek."*

—Psalm 110:4 (emphasis added)

This is why this discussion regarding the true nature of Jesus Christ cannot be lightly cast off by anyone who calls himself or herself a Christian. This isn't some theological discussion carried out only in the hallowed hallways of the major seminaries of the world. In the depths of the answers that result from this discussion are very real, very palpable, very tangible consequences that will have a direct impact on each and every one of our eternal destinies.

Let us also remind ourselves at every step of this journey of the delicacy of this discussion. We walk a razor thin ridge between the magnificent expanse of the true knowledge of God, and heresy; between honoring Jesus as He truly is, and blaspheming the only Name that is written on the very bedrock of our hearts.

But our deep hearts still cry out for the answers to these questions posed by the very Word of God to man. Could Jesus have been the messenger of the first part of Daniel 10 who is described nearly exactly as Jesus is described in Revelation and at the transfiguration? Certainly. But is Jesus the very same man who then recounts how He has just come from doing battle with the Prince of Persia for three weeks—and further still that the only reason He actually got here was because Michael, the great prince, came to help Him? The complete nature of Jesus is unknowable without the answer to this question.

Chapter 6

Fully Emptied...Forever
Faith: The Hinge Point of Everything

In the salvation of those who would be saved—those who would spend eternity as the princes and princesses of the eternal kingdom of God—a redemptive price had to be paid. Since human life was that which was being redeemed, human life was the payment due. Jesus had to really become a human being in order for His sinless life to count in the ultimate redemptive act of the crucifixion. He had to be 100% man. He had to confront 100% of the battles that we face in our lives in the battle that He faced on the cross of Calvary.

> *Since the children have flesh and blood, he too shared in their humanity so that by his death he might destroy him who holds the power of death—that is, the devil—and free those who all their lives were held in slavery by their fear of death. For surely it is not angels he helps, but Abraham's descendants. For this reason he had to be made like his brothers in every way, in order that he might become a merciful and faithful high priest in service to God, and that he might make atonement for the sins of the people. Because he himself suffered when he was tempted, he is able to help those who are being tempted.*
>
> —Hebrews 2:14-18 (emphasis added)

Jesus was born of Mary—but *not* of Joseph. The evidence presented in the Bible is clear in making this point. This is not some random quirk in the story of the birth of Jesus. Quite to the contrary, this was by very precise design. We are assured by God's nature that everything He does has a very precise intention behind it. The fact that Jesus was born of Mary and not of Joseph means that Jesus did not share the same sinful nature of every other man. This is critical. It means that the paternal bloodline of Jesus came directly from His Father in heaven—not from Adam. It means that Jesus had the chance to do life on earth as a man precisely as God originally planned it.

In other words, Jesus—fully man—had the chance to live a full human life perfectly in step with the Father. Jesus had the chance to live every moment of His life as a human being while simultaneously being fully indwelled by the full empowerment of the Holy Spirit. Jesus had the chance to spend every moment of His life centered in the middle of the Father's will for His life. Only Jesus—free from the sinful nature of Adam—had the chance to stare at every trial of every day of His life while simultaneously staring at the face of His Father. Only Jesus continually saw the true reality behind the false facade of this world. Jesus had the chance to do it right.

Jesus' vision, therefore, was not clouded by the sinful nature of man that makes each of us see the world and its standards *before* we see the Living God, the only True Standard. His vision was the crystal clear vision of a man whose heart is fully and continually aware of, directed by, and empowered by the Holy Spirit of the living God. This is the life Adam was intended to live. This is the life each of us was intended to live. But, it is also the life we are all incapable of living because of the sinful human nature passed onto us through our father Adam.

> *The LORD smelled the pleasing aroma and said in his heart: "Never again will I curse the ground because of man, even though every inclination of his heart is evil from childhood. And never again will I destroy all living creatures, as I have done.*
>
> —Genesis 8:21 (emphasis added)

When Jesus became man, He never quit being God. He never quit being 100% fully God. This simply could never happen. God can never change. And yet at the same time the Word of God teaches us about *limitations* that seem to have been placed on the knowledge and power of Jesus the man. For example, Jesus Himself told us that He did not know the time of His second coming. The statement by Jesus that only the Father knew the exact time was in fact documented in two of the gospel accounts (Matthew 24:36; Mark 13:32).

We are also told that there were times when Jesus could not perform miracles.

> *He could not do any miracles there, except lay his hands on a few sick people and heal them.*
>
> —Mark 6:5

It is important to note that the terminology utilized in the passage above is *"could not,"* not *"would not."* In other words, the power or ability to perform miracles was not there, even if the will to perform them was. In a similar fashion, we are also told that when Jesus *could* perform miracles it was in fact precisely because of *"the power of the Lord."*

> One day as he was teaching, Pharisees and teachers of the law, who had come from every village of Galilee and from Judea and Jerusalem, were sitting there. And <u>the power of the Lord was present for him to heal the sick</u>.
>
> —Luke 5:17 (emphasis added)

> Jesus answered, "I did tell you, but you do not believe. <u>The miracles I do in my Father's name</u> speak for me, but you do not believe because you are not my sheep."
>
> —John 10:25-26 (emphasis added)

We are also reminded of times when Jesus did not demonstrate the omniscience that one would normally attribute to God. When a woman in the crowd touched Him, for example, He was compelled to ask, *"Who touched me?"* (Mark 5:31; Luke 8:45). Jesus is no liar. He is no deceiver. He did not know.

In a similar fashion, we are continually reminded of the importance of Jesus' recurring retreat to prayer with the Father. We are also repeatedly told of the indwelling of God's Spirit in the man, Jesus. These passages necessarily stir questions in our hearts. Why would a member of the Triune Godhead—being clearly equal to the other members—*need* to be in continual prayer? Why also would there exist a need to be indwelled by or get support from another member of that same Godhead?

> "Here is <u>my servant</u> whom I have chosen, the one I love, in whom I delight; <u>I will put my Spirit on him</u>, and he will proclaim justice to the nations."
>
> —Matthew 12:18 (emphasis added)

But even if we do not grasp the importance of all of these not-so-subtle hints, it is hard to mistake Paul's intent in the letter to the Philippians. Paul speaks boldly of the nature of the infinitely perfect meekness of Jesus. Jesus, he tells us, *fully* emptied Himself of the power that made Him equal to God:

> Your attitude should be the same as that of Christ Jesus: Who, being in very nature God, <u>did not consider equality with God something to be grasped</u>, but made himself <u>nothing</u>, taking the very nature of a

servant, being made in human likeness.   And being found in appearance as a man, he humbled himself and became obedient to death — even death on a cross!

Therefore God exalted him to the highest place and gave him the name that is above every name, that at the name of Jesus every knee should bow, in heaven and on earth and under the earth, and every tongue confess that Jesus Christ is Lord, to the glory of God the Father.

—Philippians 2:5-11 (emphasis added)

Paul's words are not subtle in their meaning. He could not state it any clearer. Further still, the apostle Peter also expands our understanding of the nature of the relationship of the fully emptied Jesus to the other two Persons of the Triune God in his speech to the centurion Cornelius in Acts 10. Peter also is not subtle in his declaration. Jesus is characterized as being in need of anointing by the Holy Spirit. We are told that Jesus healed those who were *"under the power of the devil"* only *"because God was with him."*

You know what has happened throughout Judea, beginning in Galilee after the baptism that John preached — how God anointed Jesus of Nazareth with the Holy Spirit and power, and how he went around doing good and healing all who were under the power of the devil, because God was with him.

—Acts 10:37-38 (emphasis added)

So once again we come back to this nagging question in regard to Jesus. Why would He need to be indwelled by the Holy Spirit? Why would an equal member of the Trinity—fully God Himself—*need* to be indwelled by another member of the very same Godhead? The answer is becomes clearer and clearer as all of the evidence is examined. Despite the hesitancy of our hearts in this regard, we must acknowledge the depth of the emptying of our Redeemer. Just because it does not fit with our comfortable theology doesn't negate the truth found here. Just because we are—by our own weakness—uncomfortable with this truth doesn't really matter. We are not empowered to rewrite the Word of God—and the Word of God tells us of the fact of the full emptying of the Son of God.

Jesus was emptied of His Godly power so that He could face precisely the same trials that we do. The difference between His life and ours is that He lived His with the perfect indwelling of the Holy Spirit. From the moment of His baptism (or possibly before) until this very moment, the 100% man Jesus has been and is fully indwelled with the Spirit of God. In this, Jesus has perfectly modeled the life that we are supposed to lead. He never spent even a single millisecond of time outside of the presence of the Holy Spirit. This is the way it was supposed to be done. This is the way that Adam was supposed to do it and this is the way that we were supposed to do it. This fact is exactly what David tells us in the first three verses of Psalm 26:

> *Vindicate me, O LORD, for I have led <u>a blameless life</u>; I have <u>trusted</u> in the LORD <u>without wavering</u>. Test me, O LORD, and try me, examine my heart and my mind; for your love is ever before me, and I walk <u>continually</u> in your truth.*
>
> —Psalm 26:1-3 (emphasis added)

There is absolutely no chance that David is speaking of himself in this sacred psalm. He had not *"led a blameless life."* David is referring to the Messiah. He is anticipating the life of Jesus Christ. He is speaking the words of Jesus. Nowhere else in Holy Scripture is the importance of the life Jesus led so clearly delineated. David is telling us that Jesus did it like we are supposed to do it. His life was blameless because He trusted the Father *"without wavering"* and walked *"continually"* in God's truth. David is describing a life led entirely and all inclusively by the Holy Spirit. This passage describes perfection in Jesus' faithful walk with the Father—He never wavered and walked continually, as a man, in the guidance of the Holy Spirit. There was never a single moment spent outside of the Spirit—not a single moment.

And this, most importantly, explains why Jesus could do all of the incredible things that He did while He was on earth despite being fully emptied of His Godly power. His perfect life, all of the healing, all of the prophecy, all of the acts that set Him apart from any other man—were all *of* the Holy Spirit. Look carefully at the Word of God. Look carefully at the gospel accounts. Almost every gospel account of a miracle—and the whole of Jesus' life itself—are all about going to the Father first. And in the Father—in the act of turning to the Father—is the fullness of the gift of the Holy Spirit given to the fully emptied Jesus.

This same gift of the Holy Spirit is offered to us. The Holy Spirit is available to us by way of Jesus, by way of the Father, if we will only accept the offer. I don't need to tell you the problem in this, however. We don't accept it. We want to do things by ourselves. We want to do things *our* way. We want to figure out *our* solution to the problem. We want to fix things by *our* strength. We are swayed by the deceptiveness of the world into believing that we are capable of fixing everything by our own strength. We are convinced not only that we *can* do it our way, but also that our way is the best way. We *want* to do it our way.

And that is the very definition of sin—*doing it our way*.

And precisely in sin—in this sin of not turning to God in every circumstance—is the squelching of the power of the Spirit in our lives. It is a vicious cycle that feeds on itself. We sin which leads to blindness, which leads to more sin, which leads to more blindness. We swirl hopelessly into a blind spiral of sin, as spiritual blindness is the consequence of shutting the Spirit out of our lives.

The exact opposite of this is the hallmark of the life of Jesus. There simply was no sin. He never did it *His* way. Through the Holy Spirit, he did it the Father's way in every single millisecond of His life. The absence of sin equates with the absence of the squelching of the Holy Spirit, which means no blindness. Jesus always knew the will of the Father because He was always under the full influence of the Holy Spirit. Instead of being blind, He saw things through the eyes of the Father. As a feedback cycle spins, it picks up momentum. But this time holy reinforcement feeds on itself in the only righteous life, as the Holy Spirit is found in the middle of every thought, word, and deed.

> *How much more, then, will the blood of Christ, who through the eternal Spirit offered himself unblemished to God, cleanse our consciences from acts that lead to death, so that we may serve the living God!*
>
> —Hebrews 9:14 (emphasis added)

This pattern established by Jesus is precisely what our sanctification is supposed to be about. We seek to live like Jesus. We seek to do things the way that Jesus would do them. With Jesus in our hearts, we seek to spend every moment in the presence of God through His Holy Spirit. Jesus is our role model precisely because in this *He was perfect*. The Holy Spirit of God is the force behind the perfect life.

Precisely in being indwelled perfectly, continuously, eternally is found our future as sons and daughters of God. Through His modeling of this perfect life, Jesus has shown us what our eternity will be like. He modeled it perfectly. He didn't just model our present, but also our future. The Word of God tells us exactly this.

"As for me, this is my covenant with them," says the LORD. "My Spirit, who is on you, and my words that I have put in your mouth will not depart from your mouth, or from the mouths of your children, or from the mouths of their descendants from this time on and forever," says the LORD.

—Isaiah 59:21

In exactly this is found blessed assurance of our eternity in heaven. It will be spectacular. No matter where we go, no matter what we are doing, we will *always* be in the presence of God through the Holy Spirit. In this, we will live in eternity in heaven like Jesus lived on earth. In this we will be like Jesus. No matter what we face, the Holy Spirit will always be there to guide us in the way of the Lord.

Whether you turn to the right or to the left, your ears will hear a voice behind you, saying, "This is the way; walk in it."

—Isaiah 30:21

When all of these scriptural passages are pieced together, their overarching meaning becomes readily apparent. The Holy Spirit is trying to convey a fact that has critical importance in understanding the nature of the incarnation of our Redeemer. Jesus, the Son of God, *fully* emptied Himself when He took on the flesh of mankind. There are too many scriptural passages that speak of Jesus being limited beyond what we would expect of the Son of God. We can't ignore the clear intent of these passages. They tell us that in regard to His *power*, Jesus became like us—*totally like us*.

Indeed, there was only one pathway by which Jesus could become the reconnection to God that was lost in Adam's sin. He *had* to become like us. The infinite Son of God had to become infinitely emptied in the surrendering of His divine power. Becoming like us—to whatever degree that transformation occurred by the decree of the fullness of the wisdom of God—was critical to making the sacrifice of Jesus worthy to fulfill the terms of the redemptive contract.

Then I saw a Lamb, looking as if it had been slain, standing in the center of the throne, encircled by the four living creatures and the elders. He had seven horns and seven eyes, which are the seven spirits of God sent out into all the earth. He came and took the scroll from the right hand of him who sat on the throne. And when he had taken it, the four living creatures and the twenty-four elders fell down before the Lamb. Each one had a harp and they were holding golden bowls full of incense, which are the prayers of the saints.

And they sang a new song: "You are worthy to take the scroll and to open its seals, because you were slain, and with your blood you purchased men for God from every tribe and language and people and nation. You have made them to be a kingdom and priests to serve our God, and they will reign on the earth."

—Revelation 5:6-10 (emphasis added)

The critical issue, then, focuses on the nature of the *power* inherent in God that Jesus had to empty Himself of in order for His trial on earth to "count" on our behalf. In other words how completely emptied into the shell of ordinary man did Jesus have to be for His conquest over sin to count on our behalf, to pay our debt to a perfectly just God, to *"purchase"* us for God? After all, *our behalf* is really what His mission on earth was all about. To teach us about the Father and in so doing to live a perfect life and therefore become the only perfect sacrificial lamb was *the* gospel mission of Jesus Christ.

In this mission, Jesus could not be assisted. He could not be totally assisted and He could not be partially assisted. *He had to be just like you and me.* He had to become the fullness of the weakness of mankind. He had to empty Himself to the point that he was truly...*a man.* Anything less than the total emptying of the Son of God would mean that He was in fact not like us when He faced the crucifixion. In other words, one could say, "Of course He went through all that suffering, but He didn't really feel it and there was no chance of failure because He was, after all, *God.*"

But that of which the gospel accounts so readily assure us is clear in this regard. The commitment of the Son of God was wholehearted. There can be no question in our minds. Jesus felt every blow of the hammer on the nails that pierced His hands. He felt every point of every thorn of His bloody crown. Anything less would be so much less than that which we know of the perfection of the Son of God.

Yet before we limit the crucifixion to being only about the death of a man, we must also acknowledge the fullness of the divinity of Jesus. The fact that Jesus is 100% man, yet simultaneously nothing less than 100% God, made His crucifixion even so much worse—infinitely worse. The nature of the *"second death"* (Revelation 20:6), which is what Jesus endured for us, is the complete and utter alienation from

God the Father. The second death with its separation from the Father is the only possible divine response to rebellious sin, for God cannot tolerate sin in His presence. He cannot even look upon it.

> *Your eyes are too pure to look on evil; you cannot tolerate wrong. Why then do you tolerate the treacherous? Why are you silent while the wicked swallow up those more righteous than themselves?*
>
> —Habakkuk 1:13

The separation from God the Father, which is true death for us, was immeasurable, infinite death for the Son of God. In becoming our sin, Jesus became that which is most abhorrent to the Father, the One that He has loved for all eternity. He became the embodiment of evil. The Father's *"eyes are too pure to look on evil."* The Father *had* to look away from His son for the first and only time in all eternity. We have no concept of what this really means. We do not have the capacity, as created beings, to even remotely comprehend. We cannot even approach it in our imaginations.

There can be no confusion here. In the moment that the Father looked away, Jesus endured the *infinite* wrath of the Father, the only fitting response to the equally infinite darkness of the sin that Jesus had become for us. He took upon Himself *all* of the sin of the world. In this combination of the 100% man and 100% God nature of the death of Jesus Christ is embodied the incomprehensible. And yet from the depth of that incomprehensible price is found the equally incomprehensible redemption of all who would become sons and daughters of God. From that unfathomable price alone springs the joy of the hope of eternal *life*.

In this death, Jesus had to be emptied 100% of His Godly power. In anything less than 100% is found imperfection. Anything less is unworthy of the Son of God. In the infinite completeness of His emptying is found the infinite power of His perfect strength as the only Son of God.

> *But he said to me, "My grace is sufficient for you, for my power is made perfect in weakness."*
>
> —2Corinthians 12:9

So what power did Jesus give up in His incarnation? It can only be described in infinite terms—for the gap between the uncreated and the created is infinite. In this act of infinite selflessness lies the heart of God. Infinite emptying of divine power is an act that only God could perform and an act of which God could do no less. In the voluntary surrender of infinite power is the demonstration of infinite love, infinite faith. It is the singular act that tells us—more than any other act—that Jesus is the Son of God. Only the Son of God could accomplish this.

Jesus cannot become something that He was not, for in doing so, He must either improve or worsen—neither of which is He capable. Jesus, the eternal partner of the Father and the Spirit *did not change* to become man. This did not happen because it cannot happen. This we know by the knowable attributes of the *immutable*, infinite, omnipotent, omnipresent, eternal Godhead as taught in the written Word of God. Instead, that which Jesus did had to be *inherent to His nature*. What Jesus did was the only thing He *could* do. What Jesus did was mandated by Who He was—the Son *of God*.

In response to the attributes inherent to His very nature—which mandated perfect submission to the Father's will—Jesus voluntarily took on the weakness embodied by the incarnation. The meekness, the humble servitude toward the Father, the humble nature that would allow Him to become man, the willingness to place the Father's will above His in the deepest of all acts of humility—these were all attributes that the eternal Son of the living God *has always had*, for eternity past. These are all attributes that characterize the eternal love for the Father that has always existed in the heart of the Jesus, the Son of God.

> *The reason my Father loves me is that I lay down my life—only to take it up again.*
>
> —John 10:17

It is these attributes of meekness and submission that guide our discussion now. The Bible assures us in its description of Jesus that the Son of God doesn't do anything halfheartedly. Once again, he can't—He is by very nature God. He is perfect. Everything He does is perfect. He is by His very nature infinite. Everything about Him is infinite, including His perfection. This tells us many things. Perhaps the most important of these is that Jesus took on the skin of man *perfectly*. It tells us that Jesus took on the skin of man in the only manner that would make it infinitely perfect—*forever*.

Forever.

In our hearts we rebel at this thought. And yet, by its very definition, this eternal submission to the will of the Father would require the *eternal* dependence of Jesus upon the Father. Our first response is to cry out, "How can that be?" for the thought of eternally submitting to the will of another—with *no chance* of ever changing back—is contrary to our very nature. We can't imagine trusting anyone *that* much because in the depths of the darkness of our sinful nature we cannot imagine *ourselves* being trusted that much. We have never encountered anyone who can be trusted that much—because we have not known the Father for eternity like Jesus has. We are, if left to our sinful human nature, incapable of trusting someone *that* much, that *forever*.

But praise God that this infinitely perfect submission to the will of the Father is not contrary to the nature of Jesus. Praise God that what we know of His attributes consoles us that He can, in fact, *be no other way*. For the bottom line is trust and its active partner, faith. It always has been. It is what our salvation is all about—it is the hinge point of our eternity. And it is also precisely what Jesus is all about. For trust and faith in the Father—the very same trust and faith that we are asked to have—was active in every moment of the life of Jesus on Earth. Jesus has known the Father for eternity. And in that eternity He has known the Father to be infinitely perfectly faithful. In that eternity He knows—as only a fellow member of the Trinity can—the depth of the perfect faithfulness of the Father that is inherent to His very nature. *Only* in infinite perfect faithfulness can one place infinite perfect faith—and that is exactly what Jesus was asked to do. In His incarnation and crucifixion—the great rescue of those men and women who would become sons and daughters of the Living God—Jesus demonstrated perfect faith by agreeing to accept His humanhood *for eternity*.

Deep in the back-most reaches of our hearts, most of us hide a dark fear. In the depths of the limitations of our untrusting human nature, we fear that this *manhood* thing is just a part-time, short-lived chore for Jesus. Deeply embroiled in our very human nature, we can't imagine that the manhood of the Only Son of God *is* eternal. Surely, we plead, Jesus only *temporarily* became a man to enter His creation and rescue the sons and daughters of His eternity. Surely this could only be a temporary state. From these beliefs it is only a short step to the fear in the back of the distrusting heart of man that Jesus will ultimately get tired of us and just call off that unknowably wonderful thing that we so casually refer to as *our eternity*.

We fear that Jesus will get tired of being *a man* and will wander off to do something else, leaving us in the eternal lurch. But, what we know of the attributes of God—that which He has revealed in His Holy Word and by the revelation of the Living Word, Jesus—assures us that this cannot be true. The Bible repeatedly assures us—over 40 times to be exact—that God's love (and faithfulness) endures forever.

> *Give thanks to the God of heaven. His love endures forever.*
> —Psalm 136:26

> *For great is his love toward us, and the faithfulness of the LORD endures forever. Praise the LORD.*
> —Psalm 117:2

We must remember that this earth, this universe, this creation, this eternity is indeed the whole show for the three Persons of the Triune God. They exist outside of the constraints of time so there can be no *next* creation for them. There can be no *next* incarnation for Jesus. *Next* would imply the sequential ordering of events in time and God exists outside of any such constraints. Since God cannot change, He cannot be *God before He created the earth* and then in the next moment *God after He created the earth*. That would imply change, that would imply time—and God does not change or exist in time.

> *"I the LORD do not change."*
> —Malachi 3:6a

The fact that God cannot change means that *we* have *always* been a part of God's plan throughout the unknowable depths of eternity. This means that the rescue of man through the mechanism of the incarnation of Jesus has *always* been within the knowledge, within the Being of the eternal Triune God.

And praise God that the very definition of the Father as being infinitely, perfectly faithful is that one can place *eternal* faith in Him—more specifically, that one can have faith in Him *for eternity*. *That* is exactly what Jesus has done. *He has become man for all eternity*. He emptied Himself *for all eternity* in the act of His incarnation. And in so doing, He placed His faith *infinitely* and *perfectly* in the Father, in the One Who is infinitely and perfectly faithful.

> *But I am like an olive tree flourishing in the house of God; I <u>trust</u> in God's unfailing love <u>for ever and ever</u>. I will praise you <u>forever</u> for what you have done; in your name I will hope, for your name is good. I will praise you in the presence of your saints.*
> —Psalm 52:9 (emphasis added)

In the act of trusting in the Father forever, Jesus demonstrated perfect faith. In this statement is our salvation. In this statement is the embodiment of the will of the Father for His precious Son—that He become perfect man by being perfectly faithful. It is this perfection of faith that made Jesus the perfect substitute for us. It empowered Him as the perfect Lamb of God. After all, it was the act of becoming unfaithful—of not trusting the heart of God—that was the embodiment of the fall of man, of the sin of Adam.

This is why the salvation of every single man is dependent upon only one thing: *faith*. It is dependent upon the literal hinge point of all mankind, of all creation— *faith*. Did you ever wonder why our salvation is dependent upon only one thing, a heart deep commitment of faith? It wasn't just because the Father was sitting around one day and asked the Son and the Holy Spirit, "What should I make their eternal salvation dependent upon? Hmm. How about faith? Maybe I will make it faith."

Quite to the contrary, there really was no choice. *Faith* is what *any* relationship with God is all about. Faith is what Jesus Christ is all about. Faith was what the greatest act of all eternity—the crucifixion of the Son of God—was all about.

Of equal importance, faith is also what *sin* is all about. Turning from God occurs only from failure in faith. It occurs only in the failure to believe and have faith that God is exactly Who He says He is—perfectly good, perfectly faithful, perfectly powerful and perfectly loving toward mankind. Sin, by its very definition, is *not* having faith in the heart of God. There is no need to turn anywhere else if one has faith in the perfect faithfulness of the eternal Godhead. Faith is the determinant of our eternity because faith is what the entirety of the creation is all about.

A lack of faith is what Lucifer had. A lack of faith is what Adam had. A lack of faith is what each of us has demonstrated. Perfect faith was—in the context of man—eternally lost with the sin of Adam, and quite logically it follows *that perfect faith was the only solution to this self-imposed deficit*. Perfect faith is what only Jesus could and did demonstrate. Perfect faith is founded in perfect knowledge of the One in whom you have faith—and only Jesus knows the Father perfectly. It was the perfect faith of Jesus in the perfect faithfulness of the Father that the focal point of all creation was all about. That focal point was the incarnation, sacrificial death, and resurrection of Jesus Christ, the Son of God.

Jesus and the Father, of course, knew this before the creation. Jesus knew at His incarnation, life, and death that these were the *irretrievable* steps of perfect faith that were needed to rescue the sons and daughters of the living God. Any less of a commitment would be unworthy of—and impossible for—the One and Only Son of God.

Chapter 7

The Infinite Perfection of Meekness
Precisely How Much Did Jesus Empty Himself When He Became Man?

When we, in our imperfection, think about the incarnation, about Jesus emptying Himself to become man, we always do it with reserve. We try to assign our human weakness—our naturally halfhearted attitude—to Jesus, the perfect Son of God. In other words, we always try to hold onto some of His power for Him. We just can't imagine Him really emptying Himself to the depth that would be required to actually become man—let alone a sword wielding Old Testament warrior.

And that is where we usually stop. We stop because we can't make it work. We cannot fit the infinitely perfect Son of God into our infinitely flawed perspective. It cannot work because we cannot figure out exactly how much power Jesus had to hold onto to actually carry this off. As we have already discussed, we cannot come up with the perfect balance that has Jesus giving up enough to make it "count"—to make Him mankind's perfect sacrificial lamb—while still holding onto some of His Godly power for Him.

To remedy this conundrum, we try to negotiate the impossible. We do what humans seem to naturally do best—we compromise. We try to extend our imperfection to God to make this dilemma somehow manageable. We try to bring Him down to our level. We try to make the infinite, finite; the perfect, imperfect; and the holy, common. We try to limit the illimitable. We assign halfhearted motivation to a Person who has never been anything but wholehearted in His devotion to the Father. We try to compromise the perfection of God, even though in the depths of our hearts we know that this is not right. We, in our very human minds (with our uniquely human tunnel vision) try to figure out which of His divine powers—and to what degree—Jesus held onto when He became man.

Our inability to see Jesus as fully, totally, perfectly, infinitely emptied in His incarnation is therefore *our* problem. Even though *we* need to have Him hold on to at least some of His power—because we in our weakness and in our lack of faith in the Father can't imagine doing it any other way ourselves—Jesus didn't see it that way. We only have to think about it for a short time, in fact, before it becomes glaringly obvious that it could be no other way.

It could be no other way precisely because Jesus is, first and foremost, the Son of God. The Father could ask for nothing less than "perfect" faith and Jesus could supply nothing less. Perfect faith—infinitely perfect faith—required infinitely perfect, eternal reliance upon the Father. It required infinitely perfect reliance, and that can only be demonstrated by infinitely perfect emptying.

Infinitely perfect emptying. That is exactly what we are describing. The distance between the uncreated God and created man, after all, is the very definition of "infinite." The Father didn't ask His Son for a halfway commitment in the incarnation. He asked for a full, total, forever commitment. There is nothing halfway about the Father. And praise God that there is nothing halfway about His Son. Jesus is, of course, every bit of the perfection of the living God. There simply can't be anything halfway about Him. It is all the way or it is nothing.

Can it be any other way? We must search our hearts—for far below the clutter of this world, in the holiest chambers our hearts, we know this is true. There, the Word of God is carved in the stone of our hearts:

> *The Son is the radiance of God's glory and the exact representation of his being, sustaining all things by his powerful word. After he had provided purification for sins, he sat down at the right hand of the Majesty in heaven.*
>
> —Hebrews 1:3 (emphasis added)

In the incarnation, Jesus emptied Himself totally, completely, infinitely, and permanently. In doing so, He demonstrated the perfect faith that the Father would do exactly what Jesus asked Him to do when He prayed:

> *And now, Father, glorify me in your presence with the glory I had with you before the world began.*
>
> —John 17:5

Jesus emptied Himself infinitely and perfectly of His might and power and became *entirely* reliant upon the Father—more specifically, the other two Persons of the Triune Godhead—for eternity. This seems staggering to us. Nonetheless, if we but knew—for even a moment—of the infinite depth of the faithfulness that is inherent to the eternal nature of the Father, it wouldn't. In Psalm 61, King David spoke of the eternal enthroning of Jesus by the Father whose *"love and faithfulness...protect him"* forever.

> *Increase the days of the king's life, his years for many generations. May he be enthroned in God's presence <u>forever</u>; appoint your <u>love and faithfulness to protect him</u>.*
>
> —Psalm 61:6-7 (emphasis added)

As we have discussed, this perfect emptying, this perfect *eternal* commitment of Jesus to the Father is repeatedly demonstrated by His life on earth. When we reread the gospel accounts and other books of the New Testament with this new perspective, we cannot help but notice how many times Jesus repeatedly and very literally tells us precisely this. Incontestable statements concerning His total reliance upon the Father and the Spirit are scattered liberally throughout all of the gospel accounts of His life.

> *<u>By myself I can do nothing</u>; I judge only as I hear, and my judgment is just, for I seek not to please myself but him who sent me.*
>
> —John 5:30 (emphasis added)

This is why the New Testament descriptions of the majority of Jesus' miracles include a reference to His first *asking* the Father. This is also why prayer—talking to God—was so very important to Jesus.

> *But Jesus often withdrew to lonely places and prayed.*
>
> —Luke 5:16

Holy scripture also repeatedly reveals that Jesus was actively *empowered* to perform supernatural acts. These episodes suggest that He did not retain these powers in Himself at all times—as God does—but rather relied upon His external source, the Father through the Spirit.

> *One day as he was teaching, Pharisees and teachers of the law, who had come from every village of Galilee and from Judea and Jerusalem, were sitting there. And <u>the power of the Lord was present for him to heal the sick</u>.*
>
> —Luke 5:17 (emphasis added)

It remains the most difficult of tasks to truly accept the fact that the perfect meekness, the perfect emptiness of Jesus—the Son of God—required that He rely totally upon the power of the Holy Spirit for the performance of all of the supernatural acts that He performed. And yet any questions that we may have in this regard are finally and completely put to rest by a most unusual and emphatic statement made by Jesus Himself. The response of the Pharisees to the miraculous healing that resulted from the casting out of demons by Jesus was to attribute these supernatural powers to Beelzebub.

> *Then they brought him a demon-possessed man who was blind and mute, and Jesus healed him, so that he could both talk and see. All the people were astonished and said, "Could this be the Son of David?"*
>
> *But when the Pharisees heard this, they said, "It is only by Beelzebub, the prince of demons, that this fellow drives out demons."*

—Matthew 12:22-24 (emphasis added)

In his response to the Pharisees, Jesus makes a statement that seems somewhat unrelated, but actually directly answers the question regarding the source of His power for such miraculous acts. Jesus attributes the power totally to the Holy Spirit by telling the Pharisees that their attribution of this power to Beelzebub is nothing less than blaspheming the Holy Spirit. Not only this, but Jesus also emphasizes the importance of knowing and acknowledging the true source of this power by stating that to blaspheme the Holy Spirit in such a manner is an unforgivable sin!

> *Jesus knew their thoughts and said to them, "Every kingdom divided against itself will be ruined, and every city or household divided against itself will not stand. If Satan drives out Satan, he is divided against himself. How then can his kingdom stand? And if I drive out demons by Beelzebub, by whom do your people drive them out? So then, they will be your judges. But if I drive out demons by the Spirit of God, then the kingdom of God has come upon you.*
>
> *"Or again, how can anyone enter a strong man's house and carry off his possessions unless he first ties up the strong man? Then he can rob his house.*
>
> *"He who is not with me is against me, and he who does not gather with me scatters. And so I tell you, every sin and blasphemy will be forgiven men, but the blasphemy against the Spirit will not be*

forgiven. Anyone who speaks a word against the Son of Man will be forgiven, but anyone who speaks against the Holy Spirit will not be forgiven, either in this age or in the age to come.

—Matthew 12:25-32 (emphasis added)

Clearly the Holy Spirit is repeatedly credited with the work of empowering the fully emptied Son of God. Why would the Son of God need to rely on the indwelling of the Holy Spirit? Why would the Son of God need to be baptized or have the Holy Spirit *empower* Him?

Then Jesus came from Galilee to the Jordan to be baptized by John. But John tried to deter him, saying, "I need to be baptized by you, and do you come to me?" Jesus replied, "Let it be so now; it is proper for us to do this to fulfill all righteousness." Then John consented. As soon as Jesus was baptized, he went up out of the water. At that moment heaven was opened, and he saw the Spirit of God descending like a dove and lighting on him.

And a voice from heaven said, "This is my Son, whom I love; with him I am well pleased." Then Jesus was led by the Spirit into the desert to be tempted by the devil.

—Matthew 3:13-4:1

In fact, all four gospel accounts include a recounting of the Holy Spirit descending on Jesus. It is hard to explain why one member of the Triune Godhead would need to be filled and empowered by another member of the same Godhead unless the fullness of the emptying of Jesus is appreciated to its *infinite* degree.

For the one whom God has sent speaks the words of God, for God gives the Spirit without limit.

—John 3:34 (emphasis added)

Indeed, we are told in the 4th chapter of Luke's account that Jesus returned from His baptism *"full of the Holy Spirit"* (Luke 4:1) and from the desert temptation *"in the power of the Spirit"* (Luke 4:14).

That same chapter in the gospel of Luke gives us another interesting bit of support to the phenomenal degree of emptying to which the Son of God subjected Himself. For in the three different recorded temptations of Jesus, twice the preamble to the temptation includes the words, *"If you are the Son of God."* Satan is truly asking for proof. For some reason—possibly because of the degree of emptying that Jesus has subjected Himself to—Satan can't believe it. Once again, the prudent reader of the Word has to ask why Satan, who was created by Jesus and has presumably known this Person of the Triune Godhead since the beginning, has to ask if this man he is tempting is really the Son of God. Truly Jesus is emptied. Truly He is limited to the powers of 100% mortal man and relying on the power of the Spirit for all that is supernatural—just like us!

Indeed, we are even told that, *"the grace of God was upon him"* (Luke 2:40) when most of us would quite reasonably ask why the Son of God would even *need* the *"grace of God."*

These examples occur too frequently in the Bible for their implications to be ignored. The Holy Spirit, the Author of the Bible, wanted us to know the heights of the true magnificence of the Son of God who gave up everything in and of Himself, in infinitely perfect submission to the will of the Father—all to gain sons and daughters of God for eternity. This is the very heart of the magnificent story that is described in the Bible and that is written on each of our hearts.

In summary, Jesus emptied Himself perfectly, voluntarily, and profoundly as the prerequisite to demonstrating perfect faith. He also emptied Himself *permanently*. He had to—permanently is the only *emptying* that is infinitely perfect. *Permanently* is the only perfect demonstration of faith. Jesus had to give up all of His power permanently with the perfect faith that the Father would restore it to Him upon the completion of the salvation of all who would be saved. Jesus had to become dependent upon the Father—fully, totally, permanently dependent—just like we are asked to in that defining moment in which we surrender the sovereignty of the throne of our hearts to Jesus. That is what infinitely perfect faith is all about. Jesus gave up His power permanently precisely because—for Him and for us—there is no other way. He could do this because He knew that He could rely on the perfectly faithful Father for the restoration and maintenance of His attributes—His glory—even for all eternity! He, in fact, told us exactly this while He was on earth. It is recorded in the gospels of John and Matthew:

> *Jesus replied, "If I glorify myself, my glory means nothing. My Father, whom you claim as your God, is the one who glorifies me."*
> —John 8:54 (emphasis added)

For the Son of Man is going to come <u>in his Father's glory</u> with his angels, and then he will reward each person according to what he has done.

—Matthew 16:27 (emphasis added)

Jesus will not come back in His own glory as God. He has chosen to give that up completely for eternity and to rely 100% on the Father. The case has also been presented that the New Testament writers are not subtle in revealing the dependence of Jesus upon the Holy Spirit for the performance of His miracles during His three years of ministry. Any remaining hesitation in accepting this premise and its eternal implications should be removed by the recognition that Jesus is *still* filled with the power of the Holy Spirit as He—the Lamb of God— ushers in the end times *"day of the Lord."*

Then <u>I saw a Lamb</u>, looking as if it had been slain, standing in the center of the throne, encircled by the four living creatures and the elders. He had seven horns and <u>seven eyes, which are the seven spirits of God</u> sent out into all the earth.

—Revelation 5:6 (emphasis added)

This dependence upon the glory of God and the indwelling of the Holy Spirit is precisely what *we* also are asked to voluntarily accept—just like Jesus—for all eternity. For in a similar fashion, we also will not come back in our own glory. We will—praise God!—be resurrected in the glory of Jesus. And, just like Jesus voluntarily became dependent upon the Holy Spirit to perform all of His miracles during His three years of earthly ministry, so also are our efforts to place our thoughts, words, and deeds squarely in the will of the Father also dependent upon the work of the Holy Spirit—now and for eternity. Indeed, when the One that we rely upon is perfectly infinitely faithful and is known to be utterly incapable of anything less, we can put our faith in Him—*forever.* We can become completely dependent upon Him for eternity. That is perfect emptying. That is the perfect sacrifice. That is perfect meekness. Jesus embodies this meekness. It is the hallmark and cornerstone of His divinity. In this, He is our perfect model. As we will review, the demonstration of His power as God is made perfect in precisely this, His sacred weakness.

Chapter 8

The Answer to the Question
Who Is the Messenger of Daniel 10?

The recognition of the fullness of the emptying of Jesus upon His entering the creation leaves us well prepared to readdress the question we posed at the beginning of this book. Could Jesus have been the man described in Daniel 10 who was detained in a fight with the prince of Persia until Michael the prince came to help Him? The answer has to be a resounding *yes*. That which seemed at first to be preposterous doesn't seem so outrageous now. As we have reviewed, a wealth of both New and Old Testament scriptures teach that Jesus fully emptied Himself to become man in His birth in Bethlehem. Do we somehow lessen our Redeemer when we see Him as similarly emptied in the thick of battle in the Old Testament also?

Quite to the contrary, Biblical truth suggests otherwise. Indeed, as this discussion has pointed out, to place Jesus anywhere else and in any status other than the fully-emptied state that He voluntarily submitted to, is to assign a *lesser* position to Jesus, fully God. For us to claim anything less than infinitely perfect submission to the will of the Father by infinitely perfect emptying to become man for eternity is nothing less than denying Jesus His place as an equal Person of the Triune Godhead. For us to claim anything less may be the ultimate in heresy, the ultimate in insults to the only Son of God.

Yet still our resistance to the full, voluntary, infinitely perfect emptiness of Jesus continues. Our weak human natures cling to *our* inability to surrender all and desperately stretch to believe that Jesus likewise held on to at least some of the power that is inherent to God. We anxiously search for middle ground. And yet to our dismay, the logical progression of the evidence in this time of our great discontent rapidly brings us to the conclusion that there can be no middle ground in this discussion.

The commitment requested by the Father is clear in its infinite perfection. Jesus could not hold on to *anything*. In grasping even a single tiny bit of *His* power, He would have been something less than the beloved Son of the Most High God. The Father requested all and Jesus surrendered all. Just like with you and me, the commitment to the will of the Father had to be total and complete. It had to be perfect and uncompromised. It had to be what God repeatedly asked of the Israelites in the Old Testament scriptures: it had to be wholehearted, single-minded, and unconditional. Jesus had to give it *all* up. In this perfect crucifixion that occurred *"before"* the creation of the world, Jesus' perfect sacrifice became manifest in the only manner that it could—in the infinite perfection of the Living God.

> *He was chosen before the creation of the world, but was revealed in these last times for your sake.*
>
> —1Peter 1:20

> *In the beginning was the Word, and the Word was with God, and the Word was God.*
>
> —John 1:1

In this recognition of the perfection of the submission found only in the perfect emptying of the Son of God in His incarnation, we exalt Jesus as precisely who He is. Most certainly we are not saying for a single moment that Jesus is not God or that the *fullness* of God did not exist in its entirety in Jesus. Quite to the contrary—most surely He is, most surely it did, and most surely that is exactly what is revealed and promoted in the recognition of infinite emptying. It is precisely in the fullness of the voluntary infinitely perfect, eternal emptying of the Son of God that the fullness of God is manifest. In the perfection of the sacrifice that was required to win our freedom is found the divine perfection of the Son of God. Only God could be the author of the perfect obedience, the perfect submission, the perfect love that is found in perfect emptying.

> *Your attitude should be the same as that of Christ Jesus: Who, being in very nature God, did not consider equality with God something to be grasped, but made himself nothing, taking the very nature of a servant, being made in human likeness. And being found in appearance as a man, he humbled himself and became obedient to death—even death on a cross! Therefore God exalted him to the highest place and gave him the name that is above every name, that at the name of Jesus every knee should bow, in heaven and on earth and under the earth, and every tongue confess that Jesus Christ is Lord, to the glory of God the Father.*
>
> —Philippians 2:5-11 (emphasis added)

The key to His sinless life was Jesus' perfect access to the Holy Spirit. Without sin, without the sinful nature of man, He was purely, totally, and unconditionally indwelled by the Holy Spirit. He always knew precisely what He needed to know. He always knew exactly what the Father's will was in every situation. He was always given the power that He needed to perform the Father's will in every set of circumstances.

But, of the utmost of importance, Jesus could be the perfect representation of meekness only in the perfection of His emptiness. Meekness is power willingly surrendered, majesty perfectly humbled. Jesus was perfectly, infinitely powerful before the creation. To be *perfectly* meek (would God settle for anything less?), He had to be willing to perfectly empty Himself of all of His Godly power. In direct contrast to the way we view things in this world, the more power Jesus gave up, the more perfectly humbled, perfectly meek, and perfectly the Son of God was He manifest. This is where the word *infinite* is utterly priceless. Jesus was uniquely capable—as the Son of God—to give up infinite power and therefore was infinitely glorified by the infinite nature of His meekness.

Indeed, we are most pointedly told precisely this by the Apostle Paul in his 2nd letter to the church at Corinth. Paul makes it clear that the agreement to give up everything—which is exactly what happened when *God* became man—was the very hallmark, the hinge point, of Christ's perfection. For in *"perfect"* weakness is Christ's power made perfect.

> *Three times I pleaded with the Lord to take it away from me. But he said to me, "My grace is sufficient for you, for <u>my power is made perfect in weakness</u>." Therefore I will boast all the more gladly about my weaknesses, so that Christ's power may rest on me. That is why, for Christ's sake, I delight in weaknesses, in insults, in hardships, in persecutions, in difficulties. For when I am weak, then I am strong.*
> —2Corinthians 12:8-10 (emphasis added)

How deep is the revelation of this verse. The perfection of Christ's power in our life is found only in the depths of our weakness. How perfectly this directly mirrors the eternal perfection of Christ's power by the weakness in which He voluntarily robed Himself for our salvation.

> *Not so with you. Instead, whoever wants to become great among you must be your <u>servant</u>, and whoever wants to be <u>first</u> must be <u>slave of</u>*

all. For even the Son of Man did not come to be served, but to serve,
and to give his life as a ransom for many."

—Mark 10:43-45 (emphasis added)

Could the infinitely loving and compassionate Son of God do anything less than attaining *perfection* in weakness, *perfection* in meekness? The answer is clear in the logic that is revealed in the facts. For we readily see that, in fact, if Jesus had held onto a single shred of His power, He would not have attained perfection. He would not be God. Only God could do this perfectly and empty Himself totally. It is, in other words, an undeniable and inherent attribute of God that is acknowledged in the fact that Jesus had to empty Himself *perfectly*. For us to claim anything less is not only to *not* exalt Jesus, but also in not exalting Him to thereby demean Him.

The Holy Spirit wanted us to know these facts about the true nature of our Savior. He wanted us to know precisely what Jesus was doing all during the time period of the Old Testament. He wanted us to know of the true nature of the infinitely perfect submission of the Son to the Father. He wanted us to know that just like Jesus emptied Himself to rescue us on the cross, so also was He emptied during the entirety of the Old Testament. He was indeed made *"a little lower than the angels"* (Psalm 8:5, Hebrews 2:7 and 2:9). This placed Jesus right in the thick of battle, with mighty archangels standing back-to-back with the Son of God, the *"commander of the army of the Lord"* (Joshua 5:14)

And then in the crucifixion and resurrection of Jesus came the pinnacle moment of the entirety of the creation. For in the resurrection of Jesus following his perfect death—the perfect sacrifice of the perfectly emptied Son of God—*everything changed*. Everything was restored.

The Son is the radiance of God's glory and the exact representation of
his being, sustaining all things by his powerful word. After he had
provided purification for sins, he sat down at the right hand of the
Majesty in heaven. So he became as much superior to the angels as
the name he has inherited is superior to theirs.

—Hebrews 1:3-4 (emphasis added)

This pivotal passage tells the whole story. These words *"After"* and *"became"* echo through eternity. They demand our focused attention. They signal a change. They can *only* apply if Jesus was indeed—at some point—*not* *"superior to the angels."* Therefore, before the crucifixion—that which *"provided purification for sins"*—Jesus was in fact *not* *"superior to the angels."* This elevation of His status only happened *after* His death and resurrection. The passage is clear in this regard—the implied change described in this passage can only be from a state *lower than or equal to* the angels. A state lower than or equal to the angels, indeed, puts Jesus—prior to His crucifixion—right in the middle of the mix, right in the middle of the heat of the battle, and right in the middle of the message of Daniel 10.

Further Scriptural confirmation of the fact that Jesus undergoes a transformation in status following his crucifixion and resurrection is found in a remarkable passage in Psalm 45 and later confirmed and reemphasized in the New Testament book of Hebrews.

> *You love righteousness and hate wickedness; therefore God, your God, has set you above your companions by anointing you with the oil of joy.*
>
> —Psalms 45:7 (emphasis added)

> *You have loved righteousness and hated wickedness; therefore God, your God, has set you above your companions by anointing you with the oil of joy."*
>
> —Hebrews 1:9 (emphasis added)

Remarkably, these passages not only speak of this transformation, but also confirm that Jesus existed in a lesser state in which he was equal to or below His *"companions."* What an incredible word is utilized in this passage. The word, *"companions,"* speaks of friends, of a band of brothers, of a band of warriors, of sharing the very special warriors' bond found only in the camaraderie of standing back-to-back in vicious battle. Jesus was not just parked on a throne issuing edicts and commands—He was in the thick of the battle. He was a tactical commander. He was a battlefield commander. He stood in the throes of battle with His *"companions"* issuing battlefield commands as the tide of battle washed to-and-fro over Him and His fellow warriors.

And thus we return to the point of this discussion and boldly answer the question posed at the beginning of this book. Yes, it was Jesus, who spoke to Daniel. Yes, it was Jesus—fully emptied of all power, yet still the Son of the Living God—who stood before Daniel and spoke boldly of His warrior exploits, of being detained by the Prince of Persia and of being assisted by the Archangel Michael. These are the cautious introductory steps in a journey toward a new perspective regarding the nature, role, and activities of Jesus in the Old Testament.

Chapter 9

The Unnamed Angel
"'The' Angel of the Lord"

Abraham, Isaac, Jacob, Moses, Joshua, David. All stood before this mysterious figure. All encountered *"the angel of the LORD."* From mountain top crags to desert wadi, from bright daylight to darkest night—anywhere, anytime, his presence changed everything. He spoke out of the infinite brightness of flame and from the darkness of the shadows. He was hidden from their sight and he stood fully embodied as a man before them. No matter the form, no matter what the reason, all sensed the gripping fear of the *Awful Uncreated*. All knew that a man spoke to them. All knew that God spoke to them.

Our hypothesis is now fully developed. Jesus Christ, the only Son of God, emptied Himself fully of His Godly powers to enter the adventures of the Old Testament in an embodied, fully physical state as the warrior Commander of the army of the Lord. Every episode and adventure of the Old Testament saints, warriors, kings, and patriarchs was indeed—as we should expect—about only one person: Jesus Christ.

Yet this hypothesis involves so much more. For with it we are declaring that the involvement of Jesus in the Old Testament went beyond the fact that He *planned* every moment—which He undoubtedly did. It went beyond His close *oversight* of every moment—which undoubtedly occurred. The involvement of Jesus—the very pinnacle of the whole of creation—went even further still.

Jesus Christ, the fully incarnate Son of God did in fact actively, physically, and palpably *participate* in every moment of the Old Testament. He was not just there in a Godly sort of oversight capacity. He was right there in the mix in every important patriarchal decision, every Israelite battle, every episode of discipline, and every episode of joyous worship.

The next step is clear. A rock solid case for the veracity of our bold hypothesis must be constructed upon the foundation that has been established. This case must be built upon evidence that not only tells us that every word of our hypothesis is true, but also serves to fully define the special role that Jesus played as the very central figure of the entire epic story. The grains of bold truth that are the clues to the mystery of the fullness of the Person of Jesus Christ are found in every chapter of every book of the Old Testament.

Several golden threads weave mysteriously and continuously throughout the deep waters of the Old Testament text. They are critical to our search for Jesus. These threads tie our quest through the Old Testament into a unified glorification of the Person of Jesus Christ. They define the role of Jesus in a very special manner. One such thread is especially critical to our quest. It involves the repeated appearance of a person referred to as *"the angel of the Lord."*

This enigmatic figure appears throughout the adventures of the Old Testament. The clues to this character's identity are critical and can be drawn together from many cryptic references to him that are scattered throughout many different Old Testament books. This figure, *"the angel of the Lord,"* is indeed but one of several spectral individuals referred to under the title of *"angel."* Yet this figure is not just referred to as *"an"* angel of the Lord; he is instead quite pointedly and repeatedly—in many different settings—referred to as *"the angel of the Lord."*

That little three-letter word *"the"* is critical to this quest. It is a word of emphasis. It is a word that tells us that in all of the circumstances in which it is used, it is speaking of only one individual. It tells us that in every circumstance it is referring to the *same* individual. There can only be one *"the angel of the Lord."* In this respect, it is in direct contrast to those accounts where the word angel is preceded by the word *"an,"* which would imply the existence of multiple such angels. The word *"the,"* in this case, is a word that sets this particular Old Testament figure apart from, even raises him above, all of the other persons of the Old Testament who are referred to under the title of *"angel."* In this regard, several critical clues have been scattered throughout the Old Testament regarding the nature of *the angel of the Lord*.

First of all, *the angel of the Lord* is not to be confused with any of the *named* angels in the Bible. Never in scripture is the title *the angel of the Lord* used in association with Gabriel, Michael, or Lucifer. In fact, as we shall discuss in more depth later, in all but one of the appearances of *the angel of the Lord*, this angel is very specifically not named. This very purposeful omission of a name for *the angel of the Lord* simply cannot be a random act by the authors of the Old Testament scriptures.

Quite to the contrary, it is the clear and purposeful intent of the Holy Spirit that this angel remains unnamed. As we will discuss, this is most dramatically pointed out as several Old Testament characters try to pry this angel's identity from him. The failure of their very best efforts to discover his name is well documented by the Old Testament authors—and it is critical to his identity. This becomes readily apparent when we ask ourselves why this name is so diligently hidden from revelation and why its secretive nature is not just revealed, but emphasized. After all, why would the Holy Spirit so carefully and thoroughly record all of the attempts to get this angel to reveal his name except that He wanted to draw attention to the fact that it was indeed a secret? From Jacob's use of a hammer-lock wrestling hold during his somewhat impromptu wrestling match, to the prying questions of Samson's mother and father, we see considerable effort being expended in attempting to extract this angel's name from him. And precisely in this effort—and well-matched resistance—is found the initial clue to his identity given. Their persistence in this quest—and his equally persistent resistance—is recorded so that we may know that his name is hidden for a very specific and very special purpose.

After all, this angel—who is right in the middle of each of these scenes—is not just some random bit part actor with a minor role in the dramatic presentation of the Old Testament adventures. This most mysterious of Old Testament personalities is not just the main character of the unfolding drama. He is the whole show. Why would the Holy Spirit make such a point of hiding the name of a "bit part" player? He wouldn't. It is only because this character is indeed the very focal point of the greatest of all of the great mysteries of mankind that such an effort is put into hiding his identity.

The answer to the question that the Holy Spirit is posing regarding the secretive identity of *the angel of the Lord* is obvious. This is no ordinary angel. This is the Son of God. This is *the One* who is to come. This is the Redeemer of Israel and the Redeemer of all mankind—and His time to burst onto the scene and be fully identified had not yet come. This is the very *"one who was to come"* whom John the Baptist will refer to when seeking the true identity of Jesus.

> *When the men came to Jesus, they said, "John the Baptist sent us to you to ask, 'Are you the one who was to come, or should we expect someone else?'"*
>
> —Luke 7:20 (emphasis added)

God in His perfect wisdom obviously decided that certain things about the great plan to rescue the sons and daughters of God should remain a mystery. For example, the church—the bride of Christ—was clearly a mystery that was held from the Old Testament writers. And yet most certainly the greatest of Biblical mysteries, without a doubt, is indeed *Christ in us*.

> *I have become its servant by the commission God gave me to present to you the word of God in its fullness—the mystery that has been kept hidden for ages and generations, but is now disclosed to the saints. To them God has chosen to make known among the Gentiles the glorious riches of this mystery, which is Christ in you, the hope of glory.*
>
> —Colossians 1:25-27 (emphasis added)

The mystery of the divine identity of *the angel of the Lord*, therefore, falls right in line with the mysteries of the Old Testament that *all* center on the most important individual in either Testament, Jesus Christ. As hidden as the angel's identity is, however, with the right perspective and the Holy Spirit as our guide, the process is readily apparent. Indeed, many clues to his identity are purposely and obviously left for us to find along the path of our quest. Since his identification process is critical in the proof of the overriding hypothesis of this book, this evidence will be reviewed in more detail.

The first and most stunning of the clues to the identity of *the angel of the Lord* is found in the encounter of Moses with the voice emanating from the burning bush. From the very onset of this visitation, the identity of the person whose voice comes from the burning bush is made perfectly clear. It belongs to none other than *the angel of the Lord*.

> *Now Moses was tending the flock of Jethro his father-in-law, the priest of Midian, and he led the flock to the far side of the desert and came to Horeb, the mountain of God. There the angel of the LORD appeared to him in flames of fire from within a bush. Moses saw that though the bush was on fire it did not burn up.*
>
> —Exodus 3:1-2 (emphasis added)

As previously mentioned, there is indeed only one time that is documented in the Old Testament when *the angel of the Lord* tells anyone his name. This is it. Only in response to Moses' request for a name to tell his fellow Israelites does *the angel of the Lord*, whose voice emanates from the burning bush, tell us his name: *"I*

AM." And as already reviewed, New Testament scripture confirms that it was indeed very specifically Jesus who was the source of that voice in the burning bush. The identity of *the angel of the Lord* is well established by the available textual evidence.

Jesus is the angel of the Lord.

There are in fact many elaborate revelations in Old Testament scripture that confirm the identity of *the angel of the Lord.* Their review is best initiated by noting some of the simpler and more direct textual confirmations of his identity. These references do not rely upon a more elaborate evaluation of evidence, but are instead just simple straightforward references to the divine nature of *the angel of the Lord.* Despite their simplicity, their impact is nevertheless profound because of the clarity of their text. In other words it is hard to argue with the uncompromising nature of their straightforward identification of *the angel of the Lord.* One great example among many is found in the book of Genesis.

> *Then he blessed Joseph and said, "May the God before whom my fathers Abraham and Isaac walked, the God who has been my shepherd all my life to this day, the Angel who has delivered me from all harm—may he bless these boys. May they be called by my name and the names of my fathers Abraham and Isaac, and may they increase greatly upon the earth."*
>
> —Genesis 48:15-16 (emphasis added)

This statement by Jacob comes near the end of his life. He is a sage patriarch by then and knows well the very specific identity of the warrior who has been at his side through every battle, even from the very beginning. This is the very same Jacob after all who actually wrestled with this angel, as we will review in detail later. The fact that this declaration comes in the midst of Jacob's blessing of Joseph is no coincidence. Jacob is passing the torch to the leader of his family. Jacob wants Joseph to know the precise identity of the individual who has been assigned the task of protecting their extended family.

For us also, the relevance of this clear declaration is not subtle. It tells us very simply and in a very concise and clear manner that *the angel of the Lord* is the incarnate Jesus Christ. It tells us that there can only be one *the angel of the Lord*— for no other heavenly being would dare use the same title held by the Son of God. It tells us in no uncertain terms that every single time that we see a reference to *the angel of the Lord* in the Old Testament that we can know that it is a description of the Son of God in action as the warrior Commander of the army of the Lord.

> **When used in the Old Testament, the phrase** *"the angel of the Lord"* **always refers to the embodied Jesus Christ.**

Another equally brief reference from the book of Genesis also confirms the divine identity of *the angel of the Lord* in straightforward terms that are hard to misconstrue. Once again the patriarch involved is Jacob and *the angel of God* is the messenger.

> *"The angel of God said to me in the dream, 'Jacob.' I answered, 'Here I am.' And he said, 'Look up and see that all the male goats mating with the flock are streaked, speckled or spotted, for I have seen all that Laban has been doing to you. I am the God of Bethel, where you anointed a pillar and where you made a vow to me. Now leave this land at once and go back to your native land.'"*
>
> —Genesis 31:11-13 (emphasis added)

Here, as *"the angel of God"* is discussing Jacob's difficulties with Laban, he suddenly makes the statement that he is in fact *"the God of Bethel."* There is no other way to interpret this than to know that *the angel of the Lord* or *"the angel of God"* (as He is referred to in this passage) is the embodied, incarnate Jesus.

Another direct, single line reference that builds this case in its declaration of the divine identity of *the angel of the Lord* is found in the book of the prophet Zechariah. There, a single line of scripture is strategically dropped into a discussion of *"the day of the Lord."* Zechariah is describing precisely how strong the inhabitants of the city of Jerusalem will be on that day.

> *On that day the LORD will shield those who live in Jerusalem, so that the feeblest among them will be like David, and the house of David will be like God, like the Angel of the LORD going before them.*
>
> —Zechariah 12:8 (emphasis added)

How easy it is to overlook this deliberate revelation of the divine identity of the *angel of the Lord*. The translators did not miss its significance though, as the word *"Angel"* is indeed capitalized. It really is hard to misinterpret this statement though, as it very clearly states that *"the Angel of the Lord"* is *"like God."*

Certainly with this precise terminology, to state that *the angel of the Lord* is *"like"* God is very clearly to state that he is God. We know that God is uncreated and entirely unlike us—set apart from us. Only God is holy. There is no middle ground here. There is no ordinary angel who fits the criteria of being *"like"* God. The prophet Zechariah is equating *"the Angel of the Lord"* with God Himself.

Another similarly brief reference to *the angel of the Lord* is found in Psalm 34. This reference is important because it further enlightens us to the precise role that Jesus, *the angel of the Lord*, played in the Old Testament.

> *The angel of the LORD encamps around those who fear him, and he delivers them.*
>
> —Psalm 34:7

Perhaps in no other place is the role of Jesus in the Old Testament more succinctly stated than here. Jesus is a warrior and His mission is to implement the will of the Father. That most certainly—and perhaps most perfectly—includes the deliverance of those who fear God. The reference to *"him"* in this passage is therefore to both the angel of the Lord and God—one in the same Person: Jesus.

Everything about this passage is military. To have the angel of the Lord encamp around them is to have the very elite personal military guard of the Mighty God standing as a protective force around them. Even as they slept, Jesus and the army of the Lord stood guard over them.

Likewise, *deliverance* itself is all about military action. It implies rescue by use of force from those who mean to harm or, at the very least, hold others against their will. The very use of the term *"deliver"* brings into mind scenes of a military force, by massive armed conflict or even by covert operations, bringing about the rescue of captives. It suggests riding to the last minute rescue of a loved one who is surrounded and in a fight for their life. Deliverance is all about military action and Jesus is all about deliverance. Deliverance was precisely His role in rescuing the Israelites from their captivity in Egypt and then again from the Babylonian captivity. It is also His role in redeeming us from the certain—and eternal—death to which our sins most justly consign us. The precise military definition of the Old—and New—Testament mission of Jesus Christ will be discussed in great detail later.

We have already touched lightly upon the cryptic answer that the warrior Jesus gave to Joshua when asked whether he was for Israel or for her enemies. The word, *"Neither,"* (Joshua 5:14) answers this question best when the role of this warrior Commander is understood to be the defense of *only* those who fear the Lord. The later apostasy of Israel is perhaps best summarily characterized by their lack of the fear of the Lord. With this key fact in mind, a review of the history of Israel easily reveals when indeed this warrior Commander was fighting for them and when he was fighting against them—much more about this later.

Still another equally obvious reference to the divinity of *the angel of the Lord* is found in Psalm 35. The author of this psalm is David, the greatest of the warrior kings of Judah. His graphic description of God leaves little doubt that David had a firm knowledge of the presence of the Lord in his life. David knew that God very literally went before him in battle. There is nothing allegorical about his depiction of God as tangibly involved in the physical battle that surrounded David. He knew that God Himself very literally fought side-by-side with him with shield and javelin, buckler and spear.

> *Take up shield and buckler; arise and come to my aid. Brandish spear and javelin against those who pursue me. Say to my soul, "I am your salvation."*
>
> —Psalm 35:2-3

David knew what we must know: that God will go physically before us in battle— if we will just ask Him. David knew that all who call upon the name of the Lord will be saved. He implored God, *"Contend, O LORD, with those who contend with me; fight against those who fight against me"* (Psalm 35:1).

David also knew the identity of the mediator of God's rescue of those who call upon the name of the Lord. Just as Jesus is the mediator of God's rescue of the sons and daughters of God, so also did Jesus, as *the angel of the Lord*, serve as the direct vector of intervention on David's behalf against the real world enemies that had positioned themselves against David.

> *May those who seek my life be disgraced and put to shame; may those who plot my ruin be turned back in dismay. May they be like chaff before the wind, with the angel of the LORD driving them away; may their path be dark and slippery, with the angel of the LORD pursuing them.*
>
> —Psalm 35:4-6 (emphasis added)

David—ever the warrior, ever the strategist, ever the tactical commander of the armies of Israel—even describes the tactics to be implemented on the field of battle by *the angel of the Lord.*

> *Since they hid their net for me without cause and without cause dug a pit for me, may ruin overtake them by surprise—may the net they hid entangle them, may they fall into the pit, to their ruin.*
>
> —Psalm 35:7-8

And before the battle is even fought—as David faces the very palpable threat before him—he will *"rejoice"* and *"delight"* in the salvation brought about by the actions of *the angel of the Lord.*

> *Then my soul will rejoice in the LORD and delight in his salvation. My whole being will exclaim, "Who is like you, O LORD? You rescue the poor from those too strong for them, the poor and needy from those who rob them."*
>
> —Psalm 35:9-10

There should be no doubt in our minds that David was imminently aware of and in full appreciation of the efforts of the warrior Commander who went before him in battle. How easy it is to just read past these clues that take on so much importance if viewed in the proper perspective.

The identity of *the angel of the Lord* is not in doubt. The illumination of the role of Jesus Christ in every battle of the Old Testament is obvious and palpable to even the most stubborn among us. There are precisely fifty verses in the NIV translation of the Old Testament that refer to *the angel of the Lord.* Every one of these fifty verses is describing the palpable, physical, Old Testament participation of the fully embodied Son of God in the lives of the patriarchs and prophets.

> *...you welcomed me as if I were an <u>angel of God</u>, as if I were <u>Christ Jesus himself</u>.*
>
> —Galatians 4:14b (emphasis added)

Chapter 10

Judges Chapter 2
The Angel of the LORD and "a Great War"

The conquest of the land should have been the purest of war. The land belonged to the Israelites by the promise of its Creator, by the promise of God. They were to move forward in faith and take possession of the land in the strength of the Lord. The command of God had been clear. Show no mercy in the utter elimination of the pagan occupants of the Promised Land.

After the initial conquest of the land by the combined army of Israel, the individual tribes had been left to complete this task in their assigned portions of the land. There were to be no survivors. Survivors would only be a source of impurity, defilement, and temptation. God had warned them of the weakness of their hearts. Unbelief and disobedience in this command would be disastrous.

Despite God's promises, the people were afraid and gave voice to their fears in their complaints. Their enemies were too numerous. Their enemies had iron chariots. Their enemies were raiders who made their living at war. How could they possibly do that which God had requested of them? How could they defeat these enemies?

Thus, the land remained untaken, the Israelites immobilized by their fear. The pagan occupants remained a thorn in their sides and their pagan gods a snare. The Israelite tribes stood before the Lord, unwilling to do that which God had asked of them.

In addition to the many simple and straightforward references to *the angel of the Lord*, the Old Testament also includes many more elaborate accounts describing his direct involvement with the nation of Israel. In these accounts, *the angel of the Lord's* involvement is described in much more detail. These descriptions are especially relevant to the search for the trail of Jesus in the Old Testament and worthy of review. The first of these accounts is a short but powerfully specific reference to an appearance of *the angel of the Lord* to the Israelites during the days of the Judges. In addition to its identification of the identity of *the angel of the*

Lord, this account has much to say regarding the specific assignments and motives of this very special warrior.

The story begins with warfare. Just as the people of God were continuously in a fight through the five books of the Pentateuch and the book of Joshua, so also do they find themselves continually in a fight in the book of Judges. But even before we are introduced to the cycle of rest, disobey, cry out, and rescue that is established in the book of Judges, we are given a brief introduction that is actually directly spoken by *the angel of the Lord*. In it he tells us that not only is this story about war, but that *he* is about war.

Indeed, *the angel of the Lord* starts out with a startling declaration in the introduction to the second chapter of the book of Judges. And yet, it is startling only if you have not yet bought into the true identity of *the angel of the Lord*. It is startling only to those of us who are still desperately clinging to the belief that Jesus spent the entirety of the Old Testament just drinking coffee at a heavenly Starbucks waiting for His birth in Bethlehem. The declaration is clear in its intent. Its meaning is easily discernible. Its impact on our search for Jesus is profound.

> *The angel of the LORD went up from Gilgal to Bokim and said, "I brought you up out of Egypt and led you into the land that I swore to give to your forefathers. I said, 'I will never break my covenant with you, and you shall not make a covenant with the people of this land, but you shall break down their altars.' Yet you have disobeyed me. Why have you done this? Now therefore I tell you that I will not drive them out before you; they will be [thorns] in your sides and their gods will be a snare to you." When the angel of the LORD had spoken these things to all the Israelites, the people wept aloud, and they called that place Bokim. There they offered sacrifices to the LORD.*
>
> —Judges 2:1-5 (emphasis added)

The angel of the Lord is clearly stating—in terms that leave little uncertainty as to his precise intention—that it was very specifically *he* who led them out of Egypt. Indeed, he reveals that he has been involved in every moment of the warfare that has engulfed the nation of Israel since his first suggestion of the exodus from Egypt. The phraseology used by the angel in the above scripture is specific and convicting.

The tone and the precisely chosen words clearly infer that this angel is in fact not merely acting as a messenger. He is claiming to be the originator of the thoughts, words, and actions of the message he is delivering. This angel is clearly speaking from the same plane as God. *A regular angelic member of the heavenly host would never use this language.* Indeed, for a regular angel to raise himself to the level of God—as this statement clearly does—would mirror that original act of most heinous rebellion by Lucifer. A member of God's heavenly host would never use words that could in any way suggest—or in any way be misconstrued to suggest—that he spoke as one empowered at the same level as God.

Quite obviously, this is no ordinary angel. This is the Lord God. This is Jesus Christ. This is the Prince of princes. This is the Commander of the army of the Lord. This is the Prince of the angelic host. As we have already reviewed, his statement that it was He, Jesus, who led the Israelites out of Egypt, should be of no surprise to any reader of the New Testament. Paul in fact specifically tells us that it was precisely and very specifically *"Christ"* who accompanied the people of Israel as they left Egypt.

> *For I do not want you to be ignorant of the fact, brothers, that our forefathers were all under the cloud and that they all passed through the sea. They were all baptized into Moses in the cloud and in the sea. They all ate the same spiritual food and drank the same spiritual drink; for they drank from the spiritual rock that accompanied them, and that rock was Christ.*
>
> —1Corinthians 10:1-4 (emphasis added)

The case for Jesus as *the angel of the Lord* is so rock solid that it is hard for even the most ardent of skeptics to deny. Indeed it is only from the perspective of the Son of God embodied as the Commander of the army of the Lord that these words of *the angel of the Lord* make any sense at all. Our theology—whatever it may be—must include *all* scripture. It cannot contradict scripture and scripture cannot contradict it. Very little leeway is left for alternative explanations to these passages.

This leads us to a very significant conclusion regarding the activities of the Son of God during the historical period that is chronicled by the Old Testament scriptures. It is becoming readily apparent that Jesus in fact not only led the Israelites into and out of Egypt, but also through the desert, into the Promised Land, and through the entirety of the rest of the history described by the Old Testament scripture. This evidence suggests that Jesus was in fact the warrior of God who fought for the Israelites behind the scenes, as well as visually and palpably leading them through the good times and the bad, through peace and through war.

In this context, these words of the angel at Bokim remind us of that which was behind all that Jesus undertook in the Old Testament. The primary mission of Jesus the Warrior of God and Commander of the army of the Lord was nothing less than the will of His Father. He was neither for the Israelites nor against them—He was *for* the Father and contended against anything or anyone who stood in opposition to the will and knowledge of the Holy God. As we will soon discuss in more detail, it was the Father's will that the remnant of Israel be preserved. Indeed, that which was already quite apparent in the five books of the Pentateuch becomes even more obvious in the book of the Judges. Jesus is telling the Israelites in the above passage that He will fight against them—or at the very least will not fight for them—if they do not obey the commands—the will—of God.

This should be of no surprise. The Lord repeatedly stated throughout His covenant discussions with the Israelites that He had placed two choices before them. In obeying God they would be blessed. But He clearly also warned them of the consequences of disobedience, of rebellion against the commands of God. He forewarned them then of precisely what He is telling them now. As we have reviewed, this is a message that is then echoed by multiple prophets throughout the Old Testament.

> *I myself will fight against you with an outstretched hand and a mighty arm in anger and fury and great wrath.*
>
> —Jeremiah 21:5 (emphasis added)

> *If you fear the LORD and serve and obey him and do not rebel against his commands, and if both you and the king who reigns over you follow the LORD your God—good! But if you do not obey the LORD, and if you rebel against his commands, his hand will be against you, as it was against your fathers.*
>
> —1Samuel 12:14-15 (emphasis added)

This second chapter of Judges also supplies detailed insight into exactly what the day-to-day role of Jesus seemed to involve. Over and over in the Old Testament we are treated to the intriguing statements by the Lord that He *"has driven them out before you"* (Deuteronomy 9:4), *"has given them into your hand"* (Joshua 10:8), or *"goes before you"* (Deuteronomy 31:8). How often in the Old Testament text have these lines been so easily dismissed as just allegorical descriptions of God's role in the trials faced by Israel. We readily recognize that we do not overcome anything in our lives, let alone the mighty armies of our enemies, without God's help. We think of these stories as just God's quaint way of stating this truth that we all accept. We readily recognize that we are powerless to eternally redeem ourselves as well as powerless to redeem ourselves from the physical enemies who confront us in our day-to-day lives, just like they confronted the Israelites.

But the Holy Spirit is trying to tell us so much more here. Truly the most prevalent error in the interpretation and application of Scripture has always been our desire to not take it literally. This desire to defuse the implications and impact of scripture by attributing it to allegory seems to be based mostly in our human desire to evade the demand to literally obey God's direct commands. This particular case is also a great example of the many-tiered revelation of the Word of God. We all recognize the superficial explanation that when God says He has already defeated the enemy, He is just stating that He is the strength behind us in our battle—and because of His unlimited power, the battle can already be assumed to be won.

But there is also a deeper level of revelation. *The angel of the Lord*, Jesus, wanted us to know that when Israel was in a fight, *He* was in a fight—one way or the other. Sometimes he fought for Israel. Other times, as we will review in detail later, he fought very purposely against Israel. Either way, these were not fights that He chose to win by just the word of His mouth, as He is described as doing in the book of Revelation. Instead, it was His good pleasure to empty Himself into the ultimate act of meekness and to fight side-by-side with His fellow warrior angels in every Old Testament battle.

Chapter 11

Judges Chapter 13
Samson and *The Angel of the LORD*

Zorah. The western border of Judah. It was the time of the Judges of Israel. *"In those days Israel had no king; everyone did as he saw fit"* (Judges 21:25). The abundant provision of God had been taken for granted. The Israelites had exchanged their Glory for the worship of lifeless idols. As He had promised, God had delivered Israel into the hands of the Philistines for 40 years. The subjugation of God's people was oppressive.

Yet somewhere a smoldering spark of repentance had burst into flame in Israel. The righteous remnant was on their knees before the Lord their God. They remembered. They remembered their history, their many rescues. They cried out. Their cry of repentance reached the throne room of the Mighty God.

Jesus, the Commander of the army of the Lord had been watching. He had seen the hearts of the Israelites turning slowly back to God in response to the discipline meted out by the Philistines. He had waited anxiously for the battle directive from on high, for precisely in the repentance of God's people was found the compassion and mercy of God's heart. God's discipline had its intended effect. The people of His pasture were turning from their lifeless idols. Those whom Jesus had been directed to protect—the righteous remnant of Israel—had in their repentance given voice to the cry of their hearts. They cried out to the Lord for redemption. And in this repentance of God's people was found the stirring of the army of the Lord. A rescue was being planned.

And yet the Commander of the army of the Lord had a problem. To implement a rescue was more complicated than it might seem. By God's will, that rescue would come—but only in the timing of God. Preparations had to be made. A special Israelite warrior was needed. He needed to be a rowdy, edgy, scurrilous type—it took more than just an ordinary warrior to stand up to the daunting Philistine army. At God's prompting, when the timing was right, this one had to be brazen enough to pick a fight. He had to be reckless enough to stand before the Philistines.

The outcome of this fight depended critically upon timing. It had to be precise. It was vital, therefore, that this warrior was not only a brazen, reckless bully, but also open to the direction of the Holy Spirit—a rare combination, indeed. This had to be a truly unique individual. Nefarious—and yet open to the guiding of the Spirit? This warrior had to be a Nazirite. He had to be of that very special breed of warrior, consecrated to the Lord from the moment of his conception.

To initiate God's complicated plan for rescue, therefore, the Commander of the army of the Lord had been sent on a very special mission to a very special couple. They were to conceive and parent a unique Nazirite warrior. They were Manoah and his wife—the parents of Samson.

The remarkable conversation between *the angel of the Lord* and Samson's mother and father that is recorded in Judges 13 gives us many important clues regarding the personality and personal attributes of *the angel of the Lord*. Once again, the identity of *the angel of the Lord* is pointedly confirmed. The case for the physical participation of Jesus as *the angel of the Lord* continues to build. The Holy Spirit very literally includes so many clues to the identity of *the angel of the Lord* that He falls just short of coming right out and saying that the angel is Jesus Christ.

What a delightful chapter this is. It describes the encounters of an Israelite couple with a very special messenger who tells them of the son that they would soon raise. Once again, a physical description of this messenger is included as the Holy Spirit is quick to point out that his description as a *"very awesome"* angel was in the context of appearing as *"a man of God."*

> *Then the woman went to her husband and told him, "A man of God came to me. He looked like an angel of God, very awesome. I didn't ask him where he came from, and he didn't tell me his name.*
> —Judges 13:6 (emphasis added)

Once again the issue of the angel's name takes center stage. Once again, *the angel of the Lord* is evasive in this regard. But precisely here is where the Holy Spirit then takes the whole conversation immediately to a higher level. The angel's next encounter is nothing short of profound, for when Manoah asks the angel if he is the one who talked to his wife, the answer of the angel is stark in the clarity of its meaning: *"I am."*

Manoah got up and followed his wife. When he came to the man, he said, "Are you the one who talked to my wife?"

"I am," he said.

—Judges 13:11 (emphasis added)

The phrase *"I am"* is not subtle in its implications. It is, of course, the exact phrase used by *the angel of the Lord* to identify himself when He spoke with Moses from the burning bush. As we have reviewed, Jesus clearly identified Himself as the source of the voice in the burning bush. These are sacred words. No ordinary angel would ever dare to use these words in this manner. They are simply too close to those used by Lucifer as he proclaimed himself the equal of God.

The clues continue, as the angel then states that it is in fact *He* who is commanding Manoah and His wife. His terminology includes the phrase *"I have commanded her,"* instead of using a reference to the Lord commanding them, as we would expect.

> *"She must not eat anything that comes from the grapevine, nor drink any wine or other fermented drink nor eat anything unclean. She must do everything I have commanded her."*

—Judges 13:14 (emphasis added)

The author of the book of Judges then offers an editorial comment that is included in parentheses: *"(Manoah did not realize that it was the angel of the LORD)"* (emphasis added). This comment clearly and specifically identifies the messenger. It also tells us that Manoah's realization of this fact, and his reaction to it, have much more bearing on the situation than the reader might have expected. It suggests that Manoah's attitude, words, and actions might have been significantly altered by the realization that this was *the angel of the Lord*.

> *Manoah said to the angel of the LORD, "We would like you to stay until we prepare a young goat for you."*
>
> *The angel of the LORD replied, "Even though you detain me, I will not eat any of your food. But if you prepare a burnt offering, offer it to the LORD." (Manoah did not realize that it was the angel of the LORD.)*

—Judges 13:15-16 (emphasis added)

Then comes yet a further revelation as Manoah directly confronts the angel to ask him his name.

> *Then Manoah inquired of the angel of the LORD, "What is your name, so that we may honor you when your word comes true?"*
>
> *He replied, "Why do you ask my name? It is beyond understanding."*

—Judges 13:17-18 (emphasis added)

Instead of simply replying with a name, this mysterious angel of God first asks Manoah why he asked. He then replies that his name is *"beyond understanding."* This description of his name as being *beyond understanding* is strongly reminiscent of the reference to the unknown name of Jesus described in the book of Revelation.

> *I saw heaven standing open and there before me was a white horse, whose rider is called Faithful and True. With justice he judges and makes war. His eyes are like blazing fire, and on his head are many crowns. He has a name written on him that no one knows but he himself.*

—Revelation 19:11-12 (emphasis added)

Again, no ordinary angel would claim to have a name that *"is beyond understanding."* It is interesting to note that only *the angel of the Lord* is ever asked his name in the Bible. It is only *the angel of the Lord* who likewise ever purposely avoids the revelation of his name.

After the offering of the burnt sacrifice and the angel's subsequent disappearance, Manoah then realizes *"that it was the angel of the LORD" (Judges 13:21).* He laments to his wife *"We are doomed to die!"* because they *"have seen God!"* (Judges 13:22). The revelation that this is *the angel of the Lord* is immediate and definitive. Somehow Manoah and his wife knew that *the angel of the Lord* was God incarnate. There is nothing tentative about their response. They bow down before this mysterious angel whose name is *"beyond understanding"* because they realize that the fact of their having *"seen God"* would most certainly result in their deaths.

Further still, we must be captivated by the prophetic meaning of *the angel of the Lord's* mystical response to their burnt offering. Rather than just standing by and observing, *the angel of the Lord—Jesus*—spirals up with the smoke to heaven.

> *As the flame blazed up from the altar toward heaven, the angel of the LORD ascended in the flame. Seeing this, Manoah and his wife fell with their faces to the ground.*
>
> —Judges 13:20 (emphasis added)

This act is not cryptic in its intent. It is directly prophetic of the ultimate mission of this particular angel of the Lord. It is precisely this angel—Jesus—who hundreds of years later would ascend as *the* ultimate and all-encompassing sacrifice to the Lord. This sacrifice would do perfectly, singularly, and forever, all of that which Manoah and his wife's temporizing burnt offering was intended to do. It would make us right with God, once and for all.

Although we can never yet know the full meaning behind any micro-aspect of the infinite written Word of God, surely we can safely draw several conclusions regarding the purpose of the incarnate visit of the Son of God described in the 13th chapter of Judges. This purpose lends more strength to the case we are building of Jesus Christ as an Old Testament holy warrior in the unseen otherworld that parallels ours. First of all, the visit of Jesus to Manoah and his wife has all of the trappings of a *recruiting* trip. Jesus' efforts were once again directed toward the mission of rescuing the remnant of His people from their oppressors. *Rescue* truly was His mission in every aspect of His earthly incarnation. That word, *rescue*, singularly personifies all that He was about—in the Old Testament or the New. This, of course, includes not only the very visible rescue of all who would be sons and daughters of God by His death on the cross of Calvary, but also His repeated efforts during the Old Testament era to rescue the nation of Israel from her oppressors. This latter mission will be reviewed in more depth later.

The entire book of Judges gives us a unique perspective on the military aspects of the missions of warrior Jesus. This book chronicles one after another of the most unusual military assignments for the elite army of the Lord and its one-of-a-kind Commander. Most are rescue missions and evolve out of a repeating pattern that involves the natural human tendency to turn from God when things are going well. The Israelites repeatedly turned to the ways of the people around them. In this chapter, God was again attempting to get their attention—trying to rescue them from the sinful, idol-worshiping lifestyle that they had fallen into—by sending discipline in the form of Philistine oppressors.

Again the Israelites did evil in the eyes of the LORD, *so the* LORD *delivered them into the hands of the Philistines for forty years.*

—Judges 13:1

How quickly we rise to pass judgment on the Israelites from the perspective of our perfect hindsight. And yet, how perfectly do the Israelites' actions mirror our own actions in our every day lives! Like them, we are so quick to ask why God sends trials into our lives—all the while remaining blind to the fact that we consistently wander away from God when things are going our way. It is only in the midst of disciplinary trials sent by God that we—like the Israelites—consistently turn back to the Lord.

And this is exactly the pattern demonstrated by the Israelites in this chapter of the book of Judges. The Philistines are oppressing them and they have cried out to God. God seeks, in His endless compassion and mercy, to once again come to their rescue. The point of the book remains crystal clear. The answer now is the same as the answer in the time of the Judges: Jesus.

It might be fun to use our imagination to try to flesh out exactly what is really going on here in the book of Judges—especially as it relates to that complex interface between our world and this mysterious spiritual otherworld that parallels ours. One thing upon which it might be reasonable to speculate is whether Israel's bad choices had somehow *empowered* the otherworld forces of evil. More specifically, had their worship of the gods of the Canaanites around them somehow empowered otherworld evil forces—the "gods" of the otherworld?

We might even presume that as the Israelites had paid homage to the gods worshipped by the pagans societies around them, they had also been simultaneously praying to and worshipping the powerful otherworld powers and authorities that stood behind these gods. In other words they worshipped the spiritual "gods" behind the gods of the pagan nations. It might well be presumed that there is a direct relationship between the prayers offered to these false gods and the power wielded by the evil forces in the otherworld. Given this assumption, we might also make a safe assumption that the power of the evil ones in the other world had grown as the idol worship had increased in the land of Israel.

Perhaps, given a similar relationship between the righteous prayers of the Israelites to the one true God, we can safely assume that the angelic armies led by the Son of God had, in contrast, *not* been empowered. The Israelites had not yet sought the

Lord their God in supplicated prayer. We can only imagine that Jesus and his angelic comrades may have stood by watching the surging strength of the evil forces that opposed them with dismay. How they must have wanted to be given the command from God to attack. How this must have broken Jesus' heart as He watched His beloved people suffering because of their unbelief.

In fact, Jesus hinted at this exact yearning desire later during His earthly ministry when He said, *"... how often I have longed to gather your children together, as a hen gathers her chicks under her wings, but you were not willing!"* (Luke 13:34). One can easily imagine Him standing there watching the oppression of His people and the growing power of the demonic forces on the battlefield before Him in the otherworld. He must have been chomping at the bit to pick a fight with the Philistines—in fact we know that this is exactly the case by the words of the angel to Manoah and his wife.

> *Now see to it that you drink no wine or other fermented drink and that you do not eat anything unclean, because you will conceive and give birth to a son. No razor may be used on his head, because the boy is to be a Nazirite, set apart to God from birth, and he will begin the deliverance of Israel from the hands of the Philistines."*
>
> —Judges 13:4-5 (emphasis added)

The Father has, nonetheless, granted man a free will to make these decisions, and the Israelites had by their own free will made choices that did not empower God in their lives.

Then, as Jesus and His warrior angels must have anxiously stood by, the oppression of the Israelites by the Philistines finally reached a trigger point for the Israelites. Finally they remembered the previous demonstrations of the faithfulness of God and, once again, cried out to Him to rescue them. And this was exactly that for which Jesus was waiting. He got the green light from the Father and set His tactical battle plan into action—and the initiation of that plan was precisely what was on display in this encounter between Manoah, his wife, and *the angel of the Lord.*

Jesus, the Commander of the army of the Lord, needed to recruit a warrior—a rowdy bully—from the Israelite nation. He needed to select a very special man from among the Israelites. This man had to have very special characteristics. This man needed to be kept *set apart* from the very beginning. He needed to be raised a

Nazirite such that when the time was right for the rescue of Israel, he would be equipped with the power of the Holy Spirit.

Jesus wanted just the right guy—one who lived out on that thin edge between right and wrong, one who loved to pick a fight just because he could. But, Jesus also needed a man who could easily be nudged in the direction of doing God's bidding when it came time to put the rescue plan into action. Jesus, the Commander of the army of the Lord, knew that this was a fight that was long overdue and would no longer be postponed. When called upon, this man would need to fearlessly rise in pure faith—only the pure faith of one raised in the Holy Spirit of God—to oppose the overwhelming power of the Philistines. This very special Israelite warrior needed to be raised as a man who had nothing to lose—and precisely this fearless, almost carefree abandon would trigger Jesus' tactical battle plan into full action.

This was the reason that Jesus Himself appeared to Manoah and his wife. Jesus was there to anoint the next hero of Israel before he was even born. He was there to raise up the next hero of the nation of Israel. He was there to explain to Manoah and his wife the necessity that Samson be born and raised a Nazirite in order that he be so very specially equipped—and so very open to the guiding and inspiration of the Holy Spirit—for the battle that Almighty God had staged not far into his future.

> *The angel of the LORD appeared to her and said, "You are sterile and childless, but you are going to conceive and have a son. Now see to it that you drink no wine or other fermented drink and that you do not eat anything unclean, because you will conceive and give birth to a son. No razor may be used on his head, because the boy is to be a Nazirite, set apart to God from birth, and he will begin the deliverance of Israel from the hands of the Philistines."*
> —Judges 13:3-5 (emphasis added)

As a direct result of this very direct intervention of Jesus as *the angel of the Lord*, Manoah in fact repeatedly acts in faith. His persistence in the path of righteousness seems to be in direct response to this physical and obviously impressive visitation by the Son of God. Manoah even asks the Lord to once again send the *"man of God"* to teach them how to raise the child.

> *Then Manoah prayed to the LORD: "O Lord, I beg you, let the man of God you sent to us come again to teach us how to bring up the boy who is to be born."*

—Judges 13:8

Manoah also responds in faith to the proclamation that his childless wife would conceive and give birth. He assumes that God will do exactly what He has stated He will do—for he knew this was God he was speaking to—and very specifically uses the word *"when,"* not "if," when referring to the birth of the child.

> *So Manoah asked him, "<u>When</u> your words are fulfilled, what is to be the rule for the boy's life and work?"*
>
> —Judges 13:12 (emphasis added)

This full faith commitment of Manoah and his wife to raise Samson as a Nazirite leads to the initiation of the confrontation of their Philistine oppressors. God's plan of rescue is once again set into motion with Jesus in full command and leading the way.

> *The woman gave birth to a boy and named him Samson. He grew and the LORD blessed him, and the Spirit of the LORD began to stir him while he was in Mahaneh Dan, between Zorah and Eshtaol.*
>
> —Judges 13:24-25

Chapter 12

The Hornet
A Weapon in the Hand of the Mighty God

Jerusalem, Hebron, Jarmuth, Lachish, Eglon. These were the darkest of days in the five principal cities of the Amorite tribes. A feeling of doom had slowly settled in the hearts of every man, every woman, and every child. It had started at the top. The kings knew first. They had attributed the uneasy feeling that enveloped them when they first heard of the destruction of the Egyptian charioteers in the Red Sea to indigestion, to the meal they had eaten hours before. After all, this fanciful story was exactly that, a fanciful story. There was no factual substantiation. There were no surviving eyewitnesses—for sure. Surely it had not happened the way they had described. And besides, where had the Israelites been for the forty years since then?

Similarly, the destruction of the two mighty warrior kings east of the Jordan had seemed all too easy. Their armies had been mighty and well trained in modern war. Surely this had not really happened the way they described. And Jericho—surely the walls had not collapsed with merely a shout.

The feeling of dread had started with the kings of Jerusalem, Hebron, Jarmuth, Lachish, Eglon. The change in their demeanor had been obvious to all. And then the rumors began, "What do the kings know that we do not?" Slowly a cold feeling had fallen upon them all. It was as if a *terror*—a great dark and unknown threat—loomed ominously nearby. The feeling was of cold, dark, gloom, and death. It was unlike anything that any of them had ever experienced before. Maybe the rumors of the mighty, invisible Israelite warrior God were true.

To the man, the Amorites had a very bad feeling about all of this. This feeling was something more than a thought process. It was intangible—and yet palpable. It was illogical, emotional, and very dark. They knew. Somehow they just knew. Their future was not in their hands. A mighty warrior went before the Israelites into battle...and now he was coming for them.

Is there any nastier character in the animal kingdom than the hornet? Can there be any creature on earth that more embodies the military mind than the hornet? Can there be any living thing that is more single-minded in attack? The hornet is weaponry, pure weaponry. We aren't talking insects with nice names like butterflies or caterpillars. We aren't even talking honeybees or bumblebees here. It's name strikes fear into even the most stouthearted among us. The hornet is pure weaponry. The hornet is a Delta Force warrior on steroids. The hornet is an Army Ranger with an attitude. The hornet is a Navy SEAL who doesn't like the way you comb your hair.

A hornet cannot help its nature. It cannot be anything but absolutely obedient to its nature. It is a pinnacle of purpose in God's magnificent creation. It is an air-mobile weapons platform of the finest kind. In its attack mode, it is designed for one purpose. It is single-minded in this purpose. In this respect, it is much like the U.S. air force A-10 Warthog attack aircraft. The A-10 is a mobile air platform for the most powerful rapid-fire Gatling gun ever made. The sole purpose of the airframe is to serve that gun. Its sole purpose is to air carry that gun rapidly into battle and to deploy its firepower in an accurate and effective manner. To this end, the entire aircraft was built around that gun. It is a pure air-mobile fighting machine.

The hornet is similar. When in the attack mode its entire body—its entire being— becomes subservient to the stinger. Its stinger is like the Gatling gun on the A-10. When threatened, the deployment of this very effective weapon becomes the entire purpose for the rest of the body. The rest of the body serves the purpose of the stinger. The hornet's brain becomes an attack command center. It integrates all of the battle information uploaded from all of the hornet's sensors. The eyes supply the bulk of the sensor data, although the pheromone detection sensors, which search the air for important "attack" pheromones, are also critical. The brain processes all of this sensory information and automatically formulates a direct plan of attack that will allow it to most effectively deploy its firepower toward the only acceptable outcome: the utter destruction of the detected enemy. The pinnacle purpose of the circulatory, respiratory, neuromuscular, and all other hornet systems is to support the stinger toward this directed application.

All of the hornet's bodily systems combine with its ferocious resolve in what can only be described as a furious and relentless attack against the unfortunate individual or group that has earned *target* designation. There is no emotion. It is pure business. It is pure fury. It is pure war. The hornet simply applies every capability that it has, with all of the strength it can muster, as quickly and efficiently as possible in the fanatical delivery of its powerful weapon.

Where are we going with all this? The analogy is simple and straightforward. Of all of the different terms that are used in the Old Testament to describe the embodied Son of God in His very special role as a warrior Commander, *"the Hornet"* (Exodus 23:28) demands special attention. In fact, this is such an intense analogy that it makes one wonder. It is almost as if God created hornets in the first place for the sole purpose of supplying an appropriate analogy to illustrate the intensity of Jesus in the pursuit of the will of the Father.

Can you for even a moment doubt the resolve of God's *hornet* on a military mission? Is there any human being on earth who would not flinch at the mere thought of the furious attack from what must be a terrifying, unrelenting, single-minded war machine? How perfect is this very carefully selected terminology in its description of the Warrior of warriors, the Commander of the most elite army that has ever existed? He protects the remnant of the nation of Israel like a hornet protects its queen: unrelenting, unstoppable, unquenchable in His willingness to use every capability that is at His disposal—including a willingness to die—in defense of the cause to which He, in obedience to the Father, is dedicated.

We are first introduced to *"the hornet"* in the books of Exodus and Deuteronomy.

> *"I will send <u>my terror</u> ahead of you and throw into confusion every nation you encounter. I will make all your enemies turn their backs and run. I will send <u>the hornet</u> ahead of you to drive the Hivites, Canaanites and Hittites out of your way."*
>
> —Exodus 23:27-28 (emphasis added)

> *Moreover, the LORD your God will send <u>the hornet</u> among them until even the survivors who hide from you have perished. Do not be terrified by them, for the LORD your God, <u>who is among you</u>, is a great and awesome God.*
>
> —Deuteronomy 7:20-21 (emphasis added)

The identity of this hornet is made clear in Holy Scripture. This hornet is the very same angel of the Lord who accompanied the Israelites in their travel to and conquest of the Promised Land. The identity of the hornet is made clear by the fact that the Exodus reference falls at the end of this revealing passage on this very special warrior:

> *"See, I am sending an angel ahead of you to guard you along the way and to bring you to the place I have prepared. Pay attention to him*

and listen to what he says. Do not rebel against him; he will not forgive your rebellion, since my Name is in him. If you listen carefully to what he says and do all that I say, I will be an enemy to your enemies and will oppose those who oppose you. My angel will go ahead of you and bring you into the land of the Amorites, Hittites, Perizzites, Canaanites, Hivites and Jebusites, and I will wipe them out.

—Exodus 23:20-23 (emphasis added)

God refers to him as *"my angel."* Most amazingly, God states that *"my Name is in him"* in reference to this very special warrior angel, this hornet. The words are obviously very carefully chosen. The Lord states that the Israelites must listen to *"what he says and do all that I say."* This angel speaks as the Lord Himself and the Lord's *"Name is in him"* because He is indeed the Lord Jesus Christ.

Jesus, the angel of the Lord, is God's hornet.

The description of this individual that God is going to send ahead of the Israelites as *"the hornet"* has fascinated me from the very first time that I read it. Ounce for ounce there probably is not a nastier fellow to deal with in the whole of the animal kingdom than a hornet—and this description in the Holy Scriptures is of *God's* hornet. We in fact are further assured in the first sentence from the passage from Exodus above that the hornet does indeed represent the *embodiment* of God's terror.

This is scary stuff. Can you imagine the intensity of the terror that is represented by what God refers to as *"my terror"*? The fact that the word *"my"* precedes the word *"terror"* suggests that this Person, this angel, this *"hornet"* represents the focal point of God's wrath in this world. This warrior angel is God's *"presence"* (Exodus 33:14-15) who will go before them in their travel to, and conquest of, the land.

In all their distress he too was distressed, and the angel of his presence saved them. In his love and mercy he redeemed them; he lifted them up and carried them all the days of old.

—Isaiah 63:9 (emphasis added)

Could there be any other person in the known universe who would fit the billing of *"the angel of [God's] presence"* other than Jesus Christ? Could there be any other person—man or angel—who *could* be God's most lethal weapon of His wrath, the hornet, other than Jesus Christ? We must understand that this designation as God's hornet is the most intense of *military* terminology. God is describing a weapon. He is describing a warrior.

The fact that God chooses to personify, to embody His terror in the warrior that He equates with the nastiest of his creatures—the hornet—leaves little doubt to His intent in His directed use of this very special individual. From both of the descriptions given above, it is clear that as God's very special weapon, this warrior packs a powerful punch. This solitary warrior—for the word hornet is singular, not plural—will single-handedly act as the intermediary, the interface between the two worlds—both of whom are at war. He is the embodied power of the Mighty God who will go before the Israelites and drive out the powerful warrior peoples who occupy the Promised Land. There is only one logical conclusion regarding the identity of the hornet. No other warrior angel could ever upstage Jesus in this regard. This hornet character was the Warrior of warriors. How could it be anyone other than Jesus?

Our suspicions are quite amazingly and definitively confirmed in the final of three descriptions of this hornet that are found in the book of Joshua. Once again, the very specific wording is critical in revealing the identity of the hornet, for the passage clearly tells us that it was indeed, the hornet that went ahead of the Israelites in the battle for Jericho.

> *"'Then you crossed the Jordan and came to Jericho. The citizens of Jericho fought against you, as did also the Amorites, Perizzites, Canaanites, Hittites, Girgashites, Hivites and Jebusites, but I gave them into your hands. I sent the hornet ahead of you, which drove them out before you—also the two Amorite kings. You did not do it with your own sword and bow.'"*
> —Joshua 24: 11-12 (emphasis added)

The information in this passage, combined with the previously discussed revelation that it was in fact Jesus who was the Commander of the army of the Lord at Jericho (and who confronted Joshua before the battle), gives us the confirmation that we seek. Once again, the clues are found in the very clear and precise wording of the text of the Bible. The message these clues tell us is uncontested. This hornet is the incarnate Son of the Living God, Jesus. This Warrior of warriors who goes before the Israelites into the most frightful of battles against the most intimidating of enemies is no one less than Jesus Christ. Our thesis that Jesus was physically, directly involved in all of the critical events described in the Old Testament is strongly confirmed by this revelation. That this involvement was as a most holy warrior is amazingly and delightfully confirmed.

Chapter 13

Jesus As a Warrior
The Uncompromised Truth

Jericho was a pile of smoldering rubble. The warriors sat exhausted—and yet victorious—upon the massive stones that had once formed the walls that reached to the sky. The city walls had been so intimidating. This city was like nothing they had ever encountered. How could they possibly be standing there in conquest the very same day that they had attacked? Walled cities like this were conquered only by years of siege. Their siege—if you could even call it that—had only lasted seven days. How had the entire city been reduced to rubble in a single morning?

The warriors could agree upon no rational explanation. Instead they had only the reality of the fact that their leader, Joshua, had encountered a mighty warrior who had given them a battle plan...and it had worked.

The LORD is a warrior; the LORD is his name.

—Exodus 15:3

The Promised Land at last. In obedience to the Lord's command, the nation of Israel had finally crossed the Jordan River. Then something amazing happened at Jericho. One of God's promises to Moses—a mysterious and seemingly inconsequential promise—had been dramatically and undeniably fulfilled before their eyes. The Israelites at first had not known what to make of this promise. It spoke vaguely of an unfamiliar military presence.

> *"I will send my terror ahead of you and throw into confusion every nation you encounter. I will make all your enemies turn their backs and run. I will send the hornet ahead of you to drive the Hivites, Canaanites and Hittites out of your way.*

—Exodus 23:27-28

The meaning of this promise was so much clearer following their attack on Jericho. This was God's promise of a great warrior who would fight on behalf of the Israelites. This great warrior, God's very own *"terror,"* God's *"hornet,"* would go before them into the Promised Land. This inestimable force, this unknowable weapon in the hands of God, would literally *"drive"* their enemies out of the land before them.

This promise now held new hope for the Israelites as they faced a daunting military campaign in the conquest of the rest of Canaan. For even though they still had to storm Jericho after the towering wall had collapsed, every Israelite knew that *someone* had gone before them in this first battle against the great walled cities of the Promised Land. They had first sensed this divine presence east of the Jordan. The ease of the victories over Sihon, king of the Amorites, and Og, king of Bashan had not gone unnoticed. Now, however, the sudden collapse of the wall of Jericho—precisely as predicted—had been nothing less than miraculous and supplied indisputable proof that God had sent a supernatural warrior into the battle before them.

The Israelites knew the identity of this mysterious military force. This terror of God was in fact the same shadowy figure Joshua had encountered before the battle. To those who did not recognize that the enigmatic figure who confronted Joshua with sword in hand was one in the same with this *"hornet,"* the Lord would later tell Joshua precisely this.

> *"'Then you crossed the Jordan and came to Jericho. The citizens of Jericho fought against you, as did also the Amorites, Perizzites, Canaanites, Hittites, Girgashites, Hivites and Jebusites, but I gave them into your hands. I sent the hornet ahead of you, which drove them out before you—also the two Amorite kings. You did not do it with your own sword and bow.*
>
> —Joshua 24:12 (emphasis added)

In this first battle west of the Jordan, the Israelites correctly made the crucial first step of faith. As a result, God's hornet went before them in battle. The Israelites knew they would have to repeat this step many times, for there would be many more great battles ahead of them. The nations who had claimed this land as their home for countless generations would certainly not give it up without a fight. Obviously, the presence of this hornet would therefore be critical to the military success that was necessary to claim the Promised Land.

The identification of Jesus in His role as God's hornet obviously elevates our discussion of His Old Testament warrior attributes to a whole new level. One might argue that up to this point we have been approaching His warrior status with a half-hearted commitment. Our hearts tell us we can go further. A wholehearted commitment to the *whole* truth that is revealed in Holy Scripture is the only thing that will sate our hunger for knowledge of Jesus. In this regard, the hypothesis of this chapter can be boldly revealed right from the beginning.

> *In regard to the warrior attributes that are used to describe Jesus in the Old Testament, the evidence demands that we think nothing less than spectacularly.*

There is, after all, nothing boring, ordinary, or passive about Jesus. He is God. That says it all. Everything about Him must be infinite in its perfection. He has never been some seeker of the passive mainstream or the comfortable middle of the road.

To the contrary, Jesus is the *extreme* of all things.

He is perfect and everything in all things. Everything about Him very literally abhors the lukewarm backwash of the middle ground that *we* so often seek. He has never settled for the ordinary. Instead, Jesus is the most compassionate, the perfection of mercy, and the ultimate expression of God's love. As we have described, even his humility is taken to extremes. In fact, it is precisely in the infinite depth of His humility that the ultimate height of His power and righteousness is revealed.

And yet when we think of the more aggressive aspects of the attributes of Jesus that are unmistakably revealed in the Old Testament, we invariably shy away. These attributes are no less deserving of the application of our most extreme adjectives. After all, none of the attributes of Jesus are less important than the others. In regard to His warrior attributes, therefore, He similarly embodies the most ferocious warrior, the extreme perfection of battlefield command, and the ultimate demonstration of God's wrath. In the search for truth, we cannot let our personal feelings keep us from knowing the fullness of the nature of this Warrior of God. We cannot rewrite the Word of God with our comfort in mind.

Certainly one of the focal points—if not *the* focal point—of this book must be our emphasis upon Jesus as the very center—the heart—of all creation. He is at the very center of not only every object that has been created, but also every moment of time into which those objects of creation have been submerged. He simply cannot be anything less. The facts remain that Jesus is the centerpiece of our very existence and He is that which He simply must be—spectacular in every respect.

Surely there can be no doubt that the greatest, the most extreme adjectives and adverbs ever uttered by mankind were indeed created to describe Jesus and His thoughts, words, and actions. The fact that they have been hijacked by mankind to describe that which is relegated to the merely mundane in the presence of Jesus, should not lead us to believe that a single thing, person, thought, action, or name has ever risen — or ever will in any way rise — above Jesus.

The facts therefore remain perfectly clear. As the infinitely perfect Son of God and the focal point of the universe, it is simply not in the character of Jesus to do anything halfheartedly. So, when we begin to speak boldly of Jesus as the most lethal and intense weapon in God's mighty Old Testament arsenal it is precisely because He can't be anything less. When we discuss the scriptural evidence describing the very palpable role our Savior played in the activities of the Old Testament, the fact that He indeed comes across as an almighty version of a Navy SEAL or Army Ranger is, once again, because He can't be anything less. He is God. Everything He does must express the perfection of God. In fact, I believe that the reason that Army Rangers and Navy SEALs hold such an attraction to most of us — at least the men among us — is specifically because of their similarity to our warrior King.

Further still, we should not feel as if we are totally outlandish in our consideration of the Old Testament role of Jesus as God's most lethal Warrior. In doing so, we are only placing Jesus in precisely the role that we are told He will assume in its fullness in the end-times. In both His Old Testament and end-times roles He is the same: *the* instrument of God's wrath and vengeance upon those who persist in defiant rebellion against the righteous Holiness of God.

> *I saw the Lord standing by the altar, and he said: "Strike the tops of the pillars so that the thresholds shake. Bring them down on the heads of all the people; those who are left I will kill with the sword. Not one will get away, none will escape.*
>
> *Though they hide themselves on the top of Carmel, there I will hunt them down and seize them.*
>
> *Though they are driven into exile by their enemies, there I will command the sword to slay them. I will fix my eyes upon them for evil and not for good."*
>
> —Amos 9:1, 3a, 4 (emphasis added)

As a weapon in the Father's hand, Jesus cannot be anything less than the most extreme of warriors. If truth be told, it is almost as if God has given us the modern day Navy SEAL and Army Ranger—just as He gave the Israelites their *"mighty men"* (2Samuel 23:8)—to demonstrate the extreme warriors whom Jesus must, by definition, *surpass* in His role as a warrior. How truly awesome Jesus must have been in the midst of both the overt and covert wars of the Old Testament times. How truly awesome He will be as God's righteous Avenger of blood on the most holy *day of the Lord*.

For many of us, this perspective of Jesus poses a serious problem. How can we so readily ascribe such a violent prequel to the role Jesus played during His 33 years as the humble Lamb of God, as the very embodiment of perfect meekness? After all, this Old Testament penchant toward warfare hardly fits the singular person in all of human history that most espoused extreme love and humble servanthood as the only solution to very literally any conflict.

Indeed, most of us have known the very personal mercy of our Savior in our own salvation. The Gospel narratives, the Psalms, and all of the New Testament letters assure us that Jesus is the very focal point and fullest expression of God's very personal *love* for each one of us. In Jesus we have known the embodiment of the incredible compassion and mercy of the Living God. In His example, as fully portrayed in the Gospel accounts of His life on earth, we have seen nothing less than the most extreme example of humility, meekness, and self-sacrifice. We can't help but praise God for all of these attributes that we can personally know and experience in every step of our daily walk with our Savior.

And yet we are also told that a certain day will come when the time for accepting God's free-flowing mercy will most assuredly end.

> *Seek the LORD while he may be found; call on him while he is near.*
>
> —Isaiah 55:6

In the end-times, Holy Scripture clearly tells us that Messiah Jesus will demonstrate attributes that modern day Christians may at the moment fearfully shy away from rightfully ascribing to Him. Even Jesus Himself tells us precisely this when He directly quotes the prophet Isaiah.

> *"Here is my servant whom I have chosen, the one I love, in whom I delight; I will put my Spirit on him, and he will proclaim justice to the nations. He will not quarrel or cry out; no one will hear his voice in*

the streets. A bruised reed he will not break, and a smoldering wick
he will not snuff out, <u>till he leads justice to victory</u>. In his name the
nations will put their hope."

—Matthew 12:18-21 (emphasis added)

Jesus wanted us to know that even though His New Testament presence was
hallmarked by a truly extraordinary degree of humble meekness, there would come
a day when His meekness would be put aside and the necessity of His warrior
attributes would be apparent to all as He rights every wrong by leading *"justice to*
victory."

But the focal point of this book remains our contention that those attributes are not
just about the future. They have in fact already been ascribed to Jesus throughout
the pages of the Old Testament where long years of warfare surrounding the nation
of Israel are documented. In fact, if our hypothesis is correct, the whole of the role
of Jesus in the times of the Old Testament was as a warrior engulfed in a great war.
If He truly is *the angel of the Lord* who is described as appearing mightily in battle
throughout the Old Testament, then He has in fact *already* struck many, many
times with elements of the wrath that is described in the prophetic end-times
scriptures. His warrior attributes do not just embody his end-times future; they
also embodied His Old Testament past.

The writings of the prophet Zechariah in fact tell us nothing less than precisely
this. In the midst of Zechariah's prophetic description of the manner in which the
Messiah will fight in the end-times we are also told—*in present tense*—that he is
already fighting that way in Israel's current *"day of battle."*

I will gather all the nations to Jerusalem to fight against it; the city
will be captured, the houses ransacked, and the women raped. Half of
the city will go into exile, but the rest of the people will not be taken
from the city. <u>Then</u> the LORD will go out and fight against those
nations, <u>as he fights in the day of battle</u>.

On that day his feet will stand on the Mount of Olives, east of
Jerusalem, and the Mount of Olives will be split in two from east to
west, forming a great valley, with half of the mountain moving north
and half moving south.

—Zechariah 14:2-4 (emphasis added)

This passage is most often interpreted as a clear description of the return of Jesus, who is described as standing triumphantly on the Mount of Olives. And yet it is also Messiah Jesus who is described by Zechariah as fighting in the *present* tense, *"in the day of battle."* It is hard for most of us to easily accept that *"the Lamb of God"* (John 1:29) could display such a warrior mentality. Our feelings in this regard aside, however, the Word of God is not subtle in describing these attributes. Despite the fact that this moves many of us outside of our comfort zones and may not fit well with our Sunday-school image of Jesus, we are not empowered to rewrite the truth that is found in the words of Holy Scripture.

Indeed, Jeremiah in Lamentations tells God, *"You have covered yourself with anger and pursued us; you have slain without pity"* (Lamentations 3:43). The detail of the description of God as a warrior leaves little doubt that the proper interpretation of these passages is very literal indeed. The prophet Isaiah is also detailed, specific, and graphic in a description of God's wrath that is most commonly attributed to Messiah Jesus:

> *Who is this coming from Edom, from Bozrah, with his garments stained crimson? Who is this, robed in splendor, striding forward in the greatness of his strength?*
>
> *"It is I, speaking in righteousness, mighty to save."*
>
> *Why are your garments red, like those of one treading the winepress?*
>
> *"I have trodden the winepress alone; from the nations no one was with me. I trampled them in my anger and trod them down in my wrath; their blood spattered my garments, and I stained all my clothing. For the day of vengeance was in my heart, and the year of my redemption has come. I looked, but there was no one to help, I was appalled that no one gave support; so my own arm worked salvation for me, and my own wrath sustained me. I trampled the nations in my anger; in my wrath I made them drunk and poured their blood on the ground."*
>
> —Isaiah 63:1-6 (emphasis added)

Job also knew Jesus as a warrior. The extraordinary degree of detail in his description of God as a warrior suggests that Job was not just waxing allegorical. Just as Job had foreknowledge of the gospel of Jesus Christ, so also did Job know the physical assault of God in a very palpable and personal manner. He knew God as a very real warrior.

> *All was well with me, but he shattered me; he seized me by the neck and crushed me. He has made me his target; his archers surround me. Without pity, he pierces my kidneys and spills my gall on the ground. Again and again he bursts upon me; he rushes at me like a warrior.*

—Job 16:12-14 (emphasis added)

Elsewhere, Isaiah's description of the Messiah's role as a warrior in the end-times battles is also vivid and specific.

> *The LORD will march out like a mighty man, like a warrior he will stir up his zeal; with a shout he will raise the battle cry and will triumph over his enemies.*

—Isaiah 42:13 (emphasis added)

Isaiah is not just speaking in lyrical metaphors. How easily we rush right past this description of the Lord as a *"mighty man."* We look at the adjective and we say, "Yes, of course, God is 'mighty.'" But Isaiah is telling us so much more in this passage. The use of the phrase *"mighty man"* is in fact a very specific and directed description. First of all, it relates this warrior description not just to God, but also very specifically to Jesus. This is *a man* that Isaiah is describing. This is Jesus, fully God and fully man.

Moreover, this phrase *"mighty man"* relates specifically to the Old Testament scriptures that describe a very special group of men. These powerful warriors were King David's *"mighty men."* There is nothing allegorical, and certainly nothing ordinary, about them. They were indeed a very special group of men who gathered around David during the early intense period of warfare that set the tone for the remainder of David's reign over Israel.

These were men who, like Eleazar son of Dodai the Ahohite, fought until their hand *"froze to the sword"* (2Samuel 23:10) as they slew countless numbers of Israel's enemies. They performed miraculously in the defense of Israel, like Josheb-basshebeth, a Tahkemonite, who *"raised his spear against eight hundred men, whom he killed in one encounter"* (2Samuel 23:8). These *really* were mighty men. Surely they were like Navy SEALs and Army Rangers—and yet they were even more. They were the Old Testament equivalent of the elite of the very elite combat soldiers. Indeed, David's Mighty Men were not just like Navy SEALs or US Army Rangers; they were like Navy SEALs or US Army Rangers who had won the "Medal of Honor." They were truly extraordinary warriors. But even they were not enough to even compare with Jesus, for we can know that He unquestionably exceeds them all. Truly the word *hyperbole* can never apply to our description of this Warrior of warriors, Jesus.

Therefore, like it or not, there is another side to the compassionate and loving Savior we have come to know from the Gospel narratives. From the same source of the dazzling degrees of extreme perfection in love, mercy and compassion, also comes the awful, terrifying extreme of perfect judgment and wrath for all who stand rebelliously defiant to the holiness and sovereign dominion of the Mighty God. From the moment of our acceptance of all aspects of the multifaceted role of Jesus, explaining the graphic Old Testament battle accounts of this enigmatic Warrior becomes much easier. Truly, the Old Testament prophets are not subtle in their descriptions of the unrelenting wrath of the coming Messiah.

The Old Testament prophets assure us that we are going to see this warrior side of Jesus again—soon. Although that side of Him was clothed in love and compassion during His 33 year ministry, we have been assured that His justice, judgment, and wrath will appear in the end-times just as they did during the Old Testament. It can be no coincidence that the fiery Warrior depicted throughout the multi-prophet visionary Old Testament descriptions of Jesus so closely resembles the Apostle John's descriptions of Jesus during His transfiguration and in the end-times description in the book of Revelation. They are describing one in the same Person.

The assumption of the presence and direct participation of Jesus in the day-to-day activities described in the Old Testament make it fundamentally important for us to know the details of this very important setting, this Holy landscape in which the story of the Warrior Jesus unfolds. After all, the Old Testament is what it is. It describes a time of war. The tapestry, the very fabric of the Old Testament, embodies a warrior in the middle of a great war. It documents a period of nearly continuous conflict. There is hardly a book in the Old Testament that doesn't, in one way or another, describe some sort of conflict between the nation of Israel and its neighbors. Literally every patriarch was involved in battle at least sometime in his life. The Exodus was all about war. The conquest of the Promised Land was pure war. The times of the Judges were all about battle after repeated battle. The times of the kings of Israel are embodied by war stories describing tumultuous battle for literally every king—even including King Solomon. The facts are clear; the central theme of the Old Testament is *war*.

A textual word analysis of the books of the Old Testament adds fuel to this fire. The facts speak for themselves. The word *battle,* for instance, is used in 194 verses in the Old Testament (NIV) and in only 7 in the New—with 4 of those 7 being in the book of Revelation. The word *war* itself is used in 123 verses in the Old Testament (NIV) and only in 11 in the New—with 7 of those 11 being in the book of Revelation. The word *fight* is used in 99 verses in the Old Testament (NIV) and in only 8 in the New. The word *sword* is used in over 400 verses in the Bible (NIV) with only 29 of those being found in the New Testament. It is hard to deny it—the Old Testament is a war story.

We therefore really shouldn't be surprised when we begin to unravel the amazing clues about the role of our Savior in the events of the Old Testament. The Old Testament authors described a time of war during which Jesus had the premier role—just as He must have the premier role in all aspects of all of human history. If He is to have the premier role in a time of war, it is only logical that He be a warrior. We have already established that nearly every single word, let alone chapter and book, of the Old Testament is about one single person, Jesus Christ. The major player is Jesus and the setting is battle: Jesus must be a warrior.

We can be assured that none of this is by random happenstance. The setting that we find ourselves engulfed in when we read the Old Testament has been purposely chosen in the fullness of the wisdom of God, solely for the will and purpose of God. Indeed, we read the Holy Scriptures—yes, even the Old Testament—for only one reason: to know Jesus. Holy Scripture is, at its very foundation, the full revelation of the only Person who really matters. And, for some reason, the Story Teller of the Old Testament—the Holy Spirit—has very specifically chosen the battlefield as the setting and warfare as the medium to tell us all about Jesus.

> *My shield is God Most High, who saves the upright in heart. God is a righteous judge, a God who expresses his wrath every day. If he does not relent, he will sharpen his sword; he will bend and string his bow. He has prepared his deadly weapons; he makes ready his flaming arrows.*

—Psalm 7:10-13

This setting and this medium were not just chosen for dramatic license. They were chosen as the modality of presentation for a very special and specific reason. That reason must be that *the attributes of Jesus that we are to know are best illuminated in this manner.* The Old Testament is about war because it is in the setting of war that these *other* attributes of Jesus are best illustrated. Knowing Jesus in the fullness of all of His holy attributes is the whole purpose of Holy Scripture and very literally the whole of our existence. Holy Scripture is perfect. There are no errors. It could not have been written for this purpose of the full revelation of Jesus—the purpose for which it was written—in a better manner.

And so, we circle back to the purpose of our quest. We happen again upon the reason for this book, this discussion. We seek the revelation of the full nature of Jesus that is unveiled by the evidence that is abundantly sprinkled throughout the Old Testament. And, that which becomes readily apparent—and which is of no surprise—is the fact that the singular mission of the ultimate Warrior of God, in the Old Testament and New, is *the will of the Father*. And for His good pleasure, the Father decided that *the* very instrument of His will in the Old Testament would in fact be His Son Jesus. Rather than just directly implementing His divine will—just *speaking* it into existence—Almighty God chose to implement it through His physical and very special personal interface with mankind.

> *Who is this King of glory? The* LORD *strong and mighty, the* LORD *mighty in battle.*
>
> —Psalm 24:8

Chapter 14

Jesus, Warrior Commander on a Mission
What Were the Strategic Orders for the Commander of the Army of the Lord?

A brotherhood of warriors molded into a fighting force; their leader, a warrior Commander of warriors. Fully trained, fully equipped, fully enabled for the task at hand. But what was the task at hand? What was the mission? What was the battle plan? What was the ultimate strategic goal behind the battle plan? What were the tactical orders to implement the battle plan? If all of this is for real, the answers to these questions are vital to a complete understanding of the role of the Commander of the army of the Lord.

A warrior's work, after all, becomes most critical when they are on a mission of one sort or another. Once given their orders, real warriors then live only for the mission that is defined by those orders. This is where they use the skills with which they have been gifted. As warriors, the completion of that mission becomes all encompassing in their life. That mission, at that moment, becomes the defining reason for their existence.

A warrior on a mission takes his tactical battle commands from someone in authority over him. Such is the case for the Warrior of all warriors. The military directive, the *orders*, the *strategic* battle plan entrusted to the Son of God by His Father is essential to understanding the motivation behind every move of the army of the Lord and its warrior Commander. An overall battle directive that perfectly and yet succinctly describes the strategic directive of the Son of God during the Old Testament is critical to understanding the many different scenarios in which the warrior Jesus is encountered.

Not surprisingly, therefore, the Father Himself supplied the concisely written directive for Jesus and the army of the Lord. This literal command directive regarding the specific role Jesus was to play in the great war that encompassed the Old Testament is faithfully recorded in the Bible. The unique aspect of this directive is that it supplies—in the span of a mere two verses from the book of Isaiah—not only the Old Testament directive, but also the ultimate plan that would see its complete fulfillment described only in the New Testament gospels and end times prophecies. As such, this is one of the most important passages in the Bible. It explains, summarizes, and concisely codifies the strategic directive given to Jesus by His Father. Its explanation of the activities of Jesus Christ during the time of the Old Testament is all-encompassing.

And now the LORD says—he who formed me in the womb to be his servant to bring Jacob back to him and gather Israel to himself, for I am honored in the eyes of the LORD and my God has been my strength—he says: "It is too small a thing for you to be my servant to restore the tribes of Jacob and bring back those of Israel I have kept. I will also make you a light for the Gentiles, that you may bring my salvation to the ends of the earth."

—Isaiah 49:5-6 (emphasis added)

With the precision that is known only by the all-wise God, we are given—in a mere 15 words—a precise description of the sole Old Testament assignment of the warrior Commander Jesus. In these 15 words is found a precise directive. It concisely reveals the mind and will of God. It reveals the directive that is behind very literally every activity of Jesus in the Old Testament. It explains everything, from the many military missions to the ultimate rescue of the patriarch bloodline. It even explains the need for the Shekinah Glory to leave the temple during the Babylonian captivity—to pick up and move the whole military command center of the army of the Lord to Babylon—all to guard the remnant of Israel. And in this rescue trail is seen the confirmation of the precisely stated mission—specifically not to guard and preserve all of the nation of Israel, but just the remnant chosen by God before time began.

Before entering into a discussion of the implications of this mission statement *to guard and preserve—to redeem—the remnant of Israel*, the precise identity of that remnant must be defined. This remnant is described in many different scriptural passages. Perhaps the most concise and defining passage is found in the book of Zephaniah.

"On that day you will not be put to shame for all the wrongs you have done to me, because I will remove from this city those who rejoice in their pride. Never again will you be haughty on my holy hill. But I will leave within you the meek and humble, who trust in the name of the LORD. The remnant of Israel will do no wrong; they will speak no

*lies, nor will deceit be found in their mouths. They will eat and lie
down and no one will make them afraid."*

—Zephaniah 3:11-13 (emphasis added)

Indeed the Israelites who make up the remnant of Israel are a very select group of
individuals. They are those who call upon and trust in the name of the Lord. They
are the *saved* of the nation of Israel. In exactly this, they have become the focus of
the efforts of Jesus. They are the trust, the protectorate of Jesus, *the angel of the
Lord*, the Commander of the army of the Lord.

The more that the history of the nation of Israel is reviewed, the more this
summary statement of the mission of the Commander of the army of the Lord is
revealed as both critical and foundational. The perspective provided by this
mission statement illuminates and helps explain the activities of the nation of
Israel—as well as the activities of the army of the Lord that were occurring behind
the scenes.

*The LORD will rise up as he did at Mount Perazim, he will rouse
himself as in the Valley of Gibeon—to do his work, his strange work,
and perform his task, his alien task.*

—Isaiah 28:21 (emphasis added)

The thread of the mission statement of *the angel of the Lord* winds itself through
many prophets and many passages. Once we have been made aware of this
summary statement, its presence is readily identified repeatedly throughout Old
Testament scripture. Over and over again, the point of this mission is driven home
in bold and illustrative statements such as that found in Isaiah 46.

*"Listen to me, O house of Jacob, all you who remain of the house of
Israel, you whom I have upheld since you were conceived, and have
carried since your birth. Even to your old age and gray hairs I am he,
I am he who will sustain you. I have made you and I will carry you; I
will sustain you and I will rescue you.*

—Isaiah 46:3-4 (emphasis added)

All of the Old Testament thoughts, words, and physical activities of *the angel of
the Lord*, *the Prince of princes*, *the Prince of the host*—Jesus Christ—had behind
them, in one manner or another, the very specific command *to guard and preserve
the remnant of Israel*. As the Holy Spirit unveils even more of the evidence of the
activities of Jesus—from the wooing of the Patriarchs to their ultimate destiny, to

the rescue of the fledgling nation from Egypt, the preservation in the desert, the conquering of the land, the rescue from their warring neighbors, the discipline of the wrath poured out on them by their Assyrian and Babylonian conquerors, and their final redemption from the Babylonian captivity—the ultimate motivation behind it all is the command to preserve that remnant of Israel that God has reserved for Himself.

> *In that day—"Sing about a fruitful vineyard: I, the LORD, watch over it; I water it continually. I guard it day and night so that no one may harm it.*
>
> —Isaiah 27:2-3 (emphasis added)

In all of this is the foreshadowing of the ultimate plan of eternal redemption. From the beginning of the Bible to its end, from the beginning of time until Jesus establishes His dominion over the creation, His job is *rescue*. The entirety of His Old Testament military mission is about rescue. From the grand strategic plan to the day-by-day tactical directives, the mission is always rescue—physical, tangible, breathable, hands-on, sword swinging, last minute rescue. In fact, the ultimate Old Testament rescue—of the remnant from Babylon—was undertaken entirely by the incarnate Son of God.

> *Writhe in agony, O Daughter of Zion, like a woman in labor, for now you must leave the city to camp in the open field. You will go to Babylon; there you will be rescued. There the LORD will redeem you out of the hand of your enemies.*
>
> —Micah 4:10

And from these many missions to rescue the remnant of Israel that culminated in the ultimate redemption from Babylon—all of which preserved the line of the Messiah—we see the perfect modeling or *typing* of the miraculous rescue that is behind the redemption of mankind. We must not lose sight of this. All of this— every banner raised, every sword-swinging fight—is about the redemption of the sons and daughters of God who were chosen before time to spend eternity with the Triune Godhead.

The story into which Jesus was immersed in the Old Testament is the same as the story into which we were introduced when we came into this world. This story in which we draw our every daily breath is all about only one thing: the rescue of the remnant, the whole of God's holy remnant. This grander statement is inclusive of the entirety of mankind who will accept the gift of eternal life found only in the shed blood of Jesus Christ. This grander rescue of the eternal sons and daughters of God is foreshadowed by the rescue of the remnant from Babylon. This rescue of all rescues is precisely what the last half of the above passage from the book of Isaiah so eloquently predicts. The Father states outright that the rescue of the remnant of Israel by itself was *"too small a thing."* It was not the whole story. It was merely a foreshadowing, a modeling, a typing of God's ultimate plan, His ultimate rescue.

And this is exactly what is revealed in the last sentence of this precious passage from Isaiah. We are allowed to listen in on perhaps the most magnificent conversation in all of eternity—between the Father and His only Son, Jesus. In this amazing conversation, the Son concedes that He fears that He has in fact failed in regard to saving Israel. The course chosen by the Israelite remnant leads him to state that He has *"labored to no purpose"* and spent His *"strength in vain and for nothing."*

> *Listen to me, you islands; hear this, you distant nations: Before I was born the LORD called me; from my birth he has made mention of my name. He made my mouth like a sharpened sword, in the shadow of his hand he hid me; he made me into a polished arrow and concealed me in his quiver. He said to me, "You are my servant, Israel, in whom I will display my splendor."*
>
> *But I said, "I have labored to no purpose; I have spent my strength in vain and for nothing. Yet what is due me is in the LORD's hand, and my reward is with my God."*

—Isaiah 49:1-4 (emphasis added)

The Father's most sacred response forms the very foundation of our hope and our joy. We are allowed listen in on the response that very literally determines our eternity. The Father reveals the perfection and mastery of the redemption plan—of which Jesus must be the very focal point. Indeed, very literally the whole of the purpose of the creation is revealed in this perfectly mastered summation statement. The Father tells His Son,

> *"I will also make you a light for the Gentiles, that you may bring my salvation to the ends of the earth."*

Isaiah 49:6 (emphasis added)

Can we really understand the fullness of that which took place in this timeless moment in eternity? This conversation between the Father and the Son occurred before a single moment of time had ever elapsed in the magnificence of God's creation.

So do not be ashamed to testify about our Lord, or ashamed of me his prisoner. But join with me in suffering for the gospel, by the power of God, who has saved us and called us to a holy life—not because of anything we have done but because of his own purpose and grace. This grace was given us in Christ Jesus before the beginning of time, but it has now been revealed through the appearing of our Savior, Christ Jesus, who has destroyed death and has brought life and immortality to light through the gospel.

—2Timothy 1:8-10 (emphasis added)

The detailed account of a simple conversation that is rendered so beautifully in Isaiah 49:5-6 describes the very moment that permanently sealed the eternal fates of all who would simply accept the invitation to be rescued by the Rescuer of all rescuers. As such, this passage is the culmination of the revelation of the heart of the Old Testament—as the story of *"the One who was to come"* (Matthew 11:3; Luke 7:19-20)

The true enormity of this statement is revealed in lines that follow later in this very same chapter of Isaiah. The very physical battle that must be enjoined by the Son of God on the behalf of both the remnant of Israel and all of us who would be saved by the shed blood of Jesus is revealed.

Can plunder be taken from warriors, or captives rescued from the fierce?

But this is what the LORD says: "Yes, captives will be taken from warriors, and plunder retrieved from the fierce; I will contend with those who contend with you, and your children I will save.

—Isaiah 49:24-25 (emphasis added)

In these passages God's magnificent redemption plan comes full circle. The prophecy above speaks not just of the rescue of the remnant from Babylon and of the rescue of the remnant of the gentiles on the cross. It also speaks of the end times. It also tells of the rescue of the remnant of the Jewish nation from the hands of the antichrist. In all three stages of this masterful rescue plan, captives—

"plunder" — are *"taken from warriors"* and *"retrieved from the fierce."* Can there be any other better description of our adversary Satan—he who holds us captive—than to refer to him and his minions as *"the fierce"*?

This is the real deal. This is a fight of the first order. This rescue was no sure thing. In fact, in the eyes of the world—and most certainly in the eyes of the otherworld—it had no chance of success. It is a suicide mission that was destined to failure. And yet we are told that by the power of the mighty God, *"Yes, captives will be taken from warriors, and plunder retrieved from the fierce."* This was a vicious, physical struggle. This was the Old Testament rescue of the remnant of Israel. And most gloriously it also tells of the fight of all fights, the rescue of all rescues that was the crucifixion death of Jesus Christ on Calvary—with the ultimate redemption of the eternal lives of *all* of the children of God at stake. Can we ever understand this fight, this rescue? Can we ever hope to know what it means that we are captives *"taken from warriors,"* that we are *"plunder retrieved from the fierce"*?

And all of this—very literally all of it—is based solely on a single event, a single battle. The shedding of the blood of the Lamb on the cross of Calvary was the pinnacle. The rescue of the remnant of Israel from Babylon foreshadowed it and the final scene, the return of the King and the final rescue of the end times Jewish remnant, is the capstone of the entire stunning spectacle of the manifest plan of God's rescue of those who would be sons and daughters of God for eternity. But behind them all is the cross of Christ. The moment of Christ's death on the cross of Calvary remains the singular moment of all history. It is the rescue behind all rescues.

The mission of *"the One,"*—the warrior Prince Jesus—at every scene is the same. Jesus is all about *rescue*. Jesus is all about the rescue of *the remnant*. That is His mission. It has always been His mission. It was His mission in the Old Testament. It was His mission on the cross. It is His mission now in the Body of Christ. It will be His mission on His final return.

> *Rescue—physical, hands-on, swords swinging in the sun, Jesus right in the middle of the fury of the fight—rescue.*

And that is the whole point of this book. God could have just spoken into reality the redemption of the Israelite remnant from Babylon. He could have just spoken our eternal salvation into reality. He could just speak the rescue of the Jewish remnant from the antichrist. God could have done and could do any number of things to make it easy for His Son in any and all of His warrior roles. But Jesus *alone* exists as the only physical link between that which is physical and that which is not. He alone is the impossible link between that which is simply unlinkable— God and humankind. Because of this, the incarnate, fully embodied Jesus had to get in there and actually fight the fight for the rescue of the remnant of Israel—and He had to actually physically die upon the cross the death that was necessary for the salvation of all who would be saved. And He will physically come back—in the overwhelming power of the Father—to pull off the most magnificent of all military missions—rescues—in that day of all days that lies ahead.

It is in the *physically* embodied nature of that role that Jesus is eternally and tangibly linked to all of the redeemed—for as human beings, we have been made into a physical form that is as much a part of us as our spirit. We *are* physical. And it is precisely in the palpable blows of the fight and in the lethal bleeding of the dying on the cross that the link to mankind is *physically* forged for eternity. Through Jesus, through this precise manner of rescue, the finite is linked to the infinite, the created to the uncreated, the temporary to the eternal, and the physical to the spiritual.

> *This is what the* LORD *says: "In the time of my favor I will answer you, and in the day of salvation I will help you; I will keep you and will make you…to say to the captives, 'Come out,' and to those in darkness, 'Be free!'"*

—Isaiah 49:8-9

Chapter 15

From Strategic To Tactical
The Tactical Battle Directive for the Hornet

Establishing the chain of command is the essential first step in the creation of an operational armed force. Its maintenance is critical to the timely and effective function of that military force. Once that chain of command is established, tactical battle directives can be rapidly and accurately delivered from the source to the effectors. The source is the commander in charge. The effectors are the soldiers who implement the tactical battle plans. Jesus, the fiercest warrior among the many fierce warriors in the army of the Lord, emptied and subservient to the will of the Father, received His commands from on high.

Major overarching strategic goals are always set before battle is undertaken. Every warrior—from the field commander to the foot soldier—needs to know why he or she is going into battle. That overall strategic goal, that Old Testament military mission for Jesus, the field Commander of the army of the Lord, was *to guard, preserve, and ultimately redeem the chosen remnant of the nation of Israel.* This singular mission statement is that which is behind all of His Old Testament military activities. It is the grand strategic ideation and motivation behind His every military campaign, behind His every battlefield decision.

With the overall strategic goal in hand, we now seek tactical detail. *Tactical* battle plans translate the grand strategic design into day-to-day battle directives. Once again, we want to know the details. We want to know how the field generals and foot soldiers in the army of the Lord actually carried out the ultimate directive of preserving the remnant of Israel. It is in the implementation of this directive on a day-by-day, battle-by-battle manner that the many rich attributes of this mighty warrior Commander and the army of the Lord are displayed.

One might quite reasonably expect to have to pour endlessly over the scriptures to piece together a complex patchwork tactical command quilt from many different books of the Old Testament. Such truth is often hidden in the many deep layers of the Bible. Some clues are easy to find. Some are incredibly difficult. The moment of a Biblical clue's very special revelation is always exciting. A phrase that may have been read many times suddenly springs to life. It may reveal a tiny next step on the trail of a great quest. It may reveal an answer to a question pondered for quite sometime. It also may catch us completely off guard in the sheer volume and importance of its revelation. It may indeed be one of those moments that are best described as simply exhilarating.

Such is the case with the passage to which we now turn. This passage, a string of three consecutive verses that I had read many times before, finally hit me like a thunderclap. Never would one anticipate the Holy Spirit delivering a lucid, succinct, and concise *job description*—a precise tactical command directive—that was handed to the Son of God, the Commander of the army of the Lord, from His Father. But, there it was:

> *"You are my war club, my weapon for battle—with you I shatter nations, with you I destroy kingdoms, with you I shatter horse and rider, with you I shatter chariot and driver, with you I shatter man and woman, with you I shatter old man and youth, with you I shatter young man and maiden, with you I shatter shepherd and flock, with you I shatter farmer and oxen, with you I shatter governors and officials."*

—Jeremiah 51:20-23

I don't blame myself for missing the importance and true meaning of this passage so many times before. It appears in Jeremiah's prophecy concerning the punishment of Babylon for the destruction that Nebuchadnezzar had mercilessly rained down upon Jerusalem and the Israelites. No doubt that I felt that this description was being applied to Babylon or possibly to Babylon's conquerors, the Medes and Persians. So also would most classic interpretations of this passage hold to that very easy line.

But our eyes have been opened. The unlocking scriptural passages that we have discussed tell us a new story. They open new doors. They give us a new perspective. They spread God's illuminating light into thousands of previously unsearched nooks and crannies.

How do we know that this very special passage is describing Jesus? Let's look at the evidence. First of all, this passage never really seemed to fit. It simply doesn't fit with the rest of the chapter. But of even more importance are the verses that frame this passage. They also do not fit the rest of the chapter. The verses that immediately precede it and that immediately follow it are specifically placed there to draw our attention to the job description. The verses that immediately precede this command directive are like an *off-ramp* that takes the reader temporarily out of the main story to deliver a little side comment. The story suddenly stops in the middle of its long declaration of the inequity of Babylon. Then—without warning—Jeremiah's verses suddenly make a hard left turn and begin to speak of someone different. They make a proclamation instead about *"He who is the Portion of Jacob."* They are obviously no longer speaking about Babylon.

> *"Every man is senseless and without knowledge; every goldsmith is shamed by his idols. His images are a fraud; they have no breath in them. They are worthless, the objects of mockery; when their judgment comes, they will perish. He who is the Portion of Jacob is not like these, for he is the Maker of all things, including the tribe of his inheritance—the LORD Almighty is his name."*
>
> —Jeremiah 51:17-19 (emphasis added)

Instead of speaking about Babylon, Jeremiah has now begun to speak about God. These verses describing God then lead immediately into the tactical directive. They can only be describing Jesus— *"the Maker of all things"* and the instrument of God's justice and vengeance. This introductory verse is placed there by the Holy Spirit to make sure that we recognize that the description that immediately follows—of a truly extraordinary warrior whose directive is to be a mighty weapon in the hands of God—is a command directive for the fully embodied Son of God.

So also does the passage that immediately follows the job description confirm that Jeremiah is speaking about the Commander of the army of the Lord. In it, one Person of the Trinity is speaking to another. It is clearly not addressed to either Babylon or Israel as the speaker refers to each of *them* in *second* person. Indeed if we were to take the classical interpretation that places the Lord saying the job description passage to Babylon, then the next passage simply doesn't make sense. The next passage is clearly *about* Babylon, and certainly not being addressed *to* Babylon.

> *"Before your eyes I will repay Babylon and all who live in Babylonia for all the wrong they have done in Zion," declares the LORD.*
>
> —Jeremiah 51:24

So, just like He so often does—especially in the books of Isaiah and Jeremiah—the Holy Spirit just drops a theological bombshell right in the middle of a prophetical discourse on Babylon. It is so easily passed over or attributed a different meaning. But if we look closely at the text of these three verses, we can see that it truly encompasses the role of Jesus—both in the Old Testament, as we have discussed, and also in the New Testament as the Stone who makes men stumble and the Rock who makes men fall.

> *"The LORD Almighty is the one you are to regard as holy, he is the one you are to fear, he is the one you are to dread, and he will be a sanctuary; but for both houses of Israel he will be a stone that causes men to stumble and a rock that makes them fall. And for the people of Jerusalem he will be a trap and a snare. Many of them will stumble; they will fall and be broken, they will be snared and captured."*
>
> —Isaiah 8:13-15 (emphasis added)

> *As it is written: "See, I lay in Zion a stone that causes men to stumble and a rock that makes them fall, and the one who trusts in him will never be put to shame."*
>
> —Romans 9:33

Just as in Old Testament times, the role Jesus plays in *our* life depends on our response to Him. Those who would turn to God are broken to pieces and built back up into the likeness of the King of kings. Those who rebel against God are crushed by the Rock that falls on them. Our response to Jesus determines our fate, determines which part of Jesus' job description describes his role in our particular life.

Similarly, in His Old Testament role as *the angel of the Lord,* Jesus is first and foremost a weapon in the hand of the Mighty God. Just as He will judge Mystery Babylon in the end-times, so also did He judge Babylon following its conquest of Israel. That is precisely what this command directive—this job description— passage tells us. Just as He was the instrument of God's wrath against Babylon then, so also will He be the instrument of God's wrath against Mystery Babylon on the great day of the Lord.

We have made a strong case for Jesus as the mighty warrior angel of the Lord. The evidence for this warrior role being the primary mission of the Son of God prior to Bethlehem is indeed liberally scattered throughout the Old Testament scriptures. This very special passage from the book of the prophet Jeremiah, however, is a clear and complete summation statement of the Son's job description—His detailed tactical battle plan—from the mouth of the Father Himself. In it is that which we seek. In it is related the day-to-day tactical directives that are necessary to achieve the overall strategic plan for the preservation of the remnant of Israel.

> *"You are my war club, my weapon for battle—with you I shatter nations, with you I destroy kingdoms, with you I shatter horse and rider, with you I shatter chariot and driver, with you I shatter man and woman, with you I shatter old man and youth, with you I shatter young man and maiden, with you I shatter shepherd and flock, with you I shatter farmer and oxen, with you I shatter governors and officials."*

—Jeremiah 51:20-23

Chapter 16

Who Are These *"Princes"*...
...And Who Is This "Prince of princes"?

Two Sets of Princes

One of the most difficult words in the Old Testament to fully understand and
define—especially in regard to the role of Jesus in the Old Testament—is the word
"prince." It is used quite commonly in the Old Testament to describe real world
earthly leaders, rulers, or sons of rulers in a fashion that is quite familiar to all of
us. A typical example of its use to describe such an earthly leader comes from the
book of Genesis where the Hittites refer to Abraham as a *"mighty prince."*

> *Then Abraham rose from beside his dead wife and spoke to the
> Hittites. He said, "I am an alien and a stranger among you. Sell me
> some property for a burial site here so I can bury my dead."*

> *The Hittites replied to Abraham, "Sir, listen to us. You are <u>a mighty
> prince</u> among us. Bury your dead in the choicest of our tombs. None
> of us will refuse you his tomb for burying your dead."*
>
> —Genesis 23:3-6 (emphasis added)

In sharp contrast to this easily understood use of the word *prince* is its Old
Testament use in referring to an entirely different group of leaders. These
mysterious warrior leaders seem to occupy only the shadowy *otherworld* of war
and intrigue that paralleled the *real* world of the patriarchs. One cannot help but
be intrigued, for instance, when Michael, one of only two named angels (excluding
Lucifer) in the Old Testament, is also referred to as a *"prince."* This reference
seems to not only describe this otherworld prince status, but to also define a
hierarchy among otherworld princes. Michael is not only referred to as a prince,
but also as *"the chief"* prince. Not only he is a chief prince, but we are also told
that he is *"one of the chief princes,"* inferring that there are others.

> *But the prince of the Persian kingdom resisted me twenty-one days.
> Then Michael, <u>one of the chief princes</u>, came to help me, because I
> was detained there with the king of Persia.*
>
> —Daniel 10:13 (emphasis added)

The word *"prince"* seems to be applicable in a very similar fashion to both the visible and invisible worlds. It is also readily apparent that among otherworld princes, there are definitely the *good guys* and the *bad guys*. For instance, the so-called *"prince of the Persian kingdom,"* who is described above as resisting Daniel's messenger, most likely represents an otherworld character who operates behind the scenes on the behalf of the real world leader of the Persian empire. The fact that the word *"prince"* is applied to both he and the archangel Michael suggests that they are both warrior leaders of a similar stature—but from opposing sides.

These princes of the otherworld are referred to by many different names. For example, a similar group of apparent otherworld leaders who mirror these princes in their status and motivation are also referred to as *"powers."* Are these *"powers"* one and the same as the princes of the otherworld who appear to oppose Jesus and his mighty warrior angels? The scriptures are cryptic in this regard. In fact, it is often difficult to even discern when the prophets are speaking of princes in our world and when they are speaking of princes from the otherworld. If we examine these passages closely, we are nonetheless given a strong suggestion of the existence of two entirely different types of princes—in entirely different worlds—yet whose fates seem inexorably tied together.

Take for example two separate passages from the prophet Isaiah. In both passages a single sentence combines two statements that would appear at first glance to be about the same people. In the first passage, Isaiah refers to *"powers in the heavens above"* and *"kings on the earth below."* In the second passage he then refers once again in the same sentence to *"princes"* and *"rulers of this world."*

> *In that day the LORD will punish the powers in the heavens above and the kings on the earth below. They will be herded together like prisoners bound in a dungeon; they will be shut up in prison and be punished after many days.*
>
> —Isaiah 24:21-22 (emphasis added)

> *He brings princes to naught and reduces the rulers of this world to nothing.*
>
> —Isaiah 40:23 (emphasis added)

These two passages are critical clues that clearly explain that there are two different sets of individuals to whom these passages refer. One group resides in the otherworld and the other group resides in our world. In other words, in each case Isaiah either appears to be referring to the same people on earth twice—in which case it makes no sense to repeat it—or he is referring to two different sets of individuals. Further, these two passages tell us that these two sets of individuals appear to be tied together in regard to both God's opinion of them and their ultimate fate. They nonetheless appear to be simultaneously residing in two different—yet complexly intertwined—worlds.

Discerning between these two groups is made easier by the fact that in the first reference above, Isaiah adds two geographic descriptors that place the two parties in entirely different worlds. This critical passage tells us of the presence of evil *"powers"* who reside *"in the heavens above"* who are somehow connected with *"kings"* who reside *"on the earth."* As this passage from Isaiah suggests, despite occupying an entirely different world, these evil otherworld *"powers"* have the same malevolent purpose and are headed for the same ultimate outcome as the evil *"kings on the earth below."*

The prophet Zephaniah also appears to draw a distinction between the princes of this earth (*"the sons of kings"*) and the princes of the otherworld.

> On the day of the LORD's sacrifice I will punish <u>the princes</u> and <u>the king's sons</u> and all those clad in foreign clothes.
> —Zephaniah 1:8 (emphasis added)

This passage makes no sense at all if the presence of the otherworld is not clearly implied and foundational in its meaning. After all, *all* of the sons of a king are princes. The prophet must be referring to two sets of individuals who carry the same titles—and ultimate fates—while yet residing in altogether different worlds.

The Princes of the Otherworld
Who then are these princes of the otherworld? Is there a way to positively identify them? Are these *"princes"* and doomed *"powers"* the same as the third of angels who are cast out of heaven with Lucifer?

> His tail swept <u>a third of the stars</u> out of the sky and flung them to the earth.
> —Revelation 12:4 (emphasis added)

It is difficult to definitively discern whether scripture supports this contention or not. Certainly these fallen angels would represent a ready source of such evil powers.   Either way, we are left with the impression that intrigue, strategic maneuvering, and mighty battle wages behind the scenes of our everyday world and that these dark princes are key players in the spiritual warfare of this mysterious otherworld.

Further information regarding the precise identity of these princes is found in the very same chapter of the book of Zephaniah. We are told that their connection to the real world of the nation of Israel is direct and profound. We also know their names. Two of these evil otherworld princes go by names that should be quite familiar to the reader of the Old Testament: Baal and Molech.

> *"I will stretch out my hand against Judah and against all who live in Jerusalem. I will cut off from this place every remnant of* <u>*Baal*</u>*, the names of the pagan and the idolatrous priests—those who bow down on the roofs to* <u>*worship the starry host*</u>*, those who bow down and swear by the* LORD *and who also swear by* <u>*Molech*</u>*, those who turn back from following the* LORD *and neither seek the* LORD *nor inquire of him.*
>
> —Zephaniah 1:4-6 (emphasis added)

In this key passage, *"the starry host"*—a common reference to angelic beings—are directly related to Baal and Molech. They are two of the *gods* worshiped by the pagan nations who occupied the Promised Land. They are also princes who occupy the invisible otherworld. Despite occupying an invisible world, they obviously also had a direct and influential relationship to the pagan peoples who worshiped them. Holy Scripture seems to imply that these evil angelic princes are the otherworld powers behind the idol worship of the pagan nations. Scripture also supports the contention that worship offered to these otherworld *gods* is offered to demons.

> *They sacrificed to demons, which are not God—gods they had not known, gods that recently appeared, gods your fathers did not fear.*
>
> —Deuteronomy 32:17

God's original command to the Israelites to completely wipe out every trace of the peoples who held the Promised Land was based upon His knowledge that the Israelites would not be able to resist the allure of these *gods*. The influence of these otherworld gods on the real world occupants of Israel must have been overwhelming. God's prediction regarding the susceptibility of the Israelites to the wooing of their hearts by the surviving Canaanites was right on target. It was this very powerful influence that eventually won the hearts of the Israelites, resulted in their turning from God, and ultimately resulted in their exile from the land. There is obviously more going on with simple idol worship than meets the eye. There is also more behind God's infinite dislike of the idols mankind pursues, these gods who try to steal His glory, than most of us would normally attribute to lifeless handmade wooden idols perched on pagan altars.

Most of us are conditioned to think only allegorically when reading about the *gods* that were worshipped by the pagan nations that surrounded Israel. We are led to believe that these were just imaginary gods that existed only in the minds of the pagan barbarians who inhabited the land. In this regard they resemble the surrogate gods that stand in for the real thing in our modern day efforts to fulfill the inherent need for God that exists in every human heart. The Bible, nonetheless, is clear in its reference to these gods. *They are anything but imaginary.* They are never referred to by the Old Testament authors as being merely a product of the mischievous and creative mind of man. The Bible does not let us dismiss them so easily.

The Bible never refers to these Old Testament gods as being imaginary.

Quite to the contrary, the writers of the Old Testament always refer to them as if they are real entities that are not only really there, but incredibly influential in the real world. These passages strongly suggest that the carved images of the pagan world had their direct, living, and very real counterparts in the mysterious otherworld that parallels our world.

> *"'Do not give any of your children to be sacrificed to Molech, for you must not profane the name of your God. I am the LORD.*
>
> —Leviticus 18:21

> *The LORD will be awesome to them <u>when he destroys</u> all the <u>gods</u> of the land. The nations on every shore will worship him, every one in its own land.*
>
> —Zephaniah 2:11 (emphasis added)

> *<u>Bel</u> bows down, <u>Nebo</u> stoops low; <u>their idols</u> are borne by beasts of burden. The images that are carried about are burdensome, a burden for the weary. They stoop and bow down together; unable to rescue the burden, they themselves go off into captivity.*
>
> —Isaiah 46:1-2 (emphasis added)

These references, once again, are to more than statues. They are not just to the little figurines of gold that the pagan tribes and the Israelites perched on their mantles. They are not to *fake* gods that were only a non-existent product of the imagination. The text is quite clear. These references—by God—are to the real otherworld individuals that are represented by the little gold statues. The *gods* that are worshipped by the nations that preceded Israel in the land—and subsequently by the Israelites—are very real and living otherworld characters. The Apostle Paul, in fact, tells us precisely this in the book of 1Corinthians.

> *Do I mean then that a sacrifice <u>offered to an idol</u> is anything, or that an idol is anything? No, but <u>the sacrifices of pagans are offered to demons</u>, not to God, and I do not want you to be participants with demons. You cannot drink the cup of the Lord and the cup of demons too; you cannot have a part in both the Lord's table and the table of demons.*
>
> —1Corinthians 10:19-21 (emphasis added)

If these entities—these *gods*—are really there and if they can be destroyed as suggested above then they must exist somewhere. Heaven, the otherworld, is that somewhere. These *gods* do indeed seem to be one and the same as the evil *"powers"* of the otherworld that are so intricately tied to the pagan people who reside in our world—and who will both be destroyed together on the day of the Lord.

The Real Prince
This book, nonetheless, is not about archangels and it is not about *"powers"* or Persian kings. It is about Jesus Christ. And, precisely in specific reference to Jesus is where the Old Testament use of the word *"prince"* becomes interesting. Indeed, in the 8th chapter of the book of the prophet Daniel, we are introduced to the *"Prince of the host."*

> *Out of one of them came another horn, which started small but grew in power to the south and to the east and toward the Beautiful Land. It grew until it reached the host of the heavens, and it threw some of the starry host down to the earth and trampled on them. It set itself up to be as great as <u>the Prince of the host</u>; it took away the daily sacrifice from him, and the place of <u>his sanctuary</u> was brought low.*
>
> —Daniel 8:9-11 (emphasis added)

There can be only one *"Prince of the host."* This is a clear and obvious reference to Jesus Christ. This suspicion of the identity of the *"Prince of the host"* is confirmed in the passage that immediately follows. A clear reference to the temple is made and referred to as *"his sanctuary."* Again, the reference is not lost on the NIV translators who have again utilized the capitalization of the word *"Prince"* to further assist in our identification.

We are also introduced to the phrase, *"Prince of princes"* in the same chapter. Once again the translators have capitalized this clear reference to the Son of God. This reference to the final end-times defeat of the antichrist is easily recognizable. From other end-times scripture it is well established that the reference to the champion who comes to rescue Israel and destroy the antichrist— *"but not by human power"* —can only be to Jesus Christ.

> *"He will cause deceit to prosper, and he will consider himself superior. When they feel secure, he will destroy many and take his stand against the Prince of princes. Yet he will be destroyed, but not by human power.*
>
> *"The vision of the evenings and mornings that has been given you is true, but seal up the vision, for it concerns the distant future."*
>
> —Daniel 8:25-26 (emphasis added)

Why is it necessary to belabor this discussion regarding the use of the descriptive term *"prince"* in clear reference to Jesus? The whole point of referencing these two passages in this manner is that they clearly classify Jesus as a prince among other princes—all of whom are angels. Surely the description of Jesus as a *"prince"* in these two key passages from the book of Daniel once again places Him right there in the thick of the battle alongside his fellow warriors—who are all angels. Jesus is clearly described as functioning on the same plane and with a similar status as the warrior angels—both good and bad—who are referred to as *"princes"* by the Old Testament authors.

Truly the New Testament admonition that Jesus was *"made a little lower than the angels"* (Hebrews 2:9) takes on new meaning in this context. Indeed, these scriptures further support the notion that the only Son of God was emptied to the status of a combatant, equal to the fight that pitted the mighty angels Michael and Gabriel against the dark adversaries of this mysterious otherworld of warfare.

Princes At War

It obviously becomes important to seek confirmation that these references to otherworld princes—such as the *"prince of Persia"* referred to above—are not just references to princes of our world. In other words, the case must be made that the battle that Jesus and His fellow warriors engaged in with *"the princes"* was indeed an *otherworld* battle that then had an impact in the real world. This is opposed to the possibility that it was just Jesus and his archangel warriors battling *directly* with the real world princes of *this* world. This is important. Although we can say with assurance that when *the angel of the Lord* has his sword drawn, then people die in our world, we nonetheless don't know *why* they die. They could either be dying by the direct effect of a swinging otherworld angelic sword or they could be dying because that evil otherworld force that has been supporting them has been itself dealt a deathblow at the hand of *the angel of the Lord* and his fellow warriors (thereby allowing their real world enemies to overwhelm them).

In this regard, there are many clear scriptural references that separate the princes of this world from their counterparts in the otherworld. One such passage, which is similar to the passages reviewed above, appears in the book of Isaiah.

> *Do you not know? Have you not heard? Has it not been told you from the beginning? Have you not understood since the earth was founded? He sits enthroned above the circle of the earth, and its people are like grasshoppers. He stretches out the heavens like a canopy, and spreads them out like a tent to live in. He brings princes to naught and reduces the rulers of this world to nothing. No sooner are they planted, no sooner are they sown, no sooner do they take root in the ground, than he blows on them and they wither, and a whirlwind sweeps them away like chaff.*
>
> —Isaiah 40:21-24 (emphasis added)

This passage refers to princes and rulers in a mutually exclusive manner, as if both of them had to be dealt with separately. If the *"princes"* and *"the rulers of this world"* were in fact the same individuals, it would not be necessary to mention them both. Nonetheless, as mentioned previously, their reference in the same sentence suggests that they are nonetheless somehow tied together through the complex interface between the two worlds. It suggests exactly what many authors have made the case for—specifically that these otherworld princes are the otherworld champions of the evil rulers of this world. By opposing their evil counterparts in the otherworld, Jesus and His fellow warrior angels therefore indirectly affect the evil rulers of the real world.

This becomes of even more critical importance in the many prophetic passages that refer to the coming end times. One passage in particular serves as a perfect example of the importance of these otherworld battles on the major history changing events of our world. This passage refers specifically to a coming end times battle.

> *The word of the LORD came to me: "Son of man, set your face against Gog, of the land of Magog, the <u>chief prince</u> of Meshech and Tubal; prophesy against him and say: 'This is what the Sovereign LORD says: I am against you, O Gog, <u>chief prince</u> of Meshech and Tubal. I will turn you around, put hooks in your jaws and bring you out with your whole army—your horses, your horsemen fully armed, and a great horde <u>with large and small shields</u>, all of them brandishing their <u>swords</u>.*

—Ezekiel 38:1-4 (emphasis added)

It is the *"chief prince"* Gog who leads this end times evil army. This passage, nonetheless, is widely believed to be describing a real world leader of a great end times army. Yet if this is a real world end times battle, why does the description of the weaponry refer to *"large and small shields"* and *"swords."* It is hard to believe that today's modern weaponry will be abandoned for shields and swords in the most important battle of all time. This suggests—as many writers have suggested—that Gog is instead an evil demonic warrior prince leading an otherworld army using otherworld weapons.

Further support for this argument is added by the following passage from the next chapter of that same book. Once again, the description of the defeat of this great otherworld evil prince is described in great detail. In his defeat, God speaks as if He is turning a large beast around to head him back in the direction from whence he once came. Gog will be turned around and dragged off. And yet once again, this passage is describing an otherworldly battle, not a modern day battle. This description is complete with a full military description of the disarming of a heavily armed otherworldly foe in battle, including striking the bow from his left hand and the arrows from his right. This is not an end times battle in our modern era with the highly mechanized lethal weapons of the modern day battlefield. This sounds more like the weapons and hand-to-hand battle tactics of *Star Wars* or *Lord of the Rings* than it does those of *Saving Private Ryan* or *Platoon*.

> *"Son of man, prophesy <u>against Gog</u> and say: 'This is what the Sovereign LORD says: I am against you, O Gog, chief prince of*

Meshech and Tubal. I will turn you around and <u>drag you along</u>. I will bring you from the far north and send you against the mountains of Israel. Then <u>I will strike your bow from your left hand and make your arrows drop from your right hand</u>. On the mountains of Israel you will fall, you and all your troops and the nations with you. I will give you as food to all kinds of carrion birds and to the wild animals. You will fall in the open field, for I have spoken, declares the Sovereign LORD.

—Ezekiel 39:1-5 (emphasis added)

The use of the word *"prince"* to describe otherworld warriors is not limited to the Old Testament. Even the New Testament Pharisees recognized—and named— Beelzebub as *"the prince of demons."*

But when the Pharisees heard this, they said, "It is only by Beelzebub, <u>the prince</u> of demons, that this fellow drives out demons."

—Matthew 12:24 (emphasis added)

In other words, even in their day, the Pharisees readily recognized the activity of demonic princes. They directly attributed Jesus' ability to drive out demons to the otherworldly *"prince of demons,"* Beelzebub. Likewise, Jesus Himself referred to Satan as *"the prince of this world."*

Now is the time for judgment on this world; now <u>the prince of this world</u> will be driven out.

—John 12:31 (emphasis added)

I will not speak with you much longer, for <u>the prince of this world</u> is coming. He has no hold on me, but the world must learn that I love the Father and that I do exactly what my Father has commanded me.

—John 14:30-31 (emphasis added)

When he comes, he will convict the world of guilt in regard to sin and righteousness and judgment: in regard to sin, because men do not believe in me; in regard to righteousness, because I am going to the Father, where you can see me no longer; and in regard to judgment, because <u>the prince of this world</u> now stands condemned.

—John 16:8-11 (emphasis added)

The case for the Old Testament role of Jesus as the Most Holy Warrior continues to build. These declarations of Jesus as both *the angel of the Lord* and *"the Prince of princes"* place Him among fellow warriors in a tempestuous Old Testament environment that also speaks of royalty, battle, and intrigue.

Chapter 17

Old Testament Air Cavalry: The Shekinah Glory
War Chariot of the Commander of the Army of the Lord

In the thirtieth year, in the fourth month on the fifth day, while I was among the exiles by the Kebar River, the heavens were opened and I saw visions of God. On the fifth of the month—it was the fifth year of the exile of King Jehoiachin—the word of the LORD came to Ezekiel the priest, the son of Buzi, by the Kebar River in the land of the Babylonians. There the hand of the LORD was upon him. I looked, and I saw a windstorm coming out of the north—an immense cloud with flashing lightning and surrounded by brilliant light.

—Ezekiel 1:1-4a

Babylon. The banks of the Kebar River. Ezekiel, a priest and prophet exiled with the nation of Israel could hardly believe his eyes. Out of the clear blue Chaldean sky an immense windstorm was bearing down on him from out of the North. He had never seen anything like it. It was dark and ominous, and yet brilliantly lit up with lightning—like an immense spring thunderstorm. It was huge, breathtaking, and menacing—and it was moving directly and rapidly toward him.

The scene before Ezekiel was dynamic. There was nothing static about it. The immense windstorm was not sitting still in the distance. It was mobile. It was moving toward him and in the midst of this moving force was yet another tumult of frenzied movement. The whole scene was in a state of near constant change. It was advancing, evolving, and unveiling right before his eyes. The heavens had opened and a very real storm was advancing and was upon him. And, at the center of the storm was a throne.

Above the expanse over their heads was what looked like a throne of sapphire, and high above on the throne was a figure like that of a man.

—Ezekiel 1:26

A throne? A throne in the midst of a fiery windstorm? A rapidly moving throne in the midst of billowing fiery clouds? The scene before him had immobilized the prophet Ezekiel. He was overwhelmed by fear and awe in the presence of the awful unknown. And yet, he was also filled with wonderment. He would have feared for his life except that he knew that if this overwhelming force meant him harm, he would have been dead already. So instead his mind turned to bewilderment. He had never seen anything even remotely like this before. A throne? A throne in the midst of a fiery windstorm? A rapidly moving throne in the midst of billowing fiery clouds? Who sat on this unearthly throne? Why would a throne be so rapidly mobile in the first place? Why would it be engulfed in fire and smoke? Ezekiel did not know what to think, but he knew his life had just changed forever.

A *"throne"* surrounded by a whirlwind of blazing fire, all of which can move across the desert—how many times have we marveled at these spectacular otherworld descriptions by the prophets Isaiah, Ezekiel, and Daniel? And yet everything is different now. Our new perspective of the warrior Commander of the army of the Lord changes everything. Now we can understand that which we could only speculate about before. In the illuminating light of a new perspective we can now very reasonably know that this imposing *throne room* had a very real reason for having the extraordinarily peculiar attributes that are revealed in each of its amazing descriptions.

It may best serve our purpose to state this chapter's hypothesis boldly at the beginning of this discussion. This hypothesis has at its foundation the premise that the incredible visions of the radiant throne, mighty cherubim, whirling wheels, and engulfing fire described by the Old Testament prophets represent nothing less than a fleeting glimpse into a spectacle of immense importance to our understanding of the warrior role of Jesus in the Old Testament.

These visions give us a momentary glance behind the mysterious and imposing curtain of billowing smoke that formed the perimeter of that spectacular Old Testament entity known as *the Shekinah Glory*. This Shekinah Glory accompanied the nation of Israel throughout the period of the Exodus and occupation of the Promised Land. It was often described in association with the Ark of the Covenant—especially when it resided in the Holy Temple—and intermittently made appearances throughout the rest of the Old and New Testament accounts. It is from behind this curtain of smoke that our hypothesis originates:

The dazzling scene described behind the cloud, fire, and smoke curtain of the Shekinah Glory is of nothing less than a formidable air-cavalry war chariot, a Commander's fiery battle chariot. This airborne war chariot serves as the mobile center of the command structure of the army of the Lord.

The support of this hypothesis is found in a review of the known attributes of this fiery cloud that can be compiled from the remarkably similar descriptions scattered throughout the writings of three of the Old Testament prophets. This similarity is especially noteworthy since these prophets were constrained to using common earthly metaphors to describe something that was obviously very unearthly in its origin.

Isaiah's description serves merely as a brief introduction to the mobile throne room that was the seat of command for Jesus during Old Testament times. Daniel's vision, described briefly in the seventh chapter of his prophetic book, is similarly simple. The prophet Ezekiel, on the other hand, supplies a remarkably detailed description that strongly supports a utility that goes beyond being merely a throne room. Ezekiel's account builds the case for the use of this blazing and mobile throne as a *weapons platform* and *tactical command center*. It is from his description that we are given hints regarding the real military functionality of the Shekinah Glory. But without our new perspective of the role of Jesus as a holy warrior in these times of the prophets, this vivid description by the prophet Ezekiel would remain interesting, but barren. It would pique our curiosity but leave us empty and craving yet more of the knowledge of the Lord that so obviously lies hidden in its text.

With our new perspective, however, we can see the scene described by Ezekiel in an altogether new light. Indeed in its revelation of the military functionality of this command center, this vision reveals a very important component of the mission of Jesus during the Old Testament times. As we have already discussed, the warrior Jesus functioned as the Lord of Hosts, the *Commander* of the army of the Lord. Although we will go into more discussion regarding the specifics of His military missions, His primary role was as the Commander of the army that does the bidding of Almighty God—especially in regard to the preservation, defense, and rescue of the remnant of Israel. The discussion and defense of our hypothesis begins with the development of some sort of a composite understanding of how this magnificent war chariot functioned and why it had the attributes that are very specifically detailed in the multiple sightings that are documented in the Old Testament.

"An Immense Cloud"

In his description of the menacing approach of the spectacular windstorm by the Kebar River, Ezekiel portrays it as *"an immense cloud."* This cloud seems to have its genesis in the fiery center of this entity—as if it was a giant cloud of billowing smoke. Indeed, whether a cloud in the classic sense or a billowing cloud of smoke, it serves the same tactical purpose: stealth. This cloud serves the same military functionality as a smoke screen laid down, for example, by a navy warship intent on evading submarines in the North Atlantic in World War II. Its purpose is to conceal. It conceals from any outside observer the inner workings of the enclosed command center.

> *Clouds and thick darkness surround him; righteousness and justice are the foundation of his throne.*
>
> —Psalm 97:2 (emphasis added)

Beyond the awesome and intimidating nature of this immense cloud, this is basic military stealth. It has to do with covert operation and the basic principle of concealing command structure, internal decision process, or intent from one's enemies. This function is well demonstrated in the days of the Israelites' exodus from Egypt. When the Egyptian army closed in on the fleeing Israelites, for instance, not only could they not see into the Shekinah Glory, they could not see beyond it. Its billowing clouds truly acted as a smoke screen to shield the escape of the Israelites into the Red Sea.

> *Then the angel of God, who had been traveling in front of Israel's army, withdrew and went behind them. The pillar of cloud also moved from in front and stood behind them, coming between the armies of Egypt and Israel. Throughout the night the cloud brought darkness to the one side and light to the other side; so neither went near the other all night long.*
>
> —Exodus 14:19-20 (emphasis added)

"The cloud brought darkness to the one side" just as if it were a World War II destroyer making good its escape in a horizon-obscuring trail of choking black smoke. This ominous darkness was most assuredly the *"thick darkness,"* referred to elsewhere.

> *The people remained at a distance, while Moses approached the thick darkness where God was.*

—Exodus 20:21 (emphasis added)

*Clouds and <u>thick darkness</u> surround him; righteousness and justice
are the foundation of his throne.*

—Psalm 97:2 (emphasis added)

Moses documented the effectiveness of the cloud in regard to its primary Old
Testament stealth and concealment purpose. It apparently hid the contents of the
throne room quite well. The holy inner contents of the Shekinah Glory were well
hidden from those who did not need to—or were not worthy to—see inside.

*You came near and stood at the foot of the mountain while it blazed
with fire to the very heavens, with <u>black clouds</u> and <u>deep darkness</u>.
Then the LORD spoke to you out of the fire. You heard the sound of
words <u>but saw no form</u>; there was <u>only a voice</u>.*

—Deuteronomy 4:11-12 (emphasis added)

And still, this was darkness that was more than just stealth—it was intimidation.
This was darkness that menacingly whispered, "Back off." This was darkness that
was palpable, darkness that could *"be felt."*

*Then the LORD said to Moses, "Stretch out your hand toward the sky
so that darkness will spread over Egypt—<u>darkness that can be felt.</u>"*

—Exodus 10:21 (emphasis added)

One cannot help but notice the visual similarity between the billowing clouds of
the Shekinah Glory and the clouds that repeatedly appear with such vivid imagery
in so many critical passages in both the New and Old Testaments. The Old
Testament is literally flooded with such references to clouds in association with the
movements of God. The prophet Nahum, for example, clearly describes the
presence of this cloud enshrouded battle transport during his prophetic description
of the destruction of Assyria. This is obviously a weapons platform that is being
described and it very effectively wields God's wrath and vengeance against
Assyria.

*The LORD is a jealous and avenging God; the LORD takes <u>vengeance</u>
and is filled with <u>wrath</u>. The LORD <u>takes vengeance on his foes and
maintains his wrath against his enemies</u>. The LORD is slow to anger
and great in power; the LORD will not leave the guilty unpunished.
<u>His way is in the whirlwind and the storm, and clouds are the dust of</u>*

his feet. He rebukes the sea and dries it up; he makes all the rivers run dry. Bashan and Carmel wither and the blossoms of Lebanon fade. The mountains quake before him and the hills melt away. The earth trembles at his presence, the world and all who live in it. Who can withstand his indignation? Who can endure his fierce anger? His wrath is poured out like fire; the rocks are shattered before him. The LORD is good, a refuge in times of trouble. He cares for those who trust in him, but with an overwhelming flood he will make an end of [Nineveh]; he will pursue his foes into darkness.

—Nahum 1:2-8 (emphasis added)

This description is of the fury and confusion of battle. It describes a literally ground shaking and menacing threat. The armament of the Shekinah Glory literally shakes the mountains before it and melts the hills in its presence. Its night vision capabilities allow it to pursue its enemies under the cover of *"darkness."* This is war and the Shekinah Glory is a very capable weapon in the hands of its Commander.

The many such Old Testament references to God *traveling* in association with clouds can, of course, be left to the allegorical interpretations that have so often been attributed to them. Nonetheless, in the light of our new perspective these passages do indeed take on a new meaning when viewed in a very literal manner.

"There is no one like the God of Jeshurun, who rides on the heavens to help you and on the clouds in his majesty.

—Deuteronomy 33:26 (emphasis added)

Sing to God, sing praise to his name, extol him who rides on the clouds—his name is the LORD—and rejoice before him.

—Psalm 68:4 (emphasis added)

In one verse the psalmist actually states that not only does the Lord ride *"on the wings of the wind,"* but also literally *"makes the clouds his chariot."*

He wraps himself in light as with a garment; he stretches out the heavens like a tent and lays the beams of his upper chambers on their waters. He makes the clouds his chariot and rides on the wings of the wind. He makes winds his messengers, flames of fire his servants.

—Psalm 104:2-4 (emphasis added)

One Old Testament reference to this cloud-encompassed chariot is just too vivid to dismiss as anything less than a direct reference to the functionality of the Shekinah Glory as the principal air cavalry capability of the army of the Lord. Although this will be discussed again later, we must make note of David's vivid imagery in our discussion regarding the attributes of the Shekinah Glory and its specific use as a command post and weaponry platform for the Commander of the army of the Lord.

> *In my distress I called to the LORD; I called out to my God. From his temple he heard my voice; my cry came to his ears.*
>
> *"The earth <u>trembled</u> and <u>quaked</u>, the foundations of the heavens <u>shook</u>; they trembled because he was angry. <u>Smoke</u> rose from his nostrils; <u>consuming fire</u> came from his mouth, <u>burning coals blazed out of it</u>. He parted the heavens and came down; <u>dark clouds were under his feet. He mounted the cherubim and flew; he soared on the wings of the wind. He made darkness his canopy around him—the dark rain clouds of the sky. Out of the brightness of his presence bolts of lightning blazed forth</u>. The LORD <u>thundered</u> from heaven; the voice of the Most High resounded. <u>He shot arrows and scattered [the enemies], bolts of lightning and routed them</u>. The valleys of the sea were exposed and the foundations of the earth laid bare at the rebuke of the LORD, at the <u>blast</u> of breath from his nostrils.*
>
> *"He reached down from on high and took hold of me; he drew me out of deep waters. <u>He rescued me from my powerful enemy</u>, from my foes, who were <u>too strong for me</u>. They confronted me in the day of my <u>disaster</u>, but <u>the LORD was my support</u>. He brought me out into a spacious place; he rescued me because he delighted in me.*
>
> —2Samuel 22: 7-20 (emphasis added)

The imagery utilized to describe what is obviously nothing short of the full-scale air-cavalry assault on David's enemies is much too vivid and battle-specific to allow us the comfort of limiting it to the allegory that is classically ascribed to it. These clouds are the same clouds that are repeatedly described in countless different places in the Old Testament. In each description of the fiery clouds of the Shekinah Glory they are functioning to conceal a highly capable weapons platform that is directly connected to the otherworld activities that parallel our world.

In much the same way, the New Testament references to the clouds that envelop or shield Jesus at several key junctures are very suggestive of a similar use of this cloud-encompassed, mobile *holy ground* as a direct portal into the otherworld. Matthew's description of the transfiguration of Jesus on the mountain, for instance, reveals many similar characteristics to those described by the Old Testament prophets, especially regarding the enshrouding capabilities of the Shekinah Glory.

> *After six days Jesus took with him Peter, James and John the brother of James, and led them up a high mountain by themselves. There he was transfigured before them. His face shone like the sun, and his clothes became as white as the light.*
>
> *Just then there appeared before them Moses and Elijah, talking with Jesus. Peter said to Jesus, "Lord, it is good for us to be here. If you wish, I will put up three shelters—one for you, one for Moses and one for Elijah."*
>
> *While he was still speaking, a bright cloud enveloped them, and a voice from the cloud said, "This is my Son, whom I love; with him I am well pleased. Listen to him"*

—Matthew 17:1-5 (emphasis added)

In a similar fashion, even the ascension of Jesus is associated with His disappearance into a cloud.

> *After he said this, he was taken up before their very eyes, and a cloud hid him from their sight.*

—Acts 1:9 (emphasis added)

This description seems to further emphasize the role of the Shekinah Glory as an interface or portal or holy passageway between the otherworld and our world. At the very least it seems to be a transport vehicle—a chariot—that ushers its holy occupant between heaven and earth. Understanding this use of the Shekinah Glory in the Old Testament helps us realize that in the description of the ascension of Jesus, the appearance of a cloud that subsequently hides Jesus from his disciples is also most certainly no coincidence.

Even more startling is the amazing revelation that we can expect even further appearances of the Shekinah Glory in the not too distant future. In almost every description of the second coming of Jesus Christ—from the book of Matthew to the book of Revelation itself—He is described as *"coming on the clouds"* of the Shekinah Glory.

"At that time the sign of the Son of Man will appear in the sky, and all the nations of the earth will mourn. They will see the Son of Man coming on the clouds of the sky, with power and great glory.
—Matthew 24:30 (emphasis added)

"Yes, it is as you say," Jesus replied. "But I say to all of you: In the future you will see the Son of Man sitting at the right hand of the Mighty One and coming on the clouds of heaven."
—Matthew 26:64 (emphasis added)

"I am," said Jesus. "And you will see the Son of Man sitting at the right hand of the Mighty One and coming on the clouds of heaven."
—Mark 14:62 (emphasis added)

Look, he is coming with the clouds, and every eye will see him, even those who pierced him; and all the peoples of the earth will mourn because of him. So shall it be! Amen.
—Revelation 1:7 (emphasis added)

Indeed, why would we think that it would be any different for us in the end times than it was for the nation of Israel in Old Testament times? The Shekinah Glory factored heavily in the redemption from Egypt, as well as from Babylon—both events being well-recognized *types* of the end times rescue of the Jewish remnant. Would God just discard the Shekinah Glory, as one would discard an outdated automobile? God's works never go out of style. Quite to the contrary, if the Bible teaches anything, it is that God is persistent and consistent—He never changes. When Jesus needs a magnificent chariot on the day of the Lord, the faithful cherubim will still be standing next to the *"whirling wheels"* (Ezekiel 10:13) with their powerful wings uplifted. The clouds will once again herald His arrival. We can count on it—we will be seeing the Shekinah Glory again.

The Accompanying Presence of God
The mysterious Shekinah Glory appeared repeatedly and consistently during the formation and preservation of the fledgling nation of Israel. Its spectral image is continually described as the visible mediator of God's guidance of His people through the Exodus and desert journeys. As such, the billowing smoke and clouds of the Shekinah Glory represent the focal point of God's *"Presence"* among His people during this critical period of time.

The LORD replied, "My Presence will go with you, and I will give you rest."
Then Moses said to him, "If your Presence does not go with us, do not send us up from here.

—Exodus 33:14-15 (emphasis added)

Despite the physical presence of God in their midst, however, all that is seen by the overwhelming majority of Israelites is the outer surface of the Shekinah Glory.

Then Moses entered the cloud as he went on up the mountain. And he stayed on the mountain forty days and forty nights.

—Exodus 24:18 (emphasis added)

In the Exodus from Egypt, all that they know is that it shields them from the sun during the day and glows with fire to provide light and warmth at night. During the desert portion of the Exodus journey, the people cannot help but be aware of their vulnerability. They are in continual need of guidance and protection and provision. The Shekinah Glory hovers above them at all time. They cannot look up without being made aware of its protection. The Shekinah Glory, along with its holy occupant, is always with them.

So the cloud of the LORD was over the tabernacle by day, and fire was in the cloud by night, in the sight of all the house of Israel during all their travels.

—Exodus 40:38 (emphasis added)

As Moses went into the tent, the pillar of cloud would come down and stay at the entrance, while the LORD spoke with Moses.

—Exodus 33:9 (emphasis added)

Then the LORD came down in the cloud and stood there with him and proclaimed his name, the LORD.

—Exodus 34:5 (emphasis added)

Even though he wrote the entire first five books of the Bible, Moses had very little to say about what he encountered on the other side of the billowing clouds of the Shekinah Glory. This is despite the fact that he—according to his own account—spent a large amount of time in the *"presence"* of the Lord—*"face to face"*—inside the Shekinah Glory.

And whenever Moses went out to the tent, all the people rose and stood at the entrances to their tents, watching Moses until he entered the tent. As Moses went into the tent, the pillar of cloud would come down and stay at the entrance, while the LORD spoke with Moses. Whenever the people saw the pillar of cloud standing at the entrance to the tent, they all stood and worshiped, each at the entrance to his tent. The LORD would speak to Moses face to face, as a man speaks with his friend. Then Moses would return to the camp, but his young aide Joshua son of Nun did not leave the tent.

—Exodus 33:8-11 (emphasis added)

Can there be any doubt that Moses was meeting with the incarnate, fully embodied Son of God on these many occasions? A strong case can be made for the fact that the Shekinah Glory functioned as the command seat of the military operations surrounding the nation of Israel. Apparently Jesus, the Commander of the army of the Lord, took a direct *hands-on* approach to His shepherding of Israel through these difficult times. The text seems to suggest that face-to-face meetings best served this command mission when His direct intervention was necessary.

Despite this repeated exposure to the Shekinah Glory, on only one occasion does Moses offer us a description of that which he encountered while inside the cloud. On this occasion he and the elders of Israel had been called before the Lord and were allowed to *see* the Lord.

Moses and Aaron, Nadab and Abihu, and the seventy elders of Israel went up and saw the God of Israel. Under his feet was something like a pavement made of sapphire, clear as the sky itself. But God did not raise his hand against these leaders of the Israelites; they saw God, and they ate and drank.

—Exodus 24:9-11 (emphasis added)

How can we reconcile the above statement that *"they saw God"* except that it was Jesus they were seeing? After all, Jesus Himself later told us that, *"No one has seen the Father except the one who is from God; only he has seen the Father"* (John 6:46) and we know that Holy Spirit is spirit and has no form. What other interpretations are left open to us when the direct and incontrovertible statement, *"they saw God"* is used in the description of this meeting?

Further still, the description is of a person who was fully embodied even to being described as having *"feet"*! The single additional descriptor that we are given—of

God above a clear blue sapphire *"pavement"* — is undeniably similar to the previously discussed vision by Ezekiel. The conclusion is obvious. Moses is describing a face-to-face meeting with none other than Jesus. Moses and the elders of Israel must have been in the presence of the physical, fully incarnate Jesus Christ inside the Shekinah Glory, presumably seated upon the throne. This is Jesus as warrior and as Commander of the very same Shekinah Glory that had landed on top of Mount Sinai and filled the mountain top with fire and smoke.

> *When Moses went up on the mountain, the cloud covered it, and <u>the glory of the LORD settled on Mount Sinai</u>. For six days <u>the cloud covered the mountain</u>, and on the seventh day the LORD called to Moses from within the cloud. To the Israelites the glory of the LORD looked like <u>a consuming fire on top of the mountain</u>. Then Moses entered the cloud as he went on up the mountain. And he stayed on the mountain forty days and forty nights.*
>
> —Exodus 24:15-18 (emphasis added)

Moses had face-to-face contact with *"the LORD"* throughout the redemption of Israel from Egypt and the forty years of wandering in the desert. Yet despite the fact that Moses met with the Lord face-to-face throughout this time, we have been given only this single description of the internal aspects of the Shekinah Glory from Moses. The Pentateuch, nonetheless, clearly relates many other vivid descriptions of the *external* aspects of the Shekinah Glory, as well as the stealth and intimidation capabilities of this holy war machine.

In fact, we know that Jesus ramped up the *"thunder"* and *"fire"* and billowing *"smoke"* capabilities of the Shekinah Glory in His first formal meeting with the people of Israel. This demonstration of His *"Presence"* was meant to leave a lasting impression on the Israelites. It did. It must have been an overwhelming sight. One can easily understand the reaction of the people as they saw the mobile battle chariot descending slowly onto Mount Sinai. We can only imagine the earthshaking power emanating from the powerful *"whirling wheels"* that caused both the mountain and the people to tremble *"violently."*

> *On the morning of the third day there was <u>thunder</u> and <u>lightning</u>, with a <u>thick cloud</u> over the mountain, and a <u>very loud trumpet blast</u>. Everyone in the camp <u>trembled</u>. Then Moses led the people out of the camp to meet with God, and they stood at the foot of the mountain. Mount Sinai was covered with smoke, because the LORD <u>descended on it</u> in <u>fire</u>. The <u>smoke billowed up from it like smoke from a furnace</u>,*

the whole mountain trembled violently, and the sound of the trumpet grew louder and louder. Then Moses spoke and the voice of God answered him.

—Exodus 19:16-19 (emphasis added)

When the Shekinah Glory needed to *crank it up* to make an everlasting impression, it had the necessary capacity to shake a massive mountain like Mount Sinai. These are indeed mighty *engines* that supernaturally power the command chariot. The message to the people gathered before the mountain was perfectly clear—the ground upon which the Shekinah Glory rested was holy. As if this wasn't clear enough, God nonetheless warned Moses to tell the unconsecrated people to stay away from the Presence of God on earth.

The LORD descended to the top of Mount Sinai and called Moses to the top of the mountain. So Moses went up and the LORD said to him, "Go down and warn the people so they do not force their way through to see the LORD and many of them perish. Even the priests, who approach the LORD, must consecrate themselves, or the LORD will break out against them."

Moses said to the LORD, "The people cannot come up Mount Sinai, because you yourself warned us, 'Put limits around the mountain and set it apart as holy.'"

The LORD replied, "Go down and bring Aaron up with you. But the priests and the people must not force their way through to come up to the LORD, or he will break out against them." So Moses went down to the people and told them.

—Exodus 19:20-25 (emphasis added)

Once again, the capabilities of the command chariot served God's purpose well. The Israelites were so afraid that they begged Moses to go and meet with God alone. They had no desire for further confrontation with this threatening and ominously thundering fiery presence. The stealth and intimidation military capabilities of the Shekinah Glory were there for a reason and worked effectively for that purpose. God wanted them to know with whom they were dealing.

When the people saw the thunder and lightning and heard the trumpet and saw the mountain in smoke, they trembled with fear. They stayed at a distance and said to Moses, "Speak to us yourself and we will listen. But do not have God speak to us or we will die."

—Exodus 20:18-19 (emphasis added)

The Throne

Once we are allowed past the concealing smoke screen into the inner workings of Shekinah Glory, our attention is immediately drawn to the most important of the attributes of this powerful chariot. At its center is a throne. This is the command seat. This is the center and focal point of the whole spectacular scene. All other attributes of this command center point toward the throne and serve *the One* who sits upon it.

Above the expanse over their heads was what looked like a <u>throne</u> of sapphire, and high above on the <u>throne</u> was a figure like that of a man. I saw that from what appeared to be his waist up he looked like glowing metal, as if full of fire, and that from there down he looked like fire; and brilliant light surrounded him. Like the appearance of a rainbow in the clouds on a rainy day, so was the radiance around him. This was the appearance of the likeness of the glory of the LORD. When I saw it, I fell facedown, and I heard the voice of one speaking.

—Ezekiel 1:26-28 (emphasis added)

The Guardian Cherubim

Directly below the throne are the *"four living creatures,"* the cherubim. This mobile command center comes complete with a command seat that is unique in the fact that it is surrounded by an elite guard—mighty guardian cherubim.

I looked, and I saw a windstorm coming out of the north—an immense cloud with flashing lightning and surrounded by brilliant light. The center of the fire looked like glowing metal, and in the fire was what looked like four living creatures. In appearance their form was that of a man, but each of them had four faces and four wings.

—Ezekiel 1:4-6

We know from the book of Revelation that these four cherubim, day and night, continue to say, *"Holy, holy, holy is the Lord God Almighty, who was, and is, and is to come"* (Revelation 4:8). They proclaim to any who dare venture near the throne that they, the created, approach the uncreated fire of God. These are *warrior* cherubim. Their very specific mission is to surround the throne as *"guardian cherubim"* (Ezekiel 28:16).

In this guardian role, the cherubim stand with *"four faces"* directed perpendicular to each other—thereby essentially scanning all possible avenues of approach to the throne. Vision thus occurs simultaneously in all directions by use of a multi-face configuration that allows the concurrent confrontation of multiple threats from multiple directions. Why the mighty Son of the omnipotent God would need to be *guarded* in such a manner once again speaks directly to the fullness of the emptying of Jesus in His incarnation. The Son of God certainly doesn't *need* guardians. But, He doesn't need us either—and yet look at the extent to which He went to eternally rescue us from our sin.

Rather, just as it pleased Jesus to rescue us, so also is it His good pleasure that the fullness of the emptying of His power would mandate that these, the most powerful of created beings, surround and guard His throne. The Old Testament chronicles a time of war and Jesus is continually in the middle of the fight. These mighty cherubim—we can only assume—are the elite personal guard of the Commander of the army of the Lord. Just as all military commanders of those days, from Sennecherib to Nebuchadnezzar, surrounded themselves with an elite, highly trained, formidable personal guard whose loyalty was unquestioned, so also did Jesus place his command throne in the midst of the mightiest of created beings. They serve to remind all who approach of the holiness of this ground, this throne, and this Leader of warriors.

Much can be known about these guardian cherubim by the detail of their description. We can know, for instance, that the detailed depiction of the countless eyes that cover every aspect of their bodies is not random.

> *Their entire bodies, including their backs, their hands and their wings, were completely full of eyes, as were their four wheels.*
>
> —Ezekiel 10:12

The interpretation of this attribute by most Biblical scholars leans heavily toward allegory. Quite to the contrary, however, this detail of the description of the cherubim can also be taken very literally. Isaiah's description of eyes covering every aspect of their bodies may well describe a very specific military functionality of a complex omnidirectional sensor array. This sensor array, that can only have military defense implications, is surely more elaborate than any found on our most advanced modern day warplanes or warships, such as the Aegis line of U.S. Navy battle cruisers. There is no threat that can approach undetected the holy ground guarded by these warriors.

As they moved, they would go in any one of the four directions the cherubim faced; the wheels did not turn about as the cherubim went. The cherubim went in whatever direction the head faced, without turning as they went. Their entire bodies, including their backs, their hands and their wings, were completely full of eyes, as were their four wheels. I heard the wheels being called "the whirling wheels." Each of the cherubim had four faces: One face was that of a cherub, the second the face of a man, the third the face of a lion, and the fourth the face of an eagle.

—Ezekiel 10:11-14 (emphasis added)

A Consuming Fire

As we approach the cherubim, we cannot help but feel the heat from the intense fire that engulfs every aspect of, and spreads in all directions from, this holy chariot of fire. The blazing uncreated fire of God engulfs the cherubim who seem unaffected by its consuming flames. Indeed the ground upon which the war chariot rests—wherever it travels—is subjected to a holy and consecrating destruction by the uncreated fire of the Shekinah Glory. In every setting, no matter how pedestrian or even evil, purest holiness surrounds this throne and sets ablaze this ground made holy.

For the LORD your God is a consuming fire, a jealous God.

—Deuteronomy 4:24

The fiery furnace that engulfs the entirety of this mobile holy setting has pure military functionality. This is nothing less than the ultimate manifestation of the *scorched earth* policy made famous by Civil War General William Tecumseh Sherman as he blazed his infamous trail through the South. Nothing of earthly value remains where this chariot and its holy Commander have even momentarily rested.

Clouds and thick darkness surround him; righteousness and justice are the foundation of his throne. Fire goes before him and consumes his foes on every side.

—Psalm 97:2-3 (emphasis added)

The Commander himself reminds any who approach this glory of the holiness of His presence. In settings ranging from the fire of the burning bush encountered by Moses to Joshua's holy battlefield at Jericho, Jesus admonishes His earthly counterparts to remove their sandals.   The mere presence of Jesus and the uncreated fire of the Mighty God make the ground upon which His sandals rest holy indeed.

> *The commander of the LORD'S army replied, "Take off your sandals, for the place where you are standing is holy." And Joshua did so.*
>
> —Joshua 5:15

Air-Mobile

Another intriguing aspect of the prophet Ezekiel's visions goes beyond mere sight. Ezekiel is thorough and all encompassing in his description. He also introduces both sound and touch to his narrative. Ezekiel describes not only the sight of the enormous wings of the cherubim, but also the powerful sound and pounding subwoofer feeling of the thunder-like rumbling of the gyroscopic wheels that sit beside them. The size and power of the cherubim wings speak convincingly of the extreme combat maneuverability of this powerful mobile command post. Surely it would put our most advanced U.S. Army air cavalry units to shame.

> *Under the expanse their wings were stretched out one toward the other, and each had two wings covering its body. When the creatures moved, I heard the sound of their wings, like the roar of rushing waters, like the voice of the Almighty, like the tumult of an army. When they stood still, they lowered their wings.*
>
> —Ezekiel 1:23-24 (emphasis added)

Combat tactical mobility and maneuverability over essentially any terrain—and this at lightning quick speeds—is made possible by the combination of both wheels and wings. Indeed the cherubim are described exactly as such as they move *"back and forth like flashes of lightning"* (Ezekiel 1:14). This is a time of war. Jesus is the Commander of the army of the Lord and everything about Him speaks of the rigor of swift, armed assault and combat mobility.

> *I looked, and I saw a windstorm coming out of the north—an immense cloud with flashing lightning and surrounded by brilliant light. The center of the fire looked like glowing metal, and in the fire was what looked like four living creatures. In appearance their form was that of a man, but each of them had four faces and four wings.*
>
> —Ezekiel 1:4-6 (emphasis added)

Further still, this air combat mobility speaks most directly to the battle functionality of this command center. The warfare involving the nation of Israel was spread over a large area—from Egypt through the Promised Land to Babylon. The forty years of desert wandering by the nation of Israel alone required extreme, often daily mobility. Accomplishing the many missions of the Son of God, by necessity therefore, involved moving His command structure over large distances. When the nation of Israel moved, the remnant under His protection moved. And when the remnant moved, so also did Jesus and His central command move.

> *While I watched, the cherubim* <u>*spread their wings and rose from the*</u> <u>*ground, and as they went,*</u> <u>*the wheels went with them*</u>*. They stopped at the entrance to the east gate of the LORD's house, and the glory of the God of Israel was above them.*
> —Ezekiel 10:19 (emphasis added)

Although God certainly encompasses and fills every aspect of the creation, the actual physical presence of Jesus—as far as we can tell—is confined to a discreet position in the creation, just as it was during the 33 years described in the New Testament gospel accounts. Within these physical constraints, the time and distance requirements of tactical battle command ranging from Egypt to Babylon mandated an air-mobile throne. Jesus needed a mobile command chariot like the real world warrior kings of that era—Sennecherib and Nebuchadnezzar, for example—most certainly utilized in their campaigns of world conquest.

Indeed, this Shekinah Glory war chariot had already demonstrated its mobility as it guided the young Israelite nation through the desert. What a swirling luminescent spectacle the Israelites must have slept beneath each night, as the fiery cloud loitered in its sentinel watch above them. And what an ideal model of God's plan for each of our lives is provided by the Old Testament description of the guiding movement of the hovering Shekinah Glory. As the people arose each morning, they would turn immediately toward God's presence among them to see whether they would be breaking camp and moving on that day. During those forty years, God provided direct guidance of the nation of Israel. All that was required of the people was to put one foot in front of the other in walking with God each day. This is the only way that they could be assured that at the end of their journey they would be where God wanted them to be. The guidance of the nation of Israel by the Shekinah Glory is a perfect *type* of our every-day need to turn toward God for guidance in our life.

On the day the tabernacle, the Tent of the Testimony, was set up, the cloud covered it. From evening till morning the cloud above the tabernacle looked like fire. That is how it continued to be; the cloud covered it, and at night it looked like fire. <u>Whenever the cloud lifted from above the Tent, the Israelites set out; wherever the cloud settled, the Israelites encamped. At the LORD's command the Israelites set out, and at his command they encamped.</u> As long as the cloud stayed over the tabernacle, they remained in camp. When the cloud remained over the tabernacle a long time, the Israelites obeyed the LORD's order and did not set out. Sometimes the cloud was over the tabernacle only a few days; at the LORD's command they would encamp, and then at his command they would set out. Sometimes the cloud stayed only from evening till morning, and when it lifted in the morning, they set out. Whether by day or by night, whenever the cloud lifted, they set out.

—Numbers 9:15-21 (emphasis added)

This mobile command center also demonstrated the extraordinary swiftness of its all-terrain capabilities as it approached from the north in Ezekiel's first vision (mentioned above). To be sure, that initial vision of Ezekiel's makes much more sense when viewed within our expanded understanding of the nature of the Shekinah Glory. This spectacular scene opens with Ezekiel being approached by a menacing, rapidly moving *"windstorm"* that is described as *"an immense cloud with flashing lightning and surrounded by brilliant light"* (Ezekiel 1:4). This very same Shekinah glory— *"the Glory of the Lord"* —that accompanied Moses and the Israelites during the Exodus and throughout the forty years of wandering in the desert had moved to the new battlefield. Different stories from different prophets indeed all begin to coalesce into one as we read the many accounts of the command chariot in action.

As fire consumes the forest or a flame sets the mountains ablaze, so pursue them with your tempest and terrify them with your storm.

—Psalm 83:14-15

Even Isaiah gives a clear description of the rapid air mobility of this command post as Jesus moves to Egypt on yet another mission.

An oracle concerning Egypt: See, the LORD <u>rides on a swift cloud</u> and is coming to Egypt. The idols of Egypt tremble before him, and the hearts of the Egyptians melt within them.

—Isaiah 19:1 (emphasis added)

Air mobility requires a power source. The immediate sources of power and mobility that appear to actually physically propel the Shekinah Glory about on its various missions are nothing less than the wheels and wings of the mighty cherubim.

When the living creatures moved, the wheels beside them moved; and *when the living creatures rose from the ground, the wheels also rose.*
—Ezekiel 1:19 (emphasis added)

When the creatures moved, I heard the sound of their wings, like the *roar of rushing waters, like the voice of the Almighty, like the tumult* *of an army. When they stood still, they lowered their wings.*
—Ezekiel 1:24 (emphasis added)

How delightful it is that God would make the powerful wings of the cherubim, which sound *"like the roar of rushing waters, like the voice of the Almighty, like the tumult of an army"* (Ezekiel 1:24). Clearly they are the motor behind the mobility of His most holy airborne command center. This cherubim-powered chariot is indeed the spectacular mobile air cavalry of the great war that was the centerpiece of the Old Testament.

The Focal Interface Between Two Worlds
All of these very descriptive passages begin to make more sense when we understand that the fiery cloud that accompanied the nation of Israel is one and the same with the brilliant throne room visions of Ezekiel, Isaiah, and Daniel and that it served the same common purpose in every setting. Indeed, as the many different attributes of the Shekinah Glory coalesce into a unified picture, even so much more is revealed. Their combination results in so much more than the mere summation of its parts, for these visions speak most profoundly of the holiness of the most holy Warrior, Jesus.

Indeed, within this fiery setting—which seems to serve as a window between the two worlds—so also does Jesus serve as the focal interface between the Uncreated and the created. Though He leads His warriors in pitched battle against the dark forces of angelic powers of His world, He alone remains singularly and uniquely holy. Though emptied into this role, He *remains* the only Son of the Most High God. Though mobilized to many different places He *remains* always in full contact with the Father. Even when His sword swings in clanging contact against the swords of the heavenly enemies of God, He retains this constant union with His Father. He is holy. He remains the most holy interface, the connection. And this Shekinah Glory, this chariot of fire, is where He centers His command over the Old Testament warfare that engulfs the army of the Living God.

We know that the Shekinah Glory rested above the tent of meeting when it was reconstructed at each of the Israelite rest stops during their 40 years in the desert. The Shekinah Glory later traveled with the Ark of the Covenant into the Promised Land and ultimately rested above the mercy seat as the Ark inhabited the Most Holy Place of Solomon's Temple. Surely the meetings of Moses and Joshua and any number of other Israelite leaders, priests, and prophets took place in this same setting of a throne surrounded by cherubim, all engulfed in fire. Still, only in the visions of the prophets Isaiah, Ezekiel, and Daniel are we given an inside view of this amazing focal point of the daily Old Testament habitation of the Glory of the Lord.

In summary we can conclude that the holy fire that engulfs the throne and is encompassed by the bright clouds of the Shekinah Glory is the most holy ground that exists as the interface between our world and the spiritual otherworld that parallels ours. From this localized breech in the wall between the two worlds, the warrior Commander Jesus directed the defense and preservation of the remnant of Israel during the events of the Old Testament. Although this focal point of holy fire spent the majority of its Old Testament time in the holy temple in Jerusalem, centered above the Ark of the Covenant, it also served as a very mobile command center. Not only did it move with the Tabernacle during the Exodus, but it also served as a rapidly mobile tactical command center, a Commander's war chariot, during the period of the Babylonian captivity and subsequent periods of temple defilement. In its role as a mobile military command post, it transformed every battleground into holy ground. It also demonstrated real world battle capabilities that would put to shame any of our much-vaunted modern day U.S. Army air cavalry units in the extremity of its command, mobility, sensor array, weaponry, and battle defense capabilities.

Chapter 18

The Shekinah Glory Shows Its Stuff As a Weapons Platform
The Rescue of King David by the Air Cavalry Division of the Army of the Lord

All was lost. The battle had originally been enjoined with such hope. True, the enemy had been fearsome. But this fearsome enemy had on this day squared off with the army of the Living God. King David, the commander of the army, was the anointed of God.

The two battle lines had clashed violently together. A chaotic brawl had followed. The carefully crafted battle plans had been an early casualty. That which had initially felt like victory had rapidly soured. David's battle formation had already partially collapsed. The tide had turned. The battle was being lost.

Then it got worse.

The enemy had fresh warriors in reserve. When they threw themselves into the fight against the beleaguered army of Israel, the entire battle line had collapsed. Overwhelming enemy forces had completely surrounded them. Hopeless. All was lost. They were all going to die.

And then a cry was heard.

Ezekiel, Isaiah, and Daniel are not the only prophets to provide detail regarding the remarkable airborne capabilities of the Shekinah Glory and its powerful cherubim. In Psalm 18, King David gives us a description of the battle chariot of the Commander of the army of the Lord in an actual fight. What makes this account especially exciting is that we are allowed to actually see the Shekinah Glory in combat being utilized in one of its most fascinating capabilities — as an air cavalry weapons platform. This encounter begins with a vivid description of warrior King David's moment of greatest need. In the throes of a vicious battle in which his enemies were obviously overwhelming him, David cries out to God.

I love you, O LORD, my strength. The LORD is my rock, my fortress and my deliverer; my God is my rock, in whom I take refuge. He is my shield and the horn of my salvation, my stronghold. I call to the LORD, who is worthy of praise, and I am saved from my enemies. The cords of death entangled me; the torrents of destruction overwhelmed me. The cords of the grave coiled around me; the snares of death confronted me. In my distress I called to the LORD; I cried to my God for help.

—Psalm 18:1-6 (emphasis added)

The very desperate nature of David's situation is made clear from the graphic language that he uses to inform his Central Command—God—of his plight. The ominous nature of his call stirs the heart of every man. This is the cry that has emanated from desperate men in every war in every generation in one form or another. Our generation is no different. We have heard this cry before. It is eerily reminiscent of that which was heard from the isolated forward firebases in the early days of the war in Viet Nam and is being heard now in the forward operating bases of Afghanistan. This is the cry that signals the collapse of the defensive perimeter. It means only one thing. The defenses are being overwhelmed—the enemy is behind the wall and overrunning the base. All is lost.

Indeed, David's words leave little doubt. In his life and death struggle, he had lost. His death was imminent. These were precisely the circumstances that led to the *broken arrow* call of the overrun American firebase in Viet Nam. The dire and truly hopeless condition of the warriors who manned the firebase in those rare situations justified the immediate and unrestricted direction of all available airborne and artillery firepower into the firebase, *inside* the defensive perimeter.

These were truly desperate times. The *broken arrow* call signaled all nearby airborne weapons platforms to abandon their primary targets and drop their ordinance within the confines of the collapsing defenses. It signaled the nearby artillery installations to do that which they had never done: to direct their firepower onto the sectors of their targeting grid that were marked *safe*. It signaled to all surrounding forces that the remaining survivors of the firebase were to be considered lost. They would seek shelter as best they could, but all available weaponry should now be concentrated on inflicting maximal losses on the enemy without regard for the remaining firebase defenders.

What was needed—in the Viet Nam scenario and in David's plight—was a miraculous last minute rescue. And that is what Jesus and the Air Cavalry Division of the army of the Lord were all about—*rescue.*

King David's choice of words in his description of God's response to his distress call cannot be dismissed as mere random metaphor. We might be tempted to consider this just the enthusiastic use of vivid battle allegory by the Israel's poet laureate. Maybe King David was just trying to embellish an otherwise reality-based last minute rescue by the Mighty God. After all wouldn't Jesus just carry out such a rescue in a manner that is fitting of God—by a simple command? Most of us naturally just visualize Jesus sitting on His throne using a simple word to dispatch the solution to every such problem. Surely He would not be troubled. He would send His minions to deal with this problem.

But now we know differently. From our new perspective we know that the truly vivid and extraordinary terminology used by David is precise and it is literal. It is to be taken as literally as any other real world battle description in the Bible. In addition, we cannot help but notice that it too closely mirrors the descriptions by other prophets of their visions of the Shekinah Glory. David even uses some of the same descriptors as Ezekiel in this recounting of God's response to his desperate plea. Indeed, David focuses his description of God's rescue on *"fire"* and *"burning coals,"* just as Ezekiel does in his extraordinarily detailed description of the Shekinah Glory (see previous chapters).

> *From his temple he heard my voice; my cry came before him, into his ears. The earth trembled and quaked, and the foundations of the mountains shook; they trembled because he was angry. Smoke rose from his nostrils; consuming fire came from his mouth, burning coals blazed out of it.*
>
> —Psalm 18:6-8 (emphasis added)

If the words of this psalm are taken literally, we cannot help but come to a stunning conclusion. David's Psalm 18 is nothing less than a vivid, full action description of the incarnate Son of God in His role as a warrior and Commander of the army of the Lord. We are indeed treated to graphic imagery of the powerful wings of the cherubim raising this war chariot and to soar *"on the wings of the wind"*—as fast and as maneuverable and with as devastating an end result as any air cavalry gunship attack.

He parted the heavens and came down; dark clouds were under his feet. He mounted the cherubim and flew; he soared on the wings of the wind. He made darkness his covering, his canopy around him— the dark rain clouds of the sky. Out of the brightness of his presence clouds advanced, with hailstones and bolts of lightning. The LORD thundered from heaven; the voice of the Most High resounded.

—Psalm 18:9-13 (emphasis added)

Note that the pleural of cherub, *"cherubim,"* is used in this description of Jesus coming to David's rescue. This is not just a colorful description of a rider mounting a battle steed. Instead, this is the whole battle command chariot— supported by the powerful wings of *four* cherubim—that is thundering down to David's rescue. The 1st of the 9th Air Cavalry helicopter gun ship assault scene from the movie *Apocalypse Now*—complete with Wagner's *Ride of the Valkyries* booming in the background—has nothing on this military air assault by the mighty warrior Commander of the army of the Lord.

We don't just see and hear this otherworld battle, we *feel* it as the weaponry *"thundered"* and *"resounded."* The *"hailstones"* and *"bolts of lightning"* were poured down on the enemy as surely as the machine gun fire and rockets were unleashed in that famous helicopter attack from *Apocalypse Now*. One can almost hear the powerful wings of the cherubim—like the pulsating and ominous subwoofer thumping of helicopter gunship rotors—as they soar over, hidden in the night sky as they make *"darkness [their] covering."*

As if this description were not vivid enough, David goes even further in his graphic description of the actual weaponry utilized in this otherworld battle. This is war. This is *the* Commander. It is hard to interpret such a comprehensive and detailed description in a classic allegorical sense. This description is too literal in its detail. David's description of his rescue is vivid, exciting, definitive—and it seems purposely precise in its attempt at literal accuracy.

He shot his arrows and scattered [the enemies], great bolts of lightning and routed them. The valleys of the sea were exposed and the foundations of the earth laid bare at your rebuke, O LORD, at the blast of breath from your nostrils.

He reached down from on high and took hold of me; he drew me out of deep waters. He rescued me from my powerful enemy, from my foes, who were too strong for me. They confronted me in the day of

my disaster, but the LORD was my support. He brought me out into a
spacious place; he rescued me because he delighted in me.

—Psalm 18:14-19 (emphasis added)

These are not random verses sung metaphorically in the courts of King David merely for the purpose of entertainment and song. David is sharing an *eyewitness account* of the actual rescue carried out by the Warrior of all warriors. And remember that David wrote these verses long before the visions of Ezekiel, Isaiah, and Daniel revealed the actual visual attributes of this powerful war chariot. Our conclusion must be that somehow David had been allowed to see the actual otherworld mechanics of his rescue. Truly David knew Jesus in His role as the Old Testament's incredible *angel of the Lord,* who despite being made *"a little lower than the angels"* (Hebrews 2:7) served as a more powerful warrior than any modern day Army Ranger or Navy SEAL.

It is understandable that many would still have difficulty with the fire, dark clouds, throne, and guardian cherubim of the Shekinah Glory being described as the air-mobile battle *chariot* of the Commander of the army of the Lord. Classic interpretations have simply viewed the colorful descriptions of the contents of the Shekinah Glory as a throne room—never attaching military utility to it. King David, on the other hand, had no trouble in doing precisely that. He had seen this chariot in action. In 2Chronicles David himself uses precisely this *"chariot"* terminology in describing the plans for the *"most holy place"* (Psalm 28:2) of the temple—the residence of the Shekinah Glory.

He also gave him the plan for the chariot, that is, the cherubim of gold
that spread their wings and shelter the ark of the covenant of the
LORD.

—1Chronicles 28:18B (emphasis added)

Further still, David's vivid Psalm 18 description of the use of the overwhelming firepower of the Shekinah Glory is, of course, not the only such description in the Old Testament. There are countless episodes where fire was described as coming down from heaven to ignite sacrificial offerings or to destroy the enemies of God. One cannot know for sure, but it is not an unreasonable reach to attribute these vivid episodes to the intervention of this weapons platform.

One such account occurs in the book of Joshua. The five Amorite kings have squared off at Gibeon against the Joshua-led Israelites. That which is unique about this particular account is the visible intervention of an otherworldly force into the actual mechanics of the battle. In other words, we are not just speaking of an otherworld battle that occurs and then has some sort of secondary influence on the Israelite's real world battle. In this case we are treated to a miraculous intervention in which the otherworld Shekinah Glory itself actually delivers ordinance upon the real world enemy troops who were physically fighting with the Israelite army.

> *After an all-night march from Gilgal, Joshua took them by surprise. The LORD threw them into confusion before Israel, who defeated them in a great victory at Gibeon. Israel pursued them along the road going up to Beth Horon and cut them down all the way to Azekah and Makkedah. As they fled before Israel on the road down from Beth Horon to Azekah, the LORD hurled large hailstones down on them from the sky, and more of them died from the hailstones than were killed by the swords of the Israelites.*

—Joshua 10:9-11 (emphasis added)

Surely the weapons deployed from this advanced assault platform must have overwhelmed the relatively primitive Old Testament weaponry. Once again *"hailstones"* are mentioned. Their repeated mention suggests that they may have been the primary ordinance delivered by the Shekinah Glory. One can easily imagine that the impact of *"hailstones"* and *"bolts of lightning"* (Psalm 18:9-13, see above) would have had devastating effects on human targets. The accuracy of their delivery and the lethality of their impact are well described in the quote above.

Another particularly vivid example of the devastating firepower of the Shekinah Glory involved the rebellion of Korah against Moses and Aaron (Numbers 16). The weaponry deployed from the Shekinah Glory dealt with the 250 rebellious leaders who had accompanied Korah in his rebellion suddenly and thoroughly:

> *And fire came out from the LORD and consumed the 250 men who were offering the incense.*

—Numbers 16:35

The complete, utter, and sudden lethality of the armament deployed from the Shekinah Glory is assured by the detail and somewhat grisly description of the resulting human carnage.

> *The LORD said to Moses, "Tell Eleazar son of Aaron, the priest, to take the censers out of the smoldering remains and scatter the coals*

some distance away, for the censers are holy—the censers of the men
who sinned at the cost of their lives. Hammer the censers into sheets
to overlay the altar, for they were presented before the LORD and have
become holy. Let them be a sign to the Israelites." So Eleazar the
priest collected the bronze censers brought by those who had been
burned up, and he had them hammered out to overlay the altar, as the
LORD directed him through Moses. This was to remind the Israelites
that no one except a descendant of Aaron should come to burn incense
before the LORD, or he would become like Korah and his followers.

—Numbers 16:36-40 (emphasis added)

God could have just had the fire just come out of nowhere. Instead, He chose to surround His fully emptied Son with a platform whose characteristics and military attributes are familiar to our generation. All of us who live in the era of the sudden lethality of air mobile warrior forces and the vital devastation of air cavalry helicopter gunships can directly relate to what happened in the very real historical account of the rebellion of Korah and the 250 Israelite leaders. What a delight it is that the Master Designer of every event that has unfolded in our world since its beginning has chosen such an intense, physical, hands-on approach to His interaction with His creation. Jesus, the link between the unlinkable, was fully engaged in a very physical manner with the creation into which He was emptied.

A discussion of modern-day corollaries with the Old Testament battle capabilities of the Shekinah Glory would not be complete without mention of one other peculiar Old Testament event. In 1Samuel 7 we are treated to a description of the defeat of the Philistines by what is described as a direct assault carried out by God. The description of this unique attack sounds suspiciously like yet another account of another novel use of the Shekinah glory as a battle command and weapons platform.

While Samuel was sacrificing the burnt offering, the Philistines drew
near to engage Israel in battle. But that day the LORD thundered with
loud thunder against the Philistines and threw them into such a panic
that they were routed before the Israelites. The men of Israel rushed
out of Mizpah and pursued the Philistines, slaughtering them along
the way to a point below Beth Car.

—1Samuel 7:10-11 (emphasis added)

This account is eerily reminiscent of similar modern day accounts that accompanied the previously mentioned descriptions of the Viet Nam era use of the *broken arrow* emergency call. Along with these accounts came descriptions of United States Air Force fighter pilots who adopted a unique solution to the problem of having no remaining ordinance aboard their fighter aircraft when they received such an emergency call. They would simply take their Phantom jets to near-Mach speeds, swoop down, and fly directly over the heads of the enemy troops who were overrunning the forward American bases.

In high-speed dives that would carry them down to altitudes below 500 feet, these brave American pilots would blast the enemy troops with the only weapon available to them after emptying their cannon and wing mounts—the deafening noise from their thundering jet engines. Their hopes—that the blasting sound of twin jet engines lit up with full afterburners would frighten and dishearten the attacking enemy—were well founded. The enemy Vietnamese soldiers were described as cowering under the noise assault—and even running away in complete disarray.

In a similar fashion, the account from 1Samuel 7 may well be describing a supersonic, low level flyby of the Shekinah Glory. Admittedly, this may be assigning more than is due. And yet the resulting panic of the Philistine soldiers not only mirrors the resulting commotion following the F-4 Phantom maneuvers, but also speaks volumes regarding the thunderous presence of what must have been an awesome Old Testament spectacle.

The convicting evidence that the Son of God was an embodied participant in the great war of the Old Testament is well substantiated by scripture. That embodiment was real and physical. By God's precise design, these physical attributes—including the limitations—required that warrior cherubim guard Jesus. Further still, the tactical requirements of this warrior Commander were satisfied by a stealthy, rapidly air-mobile weapons platform that was capable of laying down the devastation that is worthy of He who *"treads the winepress of the fury of the wrath of God Almighty"* (Revelation 19:15).

Chapter 19

Battle in the Heavens
The Unseen Battle Behind the Destruction of the Egyptian Charioteers at the Red Sea

A disorganized entourage of stranded travelers stood with their backs to the tempestuous shores of the Red Sea. The newly formed nation of Israel had marched triumphantly past their Egyptian captors just days before. Their captors had been so glad to see them go that they had adorned them with the treasures of Egypt. The plagues sent by the Israelite God had been overwhelming. The death of the Egyptian firstborn had sent every household into mourning. They had been glad to see the Israelites leave.

But as the shock of the plagues wore off and the reality of a life without slaves confronted the leaders of Egypt, the charioteers had been mustered. God had hardened the heart of Egypt as He had promised. Their chariots had pursued the fleeing Israelite horde to the shores of the Red Sea. The plan was straightforward. This flirtation with freedom would end. The unarmed former slaves would be returned to their subservient position in Egypt. But first there would be slaughter.

The pages of the Old Testament are brimming with vivid descriptions of desperate battle. Some are historical accounts of real world battle between the nation of Israel and her real world enemies. Others are clearly prophetic in nature and speak of great battles yet to come. A third subset of Old Testament battle descriptions defies easy classification. It is altogether quite different. These battle accounts present a somewhat confusing combination of descriptors that seem to be both from this world *and* from the spiritual otherworld. One of these battle stories is very special. It deserves a thorough look. Of all places, this intriguing battle description is found in the third chapter of the book of the prophet Habakkuk.

Habakkuk's battle description is pivotal in importance to our quest for evidence of Jesus Christ in the Old Testament. Its uniqueness is based in the fact that it supplies *otherworld* information regarding a real world battle with which we are all quite familiar. After all, most of us learned at an early age the Exodus story of the battle at the Red Sea. For obvious reasons, it remains a favorite in Sunday schools worldwide. It fully conveys the desperate plight of the Israelites as the Egyptian charioteers bear down on them. It relates in vivid terms the miracle of the parting of the Red Sea. It tells of two towering walls of water standing on either side of a dry pathway to freedom from Egyptian tyranny. The collapse of those very same walls of water ultimately obliterates the pursuing Egyptian charioteers. It is nothing short of miraculous. And yet, as amazing as this Exodus story of wondrous redemption remains, this is not all that the Bible has to say about this pivotal battle in the history of Israel.

After all, despite its detailed account of the battle, Exodus renders few, if any, hints regarding any associated otherworld activity. The relating of the spiritual side of the battle would have to wait hundreds of years for the prophet Habakkuk to give us his perspective. His account confirms our inherent suspicions regarding the presence of furious otherworld shenanigans going on behind the scenes of this dramatic rescue. He in fact describes intense otherworld battle occurring *simultaneously* with the real world struggle.

Habakkuk was a prophet to the nation of Judah during the days just prior to the Babylonian captivity. Unlike the majority of his fellow Israelites at the time, Habakkuk was focused on God. He realized the difficult position that the nation of Israel had put itself into because of its repeated sin. He knew that severe discipline at the hand of an enemy army would be the consequence. Habakkuk's prayer, therefore, focused on a request for God to rescue them—most specifically by military intervention—from the oppressor who would be sent to discipline them.

> *A prayer of Habakkuk the prophet. On shigionoth.*
>
> LORD, *I have heard of your fame; I stand in awe of your deeds, O* LORD. *Renew them in our day, in our time make them known; in wrath remember mercy.*
>
> —Habakkuk 3:1-2

In this prayer for intervention, Habakkuk reminds God that there is precedent in the history of Israel for just such a rescue. Habakkuk reminds God of a prior time when God's mercy ruled over His wrath. Habakkuk retells the story of a great battle fought by God on behalf of the young nation of Israel. His ploy is clear. Habakkuk wants God to intervene just like He did in Israel's past. He wants God to intervene with the same suddenness and lethality upon their current enemies as He had against previous enemies. Habakkuk reminds God of the previous battle against the Egyptian army that most epitomizes God's merciful rescue of His people.

Accompanying Habakkuk's rescue request is his own version of the Exodus battle account. This is where things get even more interesting. From the very beginning, we are caught off guard by a story that seems similar and yet in many ways is startlingly different from the one we read in the book of Exodus. Indeed, the nature of Habakkuk's reference to God in verse 3 immediately gets our attention. This is hardly the classic description of God that places Him just sitting majestically on a throne in heaven.

> *God came from Teman, the Holy One from Mount Paran. Selah His glory covered the heavens and his praise filled the earth. His splendor was like the sunrise; rays flashed from his hand, where his power was hidden.*
>
> —Habakkuk 3:3-4 (emphasis added)

"God came from Teman"? From *Teman*? Teman is another reference to Edom. God came from Edom? God is in heaven. He fills the earth. He is in all of the creation and all of the creation is contained within Him. What is this reference to Him coming from a very specific geographical location? Why would the Holy Spirit make this very pointed revelation that places the Mighty God of the universe *in Teman*?

The truly spectacular nature of this reference is revealed only in our new perspective. Indeed, when we step out of our comfortable old-church beliefs and view these scriptures from the new perspective that places the embodied Son of God, Jesus, in the middle of the battles of the Old Testament, this statement begins to make sense. Only in this perspective could God possibly be seen coming from a single geographical location in His creation.

Further, why Teman? Why Edom? A barrage of Old Testament scripture liberally describes the wrath that God has poured out on Edom—and presumably will again pour out on Edom in the future. Many prophets have devoted many verses to this singular message—that God has at some time in the past settled a score with Edom and that He may well have another one to settle in the future. It is also obvious that if there was real world battle involving Edom in Israel's past, there must have been otherworld conflict also. If there was conflict, if there was battle, if there was a fight involving the remnant of Israel—which there obviously was with Edom— then you can bet that Jesus, the Commander of the army of the Lord, spent a lot of time there. So, it really should not surprise us that the scene starts with Jesus coming from Edom.

These verses from this third chapter of Habakkuk are graphic and specific and speak much of very desperate battle. The above passage tells us right from the beginning that this battle description is not just a *real world* battle description. The specific reference to God's glory covering *"the heavens"* along with His praise filling *"the earth"* places us right in the middle of both worlds. As we have mentioned, this is a very common pattern that repeatedly surfaces in the writings of the prophets concerning Old Testament battle. These dual descriptions carry elements of both real world and otherworld conflict.

This chapter in the book of Habakkuk is especially important in this regard. In few other places in the Old Testament are we given such graphic evidence that the description is of an otherworld battle and not just another of the many descriptions of real world battle involving the nation of Israel. Indeed, the otherworld references are precise and distinctly different from the known real world battle description.

In this particular case, the separation of real world battle stories from otherworld battle accounts is founded in the fact that we already have a description of the real world battle at the Red Sea. The real world battle chronology is nicely described in the book of Exodus and is familiar to all of us. In this unique account by the prophet Habakkuk, therefore, we can assuredly know *that every battle detail that did not or could not occur in the Exodus account of the real world battle must originate from the otherworld battle that accompanied it.* We just need to subtract the Exodus account from the Habakkuk account. The battle description that is left is pure otherworld battle.

This fact is what makes this battle account so instructive regarding our search for Jesus in the Old Testament. There are many battle accounts in the Old Testament where our intuition tells us that details from both our world and the otherworld are being given. But, in most, the battle details seem to be similar in both worlds. In most of those circumstances, therefore, we have no way of telling which details are specific to which world. For the most part, they could occur in either. In other words, we aren't provided with a detailed real world account (like the Exodus account of the battle at the Red Sea) against which we can contrast the details of the suspected otherworld battle (described by Habakkuk).

That is why this third chapter of Habakkuk is, in many ways, like the Rosetta Stone of otherworld battle. The Rosetta Stone supplied the characters of multiple languages side-by-side, such that interpretation between the languages was remarkably facilitated by this critical archeological find. So also does this Habakkuk battle account provide real world battle details side-by-side with otherworld battle descriptors. It can, therefore, help us interpret between descriptions of real and otherworld battle. As mentioned, there is much evidence that the battle details—such as weaponry and technique—are very similar between the two worlds. This helps in one respect as it relates *otherworld* battle in terms that are already familiar to us. In another sense, however, it complicates and compromises our effort since we are unable to separate the two when both real and otherworld descriptions are combined into one battle account.

This unique chapter, however, reveals very specific war details that most pointedly did *not* occur in the real world Exodus battle—and therefore must have occurred in the otherworld. These battle details are nothing less than stunning in their revelation regarding both the nature of battle in the otherworld and the nature of the fully emptied status of Jesus during the Old Testament. In few other dual battle accounts are we given such a surefire method to subtract out the real world battle and zero in on the details of otherworld battle. Habakkuk 3 also emphasizes the importance of the fact that the many battle descriptions that are given in the Old Testament—some of which are entirely too weird to get our arms around—are most likely hybrid descriptions that contain elements of battle from *both* arenas.

With this in mind, the first several verses of this passage can clearly be describing the prelude to battle in either world. Their relevance to a specific real world incident is brought to light only when verses 5-12 reveal that we are speaking about the Exodus of Israel from the land of Egypt. Can there be any question about this after we are given a very clear description of plagues, pestilences, cursing of the streams and rivers, and *"rage against the sea"*?

Plague went before him; pestilence followed his steps. He stood, and shook the earth; he looked, and made the nations tremble. The ancient mountains crumbled and the age-old hills collapsed. His ways are eternal. I saw the tents of Cushan in distress, the dwellings of Midian in anguish. Were you angry with the rivers, O LORD? Was your wrath against the streams? Did you rage against the sea when you rode with your horses and your victorious chariots? You uncovered your bow, you called for many arrows. Selah You split the earth with rivers; the mountains saw you and writhed. Torrents of water swept by; the deep roared and lifted its waves on high. Sun and moon stood still in the heavens at the glint of your flying arrows, at the lightning of your flashing spear. In wrath you strode through the earth and in anger you threshed the nations.

—Habakkuk 3:5-12 (emphasis added)

All of the details that are written in these verses, from the plagues and pestilences to the cursing of the water in the rivers, can be attributed to the *real world* battle account of the Exodus. That is not to say that they did not also occur in the otherworld—maybe they did. That is also not to say that they do not foretell end times battle details also—surely they do. But what we do know for sure is that they also definitely occurred in the real world, because the Exodus account from the Pentateuch also describes them in detail.

After these introductory verses, things begin to pick up in reference to *otherworld* battle details. First of all we are placed right into the middle of the heat of the battle by a graphic reference to God's *"rage against the sea,"* which refers to the parting of the Red Sea. This, once again, is a real world detail that we are familiar with from the Exodus account. But along with it comes a detail that we have not seen before. We are told in graphic fashion in the above verses that the Red Sea indeed parted because Jesus and His fellow warriors rode their *"horses and...victorious chariots"* right through the middle of it. The prophet Isaiah also seems to confirm Habakkuk's graphic visual image of a road being carved through the water by chariots of God.

Was it not you who dried up the sea, the waters of the great deep, who made a road in the depths of the sea so that the redeemed might cross over?

—Isaiah 51:10

And yet something is wrong here. There is no Exodus account of God riding horses and *"victorious chariots"* anywhere, let alone through the Red Sea. Surely we can simply dismiss these graphic battle descriptions as merely colorful allegory. But we know better than that now. These are not metaphorical muses describing God fighting battle from afar by the command of His voice while lounging comfortably on His throne. These are graphic descriptions of a tempestuous otherworld battle that involved mighty warrior steeds and great battle chariots. This is Jesus embroiled in battle against the evil powers of this otherworld who influence our world by their plotting, trade, and battle.

A vivid description of the massive wall of water that must have been roaring mightily on either side of the Israelites is rendered as Habakkuk then tells us, *"Torrents of water swept by; the deep roared and lifted its waves on high."* The Exodus description of the subsequent destruction of the Egyptian army is then echoed as the walls of water crash in upon the Egyptian cavalry. But this time we are actually told of the otherworld event that caused the walls of water to fall. Habakkuk recounts to Jesus, *"You trampled the sea with your horses, churning the great waters."* The powerful horses of the chariots of Jesus and His warriors unleashed the pent up wall of water against the Egyptian charioteers by the pounding of their powerful hooves. The result is well known to us all from the Exodus description.

> *The water flowed back and covered the chariots and horsemen—the entire army of Pharaoh that had followed the Israelites into the sea. Not one of them survived.*
>
> —Exodus 14:28

Despite the fact that the otherworld is spiritual in nature, the Habakkuk account tells us of the very physical nature of the *otherworld* battle that was fought with real weapons against real foes and paralleled the events of this Exodus account. We are told above that the Lord *"uncovered [His] bow"* and *"called for many arrows."* This is a clear and detailed description of Jesus preparing for very real battle. There is no indication that He is shooting imaginary arrows. There is no evidence that we are to take this allegorically. This is the real deal. This is battle.

Accordingly, the revelation that the *"Sun and moon stood still in the heavens at the glint of your flying arrows, at the lightning of your flashing spear"* is a further reference to the otherworld battle that accompanied Israel's desperate flight from Egypt. Jesus *"strode"* forth *"through the earth"* and in His anger has *"threshed the nations."* This is a fight. This is *"bows"* and *"flying arrows"* and *"flashing spear[s]."* It is not allegorical. It is real. And, most importantly, we know that this is *otherworld* battle being described. In the Exodus account of the real world battle there simply is no mention of bows and flashing spears and certainly no flying arrows. The Exodus account makes it clear that in fact the two real world armies never got close enough for actual battle.

> *Then the angel of God, who had been traveling in front of Israel's army, withdrew and went behind them. The pillar of cloud also moved from in front and stood behind them, <u>coming between the armies of Egypt and Israel</u>. Throughout the night the cloud brought*

darkness to the one side and light to the other side; so neither went near the other all night long.

—Exodus 14:19-20 (emphasis added)

In the subsequent verses, Habakkuk holds nothing back. It is precisely as we have suspected from the beginning. Habakkuk is telling us of the battle and the victory that accompanied the destruction of the Egyptian army in the real world. He reminds us that just as *all was lost* in the real world battle—just as the Egyptian chariots appeared to be closing in on the helpless, fleeing Israelites—Jesus stepped in to save the day. *Rescue*—it was *the* mission of Jesus in the Old Testament. The rescue of the remnant of Israel was always the driving command behind the fight in which Jesus was found. This battle is no different, as Habakkuk specifically and pointedly recounts to Jesus, *"You came out to deliver your people, to save your anointed one."*

You came out to deliver your people, to save your anointed one. You crushed the leader of the land of wickedness, you stripped him from head to foot. Selah With his own spear you pierced his head when his warriors stormed out to scatter us, gloating as though about to devour the wretched who were in hiding. You trampled the sea with your horses, churning the great waters.

—Habakkuk 3:13-15 (emphasis added)

The telling of this otherworld account by Habakkuk is masterful. Indeed, Habakkuk has much more to tell us than just that which is revealed in the book of Exodus. We knew of the water crashing in on the Egyptian chariots. We knew of the presence of God in the salvation of the Israelite remnant. But we had no idea that the embodied Son of God, Jesus, was fighting the fight in the otherworld at that very moment that would unleash that victory in the real world that was found in the *"churning"* of *"the great waters."*

In the above passage, Habakkuk even reveals the details of the accompanying otherworld battle that occurred right before the waters came crashing down on Pharaoh's chariots. As if he were trying to build even more suspense regarding the desperate nature of the Israelites' plight, Habakkuk tells us that the enemy warriors were *"gloating as though about to devour the wretched who were in hiding."* This is graphic battle. Once again, the battle is specifically detailed in this account so that we can know for sure that this was in fact very real battle—despite the fact that it is not of this world.

And most amazingly of all, up until this point we had no idea that at the very moment of the real world destruction of the Egyptian army, Jesus, the Commander of the army of the Lord, had defeated, humiliated, and killed *"the leader of the land of wickedness."* This is a pointed and obvious reference to the physical defeat of the otherworld *"power"* behind the Egyptian oppressors—no doubt an evil *"prince"* of the otherworld. There certainly was no reference in the Exodus real world battle account of *Pharaoh* being *"stripped... from head to foot."* The graphic battle description of Jesus killing this most heinously evil leader *"With his own spear"* just as *"his warriors stormed out to scatter"* the Israelites is not allegory and it is not mentioned in Exodus. It is instead a clear reference to very real, and yet otherworldly, battle.

As if to further drive home the point that this was a real life-and-death battle between Jesus and a real live wicked leader of the otherworld, the prophet Isaiah even names this powerful *"monster"* who leads the evil forces who represent the interests of Pharaoh in the otherworld. His name was *"Rahab."*

> *Awake, awake! Clothe yourself with strength, O arm of the LORD; awake, as in days gone by, as in generations of old. Was it not you who cut Rahab to pieces, who pierced that monster through?*
> —Isaiah 51:9 (emphasis added)

Amazingly, Isaiah even confirms the battle details revealed by Habakkuk. His description of the monster being *"pierced...through"* is a clear confirmation of Habakkuk's statement that Jesus killed the wicked otherworld leader with his own spear. That two witnesses (Habakkuk and Isaiah) both confirm similar graphic battle details reinforces the fact that this is a description of real hand-to-hand combat, not a poetic allegorical account. This very tangible battle clearly occurred simultaneous with the dramatic rescue that is recounted in the book of Exodus. And yet we had heard nothing of it until the prophet Habakkuk reveals that which he had been allowed to see through a briefly opened window into the history and substance of the otherworld.

By describing the real world account of battle along with the simultaneously occurring otherworld battle, Habakkuk has given us an incredibly unique and provocative revelation of the activities of our warrior King, Jesus. The purpose is clear. It is to tell us that everything that occurs in our world has an otherworld counterpart. It is to tell us that Jesus fought in that otherworld for the remnant of Israel continually throughout the Old Testament. It is to tell us that Jesus is there for us—in the same remnant-saving manner—right now.

And this revelation of the behind-the-scene exploits of Jesus was also for Habakkuk. Most certainly Habakkuk had a motive behind his recounting of this otherworld victory. He wanted Jesus to again intervene mightily on behalf of the Israelite remnant—just as He had so long before.

Indeed, the physical impact of this obviously vivid otherworld revelation on the prophet Habakkuk himself is overwhelming. This was for real.

> *I heard and my heart pounded, my lips quivered at the sound; decay crept into my bones, and my legs trembled. Yet I will wait patiently for the day of calamity to come on the nation invading us.*
> —Habakkuk 3:16 (emphasis added)

This vision was not some flowery trip into whimsical and metaphorical green Elysian Fields of eternal comfort. This was a revelation of harsh and vicious battle that left Habakkuk's heart pounding, his lips quivering, his legs trembling, and *"decay"* creeping into his bones as he waited for a similar *"day of calamity to come on the nation invading"* them at the time. When reading second hand Biblical accounts of battle, we seem to have a natural tendency to downplay the suddenness and stunning impact of shockingly violent battle. No battle, however—when the lives of the combatants are on the line—is ever anything less than simply overwhelming. Indeed, Habakkuk wanted to make sure that the readers of his account enjoyed no such luxury as the allegorical dismissal of the violent battle that he had personally witnessed.

In fact, let's take a moment together for a little field trip. Think of the most violent battle sequence from the most violent war movie that you have ever seen. Habakkuk's vision was worse. It was real. *Real* is always worse than imitation. We can be assured that what Habakkuk is describing to us was the most violent of conflicts—more so even than any of the modern day movies that almost seem to be in competition to create the most graphically real depiction of battle.

So, what can we know from this vivid Old Testament battle sequence describing *the battle that accompanied the battle*? What can we know of the otherworld conflict that is hinted at so strongly throughout the Old Testament? What can we know about the battle in the otherworld that seemed to strongly impact our world—and seemed to be so strongly impacted by our world? What can we know of the war that was the centerpiece of the real history of the Old Testament? What can we know of the setting in which Jesus Christ, the Commander of the army of the Lord, spent the entirety of the Old Testament fighting for the preservation of the remnant of Israel?

This seemingly minor chapter from one of the Minor Prophets has much to offer in regard to the many questions to which our hearts seek eternal answers. If we subtract from it the battle description of the destruction of Pharaoh's army that is given in the book of Exodus, we can make several statements regarding the battle that simultaneously took place in the otherworld. First, we can know that the parting of the Red Sea was by nothing less than a last second, whips cracking, wheels spinning, horses snorting, mad dash by the powerful angelic chariots commanded by Jesus.

We can also know that there must have been an incredible otherworld battle that took place when the Shekinah Glory—the powerful command chariot of the army of the Lord—maneuvered itself into a defensive position between the fleeing Israelites and the hard-charging, armed cavalry of the Egyptian army. Can we imagine what this must have been like? Can we picture this desperate last-second rescue of the Israelites from utter destruction? The Israelites were horrified at the approach of the Egyptian army but Moses tells them exactly what is about to happen. God is going to *"fight"* for them.

> As Pharaoh approached, the Israelites looked up, and there were the Egyptians, marching after them. They were terrified and cried out to the LORD. They said to Moses, "Was it because there were no graves in Egypt that you brought us to the desert to die? What have you done to us by bringing us out of Egypt? Didn't we say to you in Egypt, 'Leave us alone; let us serve the Egyptians'? It would have been better for us to serve the Egyptians than to die in the desert!"
>
> Moses answered the people, "Do not be afraid. Stand firm and you will see the deliverance the LORD will bring you today. The Egyptians you see today you will never see again. The LORD will fight for you; you need only to be still."

—Exodus 14:10-14 (emphasis added)

Then the fully air-mobile, flaming command chariot—the mysterious Shekinah Glory—demonstrated what it could do. This mighty weapons platform swept into a battle defense position on the wings of the mighty cherubim just in time to safely separate the defenseless, fledgling Israelite nation from the relentless Egyptian charioteers.

The result of this tactical maneuvering by the Shekinah Glory was two-fold. In our world, the very real Egyptian army was held at bay by the equally real—and awesome—presence of a giant fiery cloud.

> *Then the angel of God, who had been traveling in front of Israel's army, withdrew and went behind them. The pillar of cloud also moved from in front and stood behind them, coming between the armies of Egypt and Israel. Throughout the night the cloud brought darkness to the one side and light to the other side; so neither went near the other all night long.*
>
> —Exodus 14:19-20 (emphasis added)

But note also that once again *the angel of the Lord* is right in the middle of the battle. Simultaneous with the movement of the Shekinah Glory is the movement of *"the angel of God"*—right into battle. Simultaneous with the occurrence of the rescue in this world is a mighty battle taking place in the otherworld—just over the Israelite's heads. The Lord is their rear guard—in a very real, very physical way.

> *Then your light will break forth like the dawn, and your healing will quickly appear; then your righteousness will go before you, and the glory of the LORD will be your rear guard.*
>
> —Isaiah 58:8 (emphasis added)

Surely this movement of *the angel of the Lord* heralded a mighty otherworld battle—complete with the thundering crash of battle lines violently throwing themselves at each other. He moved for a reason. He changed position to engage the enemy. With this movement, the otherworld battle intensified with demonic angelic warriors falling in battle and the real world Egyptian charioteers suffering also at the hand of the Lord.

> *During the last watch of the night the LORD looked down from the pillar of fire and cloud at the Egyptian army and threw it into confusion. He made the wheels of their chariots come off so that they had difficulty driving. And the Egyptians said, "Let's get away from the Israelites! The LORD is fighting for them against Egypt."*
>
> —Exodus 14:24-25 (emphasis added)

At this point even the Egyptians knew that Jesus and his holy warriors were fighting for Israel! But it was too late. The Egyptians had charged in between the walls of water—the jaws of the trap—in their pursuit of the fleeing Israelites.

And then, in the tumultuous final moments of the real world battle, we now know from the account of the prophet Habakkuk that a simultaneous otherworld victory was won. For then *"the LORD,"* the Commander of the army of the Lord, struck the deathblow that would be the end. It would signal the simultaneous collapse of the massive walls of water on the charging Egyptians and the defeat of the otherworld enemies of the army of the Lord.

This deathblow was not delivered by one of His warrior angels—for Jesus was not sitting in a command post up on a hillside passively observing this battle. He was no aloof commander who had the men under His command do all of the fighting. Quite to the contrary, Jesus placed Himself voluntarily right into the middle of the fight. He wouldn't have it any other way. And in the middle of that very tangible and very real struggle, it is precisely Jesus who tears the battle armor off of *"the leader of the land of wickedness,"* grabs the spear out of his enemy's hands, and delivers a deathblow to his wicked adversary.

> *You came out to deliver your people, to save your anointed one. You crushed the leader of the land of wickedness, you stripped him from head to foot. Selah With his own spear you pierced his head when his warriors stormed out to scatter us, gloating as though about to devour the wretched who were in hiding. You trampled the sea with your horses, churning the great waters.*
>
> —Habakkuk 3:13-15 (emphasis added)

How easy it is to just assign metaphorical meaning to this very graphic description of hand-to-hand mortal combat between two powerful adversaries. How easy it is to just dismiss it as the prophet Habakkuk waxing allegorical in his reverence for the awesome work of the Mighty God. But to dismiss it is to miss the mark completely. It is to miss out on the very high adventure, the very physical involvement of the incarnate Son of God in the defense of His beloved Israel. Psalm 74 seems to confirm the very physical nature of this battle between the walls of Red Sea water.

> *But you, O God, are my king from of old; you bring salvation upon the earth. It was you who split open the sea by your power; you broke the*

heads of the monster in the waters. It was you who crushed the heads
of Leviathan and gave him as food to the creatures of the desert.
—Psalm 74:12-14 (emphasis added)

The writer of Psalm 77 also confirms that the parting of the Red Sea and the subsequent destruction of the Egyptian charioteers involved more than just two crashing walls of water.   There was nothing allegorical about the fury of the accompanying otherworld battle.   This was furious battle in which God was a hands-on active participant.

With your mighty arm you redeemed your people, the descendants of
Jacob and Joseph. Selah The waters saw you, O God, the waters saw
you and writhed; the very depths were convulsed. The clouds poured
down water, the skies resounded with thunder; your arrows flashed
back and forth.   Your thunder was heard in the whirlwind, your
lightning lit up the world; the earth trembled and quaked. Your path
led through the sea, your way through the mighty waters, though your
footprints were not seen.   You led your people like a flock by the hand
of Moses and Aaron.
—Psalm 77:15-20 (emphasis added)

Could Jesus, the Commander of the army of the Lord, taken a lesser role than I have described? Could the One whose orders were to preserve the holy remnant of Israel been satisfied with less involvement in this critical juncture of the history of Israel?   Could He have ever accepted a less physically palpable role than this? Could I have just made up a story that is actually more awesome than what really occurred?   And likewise, are the heroic acts and awesome rescues that line the pages of history just clutter in the history of the world, which must—by definition—be the epic story of the Son of God?   Are the stories of heroes, of champions of the poor and disenfranchised that fill our movie theaters, just the creation of mankind? Or do these stories of heroes reflect the very real story of Jesus, the focal point of all of creation? Indeed, Habakkuk and his fellow prophets would have much to tell us about this Rescuer of all rescuers, this Hero of all heroes.

Chapter 20

Messenger
The Angel of the Lord Comforts Hagar

The desert of Beersheba. It was there that Hagar and her son Ishmael had been sent by Abraham. The desert was unforgiving. The heat was oppressive. They were alone.

Hagar had carefully considered the facts. They, like the desert jackals that surround her, were hard to ignore. They led her to only one conclusion. All was lost. She had determined that she and her son—Abraham's son—would both die there in the desert of Beersheba. Her despair was complete as she placed her son under a nearby bush. She could not bear to watch him die.

In midst of her despair she became aware of a haunting presence. This was not over yet. She was disappointed at this. She would have gladly welcome the death to which she had resigned herself. Death seemed the easy path then. But it would not be that easy for them. She and her son were hunted. Alone in the vast desert, they were not alone. Someone stood near them. The jackals had fled from His presence. This was no ordinary creature of the desert. The Hunter of hunters stalked Hagar and her son. His search was for sons and daughters of God, and He was a relentless hunter. He hunted every man and woman. And then He hunted Hagar and Ishmael.

The foundation for the premise of this book—that Jesus took on an active and physical Old Testament role as the warrior Commander of the army of the Lord—has been laid. The new perspective that this foundation brings can now be utilized to take a fresh look at the many appearances of *the angel of the Lord* in the familiar stories of the Old Testament. Clearly, *the angel of the Lord* is a pivotal figure in the main theme of the Old Testament, which is the story of *"the One"* who is to come. If our premise is correct, a review of some of the passages describing his many appearances may be helpful in further supporting our case for his identity and the nature of his Old Testament role.

Early the next morning Abraham took some food and a skin of water and gave them to Hagar. He set them on her shoulders and then sent *her off with the boy. She went on her way and wandered in the desert of Beersheba. When the water in the skin was gone, <u>she put the boy under one of the bushes</u>. Then she went off and sat down nearby, about a bowshot away, for she thought, "<u>I cannot watch the boy die</u>." And as she sat there nearby, she began to sob.*

God heard the boy crying, and <u>the angel of God</u> called to Hagar <u>from heaven</u> and said to her, "What is the matter, Hagar? Do not be afraid; God has heard the boy crying as he lies there. Lift the boy up and take him by the hand, for <u>I</u> will make him <u>into a great nation</u>." Then God opened her eyes and she saw a well of water. So she went and filled the skin with water and gave the boy a drink.

—Genesis 21: 14-19 (emphasis added)

Once again, the evidence for the divine identity of *the angel of the Lord* is not subtle. *"The angel of God"* speaks in first person as he claims that it is *he* who is the one who will make Ishmael *"into a great nation."* No ordinary angel could make Ishmael into a great nation if he wanted to, and no ordinary angel would presume the place of God in such a proclamation. This is Jesus, the Commander of the army of the Lord, and He is on another mission.

This was not the first time that *the angel of the Lord* had found Hagar in the desert. After Hagar had first conceived Ishmael, she had then been mistreated by Sarai and had fled from her into the desert.

The angel of the LORD found Hagar near a spring in the desert; it was the spring that is beside the road to Shur. And he said, "Hagar, servant of Sarai, where have you come from, and where are you going?"

"I'm running away from my mistress Sarai," she answered.

—Genesis 16:7-8

Then as now, *the angel of the Lord*—Jesus—replaces Hagar's moment of deep despair with a message of hope. Her descendants *"will be too numerous to count"* (Genesis 16:10). But first Hagar must do that to which we are all called, for His message is the same as that which He will faithfully model after His birth in Bethlehem. *She must submit to her persecutor.*

Then the angel of the LORD told her, "Go back to your mistress and submit to her."

—Genesis 16:9 (emphasis added)

The message of the Son of God is consistent whether in the Old Testament, acting as *the angel of the Lord*, or in the New, acting as the Lamb of God. His compassion and mercy, which forms the foundation of His New Testament presence, is also on display in the desert in His message to Hagar. Despite the seemingly dire circumstances, Hagar's son Ishmael will live to be the father of a great nation. Of more significance to the discussion of the identity of *the angel of the Lord*, however, is the fact that in this statement *the angel of the Lord* again states that it is indeed *He* who will so bless Hagar.

The angel added, "I will so increase your descendants that they will be too numerous to count."

—Genesis 16:10 (emphasis added)

Once again, angels—save Lucifer—are incapable of using language that could in any way be misinterpreted as claiming credit for that which is only and exclusively the charge of God. Further still, *the angel of the Lord* then refers to the Lord in second person, once again demonstrating that this Messenger is one of the three Persons of the Triune Godhead deferring to yet another Person.

The angel of the LORD also said to her: "You are now with child and you will have a son. You shall name him Ishmael, for the LORD has heard of your misery.

—Genesis 16:11 (emphasis added)

This statement also speaks directly to the fact that it was the Father who had heard of Hagar's plight and sent the Son on yet another messenger mission. The primary motivation of Jesus never changes. It is the same in the Old Testament it is in the New. His activities are entirely motivated by the will of the Father. His message is the good news of the offer of God's salvation.

There is no doubt that Hagar knows precisely to whom she is speaking. It is not clear how, but she so obviously knows. The name she gives *"the angel of God,"* as well as the reasoning behind it are explained. She knows that she has seen God.

She gave this name to the LORD who spoke to her: "You are the God who sees me," for she said, "I have now seen the One who sees me."

—Genesis 16:13 (emphasis added)

As if this were not enough, later in the very next chapter of Genesis the divine identity of *the angel of the Lord* who spoke with Hagar is yet again confirmed. The reference is indirect, yet leaves little question that the intent of the Holy Spirit was to assure us that this message was delivered in the very physical presence of God.

> *Abraham fell facedown; he laughed and said to himself, "Will a son be born to a man a hundred years old? Will Sarah bear a child at the age of ninety?" And Abraham <u>said to God</u>, "<u>If only Ishmael might live under your blessing!</u>"*
>
> *Then <u>God</u> said, "Yes, but your wife Sarah will bear you a son, and you will call him Isaac. I will establish my covenant with him as an everlasting covenant for his descendants after him.   And as for Ishmael, <u>I</u> have heard you: <u>I</u> will surely bless him; <u>I</u> will make him fruitful and will greatly increase his numbers. He will be the father of twelve rulers, and <u>I</u> will make him into a great nation.   But my covenant I will establish with Isaac, whom Sarah will bear to you by this time next year."*

—Genesis 17:17-22 (emphasis added)

In this exchange, the Person to whom Abraham is speaking is plainly identified as *"God."* Abraham's request that his son Ishmael be blessed prompts a response from the Lord that refers directly to His meeting with Hagar described above. In His response to Abraham, the Lord claims responsibility for the blessing of Hagar and her son, Ishmael, just as *the angel of the Lord* had similarly claimed it in chapter 16. There can only be one conclusion. The Lord and *the angel of the Lord* are one in the same.

The evidence continues to build. Once again, we are assured that Abraham is speaking to an embodied, physical Person—and that this Person is no one less than *"God"*—by the reference to his departure. Only an embodied, physically present Jesus could be *"God"* who then very literally goes *"up from him"* as described.

> *When he had finished speaking with Abraham, <u>God went up from him</u>.*

—Genesis 17:22 (emphasis added)

The Son of God was palpably present as a warrior during the Old Testament. He was a soldier in the service of the Father. Although He undertook many different missions at the behest of the Father—from messenger to rescuer to fighter to avenger—His activities were directed solely by the will of the Father and aimed at the central mission *of guarding and preserving the remnant of Israel*. Our search for clues of His presence in the Old Testament leads us in a complex, winding path that travels through every incident, encounter, and battle whose details are described there. If ever there was a statement that was true about Jesus in the Old Testament, it is this: It is *all* about Him. Truly every word of the Old Testament is the story of *the One who is to come*.

Chapter 21

The Warrior Commander Leads the Army of the Lord Against Babylon
"...from the ends of the heavens..."

A great army had been summoned. Warriors from many lands had gathered, united under a single leader, united for a single purpose. Their goal was nothing short of the utter annihilation of their opposition and conquest of the land before them. They were fervent in their wholehearted quest of the will of their leader.

Their presence could not be hidden. This was no ambush. Their movement had shaken the mountains. Their voices had been like thunder. Their very presence had gripped their challengers with terror.

They were positioned. They held the high ground. Their tactical advantage was optimized. They were anxious and yet confident. They awaited the signal. The signal was by sight. A banner had been raised on a hilltop that all could see. At its sight, they moved to strike at the heart of their age-old enemy. Their path that day had been preordained from days of old.

An oracle concerning Babylon that Isaiah son of Amoz saw: Raise a banner on a bare hilltop, shout to them; beckon to them to enter the gates of the nobles. I have commanded my holy ones; I have summoned my warriors to carry out my wrath—those who rejoice in my triumph.

—Isaiah 13:1-3 (emphasis added)

There can be little doubt that the 13th chapter of the book of the prophet Isaiah has multiple levels of interpretation, relevance, and application. Like so many of the chapters of the Old Testament, its subject is yet another great battle in the Great War. This makes it particularly relevant to our subject at hand, for if there is war involving the nation of Israel, the Warrior of warriors must be there. Jesus must be involved. He could no more stay away from this fight than a mother could forbear the baby at her breast. The search for evidence of the warrior activity of Jesus in the Old Testament must include this otherworld description of the army of the Lord in action. There is little doubt that this unique description of a complex military maneuver will reveal the pathways of Jesus.

Certainly this amazing chapter tells of more than just the obvious story of the conquest of Babylon by the Medes and the Persians. No doubt that it tells that story accurately and in detail—and most amazingly, long before it actually occurred. But the battle described in this chapter also tells of the ultimate end-times conquest of Jesus over the forces of evil. In this regard, the details given in this chapter tell much about that final battle of all battles. Indeed, there is nothing in this chapter that is inconsistent with any of the many other descriptors of the *day of the Lord* that are given elsewhere in Holy Scripture. But still, this information regarding the glorious end-times battle is not the focus of our search.

Instead, our focus is upon that world that parallels ours, that *otherworld* where the incarnate Jesus seems to have spent the great majority of His time during the Old Testament. Isaiah's elegant prose describing the involvement of a fighting force—that can only be the army of the Lord—is quite revealing in this regard. To begin with, we can safely assume that Jesus, being the Commander of the army of the Lord, must have been an active participant in the otherworld battle that unfolds in this chapter of the book of Isaiah. As the Commander, Jesus undoubtedly planned and led this assault. He almost assuredly was also physically involved in what appears from the description to be actual hand-to-hand fighting—the same physical, direct, palpable involvement that has been so strongly suggested by the evidence presented thus far.

As noted in the verse above, the battle in the 13th chapter of the book of Isaiah begins with a signal. It begins with a banner raised on a bare hilltop. We must assume that this is a hilltop that, at the very least, is visible in that invisible world that runs parallel to the activities of the real world nations described by Isaiah. Indeed, from even this simple text it is difficult to restrain our imagination. We can easily visualize two great opposing armies gathered and positioned, poised for vital battle. Then suddenly a signal is given to attack. These were not the days of radio communication, E-mail, or text messages. These were the days when messengers were sent by foot. But if the message was to signal the attack of an army that was spread over a great distance, it could not be left up to the nuances or delay of a single messenger on foot, no matter how reliable or fast.

Instead, a *visual* signal was essential when an attack involving many military divisions needed to be synchronized. Timing is everything in such warfare. Catching one's enemy off guard after the careful positioning of battle forces is critical to gaining the tactical advantage. The signal therefore had to be by the fastest available means. This was not by foot, nor by a shout carried on the relatively slow waves of sound. The initial signal to engage the enemy had to come by sight. The signal had to be carried on the wings of light, the fastest of all possible message pathways.

So a high hilltop was chosen. It had to be devoid of trees that might obstruct the view of the signal banner. It had to be a bare hilltop. Then after all preparations were in place, the banner—undoubtedly a large brightly colored battle flag—was quickly raised to the top of the standard. It was the signal that all had agreed upon. It was the signal to attack.

And simultaneous with the raising of the banner, a backup signal—a *shout*—went out to all who were not in the line of sight or might have glanced away from the hilltop but were still within earshot of the echoing sound.

> *Raise a banner on a bare hilltop, shout to them; beckon to them to enter the gates of the nobles.*
>
> —Isaiah 13:2

This description of the signal is by He who commands the army. In the very next verse He tells us precisely to whom He has given the command to attack. His *"holy ones,"* his *"warriors"* have been commanded to carry out *His* wrath. He commanded *"those who rejoice in [His] triumph"* to begin the attack. There can be no doubt as to the identity of this Commander of the warriors of the otherworld.

> *I have commanded my holy ones; I have summoned my warriors to carry out my wrath—those who rejoice in my triumph.*
>
> —Isaiah 13:3

This particular verse is critical to the identification of the precise worldly location of the battlefield. If these verses were only speaking of the literal conquest of Babylon in our world, which a cursory reading and classical interpretation might suggest, then God—through the prophet Isaiah—would hardly have used the phrase *"those who rejoice in my triumph"* to describe the Medes and Persians! Rejoice? In God's triumph? Those barbarous pagans? Not hardly. The Medes and Persians were a conglomeration of rebellious, savage, war-mongering, conquering nations whose motivations, intentions, and tactics could hardly have been considered righteous or volitionally aligned with the will of God.

Instead, a much more logical answer easily reconciles this scene with our new perspective. Indeed, this verse confirms our suspicion that we are being treated to a brief glimpse of the warfare in the otherworld that accompanies the warfare in ours. The only warriors who could fit the description of rejoicing in the triumph of Jesus are His angels—His *"holy ones."* No doubt that this could also be referring to the end-times battle on *the day of the Lord.* In fact, surely it does. In that case, the identification of the identity of His *"holy ones"* who *"rejoice in [His] triumph"* could range all the way from His angelic warriors...to us.

But, the scenario to which these verses refer seems to be of so much more than even this. These verses describe a great battle that was to take place soon after Isaiah delivered these words—*but which has never yet taken place in the real world.* In other words, these verses describe the conquest of Babylon by an army that is not only loyal to God, but that *"rejoice[s] in [His] triumph."*

This has never taken place in the real world.

In this regard, both Biblical and secular historians agree—no army of warriors who were loyal to God participated outwardly in the Old Testament real world conquest of Babylon. There can be only one logical conclusion. These words of the prophet Isaiah, as his words so often did, describe events taking place in the parallel otherworld. They describe the battle exploits of the Son of God that took place in the invisible otherworld, but nonetheless had profound effects on real world history. For along with the otherworld conquest of the principalities behind the nation of Babylon by God's mighty angelic army came the real world conquest of Babylon by the combined armies of the Medes and Persians.

The visible imagery that is lavishly painted by the elegant prose of the prophet Isaiah is further enhanced by the audible sounds of war. The sound of gathering warriors is heard as many armies from many kingdoms come together at the beckoning of the Commander. A battle cry goes up from every mouth of every soldier who has gathered to do the Lord's bidding. One can easily imagine the battle cry of thousands of warriors of God as they surge forward toward the battle line.

> *Listen, a noise on the mountains, like that of a great multitude!*
> *Listen, an uproar among the kingdoms, like nations massing together!*
> *The LORD Almighty is mustering an army for war.*
>
> —Isaiah 13:4

And just when the thought has again crept slowly back into our minds that we might only be reading a description of an earthly army whose movements God is orchestrating for His own purpose (to punish the nation of Babylon for their treatment of His people), the Holy Spirit hits us with a line that is hard to misinterpret. For we are told precisely from where God has mustered this *"great multitude."* They come *"from the ends of the heavens."*

> *They come from faraway lands, from the ends of the heavens—the*
> *LORD and the weapons of his wrath—to destroy the whole country.*
> —Isaiah 13:5 (emphasis added)

Can there be any doubt that what is being described is an army of the otherworld? This is not the combined army of the Medes and Persians! This is an army that dwells in *"the heavens."* This is an army of God's mighty angels. But there is even more. In this statement we are also told precisely who accompanies His mighty ones. It is none other than the Lord Himself who accompanies them.

Jesus, the Incarnate Son of God comes with the *"weapons of His wrath"* into the fury of battle against the otherworld army of the Babylonians. How truly amazing this is. The Person speaking is God, not Isaiah. Isaiah is only His mouthpiece. God is speaking—presumably the Father or the Holy Spirit—and He is speaking about—God! God has told us that someone else—most specifically *"the LORD"*— accompanies these holy warriors in their quest for victory. Once again, the wording of this passage is precise and directed in its implications. This is Jesus Christ. Once again, Jesus has not shied away from battle. He is to be found nowhere else than dead center in the midst of the fury of the fight.

The sights and sounds of this army of the Lord have the expected impact upon their enemies. What an awesome, fearsome sight they must have been—for their presence on the battlefield gives stark warning to all who would oppose the Lord, then, now, and on the future awesome *day of the Lord.*

> *Wail, for the day of the LORD is near; it will come like destruction*
> *from the Almighty. Because of this, all hands will go limp, every*
> *man's heart will melt. Terror will seize them, pain and anguish will*
> *grip them; they will writhe like a woman in labor. They will look*
> *aghast at each other, their faces aflame.*
> —Isaiah 13:6-8

How totally immersed was the Incarnate Jesus Christ in the adventures and trials of the nation of Israel described by the books of the Old Testament. And every eye will witness Him in action on the coming day of the Lord—when the heavens will *"tremble"* and *"the earth will shake."*

> *See, the day of the LORD is coming—a cruel day, with wrath and fierce anger—to make the land desolate and destroy the sinners within it. The stars of heaven and their constellations will not show their light. The rising sun will be darkened and the moon will not give its light. I will punish the world for its evil, the wicked for their sins. I will put an end to the arrogance of the haughty and will humble the pride of the ruthless. I will make man scarcer than pure gold, more rare than the gold of Ophir. Therefore I will make the heavens tremble; and the earth will shake from its place at the wrath of the LORD Almighty, in the day of his burning anger.*
>
> —Isaiah 13:9-13 (emphasis added)

In that day, all will know of the fullness of the warrior attributes of the Son of God, as Babylon will be reminded that *"Her time is at hand, and her days will not be prolonged"* (Isaiah 13:22b).

Chapter 22

The Nature of the Fight
Was Defeat Even A Possibility for Jesus and His Fellow Holy Warriors?

Any discussion of the Old Testament role of Jesus Christ as the warrior Commander of the army of the Lord is incomplete without consideration of a persistent and troublesome question. If Jesus and His heavenly warriors were really involved in warfare in this mysterious otherworld of *powers* and *principalities,* then what was the hands-on, day-by-day, physical nature of this battle? More specifically, *could Jesus and His fellow warriors actually suffer defeat in battle?*

A million questions quickly spring from this one. Was there personal risk for them? Could they really lose? If they could be defeated, what exactly did that look like? In other words, did they actually have any skin in the game? Further, if they could lose, what determined whether they won or lost? And how did the outcomes of their battles influence the nation of Israel? If they lost, did Israel lose? And, in a similar fashion, how did the faithfulness of the nation of Israel influence the otherworld battles?

These are critical issues. Our understanding of the true nature of Jesus Christ and the Old Testament environment into which He surrendered Himself is directly dependent upon the answers to these questions. After all, is it really battle if there is no risk? Is it really a fight if you can't lose? Is it really warfare if you can't die or be injured?

To address this critical issue, it is important that we first specifically define the question we are asking. We are — most emphatically — not speaking of the ultimate outcome of this great war. We can all agree that God has not been subtle in revealing the omnipotent attributes that are the necessary foundation of His very nature. He is sovereign over every single aspect of His creation. Ultimately, God must win. Ultimately the will of God must rise above all others. The pinnacle of the creation drama—the crucifixion and resurrection of Jesus Christ—assures this.

God is over all and certainly nothing that is contained in His creation can overcome its Creator!

And yet this recognition of the guaranteed ultimate triumph of good over evil does not necessarily answer the question regarding the nature of the every day battles that were the meat of this great war. Our everyday real-world experience is an illustrative example of this: we who are covered by the shed blood of Jesus know that we have already been saved and will ultimately spend eternity with Jesus after the banishment of evil—yet still we must face daily trials. Daily, we must mirror Jesus by facing battle. Daily, we must know Jesus in His suffering by embracing our own suffering. Daily, we must demonstrate our faith by stepping forth in our belief in Jesus—in the belief that He is precisely who He says He is and will do exactly what He said He would do. Daily, we must still fight the fight.

In a similar fashion, although Jesus and His warrior angels knew they would ultimately win this fight, they still had to step into the fight in the days of the Old Testament battles. When we examine His Old Testament exploits, we know— without doubt—that ultimately Jesus will triumph. Yet still our hearts yearn to know what it was like for Him as He faced the daily battles, the skirmishes, the ambushes, and the great open field campaigns that made up this great Old Testament war.

After all, the entirety of the New Testament is a testimony to the fact that even though Jesus is fully God, He is also fully man. We are promised that He suffered all of the inconveniences, maladies, and constraints of daily life during His gospel ministry, just like we do every day of our life. And yet we know that He has and ultimately will be triumphant over all. It all boils down to the emptying of the Son of God into the day-to-day life of His creation—real world and otherworld.

In this regard, we have already discussed the emptying of the Son of God that must have occurred for Him to even enter into the fray in the first place. Jesus made Himself susceptible to the everyday struggles of the world of war into which He voluntarily submerged Himself during the epic events of the Old Testament. His commitment to this full Old Testament immersion mirrored His commitment to suffering through the physical trials that are described in the four gospels. It also mirrors the commitment that is requested of us. Just as the extent of this commitment was defined by the culmination of His ministry in the extremes of suffering that were manifest in the crucifixion, so also are we asked to surrender all.

Most would agree, therefore, that Jesus could not truly be considered a *real* warrior participant in the *otherworld* battles that accompanied the real world battles of the nation of Israel *if He could not suffer defeat*. If He and His fellow warriors could not suffer injury, could not suffer defeat, then Jesus would not have been a full participant in the fight. After all, would we consider Jesus to have truly been a man during His earthly life if He could not and indeed did not suffer? Since all humans suffer, most would say not. If Jesus could not die, would He truly have been human? If He could not die, could He stand in the place of we who were all condemned to die for our rebellion against God? This discussion once again circles back to the concept of the total emptying of the Son of God when He entered His creation. And once again, we are confronted by the stark reality that it just doesn't work unless we see Him as totally and indisputably emptied.

So, yes indeed, just as Jesus was fully emptied during the 33 gospel years, just as Jesus was the fully emptied warrior who *needed* the assistance of the archangel Michael (Daniel 10), so also were Jesus and His warrior host susceptible to defeat in the battles of this great war. A fight is simply not really a fight if one cannot suffer loss and defeat. The only conclusion supported by the facts that are revealed in the Word of God is that they could and indeed did suffer.

In examining the Biblical evidence that characterizes the true nature of this tumultuous otherworld war, considerable support for the lethality of the accompanying combat is easily found. The evil otherworld warriors who stood in opposition to Jesus and His warriors could not only suffer defeat, but could and did suffer *death* at the hands of the warrior princes of the army of the Lord. Clearly the warrior kings who rise to greet the fallen Lucifer arise very specifically from *their graves*.

> *The grave below is all astir to meet you at your coming; it rouses the spirits of the departed to greet you—all those who were leaders in the world; it makes them rise from their thrones—all those who were kings over the nations.*
>
> —Isaiah 14:9 (emphasis added)

These otherworld warrior princes have fallen, presumably in war, and await the arrival of the defeated Satan even as we speak. If this is not evidence enough, the prophet Isaiah spells it out in black and white for us. The evil enemy spirits could die.

O LORD, our God, <u>other lords</u> besides you have ruled over us, but
your name alone do we honor. They <u>are now dead</u>, they <u>live no more</u>;
those departed <u>spirits</u> do not rise. You punished them and brought
them to ruin; you wiped out all memory of them.

—Isaiah 26:13-14 (emphasis added)

Isaiah's reference is clearly to *"spirits"* and they are clearly *"now dead."* It
doesn't get any plainer than that. The evil warrior princes who stand in opposition
to Jesus and the army of the Lord can clearly suffer defeat and death. Many
questions arise as a natural consequence of such revelation. For instance, one
might well wonder who replaces these fallen spirits. Clearly the battle goes on. Is
there a natural progression of demon hierarchy to replace those who fall in battle?
The most obvious question still remains, however. If the evil otherworld enemies
could fall in defeat and death, then what about the good guys? What about the
warriors of the army of the Lord? Could they suffer a similar fate?

Before we approach this key question, however, we must put the discussion and
the facts thus far revealed in proper perspective. The panoramic view of this great
otherworld war that is described in the Bible is coming into focus. The Biblically
substantiated facts once again lead us to the unavoidable conclusion that the
otherworld battles that accompanied the battles of the nation of Israel were in fact
the real deal. The participants most certainly found themselves steeped in vicious
battle. They were sent forward into this battle at the behest of the Mighty God and,
at His command, followed His Son into the to-and-fro surges of battle against
powerful enemies. This was not some staged battle against puppet enemies or
straw dogs. Similarly, this was not just some big bully arrogantly swaggering into
a fight that he knows he cannot lose against a vastly inferior foe. This was not
some dramatic and yet unreal movie scene of passing and minimal import.

Quite to the contrary, this was truly desperate battle. This was the high adventure
that is unique to war. This was the searing sound of flaming arrows ripping
through the air. This was facing frightening foes across smoldering, carcass-
strewn battlefields. This was one warrior facing another warrior across bloody
terrain, each with a battle-ax or sword, *"each with a deadly weapon in his hand"*
(Ezekiel 9:2). This was the real deal—and Jesus was right in the middle of it all.

If these wild assertions are to be taken seriously, we must find substantial
confirmation of them in the Word of God. If we are to base a critical balance of
our knowledge of Jesus upon this evolving foundation, we must make sure that we
are traveling down the right trail. The confirmation of this characterization of the

nature of otherworld battle is once again found in the book of the prophet Daniel. In Chapter 8, the angel Gabriel tells Daniel of events that are yet to unfold. His words describe a battle. Parts of it seem to fit subsequent near-term history quite well.

> *Out of one of them came another horn, which started small but grew in power to the south and to the east and toward the Beautiful Land. It grew until it <u>reached the host of the heavens</u>, and it <u>threw some of the starry host down to the earth and trampled on them</u>. It set itself up to be <u>as great as the Prince of the host</u>; it <u>took away</u> the daily sacrifice <u>from him</u>, and the place of his sanctuary was <u>brought low</u>.*
>
> —Daniel 8:9-11 (emphasis added)

These words have classically been interpreted to describe the prophetic exploits of both Antiochus IV Epiphanes and the end-times antichrist. The passage is appropriately rendered as a description of their treachery against Israel, Jerusalem, and most specifically against the temple—the *"sanctuary"* of the *"Prince of the host."* These words do indeed fit many of the near-term exploits of Antiochus IV and most certainly seem to fit right into, and expand upon, our understanding of the nature of the coming antichrist.

And yet something is just not right about dismissing this passage with these relatively easy interpretations. Daniel seems to be describing so much more than this. For instance, the battle that is being described seems to be occurring outside of the dimensions in which both the people of Israel and we exist. We are told that this battle *"reached the host of the heavens,"* throwing *"some of the starry host down to the earth and [trampling] on them."* Indeed, this great enemy, this great warrior who is being described fights *directly* against God's holy angels.

Further still, this great enemy facing Israel elevates himself *"to be as great as the Prince of the host."* The *"Prince of the host"* can be no one else but Jesus. We can safely conclude that this is no ordinary earth-bound real world warrior who would have the audacity to raise himself to the level of God. This enemy of the Prince of the host operates well outside of our earthly dimensions. He is *heaven*-based. He fights in the otherworld. This mighty enemy directly opposes both Jesus and the army of the Lord that He commands. Who is this enemy of God? This is not Antiochus IV Epiphanes. This is not even the antichrist. In elevating himself to the level of Jesus, this otherworld warrior gives us all of the information we need to identify him. This can only be Lucifer. This can only be Lucifer surrounded by his demonic horde.

Have we been forewarned of the great conflict that unfolds in these verses? Have we been told elsewhere of the impending rise of this evil warrior and this battle? Many things are beginning to fall into place. We only have to remember back to our discussion regarding the messenger of the 10th chapter of the book of Daniel to find our answer. Could this be the *"prince of Greece"* referred to in Daniel chapter 10?

> *So he said, "Do you know why I have come to you? Soon I will return to fight against the prince of Persia, and when I go, <u>the prince of Greece</u> will come; but first I will tell you what is written in the Book of Truth. (No one supports me against them except Michael, your prince. And in the first year of Darius the Mede, I took my stand to support and protect him.)*

—Daniel 10:20-21 — 11:1 (emphasis added)

Most assume the obvious regarding this passage. Most assume that the messenger in the 10th chapter of the book of Daniel was further expanding upon the progression of the conquering empires that is indeed the core topic of the book of Daniel. Most therefore assume that this *"prince of Greece,"* who the messenger will soon confront, is the power behind Alexander the Great. Alexander the Great, after all, was the face of the Greek/Macedonian Empire that conquered the Persians and was subsequently conquered by the Romans.

But perhaps we are too quick to assume that Daniel's unnamed messenger speaks of Alexander the Great. Perhaps he is describing the menacing threat of Antiochus IV Epiphanes instead. Indeed, it is becoming readily apparent that the otherworld forces behind Antiochus IV Epiphanes leveled more havoc upon the army of the Lord than those behind Alexander the Great. Jesus and His warriors, after all, stand in defense of the remnant of Israel. Certainly Antiochus inflicted more damage upon the Israelite remnant than did Alexander the Great. It is even possible that the same demonic power—namely Satan—was behind both of these real world conquerors and was truly the powerful enemy who is being described.

Either way, it is clear from these passages that the otherworld battle that is being described definitely sways in favor of this fierce enemy of God. The daily sacrifice is taken *"away"* from the *"Prince of the host"* and the very sanctuary of the *"Prince of the host"* is brought low. Indeed, the very intentional use of the terminology *"took away"* implies that the sacrifice was surrendered only by actual vital combat between the warring parties. Furthermore, the loss of *"his sanctuary"* is reminiscent of the loss of a secret mountain hideaway or military fortress. This is a major battle. The daily sacrifice and the sanctuary of the Commander appear to be the plunder that goes to the victor. Their otherworld sanctuary must be directly associated with or contained within the Most Holy Place in the Holy Temple (where this world and the otherworld seem to interface when the Shekinah Glory fills the Temple). The real world defilement of the sanctuary of the Holy Temple thus has an otherworld correlate: the loss of the sanctuary of the *"Prince of the host"* to the evil armies of the otherworld.

The implications of these passages are not subtle. This dark leader of the evil opposition appears to overpower the *"Prince of the host"* and His holy angels— even on their own territory! The *bad guys* clearly win this battle. The central fortress— *"the sanctuary"* —of the Commander is at stake and is lost. The evil princes now occupy the sacred sanctuary of the Commander of the army of the Lord.

> " 'The people of Judah have done evil in my eyes, declares the LORD. They have set up their detestable idols in the house that bears my Name and have defiled it.
>
> —Jeremiah 7:30 (emphasis added)

Further still, we are informed of the comprehensive nature of the defeat. With the loss of the Holy Temple, so also is the *"daily sacrifice"* lost. It is hard to call the outcome of this battle anything other than defeat for the army of the Lord. But if there is any question in the mind of the reader regarding the outcome, the full manifestation of this defeat is yet further revealed. In this second statement regarding the outcome of this great conflict, the word *"surrendered"* is used in a very military sense to further characterize the meaning of *"brought low."*

> Then I heard a holy one speaking, and another holy one said to him, "How long will it take for the vision to be fulfilled—the vision concerning the daily sacrifice, the rebellion that causes desolation, and the surrender of the sanctuary and of the host that will be trampled underfoot?"
>
> —Daniel 8:13 (emphasis added)

Not only are we told of the loss of the sanctuary and daily sacrifice, but we are also informed that in the thick of the battle heavenly host suffer loss! They *"will be trampled underfoot."* In the midst of this confrontation of the *"Prince of the host,"* this storming of His sanctuary, this battle with the army of the Lord, the enemy in fact *"threw some of the starry host down to the earth and trampled on them"* (Daniel 8:10). Although many interpretations of this passage have suggested that it refers to the well-known loss of a third of the angels to Satan or to a loss of some earthly army of the nation of Israel, these explanations really do not fit the specific details of the passage. In the light of our understanding of the emptied Jesus and the army of the Lord, this passage seems to refer to precisely what it says it refers to—the defeat of heavenly angelic warriors. Being *"trampled underfoot,"* after all, can hardly be interpreted as victory.

The mechanism behind this powerful evil enemy's ability to overpower Jesus and His mighty angels is not clear. We are, however, given a hint that the power of the demonic forces over the good angelic host appears to be tied in some way to the actions of the Israelites. We are told that this defeat all comes about as a direct consequence of *"rebellion."*

> *Because of rebellion, the host [of the saints] and the daily sacrifice were given over to it. It prospered in everything it did, and truth was thrown to the ground.*
>
> —Daniel 8:12 (emphasis added)

These passages most certainly refer also to the rise of the antichrist through his indwelling by Satan in the end-times. But it is not hard to see how this scriptural revelation is of much more than just our world. It describes a battle in an epic conflict that involves much more than that which is visible to the human eye. Indeed, we are directly told that behind that which is visible to the human eye is the otherworld conflict involving far darker powers than we can even imagine. The consequences in both worlds are devastating.

> *"In the latter part of their reign, when rebels have become completely wicked, a stern-faced king, a master of intrigue, will arise. He will become very strong, but not by his own power. He will cause astounding devastation and will succeed in whatever he does. He will destroy the mighty men and the holy people."*
>
> —Daniel 8:23-24 (emphasis added)

Although the initial battle is lost as the sanctuary and sacrifice are surrendered, we are assured that this demonic warrior's final-stand against the *"Prince of princes,"* Jesus, ends as promised.

He will cause deceit to prosper, and he will consider himself superior. When they feel secure, he will destroy many and take his stand against the Prince of princes. Yet he will be destroyed, but not by human power.

—Daniel 8:25 (emphasis added)

In summary, we can know that this is very real battle. It occurs during the times described by the Old Testament Scriptures and the Son of God has voluntarily placed Himself in the midst of the fray. The battle has palpable consequences. It is violent fare. It appears to be influenced by events in our world and it definitely also appears to influence events in our world. The complex interface, the intricate mechanism by which these two worlds affect each other, is not defined for us as precisely as our hearts would desire. Yet we can nonetheless be assured that it is violent conflict of dire consequence—and Jesus Christ is right dead center in the middle of it.

Chapter 23

Prequel to the Destruction of Sodom and Gomorrah
The Evacuation of Noncombatants

It was a time of eating and drinking. It was a time of buying and selling. It was a time of planting and building. To the people of Sodom and Gomorrah, it was life as usual and it was the best of times.

And yet it was also the worst of times—a time of great immorality. Immorality cannot help but breed oppression. The cry of the oppressed of Sodom and Gomorrah had reached the ears of the Most High God. Judgment was overdue. They would be given one last chance at repentance, one last chance at grace. If the cries of the oppressed were founded in truth, then the city dwellers were far past retrieval. Judgment had to result. The cities would be destroyed. And yet righteousness reigned in the hearts of a very few.

This was a problem. The utter destruction that would be rained down on Sodom and Gomorrah would be complete. All life would be destroyed. The devastation would so saturate the cities and their surrounding countryside that no living thing could even hope to survive. There was only one solution: reconnaissance and rescue. The mission was simple. The people of Sodom and Gomorrah would have one last chance to repent of their sin. Their response would be the determining factor—one last chance. If even by God's grace they were irretrievable, then the reconnaissance mission would become a rescue mission. Righteous Lot did not belong in the maelstrom of fire that would follow. His family would be shown the path to rescue. With this mission in mind, three warriors of the army of the Lord were dispatched to Sodom.

On the pages of the Old Testament, the warrior Commander of the army of the Lord appears to undertake many different mission types. Perhaps the most unusual of these mission types is the *covert* military operation that occurs as a prequel to the destruction of Sodom and Gomorrah described in Genesis 18-19.

In this special class of mission, the Commander of the army of the Lord appears to assume a role that is similar to that of a modern day Army Ranger or Navy SEAL. In fact, in modern day terminology, this mission would be classified as a "special ops" assignment. These special ops missions commonly involve the insertion of a small elite warrior group into a combat zone before a planned major assault. This is exactly the case in Genesis 18-19. The express purposes of this particular mission are first to perform vital reconnaissance and then to deliver noncombatants from a targeted *free fire* zone. The latter portion of this mission, being yet another military *rescue*, is a perfect fit for the unique skill set of Jesus and His warrior angels.

Much has been written about the Biblical description of the destruction of Sodom and Gomorrah. The Biblical account of this very real historical event serves as a stark warning of the utter fury of the righteous wrath of God. The wrath of God is as much a part of His righteousness and justice as are His compassion and mercy. And yet this story also reminds us that God's compassion and mercy reach to such extremes—typifying the gospel story itself—that He would send His warrior angels into harm's way to rescue a righteous remnant from His impending wrath. The rescue of the righteous remnant of God was what these warriors were all about. As has been previously emphasized, this was in fact their primary assignment during the years chronicled by the Old Testament.

Even more important to the premise of this book is the fact that this carefully told story details the direct role of Jesus Christ in the every day events of Old Testament history. The Holy Spirit has carefully crafted the words of this story in this regard. A critical example of the textual specificity of the account of this event is found in the very first verses of chapter 18. Genesis 18 begins, *"The LORD appeared to Abraham near the great trees of Mamre"* (Genesis 18:1; emphasis added). It then describes *three* *"men"* who approached Abraham. The LORD spoke with Abraham about the destruction of Sodom and Gomorrah and then, in verse 22 *"The men turned away and went toward Sodom, but Abraham remained standing before the LORD"* (Genesis 18:22; emphasis added). To reinforce the precision of this identification process, the first verse of chapter 19 then states, *"The two angels arrived at Sodom in the evening"* (Genesis 19:1; emphasis added).

Several reasonably conservative conclusions can be drawn from these carefully crafted verses. First of all, *"the LORD"* and the *"two angels"* appeared as *"men."* Once again, this appearance of *"the LORD"* was not as some free floating apparition that mysteriously appeared in the sky above the trees of Mamre. The Lord appeared before Abraham as a *man*. These clear descriptive references are important clues that continue to build the case for the physical involvement of the incarnate Son of God in the Old Testament.

In addition, the Holy Spirit's use of the word *"men"* in describing these visitors continues to build a visible image of the literally physical form in which they also participated in the battle events of the otherworld. The fact that these combatants can easily enter the world in physical form as men suggests that even in the otherworld they may have bodies that look like ours. They have hands that grasp swords. They walk and apparently eat real food just like we do—at least when they enter our world.

The careful crafting of these verses is specific and direct. God was not only *incarnate* in the New Testament, but also in the Old—even very early in the book of Genesis. It is difficult to draw any other conclusion from the stated facts. Three *"men"* came to speak with Abraham and two men proceeded to Sodom while *"the LORD"* stayed to speak with Abraham. *"The LORD"* was the third *"man."*

As previously discussed, the Bible tell us that there is no other incarnate form of God other than in the Person of Jesus Christ. In addition, we are once again drawn to the foundational truth of the New Testament—that the whole of scripture is about Jesus, that Jesus is the only Son of God, that the Name of Jesus is above all others, and that Jesus is, very literally, the whole point of everything. This further strengthens the argument that the incarnate appearances of *"the LORD"* in the Old Testament are none other than pre-Bethlehem appearances of the incarnate Jesus Christ.

Abraham therefore carries on a long and revealing conversation *with Jesus* under the trees of Mamre. Two angels, the fellow warriors that accompany Jesus on this mission, then proceed to Sodom to save the only righteous people that live there. That salvation, mirrors the gospel of Jesus Christ. The salvation of the righteous of Sodom, like that of the members of Christ's church, occurs only for those who will believe the revelation of God—and who will never look back to the old ways once having tasted of the salvation of the Lord. Truly this story is all about Jesus Christ.

Still the account of this covert mission has even more to reveal about the role that Jesus assumed in His interactions with the key people and events of the Old Testament. This is a war story. It describes the activities of three warriors who have been sent on a mission. In its initial phase, this account describes a reconnaissance mission. Jesus, the Creator of the entire universe, has apparently emptied Himself to the degree that He must literally go down to Sodom and Gomorrah to check out whether things have deteriorated as badly as has been reported. He is not fabricating a story when He tells Abraham precisely this. He is not a liar and deception is never His purpose—we can rule those possibilities out right from the beginning. Jesus is on a reconnaissance mission. He clearly states that the initial phase of their mission is aimed at the gathering of this vital information. We can know that the perfectly efficient Son of God says precisely what He means and means exactly what He says.

> Then *the* LORD *said, "The outcry against Sodom and Gomorrah is so great and their sin so grievous that I will go down and see if what they have done is as bad as the outcry that has reached me. If not, I will know."*
>
> —Genesis 18:20-21 (emphasis added)

The Person speaking in the above passage is once again clearly identified as *"the* LORD*."* This is not subtle in its implication when combined with His next statement. He then discloses that He *"must go down and see if what they have done is as bad as the outcry that has reached"* Him.

Our days of accepting this statement as just a cute, albeit somewhat quirky, attempt by God to make us feel more comfortable around Him are over. This is not a folksy recounting of an ancient myth. It is a true historical account of an actual event. The Holy Spirit has carefully documented this story in Old Testament scripture to reveal something of critical importance about Jesus. This statement would not be included if it was not essential to understanding the full revelation of Jesus—the point of all scripture. The Holy Spirit wants us to know that Jesus—*"the* LORD*"*—fully emptied Himself not only during the ministry documented by the gospel accounts, but also during the times of the Old Testament.

What other explanation could clarify this statement? The Lord must go down with two fellow warriors to see if Sodom and Gomorrah are as bad as the reports they have received. How can Jesus truthfully make this statement and *not* be fully emptied? To assume that He is not emptied would lead to an enormous contradiction—that the omniscient Son of God who created Sodom and Gomorrah out of absolutely nothing really has to go see if the reports are correct. Can we believe that the all-knowing Son of God really doesn't know? How can He not know? How can the Creator and Sustainer of all *keep* from knowing? There is only one explanation and it speaks once again to the heart of the issue—the utter emptying of Jesus Christ in His incarnation at the creation of the world.

This passage is therefore a challenge to the reader. We must decide whether God has in fact just written an elaborate fairy tale for the purpose of illustrative teaching—or whether every single word is literally true. If this isn't just an allegorical fairy tale, then somehow the Son of God *"Through [whom] all things were made; without him nothing was made that has been made"* (John 1:3) really doesn't know whether the reports He has received are true or not. He really does have to go check it out Himself. The only explanation is that the Son of God emptied Himself so perfectly, so infinitely, in becoming man that He really didn't know whether the reports were true and really did have to check it out Himself. This demonstrates the complete immersion of the only Son of God into the frailty—the emptiness—of the humanity that is the centerpiece of His creation.

Jesus, for reasons that are sometimes a bit difficult to grasp, chose to be innately involved in an incredibly *hands-on* manner in the day-to-day workings of the Old Testament patriarchs. He chose to be so completely engrossed in this epic story that He actually went along with the two other warriors to inform Abraham of the events that were to occur. He even felt it necessary to discuss with Abraham the rationale behind destroying Sodom and Gomorrah in the first place. His immersion into the scene is so complete that He literally bargains with Abraham regarding the potential impact of the presence of righteous individuals in the target cities.

The other two warrior angels who accompanied Jesus were obviously also *covert* on this mission to rescue Lot and his family. They must not have been in the full battle dress that typified angelic warriors in the Old Testament. The human response to the fully unmasked display of such angelic power is recorded in many frightening accounts in the Bible. A typical example was the response of King David—one of the greatest of all Israelite warriors—to *the angel of the Lord* who held his drawn sword over Jerusalem.

> *David looked up and saw the angel of the LORD standing between heaven and earth, with a drawn sword in his hand extended over Jerusalem. Then David and the elders, clothed in sackcloth, fell facedown.*
>
> —1Chronicles 21:16 (emphasis added)

> *The tabernacle of the LORD, which Moses had made in the desert, and the altar of burnt offering were at that time on the high place at Gibeon. But David could not go before it to inquire of God, because he was afraid of the sword of the angel of the LORD.*
>
> —1Chronicles 21:29-30 (emphasis added)

The response of the inhabitants of Sodom to the two warrior angels was quite different. In fact, instead of being afraid of them, the irreverent townspeople were given over to lust for them. When necessary to complete this mission, these *covert* angelic warriors retrieved Lot from the townspeople with the application of angelic *nonlethal force*. When things began to get out of hand after the all-too-accommodating and ever-compromising Lot attempted to negotiate with the crowd, the angels took decisive action to neutralize the threat. Their covert appearance belied their powerful warrior capabilities. These *"men"* were warriors, and they were in the army of the Lord.

> *But the men inside reached out and pulled Lot back into the house and shut the door. Then they struck the men who were at the door of the house, young and old, with blindness so that they could not find the door.*
>
> —Genesis 19:10-11 (emphasis added)

Whatever weaponry the angels chose to deploy against their unruly assailants at that critical moment, its effectiveness rivaled that of the *flashbang* concussion grenades utilized by current urban assault warriors in similar circumstances. The blindness that presumably resulted from the flash of bright light essentially rendered the enemy forces ineffective against the angelic warriors and their charges.

Immediately following this action, it became readily apparent that the reconnaissance portion of this angelic mission was over. The actions of the lustful crowd supplied a clear answer regarding the true status of Sodom and Gomorrah. The angels knew the plan. They immediately implemented the next two stages of their mission: the rescue of the righteous noncombatants and the destruction of Sodom and Gomorrah.

> *The two men said to Lot, "Do you have anyone else here—sons-in-law, sons or daughters, or anyone else in the city who belongs to you? Get them out of here, because we are going to destroy this place. The outcry to the LORD against its people is so great that he has sent us to destroy it."*
>
> —Genesis 19:12-13 (emphasis added)

These angels do not shy away from getting even more physical in the completion of the extraction of the righteous. When Lot hesitates in the evacuation of his family from the city, the angels very literally use physical force to move things along.

> *With the coming of dawn, the angels urged Lot, saying, "Hurry! Take your wife and your two daughters who are here, or you will be swept away when the city is punished." When he hesitated, the men <u>grasped his hand and the hands of his wife and of his two daughters and led them</u> safely out of the city, for the LORD was merciful to them.*
>
> —Genesis 19:15-16 (emphasis added)

These are decisive, powerful angelic warriors on a mission from God. In the service of the army of the Lord, their mission is their uncompromised top priority. A total, wholehearted devotion to obedience to God's commands supplies all of the motivation that they need. Their clandestine mission to rescue the remnant out of Sodom and Gomorrah is obviously not finished until their charges are removed completely from harm's way.

Interestingly, in completing this mission, these angelic warriors demonstrate a detailed knowledge of the precise blast radius of the weaponry that is to be deployed in the destruction of the target cities. They forcefully warn Lot and his family to flee out of the plain and up into the mountains or they *"will be swept away"* by the blast-effect shock wave of the deployed ordinance.

> *As soon as they had brought them out, one of them said, "Flee for your lives! <u>Don't look back</u>, and don't stop <u>anywhere in the plain</u>! Flee <u>to the mountains</u> or you will be <u>swept away</u>!"*
>
> —Genesis 19:17 (emphasis added)

Many have made much of the metaphorical significance of the angel's command to not *"look back"*—and every word of these valuable interpretive commentaries is undoubtedly true. Nonetheless, from a slightly different perspective of viewing this scene as a military rescue, this might simply have been further evidence of the combat skill-set of these angelic warriors. They demonstrated a working knowledge of the kill radius and blast effects perimeter of the ordinance to be deployed, as well as the detrimental effects of unshielded exposure to the white-hot fireball flash that accompanied their detonation.

> *But Lot's wife looked back, and she became a pillar of salt.*
>
> —Genesis 19:26

What amazing insight is afforded by this unique revelation of the workings of God's angelic *Special Forces*. This elite warrior strike force was sent to recon an enemy stronghold, rescue the righteous non-combatants, and then direct lethal firepower upon those who remained unrepentant in their steadfast rebellion against the Holiness of God. This is war. Its impact upon the individuals involved is lethal, thorough, and palpably real.

> *Early the next morning Abraham got up and returned to the place where he had stood before the LORD. He looked down toward Sodom and Gomorrah, toward all the land of the plain, and he saw dense smoke rising from the land, like smoke from a furnace.*
> —Genesis 19:27-28

This detailed battle account also speaks volumes about the camaraderie and code of conduct shared by these angelic warriors. The rigors and extreme challenges of dangerous military missions such as this bring out the best in the warrior participants. The vital reconnaissance information gathered by these warriors made it obvious that the destruction of Sodom and Gomorrah was long overdue. Even so, Jesus and the army of the Lord patiently waited for Lot—who is called *"a righteous man, who was distressed by the filthy lives of lawless men"* (2Peter 2:7)—and his family to be removed from the target grid. What honor among warriors of God is demonstrated by these actions, such that no man or woman in the family of God should be left behind on the battlefield. The gospel likewise assures the same to those made righteous by the shed blood of Jesus Christ.

> *For I am convinced that neither death nor life, neither angels nor demons, neither the present nor the future, nor any powers, neither height nor depth, nor anything else in all creation, will be able to separate us from the love of God that is in Christ Jesus our Lord.*
> —Romans 8:38-39

The precise role of Jesus in the latter stages of this operation is not clear. It appears that Jesus did not accompany the other two angels when they went down to gather reconnaissance information in Sodom. The precise whereabouts of the Commander of the army of the Lord during the rest of the mission are unknown. Obviously with one of the most significant events of the Old Testament evolving before Him, we can safely presume that Jesus played a major role that placed Him right in the middle of the fight.

What was His role in the final completion of this mission? We can only speculate. His assignment most likely included further covert special ops that were critical to the tactical battle plan. In light of the pattern of His participation that is documented throughout the Old Testament, Jesus was almost assuredly deployed near the front lines. In His role as a covert warrior, this may have included activity as a forward air observer and air operations commander. In other words, it was almost assuredly His command that at last unleashed the coordinated air support that then rained its torrential cascade of fiery destruction on the inhabitants of these two cities. Indeed, Jesus may have performed at least a portion of His mission from His air-mobile command craft, the Shekinah Glory. One way or the other, we can know for sure that Jesus was a physical participant in this *special warfare* team sent from the realm of the otherworld to carry out God's will.

Jesus once again placed Himself right in the thick of the battle. There is simply no chance that any of His decisions and subsequent actions in this regard are somehow unimportant, unnecessary, or superfluous in the full revelation of the knowledge of Jesus that is available to all. In fact, our knowledge of Him—and therefore our reverence of Him—would be incomplete without the appreciation of the fullness of His nature revealed in the 18th and 19th chapters of the book of Genesis.

Chapter 24

When World's Collide:
Elisha's Chariots of Fire and the Presence of An Evil Otherworld Army

---

Dothan. Northern Israel. Israel and Aram were at war.

The Aramean king had long grown tired of setting traps for the king of Israel only to have the Elisha prophetically reveal the carefully crafted plans. It was as if the Elisha had full access to the words the Syrian king spoke even in the privacy of his bedroom! This would all end with the capture of the prophet and his delivery to the court of Aram.

The Aramean cavalry had arrived under the cover of night. The noise of their chariots had not disturbed the sleep of Elisha and his servant. Hidden behind darkness, the ambush had been crafted and carefully set. Its purpose was singular: to capture the eyes of the king of Israel.

The first rays of light filtered through the closed curtains and fell upon Elisha's servant. He awoke and went outside. He had barely rubbed the sleep from his eyes when he sensed that something was different. Something was very wrong.

When the servant of the man of God got up and went out early the next morning, an army with horses and chariots had surrounded the city. "Oh, my lord, what shall we do?" the servant asked.

"Don't be afraid," the prophet answered. "Those who are with us are more than those who are with them."

And Elisha prayed, "O LORD, open his eyes so he may see." Then the LORD opened the servant's eyes, and he looked and saw the hills full of horses and chariots of fire all around Elisha.

—2Kings 6:15-17 (emphasis added)

We seek knowledge of the mysterious spiritual otherworld because it was the habitat of Jesus during the Old Testament. Unfortunately, the windows in Holy Scripture that open into this mysterious world of war are all too infrequently and only briefly opened. This is what makes our brief encounter with the otherworld that is described in 2Kings 6 so important to the subject of this book. This passage provides a momentary fusion of the parallel activities of the real world and the spiritual otherworld. For our benefit, these two worlds are melded into a single landscape from which important clues can be gleaned.

As is the case so often in Biblical history, timing is critical. In fact, the timing of the Old Testament appearance of yet another sliver of light cast from the bright sunshine of the otherworld is as revealing as the vision itself. In this confrontation, a palpable real world enemy threatened the prophet Elisha and his servant. An army, whose expressed goal was to eliminate Elisha, had completely surrounded them.

This was a test. In its timing and in its form it is similar to God's daily testing of our hearts. For Elisha and his servant, the question was precisely the same as that posed to every one of us every day. They had a choice. They could act in faith and trust in God. Or, they could handle the situation on their own, guided only by a worldly perspective founded in fear and desperation.

The threat to Elisha and his servant was real and immediate. A very specific and palpable opportunity to trust in God and rely on Him was thrust into their path. As is always the case, God's omnipotent intervention was theirs for the asking. This godly choice was in fact quite obviously Elisha's plan. Never are we given any evidence suggesting that he was anxious or fearful about their circumstances. He knew things were under control. He knew that God had promised to never leave him and that the forces of the Mighty One were far in excess of those opposing them.

Elisha's servant, on the other hand, reacted like most of us so commonly do. All he saw was the opposing warriors and their horses and chariots. He lost focus. He had taken his eyes off of the only One who could save.

> *When the servant of the man of God got up and went out early the next morning, an army with horses and chariots had surrounded the city. "Oh, my lord, what shall we do?" the servant asked.*

—2Kings 6:15

Elisha intervened in supplicated prayer before God. His statement is profound and confirms the hypothesis of this book. More importantly, however, his statement also directly and unquestionably *confirms the very real presence of the dark army whose existence has so far only been presumed in our discussions.* Indeed, we are given very few scriptural references regarding the identity of the intended target of the sword that we have seen in the hand of *the angel of the Lord.* As discussed before, it is sometimes hard to tell whether that sword is used to inflict injury on real world or otherworld evil warriors. Although we are given many hints and clues, we are given precious little tangible evidence for literal warfare that pits the angels of the army of the Lord against evil *otherworld* warriors.

This passage is therefore critical in this discussion since it refers not just to the angelic warriors who stand in the parallel otherworld in alliance with Elisha, but also to *"those"* who are *"with"* their opponents. In this regard, the text is very specific. Elisha is not referring to the Aramean soldiers, but rather *to those who are the otherworld accompaniment of the real world Aramean soldiers.*

> *"Don't be afraid," the prophet answered. "Those who are with us are more than those who are with them."*
>
> —2Kings 6:16 (emphasis added)

The wording of this passage is precise. It is meant to convey the presence of both good and bad forces in the otherworld (those who stand with Elisha versus those who stand with the Arameans) that parallel the good and bad forces that are at war in the real world (Elisha versus the Arameans). It clearly refers specifically to otherworldly forces that fight on behalf of Elisha's real world enemies, the soldiers of the king of Aram's army. This evil otherworld force must be at least a component of the dark army that Jesus and His army were pitted against in the many Old Testament battle descriptions.

The possibility that Jesus and His otherworld forces somehow battled directly with the *real* world opponents that surrounded Elisha seems much less likely with this evidence in hand. This is critical. The mode of real world implementation of the will of God by the army of the Lord seems to have been in their encounter—*in the otherworld*—with a similar, yet evil otherworld army. In its revelation of these facts, this scriptural passage from 2Kings 6 becomes pivotal in the focus of this book.

> *During the times of the Old Testament, Jesus led the army of the Lord in an otherworld battle against an equally impressive — yet evil — otherworld army.*

These two parallel worlds, each with their two opposing forces, seem to be linked in time and, at least in some respect, in regard to geographical position. The fact that events in one world appear to be tied directly in time to events in the other appears very well established. Elisha's comment above also presumes that the events in both worlds are tied together not only in time and space, but also in cause and effect. But there is even more. For immediately after setting the stage in regard to time, space, cause, and effect comes an equally startling revelation. God in His divine providence chooses to open up that invisible curtain that separates our world from the other. For a brief and incredibly unique moment in time Elisha and his servant receive confirmation of Elisha's faith and provide the reader with a most critical visual image of the otherworld battlefield.

> *And Elisha prayed, "O LORD, open his eyes so he may see." Then the LORD opened the servant's eyes, and he looked and saw the hills full of horses and chariots of fire all around Elisha.*
> —2Kings 6:17 (emphasis added)

The lifting of the veil between our world and its counterpart otherworld reveals nothing less than *weapons of war*. These are not just warriors, but mounted cavalry — and the hills are *"full"* of them! There are horses and chariots — the Old Testament equivalent of modern day main battle tanks and attack helicopters. This is the real deal. This is serious battle with serious weaponry engaged in very real conflict. The use of the adjective *"fire,"* as always, adds vivid coloration to the visual image that is engendered by this battlefield description in 2Kings.

Our desire to apply only allegorical explanations to the vivid descriptions given in the Old Testament scriptures somehow assuages the fears that we commonly associate with these descriptions of powerful supernatural warriors. We are, nonetheless, repeatedly given very literal descriptions with very literal application to our lives. A little guided introspection reveals that only our own weakness makes us cling to mystical metaphorical excuses instead of taking the descriptions *literally*, in the manner in which they are given and in the manner in which they are meant to be applied.

The facts are clear. There was very literal, very physical warfare occurring in the otherworld that paralleled the real world battles of the patriarchs and prophets.

The implications of these otherworld battles were palpable and immediate to the Israelites. This warfare involved horses and chariots and they were fiery in their appearance. We are not told whether any of the horses and chariots of fire that Elisha and his servant were allowed to see belonged to their enemy's otherworldly counterparts or not. We are not told whether the horses and chariots of fire that they saw were the only combatants on the otherworld battlefield or whether Elisha and his servant were only allowed to see the fiery chariots of the army of the Lord. We are not told whether they were actually allowed to visualize combat between these forces or not. We are simply not told the details that our hearts crave regarding this amazing scene. We can nonetheless be assured that we were told exactly what God wants us to know—just enough, always just enough. And in that knowledge, we can most assuredly know that the sacred role of Jesus in the Old Testament placed Him right in the middle of a very real fight with palpable consequences for the remnant of Israel.

Chapter 25

The Battle That Preceded Every Battle:
"...the Sound of Marching in the Tops of the Balsam Trees..."

The Philistine nation had been unnerved by the news. A new king reigned in Israel. He was of the house of Jesse and of the tribe of Judah. His name was David.

That name was all too familiar to them. They knew he was the shepherd boy who had slain Goliath their champion.

They also knew that the naming of a new king called for immediate action. The early Israelite victories had been reversed and this was to be Philistia's time. This young upstart king needed his first lesson in Philistine dominance—and the army of the Philistine nation had been more than happy to oblige. They had assured each other that his defeat would usher in another generation of Philistine dominance. They met this new king in battle in the Valley of Rephaim.

The Philistine army had reeled from the sting of the relentless Israelite attack. But the retreat of the Philistine army from the rout in the Valley of Rephaim would be brief. They had been caught off guard. It would not happen again. They were not accustomed to losing and vowed that this Israelite victory would be short lived. To this end, they gathered their scattered army and once again went into the Valley of Rephaim. The time for licking their wounds was over. The time for revenge had arrived.

In the camp of the army of Israel, King David had a choice. The toughest choices always seem to follow victory. Such was the assuredly the case as the Philistines once again taunted David and his warriors from the valley walls. How tempting it was for the Israelites to just charge into battle. After all, they just met these same Philistines in battle and had overwhelmed them. By all accounts they would do it again. But this new Israelite king was different. David would not let overconfidence be his downfall like so many Israelite leaders before him. He would instead do that which he had made habit in his life. He would inquire of

God. He would not fall to temptation. He would not rely upon the strength of his *Mighty Men*. Instead, he would treat God precisely as if He were in fact God, omnipotent Creator of all. David would choose to submit. David would once again walk with God and once again surrender his strength to the will of God. David would meet with God before he met with the Philistines.

The words of Miriam rang in David's ears: *"the Lord is a warrior"* (Exodus 15:3). In David's submission before the Lord, warrior met Warrior. God had a plan. That plan became David's plan.

As we have discussed, a strong Old Testament case can be made for the existence of a mysterious otherworld of warfare shrouded in a reality that is separate from ours—and yet somehow simultaneously and delicately intertwined with ours. The events taking place in this otherworld appear to have a direct impact upon events in our world. The very thought that great battles have taken place around us and our forefathers—with God's warrior angels clashing against their dark warrior counterparts—cannot help but motivate a diligent search of the Bible for details defining the very important interface between our two worlds.

The interface between our world and this shadowy otherworld is surely complex. And yet we cannot shy away from the difficult task of defining it because nothing is more foundational to our quest than its exploration. Precisely how do the events of the otherworld relate to the events taking place in ours? The answer to this question is found in a single thread that weaves through the colorful and complex tapestry of Old Testament history. There seems to be a single common denominator shared by all of the Biblical accounts that describe the otherworld. This thread speaks of a mechanism and a mechanism is precisely what we seek.

The events that occur in this world of warfare that parallels ours seem to have a very specific mechanism aimed at an equally specific purpose. Specifically, this complex interrelationship between the two worlds appears to be the precise mechanism *by which* God has chosen to answer the prayers of His saints.

This mechanism becomes clearer in the light of our new perspective. When we go to God in prayer—when we ask Him to intercede for us—these face-to-face meetings with God take place between the outstretched arms of the cherubim in the dark inner sanctum of the Most Holy Place of our heart. This is the definition of prayer—meeting with God. These meetings, which take place many times during the course of a normal day, are the *real* substance of our life. Going there to meet with God matters. It really matters. It may well be *all* that matters.

Going to God with our concerns and troubles is indeed the very first—and most critical—step in the process by which we are to handle these difficult issues. This is a process precisely defined by the Creator of the very problems we face.

> *I form the light and create darkness, I bring prosperity and create disaster; I, the LORD, do all these things.*
>
> —Isaiah 45:7 (emphasis added)

Each and every trial in our life is a test. They are preordained in our life by God for a specific purpose. God wants to know—and wants us to know—how we will respond to a choice between His way and the way of the world. He wants to know which way we will turn. When we go to Him in prayer and in faith, we turn to Him instead of turning to the world. We seek God's way rather than our own way, rather than the world's way.

Going to God in prayer is the correct response to the difficult tests—every time.

When we choose this correct response to the challenges that God has orchestrated in our life, this action places Jesus squarely on the throne of our hearts with sovereign dominion over the kingdom of our will. In this act, we are seeking God's will by our prayer.

We cannot miss this. This is the essence of what our life is all about. God seeks to be our God. He wants us to be His people. The importance of defining precisely what that means cannot be overestimated. This is the crux of our lives and it is found, very simply, *in the act of turning to God*. If God is really our God (if we really believe He is precisely who He says He is) and if we are really His people (if we have really placed Him on the throne of our heart), then God wants and expects us to think of Him first in every situation in which we find ourselves challenged with a choice.

This is precisely what we do when He really is *our God*. He wants us to refrain from turning to the world and its version of reality and truth, and to instead turn to Him and the truth found in His holy Word. He wants us to turn to Him in every circumstance. He wants us to do it so often and in every setting and circumstance such that it becomes an innate part of us. When we do it His way, this immediate turning to Him becomes ingrained. It becomes automatic. It becomes something that we don't even have to think about. It becomes a reflex action. It becomes easier. God wants us to turn exclusively to Him and thereby to bring glory to Him by celebrating the goodness and faithfulness of His heart. He wants us to do this in the good times. He also wants precisely this again in the bad times.

God wants us to cry out to Him in the desperate times—every time. This requires us to remain undeterred in the vigor of our request by the fact that we totally forgot to invite Him along in the first place. In fact, God's perfect goal for our life would be continual communion with Him every single millisecond—if that were possible. It is not possible in this life. It will be in the next. In fact, this continual communion with God is exactly what differentiates each of our lives from the perfect life lived by Jesus. *Continual communion with the Father is what made the emptied Son of God so totally unlike us.* He spent every moment of His life on earth in direct communication with the Father. Unfortunately, we do not because we cannot. We cannot because we do not. Unlike us, Jesus did because He could—and He could because He did.

And this brings us directly to the point of this chapter. When this otherworld of war is defined as the mechanism by which God responds to our direct communication with Him, *it is huge*. The triggering of this complex two-world interplay by the correct response of our prayer is what life is all about. It is the direct and all-encompassing focus of the interface between our world and the other. And this interface—this connection between the worlds—is all about Jesus. He is the link to all that is important to us. He is the gate. He is the connection. He is the passageway. He is the truth. He is the life. He is our only chance—in every situation, every time. Jesus—He is *the interface*, the only possible connection to the Father.

Why is *prayer* the trigger for this complex mechanism by which God acts in our lives? The answer is quite simple. We can't pray unless we are focused on God. Indeed, for those brief moments when we are in prayer with God, our focus is on Him and not on ourselves. It is on Him as the answer to all the questions, problems, dilemmas, and trials of our life. It is on Him and not on the world around us. For those all-too-brief and all-too-infrequent moments, surely Jesus sits on the sovereign throne of our hearts.

So, prayer matters—every time. When we go to meet God in the dark recesses of His temple, He responds—whether we recognize it or not, whether we like the response or not, whether He does what we ask or not. He *always* responds, one way or the other, to our deep heart prayer. The Bible, and most certainly the Old

Testament is replete with examples of precisely this. He responds to our prayer just like He responded to Daniel's prayer (Daniel 10). He responds to our prayer just like He did to King David's prayer (2Samuel 5, see below). Going to Him is the correct response to the trials He sends into our life and by this critical action is God's direct intervention in our life triggered.

With this background in mind then, the hypothesis that is to be examined in this chapter can be summarized:

> *The mechanism by which God intervenes in our world as a direct response to our prayer involves warfare between the principals in the otherworld that parallels ours. The very specific reason for existence of this parallel reality, this otherworld, is to provide a mechanism by which God's specific responses to our prayers are implemented in a very palpable manner in our world. With this in mind, we can know that Jesus spent the totality of the Old Testament right in the middle of this otherworld of battle and intrigue implementing the answers to prayer—or to a lack thereof. He was Israel's interface and He is ours.*

Let there be no question in our minds that God could just wave His hand or speak a word from His mouth or have a simple passing thought and His very specific response to our prayer would indeed just happen. Instead, however, His divine reasoning has led Him to employ a very special mechanism by which His response to our prayer is implemented. This very special mechanism is an otherworld comprised of intrigue and war where His mighty warrior angels are engaged in a to-and-fro struggle against the armies of darkness led by Satan.

Perhaps no other passage in the Bible better illustrates the reality of the method of God's intervention in our world than that found in the 18th chapter of 2Chronicles. God has decided that it is time for Ahab, the evil king of Israel, to meet his demise. Instead of just commanding His will into existence, a method that is clearly at His disposal, God implements His will through an otherworld mediator. What a grand spectacle this must have been with *"all the host of heaven standing on his right and on his left"*!

> *Micaiah continued, "Therefore hear the word of the LORD: I saw the LORD sitting on his throne <u>with all the host of heaven standing on his right and on his left</u>. And the LORD said, 'Who will entice Ahab king of Israel into attacking Ramoth Gilead and <u>going to his death there</u>?'*

"One suggested this, and another that. Finally, a spirit came forward, stood before the LORD and said, 'I will entice him.'

" 'By what means?' the LORD asked.

" 'I will go and <u>be a lying spirit</u> in the mouths of all his prophets,' he said.

" '<u>You will succeed in enticing him</u>,' said the LORD. '<u>Go and do it</u>.'

"So now the LORD has put a lying spirit in the mouths of these prophets of yours. The LORD has decreed disaster for you."
                                      —2Chronicles 18:18-22 (emphasis added)

Very clearly, this scene drives home the main point. God uses the individuals of the otherworld to implement His plan in our world. And, as the rest of Holy Scripture strongly supports, this plan of His is obviously influenced by our prayer.

This line of reasoning then brings us to the illuminating scripture passage that is the topic of this chapter. Personally, I must admit that every time that I read this chapter I was fascinated. Every single time, my curiosity had been piqued and I had rocked back in my chair in wonderment. And every time I had to be satisfied with moving on in frustration, knowing that I did not have the whole story. I still don't have the whole story, but some things have become abundantly clear.

Once more the Philistines came up and spread out in the Valley of Rephaim; so David inquired of the LORD, and he answered, "Do not go straight up, but circle around behind them and attack them in front of the balsam trees. As soon as you <u>hear the sound of marching in the tops of the balsam trees</u>, move quickly, because <u>that will mean the LORD has gone out in front of you to strike the Philistine army</u>."

So David did as the LORD commanded him, and <u>he struck down the Philistines</u> all the way from Gibeon to Gezer.
                                      —2Samuel 5:22-25 (emphasis added)

Just like the scriptural passages that form the foundation of this book, this passage is hinge-point scripture. It is a critical component of the answer to the question that is the subject of this book and details a wealth of knowledge regarding the interaction between our world and the otherworld.

Surely many battles were fought by the armies of Israel before and after the battle referred to in this passage. Only here, however, does God choose to illuminate our understanding of His plan for our lives. Only here does God choose to flutter a window shade open for a brief moment to allow us a fleeting glimpse of the dazzling wonderment that is the unseen aspect of His incredible creation. In a three-sentence passage the mechanism by which God answers our prayers is confirmed.

In this colorful Old Testament incident, God has once again sent an enemy into King David's life. This is a challenge, a trial, a test sent from God. Just as God challenges us by sending daunting tasks and fearful trials into our daily lives, so also did God send the Philistines against David. Just as God tests us to reveal what our response will be, so also did He test David. Just as God tests us to reveal our true hearts, so also did He test King David.

David was given—just like we are always given—the choice of one of two options. These choices are straightforward. David could choose the world's response and march off to deal with the Philistines by his own strength. Worse yet, he could hire mercenaries to fight the battle for him. He could even pay them by selling gold that had been dedicated to the Lord. Or, in stark contrast to these worldly responses (both of which have precedent in Holy Scripture), David could do things God's prescribed way. He could turn immediately to the Lord—and then rely solely upon God's strength.

In this particular situation, David chose well—just as he did in most situations in his life. He went directly to the Lord and the Lord responded by telling him very specifically what to do. Following God's commands is the very specific manner in which God's strength is unfettered in our daily battles. David was indeed to attack the Philistines. But the very critical component of this attack is the timing and David knew that the timing is always God's dominion. We, no matter how much we think to the contrary, essentially never control the timing of God's deliverance—and how hard it is to wait on God. Waiting on God's deliverance is almost always a mandatory second step of faith that we must exercise to see the fullness of God's deliverance. It is the second test that follows the correct answer to the original test—to turn to God in prayer—and its purpose is nothing less than instilling in us the most vital sanctification goal of perseverance.

In this particular circumstance we are in fact told precisely why waiting on the Lord is so important. This is where things get very interesting and relate directly to the subject of this book. The specific event that David is to wait upon is an event that is actually taking place in the invisible otherworld. Undoubtedly, the timing is precise for the very specific purpose of drawing both David's and our attention to the role of Jesus in the Old Testament warfare.

We have to ask the obvious question. If God had indeed decided to go before David in his battle with the Philistines—which He obviously had—why couldn't God just speak the victory into immediate existence? Even if God, in His Divine wisdom decided (again, as He obviously had) to have the victory in David's world preceded by a battle in the parallel dimension, couldn't God just move His angelic forces immediately into the encounter? Why were they late in the first place? After all, David and his troops were already in position! Where was the army of the Lord? This battle could not have taken them by that much surprise. We might quite reasonably assume that the army of the Lord knew every move that the Philistine warriors were making and most certainly knew the location and movement of David and his warriors. They could long see the battle lines as they were forming. Why were they late in getting to the battlefield?

We are led to the very important conclusion that the events that occur in the otherworld are not just *filler* in the epic thriller of our life. They matter. They do not comprise just some inconsequential sideshow to the events in our world. Quite to the contrary, this very pointed example reveals that a real fight is in fact occurring in this alternate otherworld. Very real, very palpable, good versus bad to-and-fro struggles are actually taking place. These are real battles and the outcomes of these struggles have serious consequences.

Clearly God wanted David to wait on Him. Clearly God wanted David to trust wholly and totally in Him at every step of the solution to the crisis that lay on the battlefield before David. Clearly God wanted David's trust to directly impact David's actions. But how amazing—and how revealing in regard to the nature of the interface between the two worlds—that God chose to have the delay of the army of the Lord be the precise mechanism that actually placed that decision point in David's life.

One must wonder what—or more precisely, who—delayed the army of the Lord in the first place? Is this an echo of the encounter described in Daniel 10?

> *Then he continued, "Do not be afraid, Daniel. Since the first day that you set your mind to gain understanding and to humble yourself before your God, your words were heard, and I have come in*

response to them. But the prince of the Persian kingdom resisted me twenty-one days. Then Michael, one of the chief princes, came to help me, because I was detained there with the king of Persia.

—Daniel 10:12-13 (emphasis added)

Did Satan's dark army delay God's warriors from getting to the battlefield, just as the so-called *"Prince of the Persian kingdom"* delayed Daniel's messenger? Could it have been a dark prince of the Philistine nation that delayed the army of the Lord this time? Similarly, did the warriors of the army of the Lord need assistance in overcoming the evil resistance? These questions remain unanswered. We are simply not told. We can only be assured that the delay—David's waiting on the Lord—was all part of God's plan to test and mold David into the man of God that he would need to be to lead the nation of Israel. And the interaction between the two worlds is critical in implementing this important lesson.

Ultimately, in the culminating event described by this passage, David is actually allowed to hear sound coming from the invisible otherworld. Just as Elisha and his servant were briefly allowed to see the fiery chariots surrounding them, so also is David allowed to hear the sound of the warrior angels marching toward the battlefield that David and the army of Israel would soon occupy. There is obviously a physical interface between the two worlds with all human senses involved.

Further still, this passage tells us that it was not on some far off cloud that this otherworld battle took place. It was—by God's very purposeful, specific design— directly above the heads of David and his army that they heard the marching sound in *"the tops of the balsam trees."* Is this a hint as to the relationship of our universe to theirs? Is it above ours? Is it in the same relationship to the earth as ours, yet just removed 20-30 feet into the air? Other scriptural passages seem to support a similar elevation of the spiritual battlefield activity.

David looked up and saw the angel of the LORD standing between heaven and earth, with a drawn sword in his hand extended over Jerusalem. Then David and the elders, clothed in sackcloth, fell facedown.

—1Chronicles 21:16 (emphasis added)

Several other reasonable conclusions can be drawn from this *"balsam trees"* battle passage. Despite the fact that the event that David audibly witnesses is taking place in the otherworld, it is readily apparent that the outcome of the angelic battle that takes place in an entirely different dimension will have consequences that will also be manifest on the very real battlefield before David and the army of Israel. It is also clear that David will not be successful in his battle unless something first occurs in that otherworld battle toward which the army of the Lord is marching. Let there be no question in our minds, the hand-to-hand warfare that David and his men were about to face would be vicious and palpable—for there is no other kind of hand-to-hand combat. Yet still David is assured that the outcome, in some unknown manner, would be dependent upon the outcome of the presumably vicious otherworld battle that precedes theirs.

It is quite reasonable to extend that which is demonstrated in this battle account to the many other battles that the army of the Israel had faced in the past and would face in the future. In fact, a readily discerned pattern can be drawn from this and other battle episodes in the Old Testament. Specifically, warrior prayer—as demonstrated by David in this example—triggers the otherworld angelic army intervention. God's otherworldly intervention is triggered by the act of *turning to God and asking Him for help*, by the act of crying out to the Lord—by prayer. In other words, a very specific event in our world—prayer—thus triggers the intervention in the other.

The angelic armies are subsequently empowered to fight for David and the nation of Israel—or for each of us—precisely because of the faith demonstrated by first going to the Lord in prayer and then by faithfully trusting in—and waiting for—His response. David's recognition that God is precisely Who He says He is and that He is good, faithful, and has David's best interest at heart is David's empowering act of belief. But then, David still had to step into the battle. He, like you and I, still had to actually fight the fight against a vicious enemy. He still had to be brave. He still had to proceed into the fury in full confidence. He still had to be relentless and tireless in his pursuit of the enemy. He still had to remain focused to the very end. We likewise are asked to act in a similar fashion every day of our lives.

Thereby empowered by God because of David's faithfulness, we can assume that the army whose footsteps were heard above the balsam trees threw themselves against the enemy in a great otherworld battle. Presumably the opposing angelic armies represent the heart of evil itself, Satan. They must be the evil powers, authorities, demons, and/or fallen angels spoken of elsewhere in the Bible who have clearly allied themselves with Satan. But of even more significance, these otherworld evil warriors somehow influenced their evil Philistine counterpart in David's world. Very clearly we are led to believe that as goes the demon army in the otherworld, so goes the Philistine army in this world. In other words, we can summarize by suggesting that David's act of faith in this world empowered an intervention in another world that resulted in a specific outcome in his world.

In other words, the otherworld encompasses the mechanism by which God answers prayer.

Certainly, this is not the only Israelite battle that was preceded by their leader's supplication before God. In fact, a repeating scriptural pattern becomes readily apparent in this regard. When Israel and its leaders truly humbled themselves before God, honestly repented of their sin, and sought God's help in battle against an enemy army, the outcome was—presumably by the same mechanism demonstrated in this passage—uniformly awe-inspiring.

In all such cases, the Israelite army triumphed over their pagan enemy. In some cases, it took a difficult fight to achieve victory. Such was the case in the very first battle of the newly born nation of Israel following their narrow escape at the Red Sea. In that battle, the Israelite warriors, who had never been tested in battle, defeated the powerful Amalekite warriors under the field command of Joshua while Moses simultaneously held high the staff of God in intercessional prayer. In other cases, such as the defeat of Sennecherib's army by *the angel of the Lord*, the people of Israel apparently didn't have to fight at all. Hezekiah's turn to God in prayerful submission triggered that powerful result. God's victory was immediate, decisive, and complete. Once again, the otherworld was the intermediary as God's will was implemented from the otherworld by *the angel of the Lord*. The message is clear. One way or the other, when the Israelites turned first to God in prayer, they uniformly triumphed in their real world battle by way of an otherworld influence.

On the other hand, when Israel and her leaders did evil in the eyes of the Lord and did not seek God's face in supplicated prayer, the angelic otherworld army of the Lord was apparently not empowered to fight on their behalf. Thus we can safely assume that the otherworld enemy army was not defeated. The result was the disastrous defeat of the Israelite army, such as occurred in the battle at Ai or in the ultimate conquest of Jerusalem by the Babylonian army.

The Old Testament pattern of an event in this world (humble prayer before God) triggering a result in this world (victory by the army of Israel) is well established and accepted by most. Its opposite—defiance of God resulting in the defeat of the

Israelites—is also well accepted by even the most casual observer of Biblical history. It is, however, the intervening step between these linked events—the presumed empowering (or neutralization) of the otherworld angelic army of the Lord—that is the mysterious connection to the invisible otherworld that is not seen, accepted, or appreciated by most.

It is exactly that intervening step that is the focus of this book. For it is precisely in that intervening step that we see the footprints of the Son of God. The passages above beg the question regarding the whereabouts of Jesus in all of this battle. As if to drive home this point, the passage tells us that David was told to wait until he heard *"the sound of marching in the tops of the balsam trees"* before he attacked, precisely *"because that will mean the LORD has gone out in front of you to strike the Philistine army"* (2Samuel 5:24; emphasis added). The Holy Spirit's choice of words is never casual or careless—and never in error. It was none other than Jesus Christ who was going out in front of David—presumably leading the army of the Lord as its Commander—to strike the demonic counterpart of the Philistine army.

Of note, David was to wait on a real army. This was definitely not just the Spirit of the Lord leading some mysteriously floating army that resembled more fuzzy apparition than fighting force. Quite to the contrary, the passage is written in a precise manner to assure us that a fuzzy apparition is not what is being described. This is a very real, very physical army with embodied warriors whose feet generated a clearly audible *"sound of marching"* as they went forward into battle. This was an embodied army led into the vicious fury of hand-to-hand combat by the incarnate Son of the Living God.

A similar passage lends even more credence to the physical nature of the warrior armies of the otherworld. This passage from 2Kings describes a peculiar set of events surrounding the siege of Samaria by the army of Ben-hadad, King of Aram. The warriors of the attacking Aramean army turned and fled after hearing the obviously ominous and threatening sounds of what must have been a massive otherworld army.

> *At dusk they got up and went to the camp of the Arameans. When they reached the edge of the camp, not a man was there, for the Lord had caused the Arameans to hear the sound of chariots and horses and a great army, so that they said to one another, "Look, the king of Israel has hired the Hittite and Egyptian kings to attack us!" So they got up and fled in the dusk and abandoned their tents and their horses and donkeys. They left the camp as it was and ran for their lives.*

—2Kings 7:5-7 (emphasis added)

In a similar fashion, from the accounting of the 2Samuel passage involving David, we have no evidence that the angelic army of the Lord went out and physically struck down the actual real world troops that stood before David on the battlefield. According to the recounting of the story in 2Samuel, David and his army had to perform that function themselves. Nonetheless, we can be assured that the troops led by Jesus had to be fighting someone. And, of even more import, the outcome of the battle in David's world was very clearly dependent upon Jesus and His troops attacking what we can only presume is a dark angelic army. Just as the evil angelic warriors supported the Aramean troops who were after Elisha and his servant, these dark warriors presumably supported the Philistine army. Things are starting to come together.

Jesus is a warrior. His role in the battles of the Old Testament must be nothing less than as a primary participant. In this regard, His role could never have been *less than* that which is revealed in the passages from the fifth chapter of 2Samuel. It is clear that Jesus was right there in the thick of the otherworldly fight that paralleled every encounter between Israel and its enemies. The primary driver behind His participation remained His Father's will that the righteous remnant of Israel be preserved. He did not enter the fray for all of Israel, but only for the righteous remnant. In this role, Jesus and His troops appeared to be empowered by the prayer of that very remnant on whose behalf they fought. His role then—as now—was not just ancillary, but critical to, central to, and the entire point of the resulting outcome.

Chapter 26

Reconnaissance For the Army of the Lord
An Elite Cavalry Unit Takes the Field

A beleaguered remnant of the nation of Judah had returned from Babylon. Fierce enemies repeatedly threatened and thwarted their efforts to reestablish their national integrity. Silently, the call had gone out and the angelic army of the Lord was afoot. But first, vital reconnaissance was needed. Accurate reconnaissance information was critical to the formation of a tactical battle plan. Information regarding enemy troop positioning and movements was mandatory. Members of a uniquely mobile special warfare unit were given the vital reconnaissance assignment. The only question was how best to obtain the necessary information. Mounted cavalry was the answer.

One of the most fascinating periods of the history of the nation of Israel is described in the writings of the prophet Zechariah. Since Zechariah wrote during one of the most tumultuous struggle-filled times in the history of Israel, it should be of little surprise to us that the footprints of Jesus are found throughout. As we have discussed, the unique perspective of the Old Testament Scriptures that is afforded by the realization of the physical involvement of the incarnate Son of God truly changes everything. This perspective helps to shed much needed light upon the admittedly confusing scriptural passages found in the book of Zechariah.

It almost seems as if each of the prophets were purposely tasked with coming up with their own subset of cryptic passages, and Zechariah is no different. As a group, these difficult prophecies just don't seem to make sense or to be additive to the full revelation of God when viewed in the classic perspective. When viewed with a modified perspective, however, they each cleverly reveal their own unique facet of the character and person of Jesus Christ and His role in the Old Testament. No better is this displayed than in the writings of the prophet Zechariah.

The first amazing battle revelation—of what can only be of an otherworld reconnaissance cavalry unit—appears in the very first chapter of the book of Zechariah. This account begins with the fascinating description of a vision that involves the prophet's conversation with the mysterious rider of a red horse. This rider was clearly in charge of and actively involved in the immediate demands of directing a military mission.

> On the twenty-fourth day of the eleventh month, the month of Shebat, in the second year of Darius, the word of the LORD came to the prophet Zechariah son of Berekiah, the son of Iddo. During the night I had a vision—and there before me was a man riding a red horse! He was standing among the myrtle trees in a ravine. Behind him were red, brown and white horses.
>
> —Zechariah 1:7-8

These verses supply much information regarding the nature of the military mission that is being described. This rider and his companions are mounted cavalry. Mounted cavalry have specific missions for which they are best suited. They are most often utilized when the mission requires not only mobility, but also speed. The multiple different colors of their horses suggest that individual identification from a distance may also be of importance to their mission. It is most assuredly a covert mission as these riders have taken refuge in the cover offered by a ravine in a grove of *"myrtle trees."* They are hiding from someone.

Our first hint at the identity of the enigmatic person, the *"man,"* who is speaking to Zechariah in the vision is his relationship to the other riders. The other riders clearly report directly to him. He is obviously a man of rank and appears to be their field commander.

> I asked, "What are these, my lord?" *The angel* who was talking with me answered, "I will show you what they are."
>
> Then *the man* standing among the myrtle trees explained, "They are the ones the LORD has sent to go throughout the earth."
>
> And they *reported to the angel of the LORD*, who was standing among the myrtle trees, "We have gone throughout the earth and found the whole world at rest and in peace."
>
> —Zechariah 1:9-11 (emphasis added)

The commander of this group, the *"man"* speaking to Zechariah, is once again referred to with the title of *"the angel of the Lord."* From our earlier discussion, the implications of this title are well established.

We can therefore know that the mission of this mobile cavalry force is reconnaissance and that stealth was important in the acquisition of the information that was sought. We also know that *the angel of the Lord* is commanding this unit. The members of this team report directly back to him the information gathered during their cavalry reconnaissance mission.

As such, this scene is remarkably reminiscent of the use of mobile cavalry by General Robert E. Lee, the commander of the Southern army during the Civil War. It has been said that his favorite commander was the infamous Jeb Stuart, who commanded an elite cavalry unit. This unit was referred to as *the eyes* of the Army of Northern Virginia. One must remember that there was no radio communication in the days of the War Between the States—or in the days of *the angel of the Lord*. There were no surveillance aircraft. There was no satellite photography. There were no drones. The Army of Northern Virginia and its commander relied on a relatively small, crafty, and very mobile cavalry force led by Jeb Stuart to ride in front of and to be the eyes of the main force.

The critical mandate for Jeb Stuart's cavalry unit was vital reconnaissance. They were the primary source of early warning of impending attack or for information regarding the deployment of enemy troops. The outcomes of the most important battles of the Civil War were won or lost dependent upon the performance of the associated light cavalry groups. An oft-cited example is the battle of Gettysburg. Most historians believe the high ground, and therefore the battle, was lost in the early hours merely for a lack of vital reconnaissance. One is given the very distinct impression that the mobile cavalry force lying in wait in the ravine among the myrtle trees played precisely this same role for the army of the Lord.

In this regard, we discussed evidence in the previous chapter suggesting that the army of the Lord was *not* supplied with the omniscient capabilities that one might expect of an army led by Jesus Christ. The fact that David and his warriors had to wait for the army of the Lord to get into position above the balsam trees, for example, was somewhat surprising in this regard. It is becoming apparent that this epic otherworld war described on the pages of the Old Testament was a very real fight for everyone involved. There were no special favors, no unfair advantages given to the army of the Lord. They had to obtain their reconnaissance information in the same way that Robert E. Lee and the Army of Northern Virginia had to obtain it—by effective mounted cavalry.

What follows this reconnaissance report is one of the most remarkable scenes in the book of Zechariah, if not the Bible itself. Incredibly, we are given a cryptic description of a most sacred conversation between two Persons of the Triune Godhead!

> Then *the angel of the* LORD *said, "*LORD *Almighty, how long will you withhold mercy from Jerusalem and from the towns of Judah, which you have been angry with these seventy years?" So the* LORD *spoke kind and comforting words to the angel who talked with me.*
>
> —Zechariah 1:12-13 (emphasis added)

Jesus, *the angel of the Lord*, cries out to the Father on behalf of Jerusalem and the nation of Judah. He does what He truly does best. He mediates. He cries out on the behalf of the undeserving for unmerited mercy. He was the Intercessor for the Israelites, just as He is the Intercessor for us. The Father responds as He always does to His precious Son, Jesus—with *"kind and comforting words."*

The cavalry riders have just reported back to the Commander of this elite mobile cavalry unit after riding throughout the earth. We have just seen Him, in turn, report back to the Supreme Commander—His Father—with a very special request for a very special mission. This request of this particular mission was obviously spurred on by the results of the reconnaissance mission. Something about the world being *"at rest and in peace"* resulted in this very special request to His Father for mercy for *"Jerusalem and...the towns of Judah."*

This next mission for the Commander of the army of the Lord is indeed comforting to Jesus. His next mission is to militarily support the reestablishment and rebuilding of His beloved *"Jerusalem and Zion."*

> Then the angel who was speaking to me said, "Proclaim this word: This is what the LORD Almighty says: 'I am very jealous for Jerusalem and Zion, but I am very angry with the nations that feel secure. I was only a little angry, but they added to the calamity.'
>
> "Therefore, this is what the LORD says: '*I will return to Jerusalem with mercy*, and there my house will be *rebuilt*. And the measuring line will be stretched out over Jerusalem,' declares the LORD Almighty.
>
> "Proclaim further: This is what the LORD Almighty says: 'My towns will again overflow with prosperity, and *the* LORD *will again comfort Zion and choose Jerusalem.'"*

—Zechariah 1:14-17 (emphasis added)

Then, in case there are any doubts regarding the identification of *the angel of the Lord* as Jesus, the fully embodied, fully emptied only Son of God, the second chapter of the book ends all questions in this regard. There we are allowed to observe, through the eyes of the prophet Zechariah, an amazing exchange between *the angel of the Lord* who has been speaking with Zechariah and yet another messenger. This other messenger is presumably sent from God—the Supreme Commander—with tactical battle commands for the Commander of the army of the Lord.

> *Then the angel who was speaking to me left, and another angel came to meet him and said to him: "Run, tell that young man, 'Jerusalem will be a city without walls because of the great number of men and livestock in it. And I myself will be a wall of fire around it,' declares the LORD, 'and I will be its glory within.'"*
> —Zechariah 2:3-5 (emphasis added)

A casual reading of this passage can be quite confusing. The key to bringing order out of the confusion is punctuation. Indeed, the tiniest details of punctuation are critical to uncovering the special truth concealed in this passage, just as Jesus told us it would be: *"I tell you the truth, until heaven and earth disappear, not the smallest letter, not the least stroke of a pen, will by any means disappear from the Law until everything is accomplished"* (Matthew 5:18). A careful examination of the single quotation marks within the double quotation marks around this passage allows the reader to understand what is actually being said and precisely who is saying it in this very special exchange.

The messenger who has been sent from God delivers a special message. This message is comprised of a short speech that Jesus, *the angel of the Lord*, (who has been speaking to Zechariah) is to say to *"that young man,"* (i.e. Zechariah). It is a speech that has been written by the Holy Spirit of God as a declaration to the people of Jerusalem *from* Jesus. In other words, Jesus is to say to Zechariah and Jerusalem, *"Jerusalem will be a city without walls because of the great number of men and livestock in it. And **I myself** will be a wall of fire around it and I will be its glory within"(emphasis added).*

In this one passage we are given yet more confirmation that *the angel of the Lord* who is speaking to Zechariah is none other than Jesus Christ—for who else could be the *"glory within"* Jerusalem? And in that same passage we are also told of a future military command for this mighty Warrior King. Ultimately, Jesus is to be the very defense of the holy city itself—He is to be *"a wall of fire around it."* As if this clear-cut identification of Jesus in this critical role in the Old Testament adventures of Israel were not enough, the prophet Zechariah is not even close to being through with his remarkable revelations.

Indeed, when the angel messenger finishes speaking to Jesus, Zechariah himself continues with a proclamation from the Lord that further confirms the identity of this warrior who is sent *"against the nations."* Zechariah starts off by stating, *"This is what the LORD Almighty says."* However, the Person (*"the LORD Almighty"*) who is speaking then states that He (*"the LORD Almighty"*) has been sent *"against the nations"* by another from whom He takes commands. The one from whom He takes commands must obviously be a more senior Person of the Trinity. There can only be one explanation. This is Jesus (*"the LORD Almighty"*) speaking. He is telling Zechariah and the Israelite exiles that He, Jesus, has been sent *"against the nations"* **by the Father.**

> For *this is what the LORD Almighty says:* "After *he* has honored *me* and has *sent me against the nations that have plundered you*—for whoever touches you touches the apple of his eye—I will surely raise my hand against them so that their slaves will plunder them. Then you will know that *the LORD Almighty has sent me.*"
> —Zechariah 2:8-9 (emphasis added)

How could we ask for more convincing evidence from the Word of God that the very special messenger who is physically present with the prophet Zechariah is Jesus? Who else could it be? We know this messenger is *"the LORD Almighty"* precisely because He says He is. He is embodied, incarnate, and standing before Zechariah. He takes orders from a more senior member of the Trinity. The conclusions that can be drawn are straightforward. It can't be the Father. It can't be the Holy Spirit. It must be Jesus. The clues are all there and only one conclusion is reasonable.

Once again, the central theme and challenging hypothesis of this book is illuminated and accentuated by this episode. Indeed we are clearly told that Jesus has been sent *"against the nations that have plundered"* the nation of Israel. This is a warrior Commander confirming to Zechariah the nature of His latest assignment, His latest mission in the *"great war"* (Daniel 10:1).

Jesus is being sent against Babylon, the captors of the Israelite remnant. But there is more. Indeed, before Jesus can carry out the destruction that has been decreed against those who devastated the Israelites, He has been sent to warn the Israelites to flee! Note that the message delivered by Jesus is delivered with an exclamation point. There is clear urgency to the warning. It hints at military battle devastation of such a degree that collateral damage to the Israelite captives is a clear possibility.

> *"Come, O Zion! Escape, you who live in the Daughter of Babylon!"*
> —Zechariah 2:7

Many of the missions of the Commander of the army of the Lord are similar in nature. This mission is quite reminiscent of one we have already discussed in detail—the visit of *the angel of the Lord* to Abraham before the destruction of Sodom and Gomorrah. Once again, the mission that is being described by Zechariah is to warn righteous non-combatants of the impending danger of collateral damage during the assault. In each of these cases, the central theme is the same. The missions are all about the grand strategic overall Old Testament goal (Isaiah 49:5-6; see below) of preserving the righteous remnant of Israel. By sending Jesus on this critical mission to warn the righteous remnant of Judah of the impending assault, God is sending us yet another message that attests to the perfection, the extremity of His faithfulness. The code of the warrior of God is perfectly preserved. Almighty God has decreed destruction. Yet these warriors will go to extreme measures to make sure that no member of the righteous remnant of Israel is left behind on the battlefield. The warrior code and camaraderie of the army of the Lord is founded in the justice of God.

Indeed, just as we learned in the rescue of Lot and his daughters from Sodom and Gomorrah, God will pull out all stops and reserve no measure in rescuing even a single person who will call upon the Name of the Lord. Once again, we are given a glimpse in this Old Testament passage of the New Testament gospel message that we all hold close to our hearts. Just as with the church, the bride of Christ, God will do anything—including sending His only Son to die on a cross—to rescue anyone who will be rescued, anyone who will place their trust in our warrior King Jesus. As we have discussed, both of the commands to preserve Israel and to bring *"salvation to the ends of the earth"* are included in the one clear mission statement that the Father delivered to Jesus:

> *And now the* LORD *says—he who formed me in the womb to be his servant to bring Jacob back to him and gather Israel to himself, for I*

am honored in the eyes of the LORD and my God has been my
strength—he says: "It is too small a thing for you to be my servant to
restore the tribes of Jacob and bring back those of Israel I have kept.
I will also make you a light for the Gentiles, that you may bring my
salvation to the ends of the earth."

—Isaiah 49:5-6 (emphasis added)

Indeed, the prophet Zechariah confirms this. The warning of impending military action is then followed by a message of comfort and security.

"Shout and be glad, O Daughter of Zion. For I am coming, and I will
live among you," declares the LORD.

"Many nations will be joined with the LORD in that day and will
become my people. I will live among you and you will know that the
LORD Almighty has sent me to you. The LORD will inherit Judah as his
portion in the holy land and will again choose Jerusalem. Be still
before the LORD, all mankind, because he has roused himself from his
holy dwelling."

—Zechariah 2:10-13 (emphasis added)

In summary, with very literally the very same breath, the individual delivering this message to Zechariah claims not only that he *is* the LORD, but also that the LORD *sent* Him. This warrior Commander repeatedly speaks of *"the LORD"* both in the first person *and* in the second person. In the same statement where He claims He (the LORD) will live among the Israelites, He states that the LORD Almighty has sent Him to them. Only the concept of the Holy Trinity and the embodied Jesus Christ can solve this apparent dilemma.

Thus, a simple and yet intriguing set of conclusions can be drawn from this, the first of Zechariah's encounters with the warrior who sits astride the red horse in the ravine among the myrtle trees. This warrior's identity is not a mystery. There is only one individual who can possibly fit the description that is given of *the angel of the LORD* who delivers this message to Zechariah. He is Jesus. He is the Commander of the army of the Lord. And, just as was the case when he confronted Joshua at Jericho, Jesus has now been sent to intervene as a warrior in battle on behalf of the remnant of Israel.

Chapter 27

Zechariah Continues To Build Our Case
Not a Jot or a Tittle Will Fade Away

Things were desperate in Jerusalem. For many, the exile to Babylon had ended. And yet, struggle and intrigue were still the order of the day for the repatriated Israelites. The spark of the nation of Israel nevertheless glowed once again in Jerusalem. A spark, and yet there was no flame. No doubt that the heart of the Israelites was for the Lord. The rebuilding of the Holy Temple had begun. But still the will of the reborn nation waivered and collapsed like a house built on sand before the treacherous and scheming opposition. The pagan peoples of the land had no desire to see the nation of Israel rise again. In the face of the chilling wind of stiff opposition, the construction of the Holy Temple had ground slowly to a halt. A prophet was needed, a sacred messenger to fan holy spark into flame.

Israel's opponents were formidable. Some were open in their distrust and dislike of the nation that had improbably returned from what all expected to be a permanent banishment. Others were not so open in voicing their opposition. They plotted and schemed in the dark. In back rooms they wrote libelous letters and whispered slanderous lies.

No doubt a prophet was needed, one who could confirm the repentance of a nation; one who could remind the Israelites of the source of their forgiveness, their redemption; one who did not hold back in demanding the return to the Lord. The Israelites desperately needed a new direction. They needed a kinsman-redeemer. They needed the rescue that is the sole purview of the Son of God. Such was the setting as the Holy Spirit stirred the heart of the prophet Zechariah.

The 3rd chapter of the book of the prophet Zechariah starts off at an easy and yet exciting pace. Our pulse cannot help but quicken as Zechariah seems to be describing yet another Old Testament encounter with the incarnate Son of God. The initial description of this encounter once again introduces the now familiar character *the angel of the Lord*. In Zechariah's description, *the angel of the Lord* squares off against none other than his expected adversary, Satan. But this encounter is different. Just as the evidence for the vital identity of Jesus as Zechariah's embodied messenger seems to be utterly convicting, the wheels suddenly come off the cart of our expectations. In a sudden turn, the text seems to be describing someone other than Jesus.

> *Then he showed me Joshua the high priest <u>standing before the angel of the LORD</u>, and Satan standing at his right side to accuse him. The LORD said to Satan, "The LORD rebuke you, Satan! The LORD, who has chosen Jerusalem, rebuke you! Is not this man a burning stick snatched from the fire?"*
>
> *Now Joshua was dressed in filthy clothes as he stood before the angel. <u>The angel</u> said to those who were standing before him, "Take off his filthy clothes." Then <u>he said to Joshua</u>, "See, <u>I have taken away your sin</u>, and I will put rich garments on you."*
>
> —Zechariah 3:1-4 (emphasis added)

In an initial perusal of this passage, the activities that are attributed to *the angel of the Lord* seem to add further to the evidence that *the angel of the Lord* is the Son of God. Who else, after all, can take sins away? That is indeed the sole jurisdiction of Jesus Christ. Only He has authority in regard to the permanent removal of sin. Certainly no ordinary angel would ever take credit for the gospel work of Jesus Christ, take credit for an authority earned by the sacred cross of Calvary. This is holy ground indeed. No ordinary angel would—or even could—go there. In fact, this angel of the Lord not only commanded that Joshua's *"filthy clothes"* be removed, but he also stated that *he himself* would replace them with *"rich garments."* This can be nobody else but Jesus. After all, these garments sound precisely like the *"fine linen, bright and clean"* given to the saints in the book of Revelation.

> *Let us rejoice and be glad and give him glory! For the wedding of the Lamb has come, and <u>his bride</u> has made herself ready. <u>Fine linen, bright and clean</u>, was given her to wear." (<u>Fine linen</u> stands for the <u>righteous acts of the saints</u>.)*
>
> —Revelation 19:7-8 (emphasis added)

But then, right out of the blue, this very same *angel of the Lord*—(whom we have been making the case is Jesus Christ) seemingly blows our whole case to pieces. He suddenly starts speaking of *"the branch"*—a well-recognized term for the Messiah—*in second person!*

How can he do that if we have correctly identified *the angel of the Lord* as the only Son of God, Jesus? The text seems to suggest that *the angel of the Lord* and the Messiah, the Branch, are two entirely different individuals. This would be a fatal flaw for our case that *the angel of the Lord* is Jesus, since our hypothesis—if it is indeed true—cannot be contradicted by even a single line of scripture. Our identification of *the angel of the Lord* must fit all scripture—or it is errant theology.   And yet in the light of our new perspective and the overwhelming evidence that we have already reviewed, we know that this apparent contradiction simply cannot be true. There is too much convicting information to the contrary— *the angel of the Lord is* Jesus.

The resolution of this dilemma is found in close attention to the details of Holy Scripture. Once again, the punctuation in the NIV translation is the key to understanding this passage, as we identify a set of single quotation marks that is bracketed by a set of double quotation marks. The key to the correct identification of *the angel of the Lord* is in recognizing that He is in fact *quoting His Father* starting in verse 7. In other words, this is Jesus quoting His Father who is speaking about Jesus to Jesus.

> *The angel of the* LORD *gave this charge to Joshua:* "*This is what the* LORD *Almighty says:* '*If you will walk in my ways and keep my requirements, then you will govern my house and have charge of my courts, and I will give you a place among these standing here.*
>
> —Zechariah 3:6-7 (emphasis added)

Our initial confusion came only in the failure to pay close attention to the punctuation. It clearly tells us that Jesus is quoting the Father who is speaking about Jesus. This detail is revealed only with the recognition of a single tiny swoop of the prophet's pen, the single quotation mark inside the double quotation mark.

Jesus continues to quote the Father in the next three verses. Although the Father is still speaking about Jesus, this time His statement is directed to Joshua and his associates.

> '"*Listen, O high priest Joshua and your associates seated before you, who are men symbolic of things to come:* I am going to bring my servant, the Branch. *See, the stone I have set in front of Joshua! There are seven eyes on that one stone, and I will engrave an*

inscription on it,' says the LORD Almighty, 'and I will remove the sin of this land in a single day.

" 'In that day each of you will invite his neighbor to sit under his vine and fig tree,' declares the LORD Almighty."
—Zechariah 3:8-10 (emphasis added)

Lets summarize the main issues. *The angel of the Lord* is not the one who is speaking in second person about *"the Branch."* If that were true, then *the angel of the Lord* could not be Jesus (*"the Branch"*). Instead, it is the Father, not *the angel of the Lord* who speaking about the Branch. *The angel of the Lord* is Jesus and He is indeed *"the Branch."*

To further emphasize the importance of this line of reasoning, the Holy Spirit again utilizes the exact same format of *revelation by punctuation* later in Zechariah 6. Once again, confusion reigns in regard to the proper identification of *the angel of the Lord* and *"the Branch,"* until the placement of the quotation marks is properly noted and the statements made regarding *"the Branch"* are appropriately attributed to the Father and not to *the angel of the Lord*, Jesus.

The word of the LORD came to me: "Take [silver and gold] from the exiles Heldai, Tobijah and Jedaiah, who have arrived from Babylon. Go the same day to the house of Josiah son of Zephaniah. Take the silver and gold and make a crown, and set it on the head of the high priest, Joshua son of Jehozadak. Tell him this is what the LORD Almighty says: 'Here is the man whose name is the Branch, and he will branch out from his place and build the temple of the LORD. It is he who will build the temple of the LORD, and he will be clothed with majesty and will sit and rule on his throne. And he will be a priest on his throne. And there will be harmony between the two.'

The crown will be given to Heldai, Tobijah, Jedaiah and Hen son of Zephaniah as a memorial in the temple of the LORD. Those who are far away will come and help to build the temple of the LORD, and you will know that the LORD Almighty has sent me to you. This will happen if you diligently obey the LORD your God."
—Zechariah 6:9-15 (emphasis added)

The angel of the Lord is Jesus and He is the Messiah. And, once again, we have yet another confirmation that it is indeed *"the LORD"* (identified as the one who is speaking) being sent by *"the LORD Almighty."* This is a very special confirmation of the direct involvement of the Jesus in the support of the nation of Israel.

One final bit of evidence regarding the identity of the angel speaking to Zechariah is supplied in the first several verses of Zechariah 6. The *"four spirits of heaven"* are depicted as four chariots with powerful horses. They are going out from the *"presence of the Lord"* and most assuredly represent the Holy Spirit.

> *I looked up again—and there before me were four chariots coming out from between two mountains—mountains of bronze! The first chariot had red horses, the second black, the third white, and the fourth dappled—all of them powerful. I asked the angel who was speaking to me, "What are these, my lord?"*
>
> *The angel answered me, "These are the four spirits of heaven, going out from standing in the presence of the Lord of the whole world. The one with the black horses is going toward the north country, the one with the white horses toward the west, and the one with the dappled horses toward the south."*

—Zechariah 6:1-6

Several verses later this reference to the Holy Spirit serves to further confirm the identity of *the angel of the Lord* who is speaking to Zechariah. Not only does this angel command the chariots whose powerful horses strain while waiting for his command to *"go throughout the earth,"* but also this angel refers to the Holy Spirit as *"my Spirit."* He thereby claims divine nature in a manner that no ordinary angel would ever dare.

> *When the powerful horses went out, they were straining to go throughout the earth. And he said, "Go throughout the earth!" So they went throughout the earth. Then he called to me, "Look, those going toward the north country have given my Spirit rest in the land of the north."*

—Zechariah 6:7-8 (emphasis added)

Can there be any doubt regarding the incarnate presence of Jesus in the Old Testament? Can there be any doubt that He was involved in every recorded event as *the* fully embodied, yet simultaneously fully emptied, *angel of the Lord* and Commander of the army of the Lord?

Chapter 28

Abraham, Isaac, and Mount Moriah
The Absence of a Jot or Tittle

Mount Moriah. God. A father. A son. A ram. The father of a nation, trusting wholly in the promise of God was going to sacrifice the very son through whom the promise was to be embodied. The son trusted his father. The father trusted his God. God had a plan.

This was *the* mountain. Its dirt was the most hallowed dirt on the face of the earth. Two thousand years from that day, on this mountain, God would for all eternity give his heart to mankind. The blood of God's son would saturate this dirt below a wooden Roman cross. That day would have to wait. This was not that day. Instead, on this day, another man would for a moment give his heart to God. Even though his mind was not in it, his heart told him that God could be trusted. He could not comprehend how God would keep His promise. But his heart told him He would.

Just as the presence of a tiny swipe of the scribe's pen changed everything in the interpretation of the identification of *the angel of the Lord* in the book of the prophet Zechariah, so also does its absence impact the interpretation of the 22nd chapter of Genesis. Once again, our proper identification of *the angel of the Lord* is dependent upon the smallest of punctuation marks.

In this Old Testament episode, *the angel of the Lord* has just been sent on yet another rescue mission. Rescue is what he does best. This time, he is sent to specifically intervene on behalf of Abraham's son, the son of *the promise*, Isaac. His orders are to keep Abraham from sacrificing his son—once Abraham's true heart is known.

> But *the angel of the LORD* called out to him from heaven, "Abraham! Abraham!"

> "Here I am," he replied.

"Do not lay a hand on the boy," he said. "Do not do anything to him. Now I know that <u>you fear God</u>, because you have not withheld <u>from me</u> your son, your only son."

—Genesis 22:11-12 (emphasis added)

The wording is specific and, once again, quite precise. In the very careful crafting of his message, this angel once again claims to be the one *to whom* Abraham was going to sacrifice his son, Isaac. *The angel of the Lord* states that the fact that Abraham did not withhold his son *"from me"* demonstrates that Abraham *"fear[s] God."* This is combined with the fact that we already know that the original command to sacrifice Isaac came directly from God. That very command is spelled out clearly earlier in the same chapter.

Then <u>God said</u>, "Take your son, your only son, Isaac, whom you love, and go to the region of Moriah. Sacrifice him there as a burnt offering on one of the mountains I will tell you about."

—Genesis 22:2 (emphasis added)

The conclusion is straightforward. *The angel of the Lord* is God. Once again, no ordinary angel would dare to speak in a manner that ascribed the commands of God to himself personally. That was Satan's sin. No faithful angel would venture even close to the boundary of that precariously dangerous ground.

Then, *the angel of the Lord* completes the revelation of his identity by the statement of the promise to Abraham.

*<u>The angel of the LORD</u> called to Abraham from heaven a second time and said, "<u>I swear by myself, declares the LORD, that</u> because you have done this and have not withheld your son, your only son, <u>I will surely bless you</u> and make your descendants as numerous as the stars in the sky and as the sand on the seashore. Your descendants will take possession of the cities of their enemies, and through your offspring all nations on earth will be blessed, because you have obeyed **me**."*

—Genesis 22:15-18 (emphasis added)

Once again we note that the punctuation is critical to understanding to whom *the angel of the Lord* is referring in his statement to Abraham. If there were single quotation marks around his statement—in other words, if the words, *"declares the LORD"* had been *excluded* by single quotation marks—then we would have known that the angel was speaking for someone else rather than himself. In other words, in this statement the angel is directly referring to himself as *"the LORD."*

This passage is a great find in our treasure hunt. The specific clues that it adds to our quest once again confirm that *the angel of the Lord* is no one less than the embodied Son of God. This passage also confirms the very special truth of the consistency of the written Word of God. It can be taken very literally because under the microscope it always comes through. Even down to the minutiae of its punctuation, it holds fast to the truth that it alone reveals.

Chapter 29

Reconciling the Irreconcilable
Jacob Wins a Wrestling Match With God?

The ford of the Jabbok River. Jacob was returning to the land, to his inheritance. Only one thing stood in his way. Esau. His estranged brother. The meeting Jacob had dreaded for years loomed before him. That from which he had previously run could no longer be avoided.

Jacob was desperate. His plan was simple. His plan was desperate in its simplicity. Since he could no longer avoid the meeting that he dreaded, he would welcome it. He would send gifts ahead to his brother, his enemy. He would, by this action, not only placate his brother, but also place himself in a position of subservience. He would send his family ahead of him. Esau and his 400 warriors would not harm them. Perhaps Esau would be appeased, his anger at the theft of his birthright placated. It was a gamble. But Jacob had always been a gambler. Besides, there was that promise from God. Jacob would be the focal point of the genealogy of God himself. From his line—not Esau's—would the promise be fulfilled. Somehow, Jacob and his family would live. His offspring would compose the genealogy of *the One* who was to come, the anointed of God, the Messiah.

The plan was in motion. Jacob's family and possessions had been sent across the river to buffer Jacob from the meeting with his past. The preparations were complete. He had done all that he could do. In the morning all would be settled. A good night's rest was all that was left.

God had a slightly different plan. God knew that Jacob needed one more preparatory test before the pivotal meeting with his brother Esau.

God sent a warrior to ambush Jacob. They did battle. There were no weapons. It was man against man, strength against strength, cunning against cunning. It was a wrestling match. It was relatively unheralded, but it would be the pinnacle test for Jacob, the father of the nation of Israel.

Perhaps nowhere else in the Old Testament is there as startling a documentation of the direct intervention of Jesus in the history of Israel as is found in Genesis 32. Most of the Old Testament descriptions of the activities and adventures of Jesus have to do with battle against the enemies of Israel. On other occasions, however, Jesus intervenes in the setting of a confrontation with an individual warrior, patriarch, or prophet. Genesis 32 in particular has much to tell of the Person of Jesus Christ as He is revealed in the Old Testament. This chapter in the greatest story of adventure and intrigue involves, of all things, a wrestling match.

> That night Jacob got up and took his two wives, his two maidservants and his eleven sons and crossed the ford of the Jabbok. After he had sent them across the stream, he sent over all his possessions. So Jacob was left alone, and _a man wrestled with him_ till daybreak. When _the man_ saw that _he could not overpower him_, he touched the socket of Jacob's hip so that his hip was wrenched as he wrestled with _the man_. Then _the man_ said, "Let me go, _for it is daybreak_."
>
> But Jacob replied, "I will not let you go unless _you bless me_."
>
> _The man_ asked him, "What is your name?"
>
> "Jacob," he answered.
>
> Then _the man_ said, "Your name will no longer be Jacob, but Israel, _because you have struggled with God_ and with men and have overcome."
>
> Jacob said, "Please tell me _your name_." But he replied, "_Why do you ask my name_?" Then _he blessed him_ there.
>
> So Jacob called the place Peniel, saying, "It is because _I saw God face to face_, and yet my life was spared." The sun rose above him as he passed Peniel, and he was limping because of his hip. Therefore to this day the Israelites do not eat the tendon attached to the socket of the hip, because the socket of Jacob's hip was touched near the tendon.
>
> —Genesis 32:22-32 (emphasis added)

This familiar yet nonetheless baffling passage from the book of Genesis finds new life in the illuminating light of our new perspective. In fact, until this vignette is viewed from our new perspective, it reigns as one of the most confusing episodes in the Bible. This passage has the audacity to repeatedly suggest that *"the man"* with whom Jacob wrestles is of supernatural origin—namely God. The textual evidence in this regard is not subtle. To begin with, this wrestling man not only has the authority to rename Jacob but does so with a name that will ring through history. *"The man"* renames Jacob, Israel, because he has *"struggled with God and with men and [has] overcome."* Finally, in a summarizing recap of the scene, Jacob states, *"I saw God face to face, and yet my life was spared."* There can be no other conclusion from an objective review of the text except that Jacob's encounter is with God.

All sorts of allegorical explanations of this passage are available to us. None are so attractive, however, as the simple recognition that we have just been told that Jacob wrestled with *"a man"* and at the same time *"struggled with God"* and that they are indeed one in the same Person. This narrows our choices considerably! This represents a *physical* encounter between the patriarch Jacob and God. The physical nature of this encounter is critical to its explanation since, as we have discussed, the Bible is not subtle in repeatedly reminding us that the Father and the Spirit are indeed without physical body. It is an easy connection for most that *"the man"* who wrestled with Jacob was indeed the incarnate Jesus Christ. Compared to some of the more extreme metaphorical explanations, Jesus Christ is actually the easy explanation for this scene. In fact, it would take a lot of work by a truly ardent skeptic to try to explain away the facts described by this Biblical passage.

This is all well and good. Most of can cautiously go this far—except for one little problem: Jacob *wins* the wrestling match! This far into this discussion of the warrior role of Jesus in the Old Testament, most of us are already way out on an uncomfortable ledge that is well beyond most of our theological comfort zones. Even so, one is now left pondering the unthinkable. How could any man—even one as surly as Jacob—possibly defeat the Son of God—fully God—in a wrestling match?

Although most might be tempted to take the easy road and simply respond that Jesus *let* him win, it is difficult to build a scripturally justifiable case for this. There is another possible answer. This answer goes back, once again, to a primary tenet of the premise of this book: namely that not only did Jesus actively participate directly in the events of the Old Testament as a fully embodied warrior and Commander of warriors, but also that Jesus totally and completely emptied Himself in the process of His incarnation.

If one were to accept—just for the sake of argument—that Jesus was incarnate in the Old Testament as a man with the same physical strength of an average man, then that which is revealed in these troublesome passages becomes a bit more plausible. After all, if this is the case, this normal *"man"* has just squared off in a wrestling match with Jacob, a proven street fighter, who is well known for his craftiness and deception. After all, Jacob started his wrestling career in an intrauterine wrestling match with his brother Esau before he was even born.

> *The babies jostled each other within her, and she said, "Why is this happening to me?" So she went to inquire of the LORD.*
>
> *After this, his brother came out, with his hand grasping Esau's heel; so he was named Jacob. Isaac was sixty years old when Rebekah gave birth to them.*
>
> —Genesis 25:22, 26 (emphasis added)

There is no doubt Jacob was an accomplished wrestler, as are most young men who grow up with a brother of similar age and size. This is especially true when the brother is a rough and tumble outdoor guy *and a twin*—like Jacob's fraternal twin Esau. Wrestling is the order of the day in most close male sibling relationships. Jacob probably had no alternative but to become an accomplished wrestler as his combative brother undoubtedly repeatedly pounced upon him in mock battle.

The scriptural text reveals that Jacob wins the all night match against his obviously out-gunned opponent, as we are told, *"the man saw that he could not overpower him."* In fact, *"the man"* resorts to a bit of what might be called a sibling *cheap shot*, as he wrenches Jacob's hip in a last ditch effort to pull victory from the jaws of defeat. That final parting shot is almost like one of those *bro-shots* a vanquished brother takes as their parents are pulling the victorious brother off of him—classic guy stuff.

Further still, as the victor, Jacob's demand is even more of the same. That which Jacob requests of his vanquished opponent is nothing less than a statement acknowledging Jacob's superiority—classic sibling rivalry. In other words, before Jacob will release him, Jesus must first bless Jacob. Jacob asks for his blessing almost like a sibling wrestling match ends when one brother makes another brother cry, "Uncle!" before he will release him. Jacob makes the release of his opponent conditional upon an admission of his defeat!

In this regard, the text also relates another interesting fact. Jacob's opponent was on a covert operation. He clearly did not want to be seen by anyone other than Jacob. Daylight seemed to be a major problem for him. One can safely assume that both his presence and identity were secrets that he wished to guard. This was definitely another covert *special ops* mission for this Warrior of God. To his obvious displeasure—and in another stunning demonstration of the fullness of his emptying—Jesus could *not* escape into the shadows until Jacob released him. Unless this was all just a cruel ruse, the incarnate Jesus had voluntarily emptied Himself such that He was truly held captive in His creation by the grip of a wrestling hold!

So, in order to gain His freedom, Jesus blesses Jacob. Blessings as such are an act of God, or at least an act of someone who is his superior. We are clearly told this in Hebrews 7 in the explanation of why Abraham was blessed by Melchizadek.

And without doubt the lesser person is blessed by the greater.
—Hebrews 7:7

Jacob knew the man whom he had just overpowered was indeed his spiritual superior. In fact, this evidence combined with the rest of the textual evidence reviewed above leads us to the conclusion that Jacob knew that he was wrestling with the Son of God. Then, of even more importance, this *"man"* acknowledges this truth by indeed blessing Jacob. Once again, no simple angel would ever—could ever—be so presumptuous. In fact we have no scriptural evidence of an angel ever blessing anyone.

This carefully detailed scene is shaping up as either the most bizarre of circumstances or a very carefully orchestrated set of events with a very special purpose. Indeed, these events are designed specifically to give us more details regarding the precise nature of the *"man"* whom Jacob defeated. This man is simultaneously Almighty God—the only Person worthy of dispensing real blessing—while simultaneously being so completely emptied that He couldn't even win a wrestling match—despite having resorted to a cheap shot hip dislocation.

We simply cannot let this point pass. The Holy Spirit felt it was so important that we know the nature of the fullness of the emptying of our Savior and God, Jesus, that He carefully orchestrated and recorded the events of Genesis 32. They are vital to the mission of the Holy Spirit to not only explain, but also illustrate the complex nature of Jesus—of the *"man"* who was simultaneously 100% man while remaining 100% God. The illumination of this passage sheds even more light upon the scriptural passage that tells us Jesus was indeed made *"a little lower than the heavenly beings"* (Psalm 8:5).

And for all of us skeptics who refuse to accept this truth the first time around, the Holy Spirit—as is often the case—later throws in a little confirmation of this vital message in, of all places, the book of the prophet Hosea! Indeed, in the twelfth chapter of Hosea, in the middle of his pleadings with the nation of Israel, the identity of Jacob's wrestling opponent suddenly becomes the topic of discussion. In a vivid recap of the exploits of Jacob, we are not only given additional clues as to the wrestler's true identity, we are specifically and incontestably told his actual name. *"The angel"* is no one less than the *"LORD God Almighty, the LORD."*

> *In the womb he grasped his brother's heel; as a man <u>he struggled with God</u>. He struggled <u>with the angel</u> and overcame him; he wept and begged for his favor. He found him at Bethel and talked with him there—<u>LORD God Almighty, the LORD is his name</u> of renown!*
>
> —Hosea 12:3-5 (emphasis added)

This opponent of Jacob is simultaneously declared to be *"God"* and *"the angel"* and *"LORD God Almighty, the LORD."* Can there be any doubt in our minds that this is Jesus? Indeed, can there be any doubt in our minds that each and every one of the other references to *the angel of the Lord* is a reference to Jesus? Amazingly, the *"man"* is never identified in Genesis 32 as *"the angel."* Only here in the book of the prophet Hosea are we told that the divine identity of the *"man"* and of *"the angel"* of the Lord are the same.

One final point deserves attention. In this provocative passage, just like in several others that have already reviewed, much is made of the mysterious *"name"* of our angelic visitor. Once again, the angel is specifically and pointedly asked to reveal his name—this time by the patriarch Jacob. And, once again, the refusal of the angel is not just noted, but emphasized in the detail of the carefully recorded conversation.

> *Jacob said, "Please tell me your name." But he replied, "Why do you ask my name?" Then he blessed him there.*
>
> —Genesis 32:29

One must begin to wonder why the Holy Spirit would repeatedly record in the text of the Bible the very specific refusal of this enigmatic messenger to answer a very pointed question regarding his name. At the same time, in this incident as well as the many other similar incidents that we have reviewed, the Holy Spirit has not been subtle in telling us that this *"man"* is God.

> *So Jacob called the place Peniel, saying, "It is because I saw <u>God face to face</u>, and yet my life was spared."*
>
> —Genesis 32:30 (emphasis added)

So, why would this visitor not answer this request for his name? The answer to this question is not specifically revealed in Holy Scripture. Nonetheless, there is much that can be said about the real *"name"* of this repeatedly appearing mysterious Old Testament visitor. After all, the fact that Jesus was running rampant through the adventures of the patriarchs of Israel, although not obvious, is not hidden either. Indeed, as joyfully discussed in this book, the footprints of Jesus are everywhere throughout the Old Testament. But, of course, nowhere in the pages of the Old Testament is the actual name of Jesus ever specifically recorded.

At the same time, it is nonetheless clear that the Holy Spirit is specifically drawing attention to the importance of this mysterious name. Special meaning and importance is indeed ascribed to the secretive name of this enigmatic character by repeatedly pointing out that it is indeed a secret. This plays on that very special attribute of our human nature that just drives us crazy when someone purposely keeps a secret from us—and then mockingly makes a point of telling us that this is exactly what they are doing. Surely, the mocking cry of our younger sibling, "I know something you don't know" still rings in many of our childhood memories. It is not lost on the attentive reader that this very pointed and intentional hiding of this very important name occurs in the same setting where God repeatedly emphasizes to the Israelites that His *"name"* is holy and to be revered.

There is no denying that the very *Name* of God is holy. We are very specifically told in the New Testament of the importance of the holy Name of Jesus Christ. It is precisely in *"the name of Jesus"* that we are baptized:

> *So he ordered that they be baptized in <u>the name</u> of Jesus Christ.*
>
> —Acts 10:48 (emphasis added)

We are told that Jesus is the *"name that is above every name"* and that it is very specifically *"the name of Jesus"* to which *"every knee"* shall bow and *"every tongue confess"* that He is Lord.

Therefore God exalted him to the highest place and gave him the name that is above every name, that at the name of Jesus every knee should bow, in heaven and on earth and under the earth, and every tongue confess that Jesus Christ is Lord, to the glory of God the Father.

—Philippians 2:9-11 (emphasis added)

There is simply no other reason for this *"man"* to so pointedly conceal his name or for the Holy Spirit to most emphatically reveal this very pointed persistence in remaining anonymous—except that the name in question is the most holy Name *of Jesus*. Precisely in its indefatigable veiling is the exclamation of its importance. How could this passage be revealing anyone else except that Person whose *"name"* is *"above every name"*? How could the name that they seek be any other name than the most important single name in the entirety of the creation? Certainly no other single person in the Bible courses through the pages of the Old Testament with this degree of specifically annotated anonymity or importance. Only one conclusion is available to us. This is Jesus. And, once again, He is right in the middle of the action in the adventures of the patriarchs of the nation of Israel.

Chapter 30

The Destruction of the Assyrian Army
Pure Otherworld Battle

They had come from the north like a hoard of locusts. Mighty nations fell before them. Their path was paved with destruction. Hamath. Arpad. Sepharvaim. Hena. Ivvah. One after one they fell before the mightiest army the world had ever seen. Great warriors of every nation trembled before the flame-red banners of the Assyrian army.

The unstoppable juggernaut hardly hesitated in its conquest of the Northern Kingdom of Israel. One fortified city after another was ground up like wheat stubble as Samaria offered little resistance to the Assyrian onslaught. Conquered, banished, obliterated, and forgotten—forever. This was the fate of those who fell and, if the Assyrians had their way, this would also be the fate of Judah.

As predicted, the great walled cities of Judah began to fall, one by one, before the brightly colored threshing sledge of the Assyrians. The very foundation of Jerusalem quaked anew with the loss of each of the walled cities. Nothing would stop the inevitable. Nothing could stop that which seemed destined to occur. All was lost.

Isaiah's description of the invasion of the Assyrian army and its ultimate defeat at the gates of Jerusalem—found in his chapters 30-31—makes for such leisurely reading now. So far removed from the terror of hopelessly inevitable destruction, the reader is tempted to glide over these two chapters. So far removed from the day-to-day horror of this time of massive devastation, it is easy to ascribe only metaphorical meaning to the very literal detail of the amazing battle descriptions that Isaiah renders with such visual and palpable fervor.

In the light of our new perspective, however, these chapters take on new meaning. No doubt, Isaiah's great battle descriptions do indeed have allegorical meaning that applies to any number of ages and peoples. And yet our new perspective allows us to appreciate that much more is being made available to us. We, through the lens of this new perspective, are being handed an actual eyewitness description of our warrior God in combat. This vivid detail of the battle accounts rendered by Isaiah (and the others) is pure gold in our search for evidence of Jesus Christ in the events of the Old Testament. This is because these accounts are wondrously consistent in one critical aspect. The detail very definitely speaks—in every case—of real, palpable, and consequential battle. Instead of imparting a fuzzy, detached, and allegorical picture of an incident of obvious divine intervention, they instead render a vivid and very literal description of an immediate and desperate physical struggle between warring opponents.

From the very beginning of this particular battle description by Isaiah, we are given the identity of the warrior Prince who sweeps in on His fiery chariot to once again rescue the remnant of Israel. Little is left in doubt. He is *the Name of the LORD.* His mode of transport is his war chariot, the Shekinah Glory, wrapped in *"dense clouds of smoke"* and conferring holiness upon this battlefield by way of the *"consuming fire"* that engulfs his throne. This is Jesus. He is the Commander of the army of the Lord. His charge—the remnant of Israel—has been threatened by the mighty Assyrian army that has already laid waste countless kingdoms and now stands at the gate of Jerusalem itself.

> *See, the Name of the LORD comes from afar, with burning anger and dense clouds of smoke; his lips are full of wrath, and his tongue is a consuming fire.*
> —Isaiah 30:27 (emphasis added)

The account of the battle that ensues is remarkable. It is a story of great contrast. On one side are the nations that have risen up against Israel. As a result of their attack, they face the fury of the Lord. The Lord very literally overwhelms them like a flood, *"like a rushing torrent, rising up to the neck"* (Isaiah 30:28). On the other side is the protected remnant of Israel. In contrast to their enemies, the Israelites are told by the Lord, *"you will sing as on the night you celebrate a holy festival; your hearts will rejoice as when people go up with flutes to the mountain of the LORD, to the Rock of Israel"* (Isaiah 30:29).

Obviously, there is a sharp contrast between the two camps. As the Israelites are celebrating, their enemies are engaging Jesus and His warrior angels in mortal combat. The description of the hand-to-hand combat is deliberately detailed, literal, and palpable.

> *The LORD will cause men to hear his majestic voice and will make them see his arm coming down with raging anger and consuming fire,*

with cloudburst, thunderstorm and hail. The voice of the LORD will
shatter Assyria; with his scepter he will strike them down.

—Isaiah 30:30-31 (emphasis added)

The visual and auditory images of the jubilant celebration that is described in verse 30:29 above stands in stark contrast to the graphic brutality of the simultaneously occurring battle. This battle description is not the allegorical fantasy of an epic poet regarding mythical battle between imaginary foes. This is real and meant to be taken literally.

Every stroke the LORD lays on them with his punishing rod will be to
the music of tambourines and harps, as he fights them in battle with
the blows of his arm.

—Isaiah 30:32 (emphasis added)

How easy it is to take Isaiah's description of God's protection of Jerusalem as purely allegorical. After all, it speaks of God flying like a bird over Jerusalem.

Like birds hovering overhead, the LORD Almighty will shield
Jerusalem; he will shield it and deliver it, he will 'pass over' it and
will rescue it."

—Isaiah 31:5 (emphasis added)

But this is no allegorical description. This is a very literal description of an air-mobile war chariot at work. The reader is allowed to picture the Shekinah Glory in the midst of doing precisely that for which it was so perfectly designed. Its ability to fly is not just about mobility from one battlefield to the next. It is also about battlefield reconnaissance and tactical battle force positioning. The reference to *"hovering"* is literal and specifically chosen. The Shekinah Glory hovers above the battlefield—Jerusalem—just like our modern day command helicopters hover above remote battlefields as they direct warfighters below.

The intense sensor array of the Shekinah Glory, as we have previously discussed, views all aspects of the surrounding terrain and detects all threats. From the elevated position, enemy troop movements and battlefield strategies are all easily detected. Tactical decisions for the Commander of the army of the Lord are based upon the latest battlefield reconnaissance and are immediately implemented from this commanding position above the battlefield.

With the tactical battle command aspects of its role covered, the Shekinah Glory then puts its capabilities as a weapons platform into full use as is necessitated by the battle sequence unfolding below. The Commander's chariot maintains the high ground at all times.

> *This is what the LORD says to me: "As a lion growls, a great lion over his prey—and though a whole band of shepherds is called together against him, he is not frightened by their shouts or disturbed by their clamor—so the LORD Almighty will come down to do battle on Mount Zion and on its heights.*
>
> —Isaiah 31:4 (emphasis added)

The outcome of the battle is described in equally graphic terms. While the victors celebrate, the conquered go into a literal banishment whose descriptors are too tangible to not be taken literally.

> *Topheth has long been prepared; it has been made ready for the king. Its fire pit has been made deep and wide, with an abundance of fire and wood; the breath of the LORD, like a stream of burning sulfur, sets it ablaze.*
>
> —Isaiah 30:33

The terrifying threat against the city of Jerusalem ends as quickly as it began. As previously predicted by Isaiah, the judgment rendered by Jesus and the army of the Lord is swift and complete. The victory in the otherworld battle is so complete that the real world army of Assyria never even approaches the gates of Jerusalem. To drive home the true origin of the victory, Isaiah reminds us that *"A sword that is not of a man"* has fought this real world battle against the world conquering power of Assyria.

> *"Assyria will fall by a sword that is not of man; a sword, not of mortals, will devour them. They will flee before the sword and their young men will be put to forced labor.*
>
> —Isaiah 31:8 (emphasis added)

Once again, we can apply the strategy of subtracting out of Isaiah's description that which we know occurred in the real world by other Biblical accounts. What is left must be pure otherworld battle. For example, we are given no historical real world suggestion that an army with a battle standard even advanced against the Assyrian army from the Israelites trapped in Jerusalem. And yet we are told that precisely this did in fact occur:

> *Their stronghold will fall because of terror; <u>at sight of the battle standard</u> their commanders <u>will panic</u>," declares the LORD, whose fire is in Zion, whose furnace is in Jerusalem.*

—Isaiah 31:9 (emphasis added)

Once again, by the subtraction mechanism we are given a fleeting glimpse onto the battlefield of the otherworld where the fate of Jerusalem was really decided. The evil otherworld army that opposed Jesus and His army of the Lord panicked at the sight of the battle standard of the Lord. Despite the fact that no battle was visible before the Israelites who on that fateful night peered cautiously over the city wall that separated them from the mighty world-conquering Assyrian army, a battle nonetheless raged mightily above them.

There was war in heaven.

The army of the Lord—led by their Commander Jesus—in mighty armed combat, threw itself against the otherworld dark army that stood behind the Assyrians. And yet, the description of the real world *battle*—if we can even call it that—accompanying this rout of the evil forces behind the Assyrian army is described tersely in a mere four sentences, once in 2Kings 19 and again in Isaiah 37.

> *That night <u>the angel of the LORD went out and put to death a hundred and eighty-five thousand men</u> in the Assyrian camp. When the people got up the next morning—there were all the dead bodies! So Sennacherib king of Assyria broke camp and withdrew. He returned to Nineveh and stayed there.*

—2Kings 19:35-35 (emphasis added)

> *Then <u>the angel of the LORD went out and put to death a hundred and eighty-five thousand men</u> in the Assyrian camp. When the people got up the next morning—there were all the dead bodies! So Sennacherib king of Assyria broke camp and withdrew. He returned to Nineveh and stayed there.*

—Isaiah 37:36-37 (emphasis added)

Once again, the *subtraction* exercise is useful in separating real world from otherworld. Very literally all that we can know of this battle as it occurred in the real world was that the Assyrian army woke up one morning with 185,000 fewer soldiers than it had the day before.

We can also know that the description of the jubilation in Jerusalem was very literal. The Israelite remnant behind the walls of Jerusalem never raised a sword or fired an arrow in their defense. All they did was celebrate. Just as the otherworld description of the battle that is described in Isaiah 30-31 suggests, from the Israelite standpoint, this entire otherworld—and real world—battle was fought entirely by the otherworld forces of the army of the Lord.

In this regard, that which is left after subtracting out the very limited real world description is a most vivid description of battle with hand-to-hand blows being delivered by the scepter wielded by the arm of Jesus Himself. The raging firepower delivered by the Shekinah Glory adds to the very tangible fury of the battlefield fray that is described.

It is difficult to tell whether the very physical blows that were struck and the firepower that was delivered by the Shekinah Glory were only against the *otherworld* evil forces that stood behind the Assyrian army. It could well be that the very literal descriptions of physical warfare found throughout chapters 30-31 were not limited to the otherworld. We are not given any suggestion one way or the other by the very terse description of the real world death of 185,000 Assyrian soldiers given in 2Kings 19 and Isaiah 37. These blows may have been the actual real world dispatching mechanism or the Assyrian soldiers may just have died in their sleep of a silent plague. We don't know. Either mechanism has Biblical precedent.

Either way, we can know that the victory was and remains all about Jesus. He may have been a very involved tactical battle Commander leading His warriors against otherworld evil warriors whose defeat signaled the defeat of the real world Assyrian army. On the other hand, He may have very literally been the one whose finger was *on the trigger* of the battle chariot weapons systems whose fury was unleashed on all who stood opposed to God on the battlefield below. We don't know. The detail of His literal involvement is shielded from us now. We can nonetheless know that the fate of Jerusalem—and the remnant of Israel, the ward of Jesus—was at stake and the Son of God was, as always, right in the thick of things.

Chapter 31

Balaam, the Donkey, and the Angel of the Lord
A Donkey Defeats Jesus?

God's intention was clear. The Israelites ruined everything on their first approach to the Promised Land. He would not let that happen again. God's purpose, God's promise, God's plan would stand.

The nation of Israel; born in Egypt, anointed at the Red Sea, and 40 years a nation in the making. Their plan—God's plan—for the conquest of the land was simple. This time they would approach the Eastern border of Canaan. They would enter the land at Jericho. But to get there, they had to first pass through Moab.

Balak, the Moabite king, was no novice. He and his princes had seen the writing on the wall. They were worried. Panic was beginning to set in among the people. They had all heard of the power of the God of the Israelites. They had heard of that little incident at the Red Sea. They had heard of the quick and decisive victory over the very capable Amorite kings and their formidable armies. Then their hearts had really sunk. Things had gone from bad to worse. They realized that a disturbing pattern had been established by the Israelite conquests: this God of the Israelites had settled for nothing less than the utter destruction of His enemies.

The Israelite promise to move quickly through the Moabite homeland fell on deaf ears. The Moabites had no desire to allow this powerful nation to set up a permanent residence as their next-door neighbor. The Israelite proposal was obviously a deception. It would not be allowed. The Israelites would only grow stronger with time. No matter what they said their intentions were then, they would soon be flourishing in Canaan. Like all such nations, they would soon be looking to expand their borders. Then they would be looking right at Moab. The Moabite princes and their king would take their chances. They would fight the disorganized desert rabble before they grew even stronger.

And yet there was a problem. The princes of Moab knew they were powerless against the God of the Israelites. They had no chance against a God who could part the mighty waters of the Red Sea. Thus their plan was simple. They would not face this God of the Israelites in battle. Instead, they would turn His mighty strength in their favor. With a little trickery and a little luck, they would soon have Him on *their* side. After all, this talk of the Israelites being His chosen people was all relative. Everyone knew they were rebellious and stiff-necked. Surely this God of Israel would listen to reason, would play by the rules. The Moabites would simply pay a prophet—a prophet of the God of Israel—to curse the Israelites. Yes, they would use the Israelites' own God against them.

The key to the plan was simple. They needed a prophet of the God of Israel who placed more value on the things of this world than on obeying God. Moab was a wealthy nation. Surely they could purchase the services of such a prophet. Take Balaam, son of Beor for example—he could be bought. He loved the things of this world. He would curse the Israelites. He was the answer to all of the Moabite worries. The Moabite princes would make him an offer he could not refuse and he would curse the Israelites and turn their God against them. Their God would destroy them just as He has threatened so many times before.

From the opening verses of Numbers 22, the scene is rapidly set for perhaps the most fascinating appearance of *the angel of the Lord* in all of the Old Testament. The stage is set as the escapades of Balaam the prophet have turned from what were initially just the wayward wanderings of a foolish prophet to the overt opposition of the carefully crafted plan of God. Instead of blessing the young nation of Israel—which he surely knows is God's plan—Balaam begins flirting with actually siding with their declared enemies. Something about the offer from the princes of Moab is just too enticing to pass up. By even agreeing to go along with the messengers from Balak, Balaam is skirting dangerously close to derailing God's plan for Israel's second approach to the Promised Land. Balaam is clearly toying with the idea of selling out the nation of Israel and the plan of God for his own personal gain.

This choice of a *"reckless"* path is apparently all that it takes to trigger the dispatch of *the angel of the Lord* to intervene against Balaam in a direct and startling fashion. Taken at face value the scene that follows is a quirky and delightfully Disney-like interaction that could easily be dismissed by even serious students of the Bible. And yet this curious description of the confrontation of Balaam and his donkey by *the angel of the Lord* offers many valuable clues in our Old Testament quest for the trail of Jesus.

In fact, in this description of the antics of Balaam and his donkey, we are treated to one of the most theologically challenging descriptions of the activities of *the angel of the Lord* that is found on the pages of Holy Scripture. Still, if our overarching hypothesis—that every single word in the Bible is indeed really about the only focal point of all history, Jesus Christ, and that *the angel of the Lord* is none other than Jesus Himself—is indeed correct, it must hold true in *every* related Biblical passage.

Despite the fact that a convincing argument for the proof of our hypothesis has already been made, in this particular case our resolve in this regard is quite vigorously tested. To be sure, in this passage—as has been true in several previous passages—the attributes of *the angel of the Lord* are not easily ascribed to the Son of God. A familiar setting is encountered as the backdrop for this amazing passage. Jesus, in His role as *the angel of the Lord*, is once again on a military mission. He is heavily armed and looking for a fight. At the same time He obviously remains fully emptied into a state that is *"a little lower than the angels"* (Psalm 8:5; Hebrews 2:7-9).

The story begins with Balaam's decision to comply with a request to aid and abet a declared enemy of the Israelites. After having dispatched the Amorite kings and their armies, the Israelite nation is once again marching toward the Promised Land. Balak is a sworn enemy who stands in opposition to the declared plans of God for the nation of Israel. It is Balak's desire that Balaam, who he obviously respects as a prophet of God, be recruited to curse the Israelites. Although Balaam assures these *"princes of Moab"* that he can only do what God tells him to do, he nonetheless agrees to go with them to meet with Balak.

> *Balaam got up in the morning, saddled his donkey and went with the princes of Moab. But God was very angry when he went, and the angel of the LORD stood in the road to oppose him. Balaam was riding on his donkey, and his two servants were with him.*
>
> —Numbers 22:21-22 (emphasis added)

God was angry enough about Balaam's decision to render assistance to the enemies of Israel that He dispatched *the angel of the Lord*, God's *terror*, God's *hornet*, to confront this wayward prophet. We are specifically told, *"the angel of the LORD stood in the road to oppose him."* But the next line is the one that sets us reeling, as the full intent of the angel is made readily apparent.

> *When the donkey saw the angel of the LORD standing in the road with a drawn sword in his hand, she turned off the road into a field. Balaam beat her to get her back on the road.*

—Numbers 22:23 (emphasis added)

Once again, just as seen in the encounter with Joshua outside of Jericho, this warrior angel has his sword *already drawn*. In fact, this episode with Balaam occurs not long before the angel's stunning appearance before Joshua outside of Jericho. The presence of the sword in hand signals clear intent. This angel means serious harm to someone. As we previously discussed, it takes less than a moment to draw one's sword from its sheath. One does not draw one's sword therefore without one very specific reason—either fear of, or intention toward, *immediate* attack.

The angel's precise motives in this regard are revealed later after the donkey repeatedly refuses to carry Balaam into three separate and progressive ambushes that are set by *the angel of the Lord*. After the third ambush when the presence of *the angel of the Lord* is finally revealed to Balaam, the angel clearly states that the very reason his sword is drawn is that he in fact meant to kill the rebellious Balaam as a result of his *"reckless"* path. There is no uncertainty in his choice of words. His intent was *to kill* Balaam.

> *"I have come here to oppose you because your path is a reckless one before me. The donkey saw me and turned away from me these three times. If she had not turned away, I would certainly have killed you by now, but I would have spared her."*
>
> —Numbers 22:32-33 (emphasis added)

The reader of these words can hardly help being overcome by an uneasy feeling. Something is just not right here. Things just don't add up. First of all, it is not at all apparent to the discriminating reader why the angel set three separate ambushes rather than simply advancing against the hapless prophet and just finishing him off. This just doesn't make sense. After all, *the angel of the Lord*—Jesus—never lies. We can know for sure that it was in fact His full intention to kill Balaam. We can also assume that this course of action—to move directly to kill Balaam—would have been well within the capabilities of this mighty warrior angel. And yet that which is logical—based on the information that we are given—simply did not happen.

The reason that the *logical* did not occur is because it is not logic—but rather the mercy of God—that rules the day in this amazing battle sequence. God gives Balaam every chance—just as He does with every one of us, every single day. In this case, the merciful grace of God even includes allowing the donkey to see into the otherworld where the ambush has been set. For a brief period of time, the curtain that separates the two worlds comes down. By allowing the angel to be seen by the donkey, God spares Balaam from the three ambushes that have been prepared for him. The donkey avoids the angel each time—saving Balaam— despite the fact that it was not *Balaam's* intent to turn back from his reckless course. After Balaam repeatedly beats the donkey—clearly demonstrating that his intent was to defy the Lord and continue on—the Lord pushes the envelope of the overlap of the two worlds even further by allowing the donkey to actually verbally rebuke Balaam.

Then after the donkey thwarts three separate ambushes, Balaam himself is finally allowed—in yet another demonstration of God's mercy and grace—to see the mighty angel standing before him. One would be hard pressed to find another episode in the Bible where God's mercy is so preposterously displayed as in this use of a talking donkey!

It takes this truly extraordinary intervention by a talking donkey to nudge Balaam into the action that brings to fruition the mercy that is offered by God. Balaam saves his own life by immediately falling on his face in humble submission before *the angel of the Lord*. He immediately repents of his sin saying:

> *"I have sinned. I did not realize you were standing in the road to oppose me. Now if you are displeased, I will go back."*
>
> —Numbers 22:34

Once again, this angel is clearly set apart from the angel in the book of Revelation who immediately asks the bowing Apostle John to hurriedly get up from his position of reverence and submission. No admonishment for the act of humble submission comes from this angel because this angel is called by the Name that is above all names and before which every knee will bow—Jesus. Instead *the angel of the Lord* tells Balaam that he may go with the men but admonishes Balaam to, *"speak only what I tell you"* (Numbers 22:35), once again strongly suggesting that He speaks as one with authority, as One who is the only Son of God.

What is the message of this episode? Surely it is important to note that our merciful God gave Balaam every chance. There is no doubt that He takes His compassionate mercy to extremes for all of us every day of our lives.

But there must be more. There must be a reason why the Holy Spirit reveals *a detailed progression of three ambushes* that are set by *the angel of the Lord*. First of all, one critical detail regarding the three ambushes is worthy of note. We cannot help but notice that each of the angel's three ambushes is progressively more intensely planned in regard to the strategy used to entrap Balaam. The donkey is able to thwart the first ambush by simply turning off the road and into a field.

> *When the donkey saw the angel of the LORD standing in the road with a drawn sword in his hand, she turned off the road into a field. Balaam beat her to get her back on the road.*
>
> —Numbers 22:23

The attentive reader cannot help but take note of the angel's response to his foiled ambush. *The angel of the Lord* responds to this initial escape by placing the next ambush in between two vineyard walls where there is no possible exit into an adjoining field. Tactical battle decisions are being made.

> *Then the angel of the LORD stood in a narrow path between two vineyards, with walls on both sides.*
>
> —Numbers 22:24

This change of the ambush terrain to one that would not allow the donkey to turn away clearly shows that the angel's sword was not staid by the *repentant* act of turning away from the first ambush. Instead, it tells the reader that the donkey thwarted the angel's intent. The progressive placement of the ambush in settings that will not allow the donkey to turn away at all tells us that this was not just a test to see if Balaam will turn from his pathway. Rather, *the angel of the Lord* shows us that it was his clear intent to kill Balaam *regardless of his choice*. This point is well demonstrated by the outcome of this second ambush. For despite the progressive improvement of the ambush layout, the donkey once again nonetheless eludes *the angel of the Lord* a second time by simply pressing against one of the vineyard walls, thereby apparently going around the angel and somehow eluding the deadly arc of the angel's sword.

> *When the donkey saw the angel of the LORD, she pressed close to the wall, crushing Balaam's foot against it. So he beat her again.*
>
> —Numbers 22:25

It must be noted that the donkey did not turn around from its course. This evasion cannot be misinterpreted as a symbolic act of repentance like the evasion of the first ambush. Instead the donkey simply goes around *the angel of the Lord* and continues on its course. There was no turning back. Thus the angel's sword is not voluntarily held because of a repentant move by the donkey. No, the donkey simply evades *the angel of the Lord* by pressing against the wall. My point? The donkey again, somehow, outmaneuvers *the angel of the Lord*!

How can this be happening? How can the reader be expected to understand what is going on here? The inconsistencies in this story are simply overwhelming. After all, this is war. This is battle. We have an extraordinarily powerful angel who has been sent on a mission. He means to stop Balaam. In fact, as we have already noted by a peek ahead in the text, *the angel of the Lord* meant to *kill* Balaam. It is hard to fathom what we are now being asked to believe. What we have just witnessed is a donkey apparently thwarting an ambush by presumably the same angel of the Lord who in a single night slew 185,000 Assyrian soldiers (2Kings 19:35; Isaiah 37:36).

As preposterous as this seems, it gets even worse. After all, is the reader of the Word of God *really* being asked to believe that the evasive maneuver of pressing against a wall somehow placed Balaam outside of the reach of the sword of *the angel of the Lord*? Something is just not right here. At this point, we must entertain the thought that we—and apparently even the donkey—must not be privy to *all* that is going on in this scene, particularly in the accompanying otherworld of war.

To be sure, the next set of tactical maneuvers add further to our conviction that all is not as it seems. The angel further alters his tactical battle plan to attempt to thwart the evasive maneuvers of the highly trained *special ops* military donkey that has single-handedly defeated the mighty *angel of the Lord* in his first two skirmishes. *The angel of the Lord* must now move *"on ahead"* to set the final ambush in a place where there can be no turning around and no evasion. There can be no escape.

> *Then the angel of the LORD moved on ahead and stood in a narrow place where there was <u>no room to turn</u>, either to the right or to the left. When the donkey saw the angel of the LORD, she lay down under Balaam, and he was angry and beat her with his staff.*
> —Numbers 22:26-27 (emphasis added)

Are we really to believe that a donkey has thus defeated Jesus in battle three straight times? If the intentions of *the angel of the Lord* were really as later stated—to kill Balaam—then indeed the facts are clear. They can support only one conclusion. A wretched donkey that has now been beaten black and blue by its irate owner has quite readily routed *the angel of the Lord* from the field of battle by single-handedly foiling all three of his carefully set ambushes! How can this scene and these seemingly irreconcilable inconsistencies be explained?

Let's begin our attempt at reconciling the apparent facts by agreeing that things are indeed most definitely not as they seem. We must now assume that we have made the mistake of drawing conclusions based only upon that which we are being allowed to see. And in this regard, we can be assured that we are not being allowed to see the whole scene. God is giving us—just as He gave Balaam—only as much of a view of the battlefield as His intention and purpose deem necessary. In a series of progressive revelations, God opens the mouth of the donkey and then opens the eyes of Balaam. Through these revelations, Balaam is brought low to the ground in humble repentance before Jesus. He is allowed to see just enough of the whole scene in the otherworld to fulfill God's purpose. He is shown just the right amount in just the right order to make him fall on his face before Jesus.

> Then the LORD *opened the donkey's mouth*, and she said to Balaam, "What have I done to you to make you beat me these three times?"
>
> Balaam answered the donkey, "You have made a fool of me! If I had a sword in my hand, I would kill you right now."
>
> The donkey said to Balaam, "Am I not your own donkey, which you have always ridden, to this day? Have I been in the habit of doing this to you?"
>
> "No," he said. Then the LORD *opened* Balaam's eyes, and *he saw* the angel of the LORD standing in the road *with his sword drawn*. So he *bowed low and fell facedown*.
>
> The angel of the LORD asked him, "Why have you beaten your donkey these three times? *I have come here to oppose you* because *your path is a reckless one before me*. The donkey saw me and turned away from me these three times. *If she had not turned away, I would certainly have killed you by now*, but I would have spared her."
>
> Balaam said to the angel of the LORD, "*I have sinned*. I did not realize you were standing in the road *to oppose me*. Now if you are displeased, I will go back."

The angel of the LORD said to Balaam, "Go with the men, but speak
only what I tell you." So Balaam went with the princes of Balak.
—Numbers 22:28-35 (emphasis added)

Just as Balaam is brought to a clearer knowledge of the Lord by the series of progressive revelations, so also is the reader of the Word of God. Stated quite plainly, we are allowed to see the tactical outmaneuvering—the defeat—of *the angel of the Lord* by a donkey. When viewed through our new perspective, however, we are allowed to see so much more. This information is just enough to take us to the next level in our understanding of the activities—and therefore the nature—of Jesus Christ during the historical period encompassed by the Old Testament. For once again, the facts that are seen tell us much—although never enough—about that which is not seen. From this information, we can know that much more had to be going on behind the curtain that is drawn between our world and the otherworld in this simple encounter between a warrior angel and a hapless donkey. After all, we know that a donkey alone simply could not thwart the efforts of warrior Jesus—even the fully emptied Jesus.

We can therefore assuredly know that we have not been allowed to see the whole of the fight on that battlefield that day.

We have not been allowed to see the entirety of the angelic forces that were arrayed across this otherworld battlefield the day that Balaam stumbled into it. The facts can lead to no other conclusion than this: more than a donkey opposed *the angel of the Lord* on this battlefield that day. In other words, there can be no doubt that *the angel of the Lord* set an ambush for more than just a man riding a donkey. He set his ambush against the otherworld powers of darkness that must have accompanied Balaam and his entourage that day. We know the evil dark powers were behind Balaam because his actions were clearly in opposition to the will of God. In this regard, this scene mirrors the later appearance of the very same angel of the Lord to Joshua before the battle of Jericho. Surely the angel's sword is drawn against a tactical array of otherworld forces that are far more dangerous than the hapless donkey.

Recognizing the dearth of information that is available to the reader of Holy Scripture in this regard, one can only begin to imagine the real battlefield setting that surrounded Balaam as he rode down the road on his donkey. On both sides of Balaam and his entourage must have ridden the principals of the evil demonic forces of the dark and mysterious otherworld that parallels ours. These warriors had to have been the authorities, powers, and spiritual forces that backed the Moabites. Indeed, we are given no evidence that Balaam ever saw the evil forces that opposed *the angel of the Lord* that day on behalf of Balak, king of Moab. Presumably the donkey did not see them either. But we can be assured that the power and tactical capabilities required to evade the ambush set by *the angel of the Lord* most certainly came from somewhere other than the mind, heart, and legs of a donkey.

> *For our struggle is not against flesh and blood, but against the rulers, against the authorities, against the powers of this dark world and against the spiritual forces of evil in the heavenly realms.*
>
> —Ephesians 6:12

The facts are clear and they are fuel for our quest for information regarding the activities of Jesus Christ during the times of the Old Testament. A summary helps put them in the proper perspective: First of all, a donkey repeatedly outmaneuvered Jesus. A donkey—even this combat-ready, battle-savvy, *special warfare*, tactical-ride of Balaam's—can't outmaneuver a seasoned warrior, even the emptied Jesus. The implications of these two facts are unavoidable. The only explanation that is available to us is that which is strongly suggested elsewhere— that the impact on our world of the spiritual warfare that surrounds us in the otherworld is not as we might expect. In other words, the immediate results of armed brutal combat in the parallel world where Jesus and the army of the Lord do battle—may be translated into *something other than sword wounds* for the parallel combatants in this world.

To clarify, let's start with a mental exercise. Let's begin by imagining what would have occurred on the road that day if the donkey had *not* been allowed to see the angel. *The angel of the Lord* had clearly been sent on a mission to eliminate the threat to the nation of Israel that would somehow occur if Balaam were allowed to curse them prior to their entry into the Promised Land. After all, as we have previously reviewed, *the angel of the Lord* had one primary directive in the Old Testament: *the preservation of the remnant of Israel*. Presumably to this exact end, the angel clearly stated that he would have killed Balaam and spared the donkey if his ambush had been allowed to progress as he planned it.

So, we can assume that something would have occurred in front of us—in the real world—that would have resulted in the death of Balaam while sparing the donkey. What might that have looked like? Other Biblical stories render many possibilities. Balaam could have fallen off the donkey ill from *the plague* as occurred after King

David's census of the army of Israel (2Samuel 24:15-16; 1Chronicles 21:14-15). Perhaps a lion would have attacked Balaam. Perhaps a band of robbers, a lightning bolt, a traumatic fall, or a tree limb would have beset Balaam. Regardless of the mechanism of death that we might have observed, we now know from this glimpse into the parallel otherworld of near continual war that the real *cause* would have been a sword held in the hand of a mighty warrior from another world.

We can also know that almost assuredly *we* did not see the whole story through the eyes of Moses, the author of this book of the Bible. We know that a donkey did not outmaneuver *the angel of the Lord*. We know that the real battle took place above the hedgerow and vineyard country of Moab that day. And yet despite the fact that in three separate military engagements *the angel of the Lord* was frustrated in his mission to kill Balaam, God's purpose was ultimately served. Balaam humbled himself and repented. Of even more importance to the outcome of the *great war* from which this battle emerged, Balaam was made very aware that his persistence in meeting with Balak would put him dangerously close to the mortal consequences of cursing the nation of Israel.

We also know that if the donkey had never seen into the otherworld and perceived the threat of *the angel of the Lord*, Balaam and the donkey would have ridden right into the ambush. Only the donkey would have walked out of that encounter. Likewise, since the donkey and then Balaam each had their eyes opened to the otherworld threat in a progressive fashion, Balaam was allowed to take advantage of one last warning to repent. God's mercy ruled the battlefield that day. God's purpose—Balaam's repentance from cursing Israel—would not have been served to the glory of God if the donkey's eyes had not been opened.

One cannot help but note that only Balaam's immediate and unbridled repentance—after he saw *the angel of the Lord*—staid the angel's sword. What does this tell the reader of Holy Scripture about the complex interaction between the two worlds? Did Balaam's initial persistence in traveling down the path despite God's warning (made clear by the shying of the donkey) somehow empower the evil forces in the otherworld that accompanied him? Did this empowerment by Balaam's persistent disobedience allow the accompanying otherworld evil forces to overcome *the angel of the Lord* and thus allow Balaam's escape? What was the otherworld reaction to Balaam's final humble response to God's test? Did the otherworld opponents of *the angel of the Lord* run in disarray from the battlefield as Balaam fell on his face before Jesus? Did his humble repentance prevent the empowerment of the evil forces?

In light of the paucity of scriptural information regarding the interface between the worlds, one can only speculate in answering these key questions. All the reader of Holy Scripture can know for sure is that in regard to this particular challenge to the return of Israel to the Promised Land, God's will triumphed. Although Balaam would later fall back into his pattern of sin, he initially responded correctly to God's very careful and persistent orchestration of events. He submitted to God's plan, God's will in his life, by submitting to and obeying *the angel of the Lord*.

Most notably, if *we* had never been told of the presence of *the angel of the Lord* in this scene, we would have thought it a most peculiar story indeed. Surely if we had been a normal world observer at this fight with no insight into the otherworld, all that we would have observed were the antics of a bullheaded donkey followed by the untimely—and seemingly accidental—death of a prophet. This fact should leave the reader much to ponder regarding all of the other quirky scenarios described in the Old Testament, as well as the events that take place in our own lives. So very much more was taking place around this comical scene. Assuredly *so very much more* takes place around all such scenes in the Old Testament—and in our lives.

Chapter 32

Gideon

"The LORD Is With You [literally with you!], Mighty Warrior"

The Midianite raiding parties had swept out of the hills to the plains below. They freely plundered the crops and livestock of Israel. The savagery of these plundering warriors was unopposed. It was the time of the Judges of Israel and the sin of the nation of Israel had long restrained the protective hand of *the angel of the Lord*. The oppression of the Midianite raiders had become so unbearable that the Israelites hid in mountain caves and makeshift shelters. Even the most stiff-necked of peoples could only stand so much. Their hearts and their eyes turned once again to the God of their fathers, the God they had willfully abandoned just a generation ago.

God was compassionate. God was merciful. God was mighty to save. He sent *the angel of the Lord* to a man named Gideon. This was a military recruiting trip. It was God's will that a specially equipped *"mighty warrior"* lead the nation of Israel against the Midianite raiders.

The angel of the LORD came and sat down under the oak in Ophrah that belonged to Joash the Abiezrite, where his son Gideon was threshing wheat in a winepress to keep it from the Midianites. When the angel of the LORD appeared to Gideon, he said, "The LORD is with you, mighty warrior."

"But sir," Gideon replied, "if the LORD is with us, why has all this happened to us? Where are all his wonders that our fathers told us about when they said, 'Did not the LORD bring us up out of Egypt?' But now the LORD has abandoned us and put us into the hand of Midian."

—Judges 6:11-13 (emphasis added)

The Old Testament story of the Israelite warrior Gideon is found in the book of Judges. In it is found yet another characterization of the role of *the angel of the*

Lord. Once again the identity of *the angel of the Lord* is confirmed. In the scene above, there is only one other person other than Gideon. That person is *the angel of the Lord.* And yet, in the very next verse *"the Lord"* is described as being physically present performing the physical act of *turning.*

> The LORD *turned* to him and said, "Go in the strength you have and save Israel out of Midian's hand. Am *I* not sending you?"
>
> —Judges 6:14 (emphasis added)

This evidence for the identity of *the angel of the Lord* is not subtle. In this scene, just like in nearly every Old Testament scene in which he appears, he is identified as *"the LORD."* Once again, emphasis is placed upon the physical nature of the involvement of the Son of God as *the angel of the Lord* in His primary Old Testament mission. Gideon is told that despite his weakness he can have confidence against the Midianites. Jesus assures Gideon that He will be right there in the middle of the fight when Gideon strikes *"down all the Midianites together."*

> "But Lord," Gideon asked, "how can I save Israel? My clan is the *weakest* in Manasseh, and I am the *least* in my family."
>
> The LORD answered, "*I will be with you,* and *you* will strike down all the Midianites together."
>
> —Judges 6:15-16 (emphasis added)

Gideon and *the angel of the Lord* continue their conversation. Gideon makes a very strange request that reveals his suspicions regarding the nature of the person to whom he is speaking. His suspicions are the same as ours.

> Gideon replied, "If now I have found favor in your eyes, give me a sign *that it is really you* talking to me. Please do not go away until I come back and bring my offering and set it before you."
>
> And *the LORD* said, "I will wait until you return."
>
> —Judges 6:17-18 (emphasis added)

Gideon is asking this remarkable individual who is standing before him whether he really is *"the LORD."* Gideon wants to know exactly what we want to know. He knows that he is standing before God's representative who is identified in the text as both *"the angel of the Lord"* and *"the LORD."* Gideon wants to know if he is really standing before the physically incarnate God of the creation. That is precisely what he is asking and *the angel of the Lord* complies with his request.

> *Gideon went in, prepared a young goat, and from an ephah of flour he made bread without yeast. Putting the meat in a basket and its broth in a pot, he brought them out and offered them to him under the oak.*
>
> *The angel of God said to him, "Take the meat and the unleavened bread, place them on this rock, and pour out the broth." And Gideon did so. With the tip of the staff that was in his hand, the angel of the LORD touched the meat and the unleavened bread. <u>Fire flared from the rock</u>, consuming the meat and the bread. And the angel of the LORD <u>disappeared</u>.*
>
> —Judges 6:19-21 (emphasis added)

The angel of the Lord gives Gideon precisely what he asked for, a sign. He demonstrates that he is of a supernatural nature by causing fire to flare from the rock and consume the meat and bread. This sign offered by *the angel of the Lord* is enough to prove to Gideon that the individual standing before him is exactly who he suspected. Gideon knew that this physically present individual who was standing before him was indeed God incarnate. Gideon knew Jesus.

Gideon did not fear for his life until he knew that the individual, *the angel of the Lord*, was indeed God. The Israelites well knew of the implications of standing in the awesome presence of God. The stories of the terrifying fire, smoke, lightning, and thunder on the top of Mount Sinai—along with the warning that anyone who tried to see God would die—surely must have been passed down to Gideon's generation.

> *On the morning of the third day there was <u>thunder</u> and <u>lightning</u>, with a thick cloud over the mountain, and a very <u>loud trumpet blast</u>. Everyone in the camp <u>trembled</u>. Then Moses led the people out of the camp to meet with God, and they stood at the foot of the mountain. Mount Sinai was covered with <u>smoke</u>, because <u>the LORD descended on it in fire</u>. The smoke billowed up from it <u>like smoke from a furnace</u>, the whole mountain <u>trembled violently</u>, and the sound of the trumpet <u>grew louder and louder</u>. Then Moses spoke and the voice of God answered him.*

The LORD descended to the top of Mount Sinai and called Moses to the top of the mountain. So Moses went up and the LORD said to him, "Go down and <u>warn the people</u> so they do not force their way through <u>to see the LORD</u> and many of them <u>perish</u>. Even the priests, who approach the LORD, must consecrate themselves, or the LORD will break out against them."

—Exodus 19:16-22 (emphasis added)

Gideon therefore knew that he had just done that which was specifically forbidden under a penalty of death. He knew that he had looked upon the face of God.

When Gideon realized that it was the angel of the LORD, he exclaimed, "Ah, <u>Sovereign LORD</u>! I have seen the angel of the LORD <u>face to face!</u>"

But the LORD said to him, "Peace! <u>Do not be afraid</u>. <u>You are not going to die</u>."

—Judges 6:22-23 (emphasis added)

Then, just as *the angel of the Lord* promised, God went before Gideon into battle. Gideon and his army of 300 men routed the enormous army that stood before them precisely because Jesus Himself fought for them. The text is not subtle in placing Jesus in the middle of the fight.

Gideon and the hundred men with him reached the edge of the camp at the beginning of the middle watch, just after they had changed the guard. They blew their trumpets and broke the jars that were in their hands. The three companies blew the trumpets and smashed the jars. Grasping the torches in their left hands and holding in their right hands the trumpets they were to blow, they shouted, "A sword for the LORD and for Gideon!"

While each man held his position around the camp, all the Midianites ran, crying out as they fled. When the three hundred trumpets sounded, <u>the LORD caused the men throughout the camp to turn on each other with their swords</u>. The army fled to Beth Shittah toward Zererah as far as the border of Abel Meholah near Tabbath.

—Judges 7:19-22 (emphasis added)

The divine identity of *the angel of the Lord* is further substantiated by this brief visit with Gideon. In addition to the textual references that demonstrate him speaking as the Lord, this encounter also confirms several other common threads of evidence that similarly support the contention that the incarnate Jesus was present in this critical role. The people who interact with *the angel of the Lord* are often quite afraid of him. He must have been a very impressive figure. But, more importantly this fear seems to have its genesis in the belief that they are standing in the presence of God. This was certainly true in Gideon's case. He feared for his life because he had seen God. The divine presence is also substantiated by the repeated desire of those who interact with *the angel of the Lord*, like Gideon, to offer sacrifices in his presence. Jesus is *the angel of the Lord*.

Chapter 33

Mortal Missions
David, the Angel of the LORD, and the Threshing Floor of Araunah the Jebusite

---

It was spring, the time of year when kings go off to war. Joab and the army of Israel had destroyed the Ammonites. The crown of the Ammonite king had been placed on David's head.

The peace was short-lived. The Philistines now opposed them. The confidence of the Philistines in picking this fight was well founded. Their champions were massive, menacing warriors. They taunted the army of Israel. These Philistine giants were sons of Rapha—brothers of Goliath. First came Sippai; then, Lahmi; then the Philistine giant at Gath, who had six fingers on each hand and six toes on each foot.

The army of Israel would not tolerate the taunting of the Philistines any longer. They had their own champions who arose and confronted these menacing enemies face-to-face in mortal combat. On the field of battle, Sibbecai the Hushathite, Elhanan son of Jair, and Jonathan son of Shimea were lions. They did not listen to the Philistine intimidation. They fiercely stepped into the breech and slew their giant pagan opponents. Victory belonged to Israel and her king.

Pride is a stealthy predator. It hunts the hearts of men when success takes their eyes off of the Lord. Victory after victory had tempted the heart of Israel's king.

Satan was there. He asked the questions. They were questions common to the heart of every man. Exactly how big was the mighty army of Israel anyway? Surely the sheer size and power of the army of Israel—not the Lord—was responsible for David's success. After all, no other nation could field an army of this size. Pride had crept into the heart of Israel's king. A census of the army was requested.

The otherworld of spiritual battle is prominent in Old Testament scripture. Its interface with the real world is repeatedly demonstrated to be both complex and frustratingly dynamic. In fact, this interface seems to be redefined in almost every scene in which it is explored. Despite its complexities, however, one thing holds consistently true. Our choices, thoughts, prayers, and actions appear to significantly influence outcomes in the otherworld. In a similar fashion, actions that unfold in the otherworld can likewise have profound, although not necessarily direct, effects in our world. This influence in both directions, which is the hallmark of the interface between the two worlds, is especially well demonstrated by the intriguing story of David's request for a census of the army of Israel and its subsequent consequences (2Samuel 24; 1Chronicles 21).

Minimal interaction with the otherworld is documented in this account until *after* this census is requested. King David broke a direct command of God by ordering a census to be taken of the fighting men of Israel. Amazingly, he did this over the objections of the somewhat scurrilous commander of his army, Joab. Joab seemed to have no difficulty whatsoever in seeing that this act of self-centered pride on the part of its King would not end well for Judah.

This rebellious sin of David's, as expected, directly provoked activity in the otherworld. God gave David a choice of punishment. In response to David's choice, God's real world punishment was mediated by activity in the otherworld. Specifically, God sent His primary otherworld warrior, *the angel of the Lord*, to afflict the people of Israel with three days of plague. As a direct result, much devastation was wrought upon the men of Israel with literally thousands dying of this *"plague."* We are then told that only when the angel reached the threshing floor of Araunah the Jebusite, did God in His mercy command the angel to stop.

> *When the angel stretched out his hand <u>to destroy Jerusalem</u>, the LORD was grieved because of the calamity and said to the angel <u>who was afflicting the people</u>, "Enough! Withdraw your hand." <u>The angel of the LORD</u> was then at the threshing floor of Araunah the Jebusite.*
> —2Samuel 24:16 (emphasis added)

This deadly activity of the angel was described in 2Samuel as *"striking down the people"* and the very visual image that is conveyed in the text is of an angel that held his sword high and *"stretched out his hand to destroy Jerusalem."* But, in the 2Chronicles description of this event, we are told more regarding the specific activity in the otherworld that resulted in the actual plague upon the people of Israel. Indeed, in 2Chronicles we are told that although David was seeing seventy thousand of his fellow Israelites dying of the *"plague"* before him in the real world, the activity in the otherworld that was causing it was quite different.

Here once again, a leader of Israel is given a brief window into the parallel dimension inhabited by powerful angelic warriors. Just as Joshua saw a warrior with drawn sword, so also does David see *"the angel of the LORD"* with his sword drawn and extended over Jerusalem.

> *David looked up and saw the angel of the LORD standing between heaven and earth, with a drawn sword in his hand extended over Jerusalem. Then David and the elders, clothed in sackcloth, fell facedown.*
>
> —1Chronicles 21:16 (emphasis added)

What an awesome spectacle this must have been. Both David and the elders of Israel were enabled to see the otherworld activity and their response was immediate and profound: they fell face down in repentance. *The angel of the Lord*, at the very least, was a scary, intimidating, and powerful individual whose very presence commanded—and received—immediate subservient respect. At his command, David buys the threshing floor of Araunah the Jebusite—above which *the angel of the Lord* is positioned—to build an altar to the Lord. One cannot help but be impressed that *the angel of the Lord* is of such power and position that he can order the prophet Gad to so direct King David's activities.

> *Then the angel of the LORD ordered Gad to tell David to go up and build an altar to the LORD on the threshing floor of Araunah the Jebusite.*
>
> —1Chronicles 21:18

Then, only after David has sacrificed burnt offerings on the altar, does the Lord end the plague:

> *David built an altar to the LORD there and sacrificed burnt offerings and fellowship offerings. He called on the LORD, and the LORD answered him with fire from heaven on the altar of burnt offering. Then the LORD spoke to the angel, and he put his sword back into its sheath.*
>
> —1Chronicles 21:26-27 (emphasis added)

This passage offers specific evidence regarding the connection between our world and the parallel dimension inhabited by angelic warriors. The sword yielded by *the angel of the Lord* obviously looked precisely like a sword and could even be returned to its sheath—just like a real sword. Nevertheless, it was the otherworld activity of this *"sword"* that directly caused the real world *"plague"* that afflicted the people of Israel. In other words, the direct *expected* injury caused by a sharpened length of metal swung in the otherworld is specifically *not* that which kills the Israelites in the real world. Instead, the activity of the sword in the otherworld results in a deadly infectious disease—a *plague*—in Israel. Even so, this result should not surprise us. We are in fact told to expect precisely this in the original description of the three punishment choices that the prophet Gad offers King David.

> *So Gad went to David and said to him, "This is what the LORD says: 'Take your choice: three years of famine, three months of being swept away before your enemies, with their swords overtaking you, or three days of <u>the sword of the LORD</u>—days of <u>plague</u> in the land, <u>with the angel of the LORD ravaging every part of Israel</u>.' Now then, decide how I should answer the one who sent me."*
>
> —1Chronicles 21:11-12 (emphasis added)

Indeed, this *"drawn sword"* of *the angel of the Lord* is an awesome and fearful sight. David is in fact so haunted by the sight of the sword itself that we are told he was subsequently unable to offer sacrifices at *"the altar of burnt offering"* at Gibeon for fear of it.

> *The tabernacle of the LORD, which Moses had made in the desert, and the altar of burnt offering were at that time on the high place at Gibeon. But David could not go before it to inquire of God, <u>because he was afraid of the sword of the angel of the LORD</u>.*
>
> —1Chronicles 21:29-30 (emphasis added)

It is a delight to the reader of Holy Scripture that so much information can be gleaned from Old Testament text regarding the complex interface between our world and the spiritual world of war inhabited by angelic forces. Once again, finding a common definition for critical pieces of the interface that are *simultaneously common* to both worlds (such as *"the sword"* of *the angel of the Lord)* is akin to finding and interpreting tiny fragments of the invaluable language translation provided by the Rosetta stone. It is through these few hinge-points, these pieces of the puzzle that appear to possess clear impact in *both* worlds, that the complexity of the interface between the otherworld and our world can be explored and ultimately made clearer.

In this case, a critical question regarding the Old Testament world of war into which the emptied, incarnate Jesus Christ submerged Himself is directly addressed. Although the drawn sword of Jesus may indeed be used against the evil *powers* and *celestial beings* that inhabit and wreak havoc in this parallel world, *it is also used directly against people in our world.* The caveat is, however, that it does not necessarily result in death by the normal mechanism of *cutting*—as is the case in our world. Instead, we are allowed to correlate its use with the occurrence of death by what is referred to as *"plague."* This may hint at an intermediary step— perhaps the use of that sword against evil otherworld powers—that we are not allowed to see. Perhaps indeed it is war between *the angel of the Lord* and evil otherworld principalities that then results in the infectious plague in the real world. We can only speculate in this regard since we are given no obvious evidence for this in Holy Scripture.

This revelation regarding the interplay between the two worlds nonetheless offers much in regard to clarifying the nature of the events that might be occurring around us every day in the invisible otherworld. One has to ask the question whether vicious spiritual warfare—vital swordplay between angelic warriors—in the otherworld is the mechanism behind *all* such infectious disease processes in our world! Furthermore, it opens further consideration of the otherworld as God's mechanism to simultaneously test our hearts and provide the pathway of His response to our prayers.

Since it seems unlikely that this warring otherworld just ceased to exist in our so-called *modern era*, we can be assured that it currently influences our lives in one way or another. We know from scripture, for instance, that the evil powers and principalities still exist today. They may have been humiliated at the cross of Christ:

> *And having disarmed the powers and authorities, he made a public spectacle of them, triumphing over them by the cross.*
> —Colossians 2:15 (emphasis added)

But so also have these otherworld spiritual powers remained in existence and at war with us to this very day.

> *For our struggle is not against flesh and blood, but against the rulers, against the authorities, against the powers of this dark world and against the spiritual forces of evil in the heavenly realms.*
> —Ephesians 6:12

They will not be completely and finally destroyed until the end times.

> *Then the end will come, when he hands over the kingdom to God the Father after he has destroyed all dominion, authority and power. For he must reign until he has put all his enemies under his feet.*
>
> — 1Corinthians 15:24-25 (emphasis added)

Either way, the amazing revelation from the life of King David that is documented in 2Samuel 24 and 1Chronicles 21 once again demonstrates the depth of immersion of Jesus—*the angel of the Lord*—into the events of the otherworld that surrounded the patriarchs of Israel.

Chapter 34

Another Rescue Mission
The Fourth Man in the Furnace

Babylon. The Plain of Dura. The courts of Nebuchadnezzar. The vital youth of Judah. They had been gleaned from the devastation of Judah and exiled to Babylon as plunder. Their prophets had told them that this would not be a short exile. Their homeland had been utterly destroyed by the army of Nebuchadnezzar.

And yet their prophets had told them more: *fit into Babylonian society—but follow the law of God. Fit in, but do not be assimilated into the culture of your conquerors. This exile will end. Maintain that which is your history, for in your history is found your future, your God-defined destiny. You will return to the Land.*

The remnant of the nation of Israel was the charge of *the angel of the Lord*. Where they went, so also went their Defender, their Champion.

Another brief, but pointedly brilliant appearance of Jesus as an embodied warrior in the army of the Lord is documented in the 3rd chapter of the book of Daniel. Three of the exiled youth of Israel, Shadrach, Meshach, and Abednego, choose to defy Nebuchadnezzar, king of Babylon. They refuse to comply with the direct command of the king to fall down and worship the golden statue that he has constructed on the Plain of Dura. In his rage at their defiance, King Nebuchadnezzar orders them thrown into a fiery furnace that has been made seven times hotter than normal. Despite this, it becomes immediately apparent that these faithful young men of Israel remain unharmed in the fire. Not only that, but they are in fact accompanied by a fourth man in the blazing furnace.

Once again, the prophet Daniel's words have been carefully chosen. The phraseology is perfectly crafted such that the clues that we seek are well defined. Specifically our interest is drawn to the text that reveals the precise identity of that 4th man who appears in the fiery furnace with Shadrach, Meshach and Abednego:

Then King Nebuchadnezzar leaped to his feet in amazement and asked
his advisers, "Weren't there three men that we tied up and threw into
the fire?"

They replied, "Certainly, O king."

He said, "Look! I see four men walking around in the fire, unbound
and unharmed, and the fourth looks like a son of the gods."

—Daniel 3:24-25 (emphasis added)

There are many things upon which King Nebuchadnezzar could have focused his first words after viewing the climactic results of his command to throw the three young Israelites into the fiery furnace. Not only were the Israelites not immediately consumed in the fiery blast—their fate being sharply contrasted to that of the guards who had accompanied them—but also, amazingly, the three young men appear completely unharmed.

How easy it is to just blow right by the amazing fact of their preservation. When we are in the appropriate mindset, however, we see this as another profound example of God's direct intervention into the lives of the patriarchs and prophets. But can we really appreciate what it looked like to Nebuchadnezzar and the other pagans who had never known the living God? The preservation of human life in the midst of a murderous blast furnace must have shaken them to their very bones. And yet did Nebuchadnezzar say anything about this stunning fact in his immediate reaction? Why didn't he mention them and their miraculous survival? One would have quite reasonably expected that this would have been the obligatory focus of his initial comments.

Obviously, there was something—*someone*—of even more importance in the scene before him than the miraculous preservation of the three young men. Only this single startling aspect of the scene commanded King Nebuchadnezzar's immediate and undivided attention. Nebuchadnezzar was obviously a man of considerable God-given wisdom. He had enough insight at that moment to know that the most important part of this scene—and that which was deserving of his first exclamatory sentence—was the presence of a very peculiar fourth person in the furnace.

We can only assume from the nature of Nebuchadnezzar's unexpected immediate response that this fourth figure was an imposing, impressive, and perhaps intimidating individual who immediately—most likely as a direct result of his appearance—grabbed the undivided attention of anyone who might gaze upon the scene. This had to be Jesus. No one, no thing could upstage Him in this setting. This is Jesus in His role as a powerful warrior, as a mighty rescuer of men.

The fourth person in the fiery furnace is clearly described as having the appearance of a man. His sudden appearance at this time—*during what must have been a time of furious warfare in the otherworld*—is entirely fitting of the warrior role of King Jesus during the times of the Old Testament. Truly this scene is a perfect characterization of His overall mission. That mission is to stand in the gap between the remnant of Israel and the destruction wrought by the forces of evil—in both worlds. It is His role as the mighty warrior Commander of the army of the Lord to take the fight directly to the heart of all that stands opposed to the will of God. That will, that command, that purpose in this scene is the same as in every scene of the Old Testament: *the preservation of the holy remnant of Israel.*

We can only imagine what spectacular otherworld battles must have been fought that day to preserve the lives of the three Israelites in a fiery furnace that should have incinerated them within seconds. Wild, tumultuous hand-to-hand combat must have immediately ensued as the three Israelites were dragged toward the furnace. Due to the paucity of detail in regard to an actual description of this otherworldly warfare, however, our now fertile minds are left to wander through the dazzling scenes of valiant battle that form our mental archives of desperate warfare. Images of recent movies, such as the Lord of the Rings Trilogy or Gladiator or Star Wars or Raiders of the Lost Ark come immediately to mind. Truly this must have been the most desperate of warfare during the direst of times.

We are given few hints regarding the otherworld activities surrounding the furnace scene. The four men themselves are seen walking around in the furnace, but otherwise we are not given any further information regarding their activities. There is no visualization of swords, cherubim, chariots of fire, or battle horses as occurs in other notable accounts of similar Old Testament scenes.

We can be assured, nonetheless, that we are on the right trail. As if the actual miraculous and unexpected presence of a fourth man itself is not quite enough to seal our opinions in regard to his identity, the divine Author of the passage painstakingly records Nebuchadnezzar's carefully constructed exclamation. Nebuchadnezzar most pointedly focuses on the description of the fourth man. He describes him as having not just the appearance of *"the gods,"* but most pointedly as *"a son of the gods."*

Moreover, Nebuchadnezzar then describes the 4th man as being God's *"angel"* — sent by God with the express purpose of rescuing *"his servants."* In this statement, Nebuchadnezzar reminds us of the Old Testament military nature of the mission of this very special *"son of the gods."* Rescue missions were the specialty of this very unique warrior and Nebuchadnezzar describes it precisely as such.

> *Then Nebuchadnezzar said, "Praise be to the God of Shadrach, Meshach and Abednego, who has sent his angel and rescued his servants! They trusted in him and defied the king's command and were willing to give up their lives rather than serve or worship any god except their own God.*

— Daniel 3:28 (emphasis added)

Truly the Incarnate Son of God was active in very literally every detail of the adventures and trials of His people. Jesus was their defender and very special detail is given to His episodic individual saint rescues, as well as His corporate rescue of the holy remnant that survived the destruction of Jerusalem and the Babylonian captivity.

Chapter 35

When Things Go Terribly Awry
Jesus Fights For the Bad Guys

Egypt. One of the most powerful empires in history. Pharaoh Neco, ruler of the Egyptian empire. *Warrior* Neco, commander of the mighty charioteers of the army of Egypt. The fate of Egypt would be decided at Carchemish on the Euphrates River. There, Pharaoh Neco's army and the army of the Assyrian empire would join together against the army of the next great world empire, Babylon. There his fate, and the fate of the world would hang in the balance as the two mightiest fighting forces ever to march to war would do battle.

But first Pharaoh Neco had to move his army north. He had to do it quickly. Nebuchadnezzar and his Babylonian hoard would surely try to strike the remnant of the Assyrian army before the Egyptian charioteers could reinforce them. Nebuchadnezzar was a master tactician. He knew his enemies. Combined with the Assyrians, the Egyptians would be a formidable fighting force. Divided, they would surely fall. The facts were clear. Neco had to move north quickly. The fate of his empire depended upon it.

The fastest route north was up the coast. Neco set his plan into motion. He drove his army past the vast desert of the Sinai Peninsula. Past Gaza and the Philistines. The Philistines knew better. They would not oppose the movement of the mighty Egyptian charioteers. The Israelites were another matter.

Pharaoh Neco attempted diplomacy. He sent messengers to Josiah, king of Judah. Their message was clear. Neco meant no harm and was no threat to Judah. He had an appointment with Babylon. The Egyptian army would simply pass through Judah.

Megiddo. King Josiah. The army of Judah. Pharaoh Neco had no time for this. He would try another ploy with Josiah. He told Josiah that Josiah's God—the one Josiah was relying upon—had spoken to Pharaoh Neco! Neco claimed that not only had the God of Judah personally told him to march his army rapidly to face the Assyrians, but also that God was in fact actually *with* him at the time. Pharaoh

Neco warned him. That was all he could do. If Josiah insisted on a fight, then a fight he would have.

The plain of Megiddo. Furious battle. The Egyptian charioteers and archers are simply too much. With divine accuracy, they inflict a mortal wound upon the brave and yet misguided king of Judah. He would die of his wound. He had not listened to the words of God. The army of the Egyptians would move on to their fate at the battle of Carchemish.

Even though the overarching command behind all of the missions that Jesus and His warrior angels undertook was the preservation of the holy remnant of the nation of Israel, the actual day-to-day attention to this goal was manifest in many different ways during the campaigns of the Old Testament kings of Israel. Our goal in exploring these many manifestations of the role Jesus played in the events of the Old Testament is to attempt to ascertain consistent patterns that establish priorities. Unfortunately, several key Old Testament events throw a disruptive monkey wrench into any possibility of establishing a neat, clean mechanism that could consistently define His involvement in any particular Biblical setting.

For instance, it would be so much easier if the strict, consistent, and inalienable allegiance of Jesus to the nation of Israel could be firmly established. How neat and clean everything would be if we knew that Jesus *always* fought for the nation of Israel. Indeed, if we could just make this one assumption, we would always know in every situation precisely what Jesus was up to behind the scenes. Even in scenarios where the text of the Bible limits our revelation into the otherworld, we could still know that Jesus was behind the scenes wielding his mighty sword in the defense of Israel.

Unfortunately, there is no neat, clean mechanism that consistently and uniformly defines the military actions of the Son of God during the Old Testament. Although we know the overarching goal, we cannot know the details of the tactical implementation of the plan to attain this strategic goal. Certainly Jesus gave us a first hint of this when Joshua asked Him outside of Jericho whether He was for Israel or for their enemies. How nice it would have been if He had just reassured Joshua, "You bet, Joshua. Come rain or shine, good times or bad, I am your man."

The clearly ringing death knell for that simple mechanism can be logically derived from two simple and irrefutable facts. First of all, Jesus could never do anything except fight for the will of the Father. His many New Testament discourses on precisely that can leave little doubt in our minds. We can most assuredly know that every single thing that He has ever done—or will ever do—is dead center in the middle of His Father's will.

Secondly, we know that the nation of Israel was simply incapable of maintaining the single-minded focus on God that would allow their motivations, thoughts, and actions to stay in the middle of God's will. Bottom line: Jesus and Israel must have spent a fair bit of time traveling in opposite directions. In fact, these two facts lead us to the conclusion that at times, the otherworld actions of Jesus in His role as the Commander of the army of the Lord *must have directly opposed the worldly interests of the nation of Israel.* Although we can know that in an eternal sense and in regard to the ultimate mission of preserving the remnant of the nation of Israel, absolutely *all* of Jesus' actions must have been *for* Israel, some of them certainly would not have been interpreted as such by the ungodly leaders of errant Israel.

Old Testament scripture clearly assures us that Jesus was indeed the one who was sent on missions to make sure that the Father's will was not in fact sidetracked by the many different forces whose vested interests were pointedly not in line with the will of God. When the leaders of Israel blatantly and rebelliously opposed God, as they surely did in the years leading up to the final destruction of Jerusalem, then we can rest assured that Jesus was not defending their earthly cause. These difficult times, when things did not go well for the nation of Israel, were precisely those times when the Israelites loudly proclaimed that God had abandoned them.

This *abandonment* was not without its clear purpose. It was part of God's plan to get the *remnant* to turn back to God. These times would not have been interpreted as *good* by most of the Israelites and they certainly would not have felt that Jesus was fighting on their behalf—despite the fact that in an eternal sense, He most certainly was. In fact, one could argue that there was no time that He was closer and fought harder for their eternal wellbeing than during these times of seeming abandonment.

The direct parallel to our lives is obvious. God utilizes trials to bring the focus of our hearts back to Him. These are difficult times that no one likes, but their end result is to our eternal benefit and demonstrates the never changing goodness of God's heart. This rule, like its counterpart—that Jesus fought hard for the Israelites when they *did* seek the Lord—appears to be solidly supported by scripture.

We have in fact already reviewed one profound scriptural example of this Old Testament misalignment of God's will and the will of the Israelites. Ezekiel's dazzling account of the behind-the-scenes otherworldly activities during the last days of Nebuchadnezzar's destruction of Jerusalem is stunning in its clarity. In it, the Commander of the army of the Lord orders the warriors guarding the temple to slay throughout Jerusalem any who do not carry the mark of the Lord. Amazingly enough, this detailed and graphic rendering of behind the scenes battle is not the only account of Jesus and the army of the Lord doing battle *on behalf of the enemies* of the nation of Israel.

The armies of the nation of Israel are defeated in battle intermittently throughout the entire chronology of the Old Testament. Although we are not specifically told of the presence of otherworld warfare behind such hallmark routs as that which occurred at Ai, we can safely assume that it occurred. At the very least, we can be assured that Jesus and the army of the Lord did not go to war *for* the Israelites when they arrogantly attacked Ai without the Lord's help.

But, as the scripture above points out, we can know that when the heart of Israel was not focused on the Lord, the activity of Jesus and His warriors could hardly be described as passive. To the contrary, we are in fact told that the Lord actively fought *against* the *nation* of Israel in such cases—to the eternal benefit of the holy remnant. We have already discussed the powerful reminders from the books of the prophets Jeremiah and Isaiah where God emphatically states such in terms that are hard to misinterpret.

> *I myself will fight against you with an outstretched hand and a mighty arm in anger and fury and great wrath.*
>
> —Jeremiah 21:5

> *In all their distress he too was distressed, and the angel of his presence saved them. In his love and mercy he redeemed them; he lifted them up and carried them all the days of old. Yet they rebelled and grieved his Holy Spirit. So he turned and became their enemy and he himself fought against them.*
>
> —Isaiah 63:9-10 (emphasis added)

In light of these clear scriptural references to this fact, there can be little doubt that Jesus, as the warrior Commander of the army of the Lord very literally drew His sword against the *nation* of Israel. We are in fact also told of several circumstances where pagan armies moved at what *they claimed* to be the very specific command of *"the LORD."* At first reading, it is easy to just assume that these pagan leaders—being pagans after all—were just lying. Now, from a new perspective, it is clear that they were in fact most likely telling the truth.

The most notable of these occurred during the final days of one of the great kings of Judah, Josiah. As described above, Pharaoh Neco of Egypt was moving his army rapidly toward its ill-fated battle at Carchemish. In order to *"hurry"*—a command he claims to have gotten from God—Neco and his army took the shortest route toward Carchemish, which happened to be right through Judah. The logic behind the absolute necessity of choosing a route through Israel was lost on Josiah who immediately mustered the army of Judah in response. King Neco's response via messengers is stunning in its implications.

> *After all this, when Josiah had set the temple in order, Neco king of Egypt went up to fight at Carchemish on the Euphrates, and Josiah marched out to meet him in battle.*
>
> *But Neco sent messengers to him, saying, "What quarrel is there between you and me, O king of Judah? It is not you I am attacking at this time, but the house with which I am at war. God has told me to hurry; so stop opposing God, who is with me, or he will destroy you."*
>
> *Josiah, however, would not turn away from him, but disguised himself to engage him in battle. He would not listen to what Neco had said at God's command but went to fight him on the plain of Megiddo.*
>
> —2Chronicles 35:20-22 (emphasis added)

Neco claimed that God was with him! More importantly, however, the author of 2Chronicles documents that that Pharaoh Neco was in fact *not* lying. He, not Neco, assures us that Neco had indeed given Josiah this warning *"at God's command."* According to the authority of the prophet, God Himself was indeed directing Pharaoh Neco. Jesus and the army of the Lord were in the camp of the Egyptians! Josiah's hasty decision to oppose the will of God—which apparently included the rapid movement of Neco's army through Judah—did not end well for Josiah. It came to pass indeed precisely as Pharaoh Neco—presumably at the prompting of Jesus—had predicted.

> *Archers shot King Josiah, and he told his officers, "Take me away; I am badly wounded." So they took him out of his chariot, put him in the other chariot he had and brought him to Jerusalem, where he*

died. He was buried in the tombs of his fathers, and all Judah and Jerusalem mourned for him.

—2Chronicles 35:23-24

Another example where an opposing army commander stated that he was under the direct command of *"the LORD"* has the ring of yet another pagan *lie*. Sennacherib's military commanders told the leaders of Jerusalem that in bringing his army against Jerusalem, Sennacherib had stated that he was only doing what *"the LORD"* had told him to do. On first reading, this statement sounds like a self-serving misrepresentation whose only purpose was to potentially gain the surrender of the Israelites who were walled up with Hezekiah behind Jerusalem's walls.

Furthermore, have I come to attack and destroy this place without word from the LORD? The LORD himself told me to march against this country and destroy it.'"

—2Kings 18:25 (emphasis added)

And yet how is the approach of this powerful army to the embankments of Jerusalem any different than any of the other difficult tests that God brings into our lives every day. *God brings them all* with the specific purpose of testing us. So also was the army of Sennacherib brought by God against Jerusalem to test Hezekiah and his fellow Israelites.

Yet this statement suggests that there may have been a more direct involvement of the Son of God in this setting. First of all, Sennacherib specifically uses the holy name of the God of Israel, YAHWEH, which is interpreted in the NIV version as *"the LORD."* He doesn't just refer to Him as *"your god"* in this instance as he did previously. In addition, Sennacherib stresses that it was the Lord *"himself"* who told him to march against Israel, suggesting even that Sennacherib may have had face-to-face personal contact with *"the LORD"*—possibly referring to an encounter with the embodied Son of God as *the angel of the Lord.*

The prophet Micah confirms the fact that it was indeed the Lord Himself who brought this very same Assyrian army against the Northern Kingdom, against all of the fortified cities of the Southern Kingdom, and right up to the gates of Jerusalem itself.

"Therefore I will make Samaria a heap of rubble, a place for planting vineyards. I will pour her stones into the valley and lay bare her foundations. All her idols will be broken to pieces; all her temple gifts

will be burned with fire; I will destroy all her images. Since she gathered her gifts from the wages of prostitutes, as the wages of prostitutes they will again be used."

Because of this I will weep and wail; I will go about barefoot and naked. I will howl like a jackal and moan like an owl. For <u>her wound</u> is incurable; it has come to Judah. It has reached <u>the very gate</u> of my people, <u>even to Jerusalem itself</u>.

Those who live in Maroth writhe in pain, waiting for relief, because <u>disaster</u> has come <u>from the LORD</u>, <u>even to the gate of Jerusalem</u>.

—Micah 1:6-9, 12 (emphasis added)

Micah's prophecy is precise. This assault comes from *"the LORD"* who has brought this disaster *"even to the gate of Jerusalem."* Sennecherib was in fact telling the truth when he claimed that *"the LORD"* told him to attack Jerusalem! The prophet Micah confirms it. The Assyrian army approaches but does not attack the gate of Jerusalem itself just as Micah states. That it is Jesus who has led them there is again confirmed in the verse that follows.

I will bring <u>a conqueror</u> against you who live in Mareshah. <u>He</u> who is <u>the glory of Israel</u> will come to Adullam.

—Micah 1:15 (emphasis added)

Who is *"the glory of Israel"*? Only Jesus is worthy of that title. There is, therefore, no way that the *"conqueror"* in the passage above refers to Sennecherib, since there is no way that Sennecherib is *"the glory of Israel."* The conclusion that can be drawn from these statements of scriptural fact is equally clear. It is no one less than Jesus Himself who threatens Jerusalem! It is He who is the otherworld *"conqueror"* referred to in this critical passage.

The implications of this logical line of thought are not subtle. Jesus is not dutifully swayed only by the birthright of the nation of Israel. He does not blindly fight for them when they are wrong, as if their true heart's stance toward God did not matter. His actions, as revealed to us in the Word of God, are quite to the contrary. This is why Jesus responded *"Neither"* to Joshua's query outside of Jericho, *"Are you for us or for our enemies?"* (Joshua 5:13-14). Just as is true with each one of us, the desire of our Savior is that the nation of Israel follows faithfully after God. In this regard, He is not above siding with the pagan enemies of Israel at the behest of the Father's will—whose discipline of the errant Israel is aimed only at gaining their true repentance upon the righteous path of the will of God.

The plan of God does indeed work. Israel is in fact turned back to the path of righteousness, the path of repentance, as the Assyrian army marches to the doorstep of Jerusalem. Only then does Hezekiah finally turn to the Lord alone. His prior errant path, an attempt to simply buy his way out of the problem that God had laid before him, simply did not work. With the Assyrian army literally at his doorstep, he finally makes the correct decision to trust *only* in God. As previously discussed, *the angel of the Lord* then acts mightily in Israel's behalf to slay 185,000 Assyrians and forever turn the Assyrian world conquerors back from the gates of Jerusalem. The Father's plan works perfectly as Israel is finally—although not permanently—brought back to the Lord.

These important Old Testament accounts reveal much regarding a more precise definition of the role of Jesus during the Old Testament. As previously discussed, His role as the protector and rescuer of the holy remnant of the nation of Israel is further supported by these new clues. Further still, this role is tweaked ever so slightly by the clear message that suggests that almost any means is available to the Son of God in this quest. The direct testing and disciplining of the nation as a whole by the threatening advancement of a Jesus-supported enemy army was clearly available to the Son of God as a tool to draw out and precisely define the answer to the real question: Who among the Israelites was to be included in this holy remnant?

This same sort of testing and discipline is most certainly used even now in our *modern* era. As discussed, the full mission of Jesus was expanded by the Father to also include the salvation of the gentile remnant. In the fulfillment of precisely this mission, our saving faith in Jesus Christ is tested daily by trials and discipline sent from God. Indeed it is exactly these trials that turn our hearts to, and this discipline that tests our resolve in the salvation found only in belief in Jesus. Further still, it is precisely these trials that test and turn our hearts to the full fruition of that faith that is found only in our ultimate sanctification, our being turned into the likeness of Christ. Only as we are challenged daily by Jesus do we *"work out"* our faith in Him—as our only source of salvation.

> *Therefore, my dear friends, as you have always obeyed—not only in my presence, but now much more in my absence—continue to work out your salvation with fear and trembling, for it is God who works in you to will and to act according to his good purpose.*

—Philippians 2:12-13 (emphasis added)

Further still, the direct military intervention by Jesus and His army of the Lord in both the destruction of the Assyrian army and the subsequent banishment of the remnant to Babylon (rather than allowing them to be destroyed by the plague, starvation, and sword that accompanied the Babylonian army's assault), all served to preserve the precious remnant of Israel. Once again, even the most extreme of means was available to Jesus to carry out this, His primary Old Testament mission. God's will is brought about by these actions of the Son of God, as once again we find the embodied Commander of the army of the Lord, Jesus, right there—sword in hand—in the fury of the battle.

Chapter 36

That Question That Has Been Bothering You...
How Did Jesus Appear in the Old Testament As a Fully Grown Adult Warrior When He Hadn't Even Been Born in Bethlehem Yet?

The central theme of this book—that Jesus Christ spent the entirety of the Old Testament directly involved in every recorded event as the fully embodied warrior Commander of the army of the Lord—absolutely vexes many people. Their first response is characterized as an immediate resistance to one key point, a single nagging question:

Are you really asking us to believe that Jesus functioned as a fully incarnate warrior who had the embodied appearance of a fully-grown man during the Old Testament—even thousands of years before His actual birth in Bethlehem?

An explanation of this phenomenon stands as the primary concern for many readers the first time they are confronted with the central theme of this book. The apparent age/time discrepancy involving the proposed appearance of an adult Jesus thousands of years before His recorded birth in Bethlehem trumps all other logic. No matter how logical the rest of the evidence may be, this single issue blocks their acceptance of the rest of the evidence that supports the palpable Old Testament presence of Jesus. Specifically, their concern is with the paradox of how someone who apparently did not come into literal existence in this world until born as a baby in Bethlehem 2000 years ago could have started making appearances as a fully-grown adult over 4000 years prior to the recorded date of that birth.

How quickly our heart—overwhelmed by our resistant human nature—leaps to grab tenaciously to little *technicalities*, little details, while at the same time being confronted with the overwhelming evidence that opposes them. Being asked to look beyond small technicalities is nothing new to Christians, however. Indeed, this is the very definition of faith. There are countless things about Christianity and the Bible that just don't make sense. Such Biblical facts seem to fly in the face of the reality that we are confronted with every day by the world around us. We

are asked to—and most of us readily do—believe these Biblical *facts* as truth
despite the fact that we don't understand them. This is faith. We are asked to trust
that God has an answer—that His wisdom far eclipses ours—and to not let the
apparent inconsistency stand in the way of the faith that carries with it the only
hope of eternal life.

A great example of this is the plight of the unsaved who have, from our worldly
perspective, apparently never even heard the name *Jesus*. Despite the fact that the
Word of God assures us that the gospel *"has been proclaimed to every creature
under heaven"* (Colossians 1:23), we—in our seemingly boundless worldly
wisdom—just can't imagine how that could possibly be true. *Every person has
heard of Jesus?* How could that possibly occur and, therefore, how can those who
have not heard be held responsible?

We counter these inconsistencies with faith. Our faith is a gift of God such that
none of us can boast.

> *For it is by grace you have been saved, through faith—and this not
> from yourselves, it is the gift of God—not by works, so that no one can
> boast.*
>
> —Ephesians 2:8-9 (emphasis added)

Thus, by God's grace, we are saved as we accept God's saving gift of redemption
despite the fact that we don't fully understand all of the facts surrounding it. We
accept as fact that God has an answer for our questions; that He is who He says He
is and can do what He says He can do and that the Word of God is exactly that—
the Word of God. In other words, we don't let these questions stand in the way of
our acceptance of the free gift of eternal life that is found in the shed blood of Jesus
Christ.

The reader is asked to do the same thing here. We must—by God's grace—not
hold back in our search for that very special knowledge of Jesus that is to be mined
from the rich hills of this adventure into the Old Testament scriptures. This is
possible only by our reaching one faith-filled conclusion: that the facts are just too
clearly laid out before us in the written Word of God to be ignored. The
cumulative evidence presented so far is just too convincing to turn our backs on the
fact that Jesus did, indeed, appear as an adult—literal millennia before His birth as
a baby in Bethlehem. And so, like so many other things that are said in the Bible,
we accept it in faith.

In faith, therefore, we are able to accept this astounding fact as pure truth. Most of us nonetheless remain in the tenacious grasp of our inquisitive human nature and strive for an answer to this age/time disconnect that poses such a faith-challenging dilemma. We hope beyond hope that this is one of those many technicalities that the Holy Spirit will find a way to resolve for us. After all, a huge multitude of very similar faith-challenging *technicalities* from the days of our newfound faith have subsequently been eliminated by the workings of the Holy Spirit in our hearts and minds. This working in our hearts and minds comes mostly through the revelation found in the written Word of God.

And so we have come to accept—and in fact expect—that not only is there an answer to this question, but also that the Holy Spirit will fill us in on it sometime in our lifetime. This may or may not be true in this case. We may have our request for this information filled in this life—or we may have to wait until we get to ask Jesus face-to-face. Our faithful quest nonetheless continues.

In support of our premise, therefore, the previous chapters of this book have been dedicated to discussing just a small sampling of the Biblical evidence supporting the fact that the embodied Son of God made repeated profound and undeniable appearances throughout Old Testament history. We can also take note however—with some degree of great satisfaction—that the Word of God in fact actually comes right out and tells us that we are on the right trail as we seek to know the mechanism behind this apparent age/time corruption. Indeed, the book of Proverbs provides us with one of the most convincing of statements in this regard.

> *"The LORD brought <u>me</u> forth as <u>the first of his works</u>, before his deeds of old; I was appointed <u>from eternity, from the beginning, before the world began</u>. When there were no oceans, <u>I was given birth</u>, when there were no springs abounding with water; before the mountains were settled in place, before the hills, <u>I was given birth</u>, before he made the earth or its fields or any of the dust of the world. <u>I was there when</u> he set the heavens in place, when he marked out the horizon on the face of the deep, when he established the clouds above and fixed securely the fountains of the deep, when he gave the sea its boundary so the waters would not overstep his command, and when he marked out the foundations of the earth. Then I was <u>the craftsman at his side</u>. I was <u>filled with delight</u> day after day, <u>rejoicing always in his presence</u>, rejoicing in his whole world and <u>delighting</u> in mankind.*
> —Proverbs 8:22-31 (emphasis added)

Although this statement is apparently made by *"wisdom,"* the entire context of the passage clearly demonstrates that this attribute and the only One who possesses it are inseparable. Therefore *"wisdom"* speaks in the first person as one who was with God at the creation.

Since the use of this passage in resolving our dilemma is contingent upon establishing the identity of *"wisdom,"* let's consider the evidence. Clearly the *attribute "wisdom"* did not come into existence at the time of the creation. Nor was it *"given birth."* God has always been the sole possessor of wisdom as an inseparable attribute of His very nature. God never changes. Wisdom as an attribute of God was not, therefore, *"given birth"* at the creation.

Nor, also, did the Holy Spirit or Jesus, the only Son of God, come into existence at the creation. They have been inseparable members of the Triune Godhead for eternity. This leads us to the only possible conclusion—that *"wisdom,"* the speaker of these words, was the embodied, fully man, fully emptied Jesus. Only the man Jesus could be brought *"forth as the first of his works"* (Proverbs 8:22) or *"given birth"* (Proverbs 8:24).

These verses add to those of the New Testament writers, most notably Paul in his letter to the Colossians, who affirm that Jesus, fully man and fully God, was the *"firstborn over all creation"* (Colossians 1:15).

We can know even more than this. Not only was the man Jesus given birth as *"the first of his works,"* but we are also reassured in a unique passage from the book of Revelation that the very special *work* that resulted in the salvation of every man who would be saved was also *completed at the creation.*

> *All inhabitants of the earth will worship the beast—all whose names have not been written in the book of life belonging to **the Lamb that was slain from the creation of the world**.*
> —Revelation 13:8 (emphasis added)

Although much can be gleaned from these passages, at the very least we can also surely know that the *fully man, fully incarnate Jesus* was present from the very beginning.

By far the quickest and easiest solution to our dilemma regarding the appearance of an adult, fully embodied Jesus in the Old Testament is found in simply remembering that God, after all, is God. He can do anything He wants. This is simple and direct and obviously true. And yet this is not the answer that we, in our uniquely human curiosity, want to hear. Despite the fact that the sovereignty of God is so much more than is needed to answer this question, we still seek much more than this. We want to know *how* it all comes about. Indeed, in the mechanism of how God has worked in the past is found wisdom for understanding how He will work in the future—and that is what we are all about. We all want to know what we can expect from God.

Although God obviously delights in being unpredictable, we can be assured that He also—quite clearly—wishes us to know certain inalienable facts about His nature. He wants to influence our future decisions. He wants us to know precisely what we can expect from Him, for example, when we turn from Him and choose the world over Him. This also has eternal ramifications. Surely our eternity will involve high adventure with Jesus as our close friend and partner. We must run hard after knowing His heart in this life if we are to expect to know it in the next. Surely this is a significant part of the reward that is spoken about in the New Testament. The goal in this life is to *know* Jesus because the more we know Jesus now, the more our deep heart desire for Him will be fulfilled by our knowledge of Him in eternity.

Still, we need to at least attempt to step beyond the simple response of *it is like it is because God can do anything He wants* and seek to understand how and why He does what He does. *Time* is obviously the issue here. Precisely that which this book is so boldly proposing—that Jesus appeared fully-grown in the Old Testament before He was born in the New—is a problem only because it ignores the *rules* of time. Our observations in this regard suggest that God ignored the constraints of time to which *we* are undeniably and irretrievably subject. We are so constrained by time that we have difficulty even thinking outside of the consideration of time.

Once again, however, understanding the attributes of God—as always—is the key to our solution. Indeed, our understanding of how God relates to time is obviously the critical information that is needed to resolve the mechanistic issues of what appears to be a breach in the normal temporal ordering of events. We know that something outside of the laws of time has taken place since these events would normally be constrained by natural laws to occur in a particular order in time—and they didn't.

Our answer is found in understanding that Jesus—*"Who, being in very nature God" (Philippians 2:6)*—exists and functions *totally outside of the constraints of time*. This understanding supplies us with several plausible scenarios that solve our problem. The most attractive of these is that which takes a bird's eye view of the *whole* of creation. We have been clearly told in the Word of God that the creation has been *complete* since the end of the sixth day.

> *Thus the heavens and the earth were <u>completed</u> in <u>all</u> their vast array.*
> *By the seventh day God <u>had finished the work</u> he had been doing; so*
> *on the seventh day he rested from <u>all</u> his work. And God blessed the*
> *seventh day and made it holy, because on it he rested from all the*
> *work of creating that he <u>had done</u>.*
>
> —Genesis 2:1-3 (emphasis added)

What we also know (from the theory of relativity!) is that time itself is a material property. In other words, all matter has as one of its properties the *time* in which it exists. The theory of relativity teaches us that as an object's mass changes, so also does its position in time, and visa versa. God both encompasses His creation and is outside of it. He therefore overlooks the whole of creation including the entire time course of all of the events that have occurred or ever will occur. God already knows every moment of our eternity—comprising an infinite amount of *time*. Only an infinite God who is outside of time can have this knowledge. As such—as an infinite Being who is outside of time—God can obviously enter the creation at any point and leave the creation at any point. He can reenter in any form that He wishes. This includes, for example, reentering the creation 4000 years before He was *born* in Bethlehem in the transfigured body He showed Peter, John, and James or even the same glorified body that He showed to His apostles after His resurrection.

Such an explanation engenders many questions. Is it in fact the *glorified* body of Jesus that is seen when the description of *"a man"* is given in the Old Testament, such as with the visitation of *the angel of the Lord* to the future parents of Samson described in the book of Judges? Is it the unshielded body demonstrated in His transfiguration to the apostles Peter, James, and John that is being described in the fiery descriptions of Jesus given by the prophet Ezekiel? Any and all of these are interesting and relevant possibilities.

In other words, one can easily imagine any number of possible scenarios, including one that has Jesus entering the creation at a fixed point, such as at His birth in Bethlehem, and then repopulating the Biblically described events that occurred before and after that time in His adult, glorified body. God stands separate from the entire creation and can enter it at any point and just as easily go backward, as forward in time. God is most certainly not bound by the constraint that binds all humans and the entirety of the creation—specifically that of being limited to only moving *forward* in time.

In support of this, the Word of God actually hints at precisely such a mechanism of Jesus repopulating the events of the Old Testament after entering the creation at His birth in Bethlehem. A great example is found in the New Testament description of the King of Salem and high priest of God, Melchizedek (Hebrews 7). In our new perspective, it is easy to see that only one person could fit the role of this enigmatic figure from the book of Genesis. Only one person is given the title of both king and priest—Jesus. The author of Hebrews tells us that this Melchizedek had neither birth nor death, was *"without genealogy, without beginning of days or end of life,"* thereby suggesting that his appearance was precisely such a repopulating event by Jesus.

> *This Melchizedek was king of Salem and priest of God Most High. He met Abraham returning from the defeat of the kings and blessed him, and Abraham gave him a tenth of everything. First, his name means "king of righteousness"; then also, "king of Salem" means "king of peace." Without father or mother, without genealogy, without beginning of days or end of life, like the Son of God he remains a priest forever.*
>
> —Hebrews 7:1-3 (emphasis added)

Another possibility is that the fiery *physical* form of Jesus that is revealed, for instance, in the revelations of Isaiah, Ezekiel, and the Apostle John, was created at the instant of creation. The Son of God from the very beginning thereby inhabits this form, with His incarnation as a fully human child being a secondary event. This possibility most readily explains the *transfiguration* event described in the New Testament gospel accounts.

Whatever the mechanism, it is clear that the Person of Jesus Christ, fully God and fully man, left the personal signature of His very real presence on every moment of time since the instant of creation. *Everything and every moment are all about Jesus. Can it be any other way?*

Chapter 37

The Last Two—and Greatest—Battles of the Commander of the Army of the Lord
The Culmination of the Great War

The eyes of every man and every woman gazed at the sky. They had no choice. They could look nowhere else. They had been created for this very moment. Every detail that a moment before had commanded their undivided attention was now irrelevant. Receptors for every sense were flooded with saturating stimuli from that which was now before them. All else was forgotten. From the grave, from heaven, from Sheol, from everywhere, the attention of all was directed nowhere else but toward He who stood before them.

But many more eyes than even this focused their attention on Him. For there was another world—an *otherworld*—where angels, demons, powers, authorities, and principalities alike also turned and looked at that which unfolded before them.

It was not subtle, this realization of a promise. This was a promise that had been echoed from the mouth of every divine messenger since the creation of mankind. The focal point of all creation had suddenly and inescapably become precisely that. He had remained hidden—and yet available, even beckoning, to every man, every woman. Then, in a moment He had taken His rightful place. He was back—just like He had promised He would be. He had come back for the sons and daughters of God. He had come back to set everything straight, to right every wrong, to take His rightful place in the hearts of every created being. Every knee would bend, every tongue would confess. Jesus is the Son of God…and He was back.

A significant portion of the Biblical evidence for the literal and physical presence of the incarnate Jesus Christ in His Old Testament role as the warrior Commander of the warriors of the army of the Lord has been reviewed. It must be nonetheless apparent to all that there are two very significant military campaigns that have yet to be discussed. It is no exaggeration—even recounting the exciting escapades that have been discussed so far—that the two remaining military missions are the most exciting and surely the most important of all. Most certainly there is more written in the Word of God about these two missions than any of the other colorful and exciting military adventures of the Old Testament.

The Great Rescue

It is in these two missions that the broadest of the extremes of the full nature of Jesus Christ are fully explored. In the first of these final two missions—that of His birth, life, ministry, crucifixion, resurrection, and ascension—we come to know the extraordinary fullness of the humble servanthood, meekness, faithfulness, obedience to the Father, and subserviently sacrificial unconditional love of Jesus Christ.

Those are non-military adjectives, for sure. But to look upon this assignment as something other than another military mission is incorrect. Quite to the contrary, the truth is found—as is often the case—in precisely the opposite extreme from that which we would expect. This mission was in fact the greatest of all of the military assignments of the Son of God. In fact, nearly everything about it was military. In that timeless moment in eternity when the Father asked of His only Son that He undertake the most spectacular rescue mission ever conceived in the mind of God, they were indeed discussing topics that we have simply no capability to understand, let alone fully address. And yet that which we can know for sure is that the 33 years that followed His birth in Bethlehem comprised nothing less than the most rigorous, the ultimate, the pinnacle of all *military* missions.

The *rescue* of those who would be sons and daughters of God was the greatest of all military missions. In regard to special warfare, special ops, it eclipsed the most important of all SEAL Team Six missions. It was the military mission of which all others—even the most extreme that we can call to mind—are merely a faint reflection. After all, how many of us would volunteer for a military mission that carried a 100% chance of failure—at least as the world defines the word *failure*? How many of us would volunteer for a military mission that carried a 100% chance of dying? Such missions are not even called *suicide missions*. At least a suicide mission—as this phrase is most commonly used—has *some*, albeit small, chance of survival. The goal of this mission—the rescue from death of the sons and daughters of God—simply could not occur without the substitutional death of Jesus Christ. In other words, the success of this military mission—by its very definition—simply could not occur without His death.

Further still, how many of us would volunteer if this certain death would be preceded by the *most* heinous single act of total humiliation in all of recorded history and that we, the volunteer, like Jesus would be rewarded for our bravery by being placed at the very focal point of this humiliation? And the suffering—how many of us would volunteer for the mission knowing that it also included—as a critical and essential last step before death—torture beyond that which *any* man has ever endured, before or since. And yet as bad as this sounds, each of us knows all too well that these meager sentences cannot even approach the true magnitude of the dark nature of this rescue mission.

The facts in regard to this mission are clear. We, as the created, the finite, the sinful and unholy, can only grasp—and only in the extreme exercise of our wildest imagination—the tiniest morsel of the true understanding of what the cross of Calvary really means. We must accept the fact that even as hard as many of us have tried, we simply do not have the capability to understand what it means for the Father to vent—for the first, last, and only time in all eternity—His infinite wrath upon the only object of His eternal love, His only Son. Nor are we capable of fathoming what the Son of God felt when the Father turned His back on Him for the first and only time in the infinite expanse of eternity. Nor can our feeble minds and hearts understand what it was like for the Son to—very literally we are told—become that which is most abhorrent to the only One whom He has loved for eternity, to the only One whose opinion He treasures. This is knowledge, these are facts, and these are feelings that we have never and will never approach, even in the most intimate walk with Jesus.

And still we press forward with the critical question. Precisely what about this mission makes it military? *After all, this mission was about love. What kind of a military mission is about love?* No doubt that the love of God is the fire that illuminates every aspect of this mission. And yet as we have already pointed out, this assignment was also—from beginning to end—a *rescue* mission. The facts in this regard remain crystal clear. Those who would occupy timeless eternity with the Persons of the Triune Godhead were *trapped behind enemy lines* because of their sin. Their plight was hopeless. Without external intervention, they by their very nature were beyond any hope of that for which they had been created. They, in the depths of their weakness, were held captive by the very powerful usurper of God's throne on earth. Their very lives were not just threatened—they were most assuredly *lost*. During the entirety of the time course of each of their lives, they teetered at the brink of nothing less than eternal catastrophe—and the usurper himself tauntingly kept them from escaping. Indeed, a truly vicious and frightful enemy guarded them. Satan is the most ferocious and awesome of enemies. His intent has always been clear: to strike at the unguarded heart of the Mighty God. His plan is equally clear: to turn away from God the very hearts of those whom God loves through fierce, unrelenting, and unmerciful deception.

And there was war in heaven.

—Revelation 12:7

There was war in heaven. Real war. Let there be no doubt in our minds that this was a military mission that Jesus undertook. The enemy who mocks and accuses us also mocked and accused the holy Son of God. Who can deny that an otherworldly melee of incalculable size most certainly must have surrounded the crucifixion scene on Calvary? It was at that precise moment that the battle was fought and the victory won:

> *When you were dead in your sins and in the uncircumcision of your sinful nature, God made you alive with Christ. He forgave us all our sins, having canceled the written code, with its regulations, that was against us and that stood opposed to us; he took it away, nailing it to the cross. And having disarmed the powers and authorities, he made a public spectacle of them, triumphing over them by the cross.*
> —Colossians 2:13-15 (emphasis added)

Military? Most certainly—and all culminated in those final moments on the cross. In the culmination of what Satan must have considered his greatest ambush was the most crushing of blows to his earthly campaign against the Mighty God. In the midst of the ambush, the great predator became prey, the ambusher was ambushed, and the outcome of the entire war—not just a single battle—was sealed for eternity.

> *For as in Adam all die, so in Christ all will be made alive. But each in his own turn: Christ, the firstfruits; then, when he comes, those who belong to him. Then the end will come, when he hands over the kingdom to God the Father after he has destroyed all dominion, authority and power.*
> —1Corinthians 15:22-24 (emphasis added)

As for right this moment—as I write these words and as you read them—it *is* war. We *are* trapped. Our plight *is* hopeless. Without the very real and daring rescue carried out by Jesus, we—like every man and woman whoever breathed—are palpably lost. Forever.

The Final Mission

But, as staggering in its eternal implications (for each and every one of us) as this great rescue mission was, the Word of God assures us that *warrior* Jesus is not finished. As you read the final chapters of this book, the final chapters of the generation of man are being played out in heaven, as well as on earth. The Warrior of all warriors, Jesus, sits next to the Father in heaven waiting for that *final* word. That word from the Father will set into motion the greatest military maneuver ever conceived in heaven or on earth. More is written in the Word of God about this final battle that is yet to come than about any other battle.

On one not-too-distant day in the future—on the much-heralded *"day of the Lord"*—the Father will turn to the Son and give Him the nod—the nod for which Jesus has been eagerly waiting since the dawn of the creation. And with that nod, the Father will tell the Son to go get His bride, the church, the body of Christ. At the very first word, the archangel Michael, the longtime warrior companion of Jesus, will be the first to arise.

> *"At that time Michael, the great prince who protects your people, will arise. There will be a time of distress such as has not happened from the beginning of nations until then. But at that time your people— everyone whose name is found written in the book—will be delivered.*
> —Daniel 12:1 (emphasis added)

This second of these final two missions will indeed be the greatest of all military campaigns in the traditional sense. In it, the returning Prince will take on the full might of all of the armies of this world *and the otherworld* in the final showdown—the biggest battle of all time—at Armageddon. This final confrontation is described in great detail in the Word of God. It is the final battle that rights all the wrongs as a prerequisite before the King of kings sets up His millennial reign. In this final battle we will see the full final fruition of many of the attributes of Jesus that He *fully* demonstrated in the Old Testament—and that we are often hesitant to acknowledge in His regard.

Surely we should not be surprised or caught off guard—*although we almost certainly will be*—by the sudden lethality, very brutal completeness, and eternal finality of the mighty warrior King's victory over the massive and seemingly invincible forces that are arrayed against Him on that day of days.

Throughout the writings of the Old Testament prophets—from Moses to Malachi—are found vivid, magnificent descriptions of the warrior Prince's victories over the enemies of God. These descriptions do indeed serve the purpose of recording the battle history of the nation of Israel and its Kings. Yet there is no denying their greater purpose of painting many small sections of a panoramic view of a massive battle—*the* battle. When they are all pieced together they provide a mosaic scene that when viewed in its entirety illuminates the fight of all fights, the battle of all battles that the Commander of the army of the Lord will take to the heart of His enemies on that day.

We are told nothing less than precisely this when the prophet Zechariah assures us that on that final day, *"the Lord will go out and fight...as he fights in the day of battle."*

> *A day of the LORD is coming when your plunder will be divided among you. I will gather all the nations to Jerusalem to fight against it; the city will be captured, the houses ransacked, and the women raped. Half of the city will go into exile, but the rest of the people will not be taken from the city. Then the LORD will go out and fight against those nations, as he fights in the day of battle. On that day his feet will stand on the Mount of Olives, east of Jerusalem, and the Mount of Olives will be split in two from east to west, forming a great valley, with half of the mountain moving north and half moving south. You will flee by my mountain valley, for it will extend to Azel. You will flee as you fled from the earthquake in the days of Uzziah king of Judah. Then the LORD my God will come, and all the holy ones with him. On that day there will be no light, no cold or frost. It will be a unique day, without daytime or nighttime—a day known to the LORD. When evening comes, there will be light. On that day living water will flow out from Jerusalem, half to the eastern sea and half to the western sea, in summer and in winter. The LORD will be king over the whole earth. On that day there will be one LORD, and his name the only name.*

—Zechariah 14:1-9 (emphasis added)

In other words—and just as this scripture so clearly states—Jesus will fight them then *precisely as he has fought them all along.* On that final day and in that final battle of battles, He will combine all that He has experienced of warfare from the countless battles that He fought during the Old Testament times as the Commander of the army of the Lord. And by His Father's strength, by the strength of His victory on the cross of Calvary, Jesus alone will vanquish the gathered armies of the nations of the world and their crown prince, Satan. He alone will be victorious on that day when *"there will be one Lord, and his name the only name."*

And don't expect this final battle to be any less graphic, any less physical, any less hands-on for the Warrior of warriors. The Bible is explicit in its rendering of the panoramic view of battle that is painted by a plethora of Old Testament prophets. This will be battle in the fullest definition of that word.

> *"See now that I myself am He! There is no god besides me. I put to death and I bring to life, I have wounded and I will heal, and no one can deliver out of my hand. I lift my hand to heaven and declare: As surely as I live forever, when I sharpen my flashing sword and my hand grasps it in judgment, I will take vengeance on my adversaries and repay those who hate me. I will make my arrows drunk with blood, while my sword devours flesh: the blood of the slain and the captives, the heads of the enemy leaders."*
>
> *Rejoice, O nations, with his people, for he will avenge the blood of his servants; he will take vengeance on his enemies and make atonement for his land and people.*
>
> —Deuteronomy 32:39-43 (emphasis added)

This will be battle on earth and this will be battle in heaven. And the battle in heaven will be every bit as physical as the battle on earth. This will be the battle of all battles in every detail. And Jesus will be right in the middle—the very focal point—of the entirety of this day of all days. The prophet Isaiah paints a particularly revealing portion of this day with his description of a battle that will involve real world armies as well as heavenly otherworld armies. Jesus will call all of His enemies to one last battle—heavenly and earthly—and will pour out upon them the full wrath of the army of the Lord.

> *The LORD is angry with all nations; his wrath is upon all their armies. He will totally destroy them, he will give them over to slaughter. Their slain will be thrown out, their dead bodies will send up a stench; the mountains will be soaked with their blood.*
>
> —Isaiah 34:2-3

Just in case we are tempted to believe that this last day will involve only real world warfare, Isaiah reminds us—using the classic idiom of *"stars"* representing angelic warriors—that the sword of the Commander of the army of the Lord will also be busy in heaven against dark angelic warriors.

All the stars of the heavens will be dissolved and the sky rolled up like a scroll; all the starry host will fall like withered leaves from the vine, like shriveled figs from the fig tree. My sword has drunk its fill in the heavens; see, it descends in judgment on Edom, the people I have totally destroyed. The sword of the LORD is bathed in blood, it is covered with fat—the blood of lambs and goats, fat from the kidneys of rams. For the LORD has a sacrifice in Bozrah and a great slaughter in Edom. And the wild oxen will fall with them, the bull calves and the great bulls. Their land will be drenched with blood, and the dust will be soaked with fat. For the LORD has a day of vengeance, a year of retribution, to uphold Zion's cause.

—Isaiah 34:4-8 (emphasis added)

How profound is the statement regarding the actions of Jesus as a warrior Commander that His *"sword has drunk its fill in the heavens."* How much more blatantly can He state it? The sword of the Lord will drink *"its fill"* that day on earth *and* in the heavens, just as it did all through the times of the Old Testament.

It is reasonable to expect that one might see the picture of Jesus that has been painted by our review of His warrior presence during the Old Testament as differing significantly from the picture we would commonly ascribe to Him from the New Testament. Nothing could be further from the actual truth. Jesus is not suddenly going to become something in the end-times battle that He has never been. *Jesus is and always has been a warrior.* Despite the fact that our traditional view of Jesus may not be entirely in line with this does not change anything. Jesus has not changed. Jesus cannot change and will never change.

As was made clear from the beginning of this book, the overall mission statement of the Warrior of warriors was two-fold. In the Old Testament, Jesus was the warrior Commander who led the army of the Lord in the preservation and outright rescue of *the remnant of Israel.* He is also the warrior who demonstrated loving and compassionate humility as only the Son of God could demonstrate it when He completed the second part of His assignment: the rescue *of the remnant of the gentiles* during the 33 years that are described by the gospel stories. The first mission directly mirrored and directly predicted the second. The Jesus who returns to rapture His bride and to face and defeat the combined enemy armies of both our world and the otherworld will be no less a warrior.

Jesus is the Warrior of all warriors and He is not through yet. There are no inconsistencies between the attributes demonstrated by Jesus during the Old

Testament and those that are described in the New Testament. And this last great mission—described as *"the day of the Lord"* (Isaiah 13:6)—will be precisely that, the day of Jesus. That which we have seen described on the pages of the Old Testament will once again describe precisely what we will see when He comes back. It is, always has been, and always will be *all* about Jesus—and He is, always has been, and always will be...*a warrior*.

> *I saw heaven standing open and there before me was a white horse, whose rider is called Faithful and True. With justice he judges and makes war.*
>
> —Revelation 19:11 (emphasis added)

Chapter 38

The Crucifixion of Jesus Christ
Psalm 68—When Everything Changed

A parade. A victory celebration. The conquering King sat astride a majestic, warhorse that stomped and snorted its approval of the celebration. The Rider of the white horse was the focal point of all. Every eye was fixed on Him. He led His victorious army into the jubilant city. The long awaited celebration had begun.

The battle had been the most dire and treacherous of all time. And yet victory was complete. Everything had been left on the field of battle that day. From that battlefield a cry had arisen. It was the cry that all creation had waited patiently upon since the closing of the gates of Eden. And then the victors of the day had led this procession, this celebration. The spattered blood on their garments spoke of the fury they had met—and been—mere hours before. Captured prisoners shuffled behind them. They were chained at the wrists and feet. They were spoils of war, the reward for great bravery, great faithfulness, and great skill in battle. They were a spectacle to all who observed this victory procession. Gifts were given to the Victor.

The entire focus of this book has been on the physical participation of the fully embodied Son of God in every moment of the recorded history of the Old Testament. His many roles, the overarching goal of His involvement, the primacy of His participation, and many of the specific missions that He undertook have all been discussed. And yet the golden strand that ties them all together is the pointed revelation that *they are the prelude to something more*. These grand adventures and captivating tales that are documented on the pages of the Old Testament are the prelude to something more, to something great.

This *something great* begins with a transition. The ending of the recorded events of the Old Testament and the appearance of John the Baptist were the immediate harbingers of this transition. From the pages of the New Testament, Jesus tells us precisely this. He stresses the importance of this transition and its timing by linking the appearance of John the Baptist to both the prophet Malachi's prediction of the return of Elijah and to the beginning of the forceful advancement of *"the kingdom of heaven."*

*From the days of John the Baptist until now, the kingdom of heaven
has been forcefully advancing, and forceful men lay hold of it. For all
the Prophets and the Law prophesied until John. And if you are
willing to accept it, he is the Elijah who was to come. He who has
ears, let him hear.*

—Matthew 11:12-15 (emphasis added)

*"See, I will send you the prophet Elijah before that great and dreadful
day of the LORD comes. He will turn the hearts of the fathers to their
children, and the hearts of the children to their fathers; or else I will
come and strike the land with a curse."*

—Malachi 4:5-6 (emphasis added)

There is no question that the spiritual landscape began to shift with the appearance
of John the Baptist. John's appearance ushered in the transition to a new status
quo. It is Jesus who is the focal point of this transition. Indeed, with the birth of
Jesus in Bethlehem, the pace of this transition quickened remarkably. At His birth,
Jesus reversed the position from which He had operated in the Old Testament. He
went from being a full time otherworld participant and occasional real world
participant to inhabiting the real world full time—while nonetheless maintaining
vision into and access to the otherworld. He appeared in flesh as a man, and yet
He remained in full contact with the otherworld. Indeed, the Gospel accounts
repeatedly give examples of Jesus communicating directly with otherworld spirits
who tormented the real world individuals He encountered.

Even then, the life of Jesus, His 3 years of ministry, His fulfillment of the prophecy
of the Old Testament saints—also pointed toward something even greater still.
Despite the fact that Jesus had made a transition from the battlefields of the
otherworld, the evil powers of the otherworld *had still not yet been defeated.* In
fact, it was not until the crucifixion of Jesus Christ that this great battle was even
fought. This progression of events and the logical conclusions that can be drawn
from them lead us to yet another critical hypothesis.

It is our hypothesis that it is in the moment of the crucifixion, this moment on a
Roman wooden cross on a skull-shaped mount, that *everything changed.*
Everything that involved the warrior conflict between Jesus and the otherworld evil
powers (whose influence dominates our world) *changed forever at the crucifixion.*

The New Testament accounts give a detailed description of the real world event that was the crucifixion of the Son of God. The events immediately preceding this pinnacle moment, as well as the actual events of the crucifixion itself, are related in tormenting detail. And yet the moment the body of Jesus is placed in a tomb, the detail ends. The single most important player in the entirety of the panoramic tapestry of the creation suddenly just disappears. He dies upon a cross, is buried, and from 3 in the afternoon on Friday until the early morning of the following Sunday, we are told little if anything of any substance regarding His whereabouts or actions.

Don't get me wrong. After all, we are told much of the *consequences* of His activities. Specifically, we know that as *Believers* we don't have to suffer the *"second death"* (Revelation 21:8) because He took our place and suffered it for us. Most assuredly this had something to do with that which He was doing—and yet we are left grasping for the details of precisely what went on behind the curtain that separates our world from the otherworld. We know that it somehow involved His descent into hell. Even then, however, we are left without a full understanding of precisely what that even means.

As little information as we have about the otherworld events following the crucifixion, there are, nonetheless, several very specific and direct New Testament references to this mysterious 40 hours. The first is a reference in 1Peter that appears to suggest that immediately following His death, Jesus was *"made alive by the Spirit"* and preached to the fallen angels who had been put in *"prison"* long ago for their part in the defilement of mankind that occurred in the time of Noah.

> *For Christ died for sins once for all, the righteous for the unrighteous, to bring you to God. He was put to death in the body but made alive by the Spirit, through whom also he went and preached to the spirits in prison who disobeyed long ago when God waited patiently in the days of Noah while the ark was being built. In it only a few people, eight in all, were saved through water, and this water symbolizes baptism that now saves you also—not the removal of dirt from the body but the pledge of a good conscience toward God. It saves you by the resurrection of Jesus Christ, who has gone into heaven and is at God's right hand—with angels, authorities and powers in submission to him.*

> —1Peter 3:18-22 (emphasis added)

Although this passage suggests a possible activity of Jesus during the enigmatic 40 hours following His death, it also certainly could have occurred any time after His resurrection and before His ascension. Still, yet another similar reference directly refers to the actual locale where Jesus spent those 40 hours.

> *For as Jonah was three days and three nights in the belly of a huge fish, so the Son of Man will be three days and three nights in the heart of the earth.*
>
> —Matthew 12:40 (emphasis added)

This passage suggests that Jesus spent the entirety of the *"three days"* in a locale whose description as *"the heart of the earth"* suggests that it is not just referring to a tomb hewn out of rock on the surface of the earth. As always, it must be assumed that the Holy Spirit's precise choice of words in this passage has a purpose. *"The heart of the earth"* seems to be describing the focal point of activity in the depths of earth—a second clear scriptural reference to hell itself. Jesus suffered the second death for mankind. In no uncertain terms, He went to hell for us.

Another New Testament reference to this period doesn't tell us where Jesus was or what He did, but rather tells us of something that He very specifically did *not* do. In his gospel account, the apostle John tells us of a peculiar conversation between the newly arisen Jesus and Mary Magdalene. In it He warns her not to touch Him because He has *not yet* returned *"to the Father."*

> *At this, she turned around and saw Jesus standing there, but she did not realize that it was Jesus. "Woman," he said, "why are you crying? Who is it you are looking for?" Thinking he was the gardener, she said, "Sir, if you have carried him away, tell me where you have put him, and I will get him."*
>
> *Jesus said to her, "Mary." She turned toward him and cried out in Aramaic, "Rabboni!" (which means Teacher).*
>
> *Jesus said, "Do not hold on to me, for I have not yet returned to the Father. Go instead to my brothers and tell them, 'I am returning to my Father and your Father, to my God and your God.'"*
>
> *Mary Magdalene went to the disciples with the news: "I have seen the Lord!" And she told them that he had said these things to her.*

—John 20:14-18 (emphasis added)

This conversation, which seems to clearly relate the fact that the risen Son of God had *"not yet returned to the Father"* at that point, gains even more importance in light of still another New Testament reference. This New Testament reference leads us once again back to the Old Testament. It specifically points to an Old Testament prophecy found in the book of Psalms.

> *But to each one of us grace has been given as Christ apportioned it. This is why it says: "When he ascended on high, he led captives in his train and gave gifts to men." (What does "he ascended" mean except that he also descended to the lower, earthly regions? He who descended is the very one who ascended higher than all the heavens, in order to fill the whole universe.) It was he who gave some to be apostles, some to be prophets, some to be evangelists, and some to be pastors and teachers, to prepare God's people for works of service, so that the body of Christ may be built up until we all reach unity in the faith and in the knowledge of the Son of God and become mature, attaining to the whole measure of the fullness of Christ.*

—Ephesians 4:7-13 (emphasis added)

This New Testament reference to an Old Testament prophecy seems to describe the precise event that Jesus is referring to in His conversation with Mary Magdalene. This passage in Ephesians is referencing Psalm 68.

> *When you ascended on high, you led captives in your train; you received gifts from men, even from the rebellious—that you, O LORD God, might dwell there.*

—Psalm 68:18

When a passage in the New Testament refers us to an Old Testament prophecy, we can be assured that it is with divine purpose. This is certainly the case in the reference to Psalm 68 that is found in Ephesians 4 above. The Holy Spirit is inviting us to explore an expanded Old Testament explanation of the event being described in the New Testament passage. In other words, in this particular reference the Holy Spirit is suggesting that if we want to know what was really going on in the early hours following the crucifixion, we should explore Psalm 68 in more detail.

Without the above-cited reference, Psalm 68's reference to the crucifixion might well be overlooked. Instead, with our attention drawn to it, Psalm 68 clearly appears to speak directly of the crucifixion and the events immediately following it. In fact, it uniquely illuminates the critical time period that occurred immediately after the crucifixion. At its core, it is nothing less than a very literal description of a triumphant entry into heaven. Old Testament triumphant entries like the one described in Psalm 68 occurred primarily following victory at war. In fact, these parades represented the primary method of celebration following victory over an enemy.

The logical conclusion is that Jesus, who is being attributed with the leadership of this triumphant entry, *has just fought a monumental battle*. The description of the celebration suggests that the battle was of particular significance. The obvious question regards the precise identity of the forces that opposed Jesus in this battle and the consequences of the victory. In Psalm 68, we are told much about both.

This Psalm celebrates the most critical juncture in the grand mission of Jesus Christ. The crucial incident that it describes is expected and the mission it addresses is well known to us. As discussed in Chapter 14 of this book, the two-part mission statement that is found in Isaiah 49 precisely predicted this mission and its conclusion.

> *And now the LORD says—he who formed me in the womb to be his servant <u>to bring Jacob back to him and gather Israel to himself,</u> for I am honored in the eyes of the LORD and my God has been my strength—he says: "It is too small a thing for you to be my servant <u>to restore the tribes of Jacob and bring back those of Israel I have kept.</u> I will also make you a light for the Gentiles, that you may <u>bring my salvation to the ends of the earth.</u>"*

—Isaiah 49:5-6 (emphasis added)

It is precisely at this juncture—at the crucifixion—that Jesus completes the transition from the limited Old Testament mission of saving the remnant of Israel to His expanded mission of saving each and every man and woman—Jew or gentile—who would ever repent and place their faith in Him. In His incarnation, crucifixion, and resurrection is seen the culmination of the transition to this broader mission, the ultimate mission.

One could easily argue that Jesus may still have been fighting the Old Testament part of the two-part mission—the battle to preserve the remnant of Israel—during

His 3 years of ministry on earth. He repeatedly prioritizes the Jewish remnant over gentile believers in multiple confrontations. And surely Jesus is continually sparring with the otherworld principalities as He repeatedly casts out demons and stands face-to-face in conflict with Satan in the desert and the Pharisees in the Holy Temple.

But something changed when Jesus went to the cross of Calvary. Surely Jesus fought the otherworld principalities and powers that stood opposed to the nation of Israel during the times of the Old Testament and during His three years of earthly ministry. But the New Testament is also not subtle in telling us that *with His death and resurrection, Jesus routed these very same enemies in battle*, defeating them *once and for all*. It was as if these powers were initially worthy opponents for the emptied Son of God, only to have this peer relationship change forever at the cross.

The support for this profound change in hierarchy following the crucifixion is once again founded in very precisely worded New Testament text. For example, Paul states that following His resurrection, Christ was raised *"above all rule and authority, power and dominion."*

> *I pray also that the eyes of your heart may be enlightened in order that you may know the hope to which he has called you, the riches of his glorious inheritance in the saints, and his incomparably great power for us who believe. That power is like the working of his mighty strength, which he exerted in Christ <u>when</u> he <u>raised</u> him from the dead and seated him at his right hand in the heavenly realms, <u>far above all rule and authority, power and dominion, and every title that can be given</u>, not only in the present age but also in the one to come. And God plac<u>ed</u> all things under his feet and appointed him to be head over everything for the church, which is his body, the fullness of him who fills everything in every way.*
>
> —Ephesians 1:18-23 (emphasis added)

The precise words chosen by Paul are critical here. He states that the Father raised Christ *"far above"* the otherworldly powers. *"Raised"* is past tense and as such implies a specific occurrence at a specific moment on the timeline of history. Further still, it implies a change from one state to another—a change in the status quo—that occurred at that specific moment in history. The implication is not subtle. Christ could not have been raised above these Old Testament otherworld warriors at His resurrection *unless He was below them before His resurrection*. We have already reviewed the Biblical verses that state precisely this.

But we see Jesus, who was made a little lower than the angels, now crowned with glory and honor because he suffered death, so that by the grace of God he might taste death for everyone.
—Hebrews 2:9 (emphasis added)

In other words, the default assumption that many of us automatically have—that Jesus was—and of course *always* had been—above these otherworld angels before His resurrection—is simply not consistent with these scriptural passages. There is only one conclusion available to us. With His incarnation into the creation, the only Son of the only true God emptied Himself into a lesser form—that of a man—that was inferior to the otherworld evil angels.

Your attitude should be the same as that of Christ Jesus: Who, being in very nature God, did not consider equality with God something to be grasped, but made himself nothing, taking the very nature of a servant, being made in human likeness. And being found in appearance as a man, he humbled himself and became obedient to death—even death on a cross! Therefore God exalted him to the highest place and gave him the name that is above every name, that at the name of Jesus every knee should bow, in heaven and on earth and under the earth, and every tongue confess that Jesus Christ is Lord, to the glory of God the Father.
—Philippians 2:5-11 (emphasis added)

The Old Testament otherworld position of Jesus relative to the angels is the topic of several key passages in scripture. His inferior position in the relative angelic hierarchy was clearly spelled out. That which is equally clear, however, is that all of this changed at the cross. The book of Colossians makes specific reference in this regard. A great battle was fought. The results of the battle were paramount and two-fold. The first direct result was the salvation of mankind. The cross was the triumphant moment of the great battle for the souls who were lost to death because of their rebellious sin against a kind and loving, yet perfectly just and infinitely holy God. The second direct result was the Father's act of elevating Jesus above everyone and everything in the creation. Both were apparently the direct result of battle. This battle at the cross on Calvary truly was the pinnacle victory of many battles for Jesus, the Warrior of warriors. In this regard, we have discussed Colossians 2:13-15 previously, but must visit it again here.

> *When you were dead in your sins and in the uncircumcision of your*
> *sinful nature, God made you alive with Christ. He forgave us all our*
> *sins, having canceled the written code, with its regulations, that was*
> *against us and that stood opposed to us; he took it away, nailing it to*
> *the cross. <u>And having disarmed the powers and authorities, he made</u>*
> *<u>a public spectacle of them, triumphing over them by the cross</u>.*
>
> —Colossians 2:13-15 (emphasis added)

One cannot help but notice that the descriptive terms used in this passage from Colossians are notably military in their connotation. For instance, the word *"disarmed"* cannot be used any other way than to describe the act of taking away an enemy's weaponry. The implications of this passage from Colossians thus become pivotal. Jesus had not disarmed the *"powers and authorities"*—the evil warrior angels—*until* the battle at the cross. Further still, the statement that Jesus *"made a public spectacle of them"* is nothing less than another direct reference to the above mentioned Psalm 68 and its description of the return of the victorious army to its home city, complete with the parading of defeated enemies behind the celebratory procession. It describes a *"public spectacle"* of the grandest form. This is Old Testament warfare at its best—and it all took place at the cross.

And this brings us back to the Old Testament prophecy from Psalm 68 that is referred to above. In this glorious psalm, the Holy Spirit is not the least bit subtle in describing a victory procession. As we have noted, the reference to leading *"captives in your train; you received gifts from men"* is a specific reference to the opposing army's defeated warriors being paraded in chains behind the victors, and the *"gifts from men"* refers to the booty rewarded to the commander of the victorious army.

Similarly, the prophet Isaiah also describes, in very military terminology, the defeat of the evil *"powers"* of the otherworld in a passage from Isaiah 24. Just like the writer of Psalm 68, he describes these evil warrior princes as being *"herded together like prisoners"* after their defeat.

> *In that day the LORD will punish <u>the powers in the heavens above</u> and*
> *the kings on the earth below. They will be <u>herded together like</u>*
> *<u>prisoners</u> bound in a dungeon; they will be shut up in prison and be*
> *punished after many days.*
>
> —Isaiah 24:21-22 (emphasis added)

All of these scriptural references support the logical conclusion that the rest of Psalm 68 has much to offer in regard to the mysterious 40-hour time period between the death and resurrection of Jesus. It tells us of a great battle. From its opening verses, it tells of a warrior God who rides a great chariot and scatters His enemies. He blows His enemies away *"as smoke is blown away by the wind"* (Psalm 68:2). It tells of a God who *"rides on the clouds"* (Psalm 68:4) and is *"a father to the fatherless, a defender of widows"* (Psalm 68:5). But, most importantly, it tells of a warrior God who *"leads forth the prisoners with singing"* (Psalm 68:6). He is mighty and when He *"marched through the wasteland"*—the battlefield—*"the earth shook"* (Psalm 68:7-8).

This psalm is telling us a story. It tells of a rescue—a great rescue. It tells the most important story ever told—of the rescue of all who would call upon the name of the Jesus. This rescue took place at the cross. Most importantly, the story also tells us that the rescue comes only as a result *of great battle*. The conclusions are obvious and foundational to our understanding of the most important moment of the entire creation. This great battle took place at the cross.

This is a battle of staggering proportions. In fact, right before the Holy Spirit tells us in Psalm 68 of the victory parade, He describes the massive nature of the military force involved in the battle.

> *The chariots of God are tens of thousands and thousands of thousands; the Lord [has come] from Sinai into his sanctuary.*
> —Psalm 68:17 (emphasis added)

The *"wasteland"* battlefield is the Sinai and—let there be no question in our minds—this psalm and this battle are about only one thing, *our eternal salvation*:

> *Praise be to the Lord, to God our Savior, who daily bears our burdens.*
> —Psalm 68:19 (emphasis added)

The skull-shaped hill named Calvary—made eternally notorious by the cross of Christ—was nothing less than the greatest of battlefields. The battle fought there was the battle of all battles and its principal was Jesus Christ. It was furious and violent and massive and it was all about us. This fight was about you and me—for in that battle and with that victory at the cross, the defeat and humiliation of the powers and authorities that have held such sway in the world, such sway over each of us, is assured. The end to this grand and epic story is written in blood in the dust of Calvary.

Truly, everything changed at the cross. The ultimate defeat of every manifestation of evil in the heavens and on the earth was assured. The implications for you and me are huge. The destruction of every otherworld *"dominion, authority, and power"* has already been assured by the singular act of the battle at the cross of Christ.

> *For since death came through a man, the resurrection of the dead comes also through a man. For as in Adam all die, so in Christ all will be made alive. But each in his own turn: Christ, the firstfruits; then, when he comes, those who belong to him. Then the end will come, <u>when he hands over the kingdom to God the Father after he has destroyed all dominion, authority and power. For he must reign until he has put all his enemies under his feet</u>.*
>
> —1Corinthians 15:21-25 (emphasis added)

It is only with this victory that the ultimate purpose of the creation—the revelation and rescue of the sons and daughters of God who will spend eternity in fellowship with the Trinity—is achieved and singularly assured by the actions of the one Person behind and above it all—Jesus. And Psalm 68 tells us nothing less.

> *Our God is a God who <u>saves</u>; from the Sovereign LORD comes <u>escape from death</u>.*
>
> —Psalm 68:20 (emphasis added)

Jesus is the Creator, the Author of the story, the primary player in the play, and the whole point of everything. He is victorious and He will demonstrate precisely that on *"that day"*—His day—*"the day of the Lord."* He is our hope and in that hope, our joy.

> *Your procession has come into view, O God, the procession of my God and King into the sanctuary. In front are the singers, after them the musicians; with them are the maidens playing tambourines. Praise God in the great congregation; praise the LORD in the assembly of Israel.*
>
> —Psalm 68:24-26

Truly, *everything* changed at the cross.

Chapter 39

The Bottom Line of This Discussion
Jesus Plus Nothing

This book was conceived from the beginning, envisioned during its writing, and implemented in its publication as a celebration of the fullness of the Person of Jesus Christ. Its purpose is first and foremost to bring glory to the most holy Name of Jesus by revealing the whole truth, by revealing as much as can be known about *the One and Only* from the pages of Old Testament Scripture.

If we were to be so bold as to summarize the New Testament as the story of the gospel of Jesus Christ, then the Old Testament can be similarly encapsulated by one thought: *It is the story of "the One" who is to come.* The full involvement of Jesus in the adventures that are described in the Old Testament is nothing less than that which we should expect of the single point of light that illuminates every moment of the history of the creation. It is in fact precisely on these pages of the Old Testament that the Messiah is fully characterized, for His activities as a warrior Commander in the Old Testament are a perfect prequel to the roles Jesus assumed in the New Testament and will assume in the end-times to come.

The whole point of this book must be, therefore, to refocus our hearts upon the fact that it really is *all* about Jesus. Even the parts that don't seem like they are about Jesus are indeed about no one else. Let this be the lasting legacy of this book: to reemphasize that it is *Jesus plus nothing* in everything, always and every time— *including Old Testament scripture.*
Whether we acknowledge it in this life or not, the very first reality that we will face when we step into eternity is that every single moment of our lives—and of every life—was about only one thing: Jesus Christ.

Can it be any other way?

He claimed to be the Son *of God.* Discussing His status as the Son of God cannot be a casual conversation. He is either absolutely nothing—*or He is absolutely everything.* There can be no middle ground.

We praise God for the magnificent complexity of the situations that we find ourselves in—and likewise praise Him for the utter simplicity of *the* solution to every one of them. In every difficulty, in every storm, in every frenzy, in every heated battle, in every darkened night we know exactly to Whom we can turn. Jesus is always there and He is *always* the answer. Even in the difficulties we face this very day, we can be assured that Jesus is all we need for this (and every) situation.

It is Jesus plus nothing for our salvation. Even with a full life of toil, we can add absolutely nothing to what Jesus has already done. And in this regard, belief *in God* is incomplete—and in that incompleteness, fatal. Without belief in Jesus, all is lost. With Jesus we get *everything*. Without Jesus we get *nothing*.

Thus, whenever we find ourselves in trouble, it has invariably resulted from our taking our eyes off of Jesus—and putting them on ourselves or on the world around us. In fact, in this life we should not ever worry about ourselves. We should not ever concern ourselves with our lives, our accomplishments, or even our heavenly rewards. We should concern ourselves with bringing glory to Jesus—and let *Him* worry about our lives, accomplishments, and our heavenly rewards.

It is Jesus plus nothing for our sanctification.

> *Let us fix our eyes on Jesus, the author and perfecter of our faith, who for the joy set before him endured the cross, scorning its shame, and sat down at the right hand of the throne of God.*
>
> —Hebrews 12:2 (emphasis added)

It is Jesus plus nothing that solves the difficult situation we face. It is Jesus plus nothing that solves every situation that we could <u>ever</u> find ourselves in—for *all* were planned and created by God, the Master of the creation of the universe, such that *every moment is about Jesus*.

Jesus is the answer to every question. He is the Savior in every battle. He is the way out of every storm. He is the water in every drought. He is the bread in every famine. He is the light in every moment of absolute darkness. He is the only truth in the sea of lies in which we find ourselves submerged. He is the only satiation of every deep craving of our hearts. He is the only voice that answers the deep cry of our hearts. He is the only *True North* by which to chart the course of our life. His is that hand that reaches down and grabs firmly hold of ours as we sink for the last time into the dark lagoon of our self-deception. He is our redemption, our only salvation.

Jesus is not "part" of the solution to anything—He is the whole solution to everything. Jesus plus nothing satisfies our hungry heart. It is Jesus plus nothing—in every moment of our lives.

Jesus is our only hope. Jesus is our whole eternity. We will romp with Jesus through the adventures of eternity dressed immaculately in the pure white righteousness of His death and resurrection, just as if we had never committed a single rebellious offense against the perfect holiness of the uncreated, mighty, and Most Holy God. For whenever the Father looks at us, He will see us through Jesus! Only through Jesus—always and everywhere. Jesus is the whole of our eternity. He is our interface, our connection, our link to the eternal, uncreated, infinite God. He is that seemingly impossible link between the temporary and the eternal, the created and the uncreated, the finite and the infinite. Jesus is our hope and in that hope our joy and in that joy, eternal life—life as we can never imagine it now.

Jesus plus nothing
        —yesterday, today and for all eternity in every setting, every time, always.

Chapter 40

So What?
You the Reader Must Decide

The central theme of this book is that Jesus Christ was a fully embodied, incarnate participant in every moment of the history recorded by Old Testament scripture. His physical participation was as a warrior Commander of warriors. As the Commander of the army of the Lord, He went to war and stood back to back with His companions in the fury of the fight on behalf of the righteous remnant of the nation of Israel.

> *The LORD struck down the Cushites before Asa and Judah. The Cushites fled, and Asa and his army pursued them as far as Gerar. Such a great number of Cushites fell that they could not recover; they were <u>crushed</u> before <u>the LORD and his forces</u>. The men of Judah carried off a large amount of plunder.*
>
> —2Chronicles 14:12-13 (emphasis added)

Much can therefore be known about the warrior attributes of Jesus by the Biblical description of His participation in this great war. Every time that *the angel of the Lord* is mentioned, the Old Testament exploits of Jesus Christ are being described. Every time Moses or Joshua or any of the other patriarchs and prophets met with the Lord in the tent of meeting, in the temple, or anywhere else, it was Jesus Christ they were speaking to, face-to-face.

> *And they will tell the inhabitants of this land about it. They have already heard that you, O LORD, are with these people and that you, O LORD, have been <u>seen face to face</u>, that your cloud stays over them, and that you go before them in a pillar of cloud by day and a pillar of fire by night.*
>
> —Numbers 14:14 (emphasis added)

> *So Moses chiseled out two stone tablets like the first ones and went up Mount Sinai early in the morning, as the LORD had commanded him; and he carried the two stone tablets in his hands.*

> *Then the LORD <u>came down in the cloud</u> and <u>stood there with</u> him and*
> *<u>proclaimed his name, the LORD</u>. And he <u>passed in front of</u> Moses,*
> *proclaiming, "The LORD, the LORD, the compassionate and gracious*
> *God, slow to anger, abounding in love and faithfulness, maintaining*
> *love to thousands, and forgiving wickedness, rebellion and sin. Yet he*
> *does not leave the guilty unpunished; he punishes the children and*
> *their children for the sin of the fathers to the third and fourth*
> *generation."*
> —Exodus 34:4-7 (emphasis added)

This means that nearly every time in the Old Testament that *"the LORD"* is described as telling somebody something, it is Jesus who is speaking. This perspective changes everything. For example, this passage from the Numbers 12 takes on a whole new light when it is recognized that it was indeed the incarnate, physically present Jesus Christ who was speaking to Moses, Aaron, and Miriam:

> *At once the LORD said to Moses, Aaron and Miriam, "Come out to the*
> *Tent of Meeting, all three of you." So the three of them came out.*
>
> *Then the LORD came down in a pillar of cloud; <u>he stood</u> at the*
> *entrance to the Tent and <u>summoned</u> Aaron and Miriam. When both of*
> *them stepped forward, he said, "Listen to my words: "When a*
> *prophet of the LORD is among you, I reveal myself to him in visions, I*
> *speak to him in dreams. But this is not true of my servant Moses; he*
> *is faithful in all my house. With him I speak <u>face to face</u>, clearly and*
> *not in riddles; he <u>sees the form</u> of <u>the LORD</u>. Why then were you not*
> *afraid to speak against my servant Moses?" The anger of the LORD*
> *burned against them, and <u>he left them</u>.*
> —Numbers 12:4-9 (emphasis added)

Indeed, when the text of the Old Testament is viewed through this new perspective, it almost seems as if the Holy Spirit took every possible opportunity to tell us in as many ways as possible that the involvement of Jesus Christ in every event was very literal—and entirely physical in every respect:

> *For the LORD your God <u>moves about in your camp</u> to protect you and*
> *to deliver your enemies to you. Your camp must be holy, so that he*
> *will not see among you anything indecent and turn away from you.*
> —Deuteronomy 23:14 (emphasis added)

Further still, we can also be assured that any angelic messenger whose face is described as being like *fire* and whose eyes are described as being like *flame* can be none other than Jesus. In fact, any Old Testament mention of any *unnamed* angelic messenger from God is describing the incarnate Jesus. God's *"terror"*, *"the Hornet"*, *"the commander of the army of the Lord"*, *"the prince of the host"*, and *"the prince of princes"* are also all descriptions used to portray Jesus in His warrior role. From this extensive array of appearances recounted in the Old Testament, it is readily apparent that Jesus was an active, fully embodied, physical participant who commanded the attention of every moment of Old Testament history.

Further still, any time that an author of the Bible renders a seemingly metaphorical description of the Lord as a *warrior*, the reader must consider the strong possibility that it is meant to be taken literally—that the author is giving a very literal, factually accurate description of the fully incarnate Jesus Christ. In fact, a strong case can be made that in the majority of the interpretations of the Old Testament by Jesus Himself (as recorded in the New Testament), He took the scripture very literally. Despite the fact that the tendency of our age is to attempt to assign these detailed descriptions to mere allegory, there is in fact nothing allegorical about the majority of them. Attributing them to simple metaphor is easy and may momentarily satisfy our anxious curiosity—for envisioning Jesus as a sword-wielding warrior most certainly moves any Believer out of their comfort zone. But an allegorical response to this literal detail underestimates and undervalues the full revelation of Jesus that is being provided by these accounts.

These detailed battle descriptions of hand-to-hand combat with the personal weapons of that day are detailed in this manner for a reason. They are not describing imaginary scenes of floating disembodied apparitions. Instead, they depict that which really took place on very real battlefields strewn with real bodies on soil that soaked up real blood from the physical struggles fought over the remnant of Israel.

> *Gird your sword upon your side, O mighty one; clothe yourself with splendor and majesty. In your majesty ride forth victoriously in behalf of truth, humility and righteousness; let your right hand display awesome deeds. Let your sharp arrows pierce the hearts of the king's enemies; let the nations fall beneath your feet.*
> —Psalm 45:3-5 (emphasis added)

Skepticism regarding these conclusions is understandable. Surely everyone who studies the Bible is individually charged with searching the scriptures to test such bold statements regarding Jesus Christ. Even if one accepts these bold conclusions as true, however, one might easily dismiss the whole idea as obscure and largely irrelevant with minimal potential to have any impact upon the daily life of the normal Christian. Indeed, one might well question: *What does this have to do with the gospel story of Jesus in the New Testament? What does that have to do with the heart of the gospel that directs and is the foundation of my life?*

These concerns are also easily understood. The focus of the New Testament is Jesus Christ. The words of the New Testament plainly detail the very special plan regarding the salvation and sanctification of the sons and daughters of eternity. The entirety of the New Testament characterization of Jesus Christ boldly claims to directly impact—in one way or another—every life on a day-to-day, moment-by-moment basis. Focusing upon this New Testament story of Jesus and its application in our lives, however, was never the function of this book. That fortress has been attacked and conquered by hundreds of writers. Nor was the goal in any way to draw attention away from the glorious message of the New Testament.

Instead, this book had the simple goal of reminding the reader that the *whole* of Holy Scripture—all-inclusively and exclusively—is about Jesus Christ. We know that if Jesus is really who He claims to be—the only Son of God—then we can take at literal face value the Apostle Paul's capstone summary statement about Him:

> *Your attitude should be the same as that of Christ Jesus: Who, being in very nature God, did not consider equality with God something to be grasped, but made himself nothing, taking the very nature of a servant, being made in human likeness. And being found in appearance as a man, he humbled himself and became obedient to death—even death on a cross!*
>
> *Therefore God exalted him to the <u>highest</u> place and gave him the name that is above <u>every</u> name, that at the name of Jesus <u>every</u> knee should bow, in heaven and on earth and under the earth, and <u>every</u> tongue confess that Jesus Christ is Lord, to the glory of God the Father.*

—Philippians 2:5-11 (emphasis added)

This passage is startling in its clarity and has directed our discussion from the very first chapter of this book. Very simply, it means that there is *nothing* in our lives that is *not* about Jesus. There is nothing in this world that, ultimately, is not about Jesus. He is the focus—the focal point—of the entirety of the creation. Taken to its radical and yet logical extreme, this statement means that there is nothing that has been created that will not be, if it hasn't already been, revealed to be *all* about Jesus Christ. He is the focal point and in being the focal point is—very literally— the *entirety* of the creation. Think logically. Think in faith. Think in truth. It can't be any other way.

If the entirety of the creation is exclusively about Jesus Christ, then the written Word of God can be no different. And indeed, it above everything else fits this description perfectly. Truly the Bible is *all* about Jesus. If Jesus is who He said He is—the only Son of God—then the written word of God must be totally and exclusively and all-inclusively about Jesus Christ *and nothing else*. It logically follows that every chapter, every paragraph, every word, every letter, and every punctuation mark must be—in one way or another—about the Person of Jesus Christ. This must include, then, the Old Testament as well as the New. In actual fact, the text of both the Old and New Testaments strongly supports precisely this:

> *Then I said, "Here I am, I have come—it is written <u>about me</u> in <u>the</u> <u>scroll</u>."*
>
> —Psalm 40:7 (emphasis added)

> *He said to them, "This is what I told you while I was still with you: Everything must be fulfilled that is written <u>about me</u> in the <u>Law of</u> <u>Moses</u>, the <u>Prophets</u> and the <u>Psalms</u>."*
>
> —Luke 24:44 (emphasis added)

There it is in black and white: *"Moses, the Prophets and the Psalms."* That encompasses the entirety of the Old Testament and it is *all* about Jesus. Surely we can agree that God is infinitely perfect in every thing that He does. We can know that the Holy Spirit is a perfectly efficient writer. We can know that not a word of Holy Scripture was superfluous or wasted. We can know that every single thing that the Holy Spirit wants to tell us in the Bible about the focus of the whole of creation—the Person of Jesus Christ—is vitally important. It must be—or the Holy Spirit would not have included it.

The revelation of Jesus that is found exclusively in the Old Testament, therefore, must not be just additive, but rather, *essential* to our understanding of Jesus. This review of the warrior role of Jesus in the Old Testament isn't just an extra credit assignment. It is definitely not just a discussion for theologians. Worse yet, it isn't a question that can be rejected because the answer is difficult to comprehend or uncomfortable. We are not empowered to tell God how He should be, what He should value, or what He should tell us about Himself. No one can pass judgment on the attributes of Jesus Christ—and not one of us is qualified to rewrite the written Word of God.

Incomplete truth is, by its very nature, falsehood. To know anything less than the complete fullness of the attributes of Jesus is to fall fatally short of the full understanding of the sacred personality and holy nature of the Son of God that is so vital to our individual sanctification and our eternity. This isn't secondary information—there is no such thing when the topic is Jesus. Incompleteness in truth is the enemy. We must fight the tendency toward the easy path—along which we leisurely pick and choose which of His attributes we will acknowledge. Only the *full* knowledge of Jesus allows one to move forward prepared for the battles we face every day. Without the full knowledge of Jesus, we move forward into the fury of battle on only one leg, with only one eye, and with one arm tied behind our back.

The whole of the Old Testament can therefore be summed up as being a testament, a story describing the fullness of *"the One" who is to come*. It is an anthology—complete in every way—describing the fullness of the Messiah, the Anointed One, the *man* who is also God. A complete knowledge of the fullness of the Person of Jesus Christ can only be obtained by understanding every word of the Bible. Just as with the New Testament, we must therefore grow in our fascination and endearment to every chapter of the Old Testament, because they are also all about Jesus.

So, where do we go from here? We move forward with an entirely new perspective. This perspective most importantly influences that which we see and hear and experience when we read the written Word of God. When I began to read and reread the Old Testament with the new perspective of Jesus Christ as a Holy Warrior who was involved in every Old Testament detail...*everything changed*. More and more evidence fully supporting this perspective simply cascaded out of the pages of both the Old *and* New Testaments. In this book, we have only bounced off of the most superficial layer of the treasures that are interwoven into the very fabric of the Bible regarding this Commander of the army of the Lord. We have only whetted our appetites for the banquet, the bounty of information about the Old Testament activities of our Savior. Truly everything changes with the correct perspective. Everything.

Now, countless new references to face-to-face meetings with the Lord, principalities behind the leaders of evil nations, warrior attributes of Jesus, and the direct military intervention of the Lord into the events surrounding Israel and its leaders suddenly take on new light. Scriptural passages that previously were simply curious become profound. Mysterious sections of Holy Scripture that previously made no sense whatsoever and in fact just seemed to have come *out of the blue* are now obvious in their relationship to their associated passages, and obvious in their glorification of Jesus Christ.

> *Then his people recalled the days of old, the days of Moses and his people—where is he who brought them through the sea, with the shepherd of his flock? Where is he who set his Holy Spirit among them, who sent his glorious arm of power to be at Moses' right hand, who divided the waters before them, to gain for himself everlasting renown, who led them through the depths?*
>
> —Isaiah 63:11-13 (emphasis added)

Best of all, I now know beyond a shadow of doubt that the incarnate Jesus Christ was literally there at every pivotal moment of Old Testament history. He was very literally *in* the cloud of fire that led the Israelites through the desert. The plainly stated fact (Ezekiel 43:1-5) that it was Jesus all along in all of the interactions with Moses—the burning bush, the Ten Commandments, the Shekinah Glory, the Tent of Meeting, the cleft in the rock—somehow just delights my heart. I don't know why, but it just brings everything all together in one easily comprehended and profoundly applicable bottom line: Jesus.

It is obvious that the New Testament is all about Jesus. In a similar fashion, everyone would agree that the end times are pointedly all about Jesus. And yet now, we can also know that every single event of the Old Testament was not just *somehow related* to Jesus (a fact every Believer already knows in their heart) but that Jesus literally and vividly ran through them *with a visible, palpable physical presence*. Further still, not only was He present, but His physical presence was critical to the outcome of every event. Even the smallest of details was impacted by the physical presence of Jesus. A great example involves the choice of Isaac's wife. At first glance, one might not see how the choice of Isaac's wife was such an earthshaking event—and yet Jesus was right there in the middle of it. Jesus went along to make sure that Abraham's servant got the right woman to be Isaac's wife.

"The LORD, the God of heaven, who brought me out of my father's household and my native land and who spoke to me and promised me on oath, saying, 'To your offspring I will give this land'—he will send his angel before you so that you can get a wife for my son from there.

—Genesis 24:7 (emphasis added)

This is a perfect example of how this seemingly obscure knowledge of fullness of the Old Testament role of Jesus impacts our day-to-day life. If Jesus felt that the choice of Isaac's wife was important enough for His personal involvement, then He most assuredly feels the same way about you and me. This realization of the involvement of Jesus in every detail of our lives is a critical reminder to me of the very personal presence of my Savior in my life.

As emphasized, the *physical* nature of the Old Testament presence of Jesus is critical to this discussion. Mankind is not just spiritual. Our physical presence in God's creation is where our spiritual being was designed to be most clearly and magnificently manifest. Jesus, our Redeemer, shares this physical presence with us through every moment of the history of His creation…and for eternity. Truly, the knowledge of the physical presence of Jesus in every event in the history of the Old Testament patriarchs somehow brings it all to completion. He was physically there—feeling it, seeing it, experiencing it, interacting with it, taking hold of it, moving it, pushing it, commanding it, judging it—making it into a truly and uniquely *human* experience.

"Go and tell my servant David, 'This is what the LORD says: Are you the one to build me a house to dwell in? I have not dwelt in a house from the day I brought the Israelites up out of Egypt to this day. I have been moving from place to place with a tent as my dwelling. Wherever I have moved with all the Israelites, did I ever say to any of their rulers whom I commanded to shepherd my people Israel, "Why have you not built me a house of cedar?"'

—2Samuel 7:5-7 (emphasis added)

And in all of this, the Person of Jesus Christ is exalted even more. The knowledge of the perfection of the emptying of Jesus in the incarnation, the knowledge of His incomparable trust and faith in His Father, and the understanding of how this knowledge impacted His crucifixion and resurrection tie everything together. Our understanding of our faith in Jesus (which is a reflection of Jesus' faith in the Father) is a hollow shell until we understand precisely why faith alone is the only answer to the dilemma of our sin. Only the insight found in examining the perfect faith of Jesus can explain the primacy of faith. This primacy is based in the faith of the Anointed One who gave up everything to be our Savior and in doing so became entirely reliant upon His perfectly faithful Father—forever.

This new perspective of ours is not just obscurely about our daily walk. In fact, it helps explain many of our deep heart feelings that seem to well up in our lives and directly influence our behavior. For example, like it or not, we *are* warriors. The desire to take up arms in defense of the truth—God's truth—runs through our every vein and is the cry of our deep heart. It is our life's blood. Much of our mainline Christian upbringing has worked so hard to suppress this. And yet, no one less than the mightiest Warrior Himself prewired *warrior* into our hearts. No one less than our warrior Savior orchestrated the battles that we face every single day. He orchestrated them directly into our daily life for a purpose. There is nothing random about this. It is purposeful. It is as if we are in training for something great.

> *These are the nations the LORD left to test all those Israelites who had not experienced any of the wars in Canaan (he did this only to teach warfare to the descendants of the Israelites who had not had previous battle experience): the five rulers of the Philistines, all the Canaanites, the Sidonians, and the Hivites living in the Lebanon mountains from Mount Baal Hermon to Lebo Hamath. They were left to test the Israelites to see whether they would obey the LORD's commands, which he had given their forefathers through Moses.*
> —Judges 3:1-4 (emphasis added)

We are in US Army Ranger or US Navy SEAL camp right now, training for God's purpose—and it is with the utmost anticipation that we await that for which we are being trained. This life alone is not the last fight for which God has been preparing us.

And best of all, this deep knowledge of battle, this drive to *be* a warrior does not arise just because it is our destiny. We are warriors because our Savior *is* a warrior. He isn't just going to be a warrior for a minute or two when He comes back. He was a warrior before the first nanosecond of the creation. Most certainly He was a warrior throughout the great war stories of the Old Testament. Further still, He will *never* stop being a warrior.

> *Jesus Christ is the same yesterday and today and forever.*

—Hebrews 13:8 (emphasis added)

Jesus has always been a warrior and will be a warrior for all eternity. It is time for the church of Christ—and especially the men of the body of Christ—to reclaim the fullness of *all* of the attributes of Christ. We can't just pick and choose the attributes that we like, the attributes that we think Jesus *should* have. The Word of God has the final say. It is the only source of absolute truth. We must accept all of the attributes of Jesus as they are fully revealed in the written Word of God. Our deep heart need for the unrestrained fullness of the knowledge of Jesus demands nothing short of this.

In this regard, the facts are clear. Battle is a part of each of us. In one form or another, it fills our every day. Deep in our hearts we know the commanding impact of war. Powerful images of desperate battle always make us turn for a second look. That is why the battle imagery utilized by the Old Testament prophets is so important. It doesn't just speak prophetically of the end-times. It tells the full story of battles that have already taken place. Jesus has *already* been fighting that fight—all through the Old Testament. In fact, His warrior role in the Old Testament makes the truth of His ministry during His 33 years on earth even more glorious. The gospel period of His incarnation was all about meekness. Meekness is *only* completely defined in a full appreciation of the power that is being suppressed in the name of compassionate, merciful love. This meekness is the heart of His rescue of the sons and daughters of God. This is the *infinite* meekness of the Warrior of warriors. The Son of God is all-capable and is capable of nothing less than the merciful restraint of His infinite power in compassionate love of the eternal sons and daughters of God.

We cannot ignore the fact that at the very heart of a huge volume of Old Testament prophecy is the greatest military mission of all time—the end times return of the King. These prophetic descriptions are vivid and literal. The story they tell is of the last minute, rescue-of-all-rescues. Every battle scene and every battle-hardened warrior of the Old Testament foreshadows the battle of battles and the Warrior of warriors. And yet they are only a hint of what lies ahead. When we think of the mighty warriors described in the Bible and the numerous accounts of their bravery and courageous warrior exploits, we are thinking of Jesus. Still, could Joshua or David or Samson or Gideon compare to Jesus? Could any of David's Mighty Men even hold a candle to Jesus? Even with their truly extraordinary feats of might and bravery in battle, they are merely a feeble reflection of the Warrior of warriors. Even the vivid, dramatic, and intriguing description of the mighty warriors who gathered at David's side in his darkest hour were recorded in the Bible merely to warm us up to Jesus and His warrior role that stands just beyond the horizon on the great Day of the Lord:

> *Some Gadites defected to David at his stronghold in the desert. They were <u>brave warriors</u>, <u>ready for battle</u> and able to handle the shield and spear. Their faces were <u>the faces of lions</u>, and they were <u>as swift as gazelles in the mountains</u>.*

—1Chronicles 12:8 (emphasis added)

Do you find this hard to believe? Let's take it one step further. Let's move beyond the Old Testament scripture and make it personal in our own life. Just think of all of the *real life* heroes whose stories put a lump in your throat every time you hear them. Think of Audie Murphy, the most decorated soldier in the history of the United States military. Think of Patton and the desperate rescue of the trapped army at the Battle of the Bulge, any of the countless World War Medal of Honor winners, or the fireman who died in the World Trade Center on 9/11/2001. Think of the Medal of Honor winners from Mogadishu and the mountains of Afghanistan. Only when we get to actually see our Warrior King in action in the maelstrom of great battle, will we fully understand that *all* of the great real life heroes of our lives were but a faint reflection of our Savior Jesus.

This is even true of our movie heroes. When we think of the dashing, brave, and swashbuckling movie heroes that move us to tears and swell our hearts with wonder for the bravery they display on the screen, *we are thinking of Jesus.* When our hearts are *lit up* by the likes of Tom Hanks in *Saving Private Ryan*, Russell Crowe in *Gladiator*, Brad Pitt in *Troy*, Keanu Reeves in *The Matrix*, or Harrison Ford as *Indiana Jones*, it is only because of their resemblance (even if only slightly) to our Warrior of warriors, Jesus.

All of these brave heroes of distant past and present—and even those in the movies we watch—had one thing in common. This is by God's very specific design for His very specific purpose. These heroes of ours, uniformly *against all odds step into the path of the oppressor in defense of those who cannot defend themselves.* Sound familiar? It is not just random happenstance that they mirror the attributes and exploits of Jesus. We must let go of the worldly illusion that these great heroic efforts somehow sprang uniquely, randomly, and without God's help from the mind and heart of man. No chance. God created everything that has been created. God is behind them all because God has focused absolutely every moment of the creation—even down to the movies we watch—*on His Son Jesus.* In your heart, consider the extraordinary bravery of these heroes of ours—skillful warriors who turn toward the battle when all others run. And then remember that they all reflect—*and pale in comparison to*—Jesus.

Search your heart on this. Search the scriptures. Could it be any other way? Could the Warrior of all warriors be eclipsed in any of His warrior attributes— bravery, cunning, strategy, stealth, strength, integrity—by the likes of the very heroes that He created? Could any of them show Him up? Could their glory out shine that of the King of kings, the Warrior of warriors? Could their accomplishments in any way diminish the luster of His? If we walk away from this discussion with nothing else, we must at least remember this. These mighty and brave warriors of every era—they are all merely a dull reflection of Jesus.

They were all created with warrior attributes and placed in the most desperate of situations for one purpose—to bring glory to Jesus. Their amazing stories are told to each and every one of us only to show us a tiny portion of the fullness of Jesus in His Old Testament and end-times role. They set a standard that thrills our warrior hearts and they set that standard magnificently high.

But they are nothing compared to the real deal.

Jesus is the mightiest of mighty warriors. He has been from the beginning of time and He will show us everything on that day of days. It is *His* heroic deeds that are written upon the sacred scrolls hidden in the deep regions of our hearts.

This knowledge of the fullness of the attributes of Jesus speaks joy into the eternity that He has written on every heart. We are reminded that what He is now and has been in the past, so shall He be in the future—and this for all eternity. Once again, *"Jesus Christ is the same yesterday and today and forever"* (Hebrews 13:8).

Our hearts experience sheer delight in the knowledge that the physical, tangible, incarnate, fully human Jesus is in this with us for eternity. He is the permanent link between all that the mighty God is—and all that we are not. He is the bridge across the unbridgeable gap that exists between the created and the Uncreated, the finite and the Infinite, the unholy and the Holy, between man and God.

> *Now there have been many of those priests, since death prevented them from continuing in office; but because Jesus lives forever, he has a permanent priesthood. Therefore he is able to save completely those who come to God through him, because he always lives to intercede for them.*

—Hebrews 7:23-25 (emphasis added)

In accepting this role, Jesus became the unbreakable and critically essential bond between the non-eternal and the Eternal. He accepted His role as our Savior forever, knowing fully that when He donned the skin of mankind, He did so for eternity. Precisely this is the hope and joy of our eternity in Him.

Indeed, exactly this sacred glowing filament has coursed through the entirety of this book—namely that everything about the Old Testament role of Jesus was *physical*. Jesus didn't just *will* the battle outcomes into being. He actually strapped on the armor, picked up the sword, and turned toward the very physical trial of hand-to-hand battle. He stepped up and fought the fight for the remnant of the nation of Israel. No longer can descriptions of the Lord fighting for Israel be taken allegorically.

> *So Joshua subdued the whole region, including the hill country, the Negev, the western foothills and the mountain slopes, together with all their kings. He left no survivors. He totally destroyed all who breathed, just as the LORD, the God of Israel, had commanded. Joshua subdued them from Kadesh Barnea to Gaza and from the whole region of Goshen to Gibeon. All these kings and their lands Joshua conquered in one campaign, because the LORD, the God of Israel, fought for Israel.*

—Joshua 10:40-42 (emphasis added)

The participation of the Son of God in these battles was anything but allegorical. When it says that God *"fought for Israel,"* it means that He literally and physically fought for Israel. Add to this the incredible story of the salvation of all mankind that required a literally physical death. Jesus very pointedly did not just wave His hand or speak a word to bring about our salvation. He became one of us and allowed those whom He came to save to put Him through the plight of every man—a physical, bodily death.

The physical nature of Jesus that has been apparent at every step since the dawn of creation has much to say about our future. We can know that when He comes back to fight the final battle on the day of the Lord, He will come back and will once again physically turn toward the fury of battle for us. He will be there—fully incarnate—to strike the blows that must be struck against all who stand in contention with the mighty God.

When Jesus comes back—when He commands the attention of every set of eyes in the creation—we can know with certainty what that moment is going to look like. Every moment that Jesus has spent in His creation—from the garden of Eden to the redemption of Israel from Egypt and Babylon, from Bethlehem to the redemption of mankind on the cross—has all been about only one thing—*rescue*. Whether we die and step into eternity or are alive to see Him return, that instant of eternal transition will be about nothing less than magnificent *rescue*. It can't be about anything less—and there is nothing more.

That moment will be the most incredible earth shaking, last minute, gut-wrenching rescue ever witnessed by anyone on the face of the earth. In that moment of moments, we will be treated to a full revelation of all that we are being rescued from—with the fullness of the very dark and awful terror that is specific to our particular life. We will, in that instant, personally know the depth of the desperation of the plight of all men—with the palpable fullness of the sheer terror of our inadequacy to do anything about it. And just as the last crushing blow of our sinful degradation is descending upon us—when all is absolutely lost—we will know the real meaning of that most holy word *rescue*. For that word *rescue* was created for only one purpose and for only one Person. In its every letter are military battle, combat, and warfare. It is the word that will describe the breathtaking, very-last-chance rescue that is the reward given to the Son by the Father in payment of a contract fulfilled. In the fulfillment of that contract, men and women who would be sons and daughters of God—princes and princesses of the kingdom—were *rescued* for the express purpose of eternal *life*.

The physical presence of Jesus in every moment of the history of the creation speaks directly to each of *our* individual eternal stories also. Just as is the case with Jesus, God did not give us bodies only for the short term. Our physical nature and the importance of our day-to-day physical activities are not lost on our Creator. To the contrary, He made us precisely this way—as beings that thrive in a physical world—for His very specific purpose. The Word of God does not speak of resurrection into eternal bodies for nothing. Just as Jesus has been very physically involved in every moment of the past, so shall He be literally physically involved in every moment of the future—and so shall we! The description of the millennial reign of Jesus details a time of physical reign in which we also will physically participate in service to the King. The eternity of life with Jesus in the New Jerusalem that follows is also a time of sumptuous eating, tireless work, glorious adventure, captivating beauty, and joyous service to the praise and glory of our Redeemer and King.

This holds abundant promise for our future. This total commitment to a physical interaction assures each of us that we also will be physically involved in the eternity of our King. Our service to Him will be physical—as messengers or warriors or servants or leaders or any number of other roles—in the millennium and beyond. Our praise of Him will be physical—in song or in deeds or in labor— in the millennium and beyond. This discussion of the Old Testament has been totally about Jesus, but it has also been about us. For in the total commitment to a hands-on, tangible, day-to-day, incarnate involvement in the Old Testament, Jesus has told us of our eternity together.

And it is with pure joy that we reflect on the hope that fills our heart—that because Jesus placed His perfect faith in the perfectly faithful Father for eternity, so also can we place our faith in Him for eternity. Our future, secured by the sacrifice of our perfect Savior, is to romp through the adventures of eternity as perfect children of the Living God *as if we never ever harbored in our heart darkest rebellion against the Holy God.* This promise speaks an eternity of praise to the compassionate mercy of the mighty God. Truly, unspeakable joy is found in the true knowledge of *every* attribute of our King.

Where do we go from here? We stop, and we listen to our heart—for inside of every one of us beats the heart of a warrior. We all know and cannot resist those feelings that tell each of us *that there is a battle yet to be fought*—and more importantly, that each of us has a very special role to play in it. In our heart of hearts, we can't wait for this fight. We have been waiting our whole life for this moment, for this fight. Battle has been our past, it is our present, and it will most certainly be our immediate future. Just as it is for Jesus, so also it is for us.

To be sure, these deep heart feelings regarding this fight—*they are not about us.* They do not originate in *our* hearts. Instead, they trace their origin back to the heart of our warrior Redeemer, Jesus. Our deep heart desire to join other Christian men as warriors in the army of the Lord—to stand back-to-back in desperate battle—exists in our hearts because it existed in His. The Commander of the army of the Lord was the first into the fray, the first into the breach, the first to stand in the gap between the Israelite remnant and the evil otherworld warriors who threatened them. With sword in hand, Jesus led His fellow warriors—His *"band of destroying angels"*—into fierce battle during the many Old Testament campaigns of the army of the Lord.

> *He unleashed against them his hot anger, his wrath, indignation and hostility—a band of destroying angels.*

—Psalm 78:49 (emphasis added)

In the same compassionate, humble embodiment of the purest love that walked the dusty streets of Jerusalem also beats the heart of a warrior. Our heart's desire is to be a warrior because Jesus is—and always has been—the Most Holy Warrior.

"At that time Michael, the great prince who protects your people, will arise. There will be a time of distress such as has not happened from the beginning of nations until then. But at that time your people— everyone whose name is found written in the book—will be delivered.
—Daniel 12:1

Epilogue

One final note seems appropriate. As amazing as all of this may seem, I would ask you to ponder just one question: *Can I outdo God in the revelation of Jesus?* Can I paint a picture that is more amazing, more fun, more spectacular than it already is? Can I make Jesus look like more of a hero, more of a warrior King, more of the focus of everything than He actually is? Can I exalt Jesus to a place that is higher than He is exalted by the Father?

No chance. Be assured that if we can even entertain such a thing as possible, then our image of the nature of God is seriously flawed. To the contrary, what we can know for sure is that as amazing as all of that which is conveyed in this book may sound to you—especially to the skeptics among us—reality, the *real* reality, is infinitely (literally infinitely!) more incredible. The real revelation of Jesus is at this very moment bursting at the seams to be revealed to the creation—and to you.

www.ingramcontent.com/pod-product-compliance
Lightning Source LLC
Chambersburg PA
CBHW072002060426
42446CB00042B/1355